You're in for a delight. This cookbook, compliments of *Food & Wine* and Pier 1 Imports, will bring you many hours of enjoyment. As a senior editor of *Food & Wine*, my involvement with Pier 1 comes naturally. I love to entertain at home, whether I'm cooking for two or twenty, and Pier 1 has a lot to offer people like me. And for those who enjoy the simple pleasure of cooking for their family, you'll find great things in store, too.

This special cookbook is an excellent resource for creating a distinctive meal for any occasion. And Pier 1 is an equally wonderful source for extraordinary ideas for entertaining and dining at home.

Whether you're planning the family meal or a dinner party, all it takes is a little imagination, a page from this cookbook, and a few of the wonderful items you'll find at Pier 1.

Enjoy!

Peter Prestcott
Entertainment/Special Projects Editor
Food & Wine

THE BEST OF Food&Wine

American Express
Publishing Corporation
New York

THE BEST OF FOOD & WINE
Editor/Designer: Kate Slate
Assistant Editor: Martha Crow
Illustrations: Steven J. Charny, Hong Chow

AMERICAN EXPRESS PUBLISHING CORPORATION
Editor in Chief/Food & Wine: Mary Simons
Art Director/Food & Wine: Elizabeth Woodson
Marketing Director: Elizabeth Petrecca
Production Manager: Joanne Maio Canizaro

Published by American Express Publishing Corporation
1120 Avenue of the Americas, New York, New York 10036

Manufactured in the United States of America

ISBN 0-916103-19-6

TABLE OF CONTENTS

FOREWORD

Welcome to *The Best of Food & Wine*. This collection, our tenth, brings you our very favorite recipes from the past year...all designed to make your meals, great and small, delicious and as easy to prepare as we can make them.

Our belief is that two of life's most sustaining pleasures are cooking and entertaining for family and friends. That is what this volume is about. What better way to express love and camaraderie than to gather round the table and savor a flavor-filled meal?

We have more Asian-inspired dishes than ever before. Foods with touches of Asian flavors are served in the best restaurants across the country, and so we have gathered recipes that mirror that trend. We promise they are easy to do and will wake up the most tired palates. And we have 50 recipes in our chapter on low-calorie dishes that keep health and waistlines in mind. They are packed with hearty taste but not with calories.

You can count on success with each of our recipes. All have been tested and often retested in our own kitchen using home equipment. At *Food & Wine* we strive to make each recipe not only as simple to prepare as possible but absolutely foolproof. There are also shaded boxes that offer fresh ideas for menus and suggestions for appropriate wines that will add a fillip to any occasion.

This year we include a guide to smart wine buying, written by our regular wine gurus, Elin McCoy and John Frederick Walker. As wines escalate in price, it has become more important than ever to know how to buy the right wines at the right prices. Our wine experts provide valuable information on what to look for, how to find it, and even on how to start a wine cellar.

For those of us who love to cook and to entertain, our kitchens and our dining tables are what center us in our hectic lives. We hope *The Best of Food & Wine* will inform, encourage...and inspire you. Here's to the myriad pleasures of cooking.

Mary Simons

Mary Simons
Editor in Chief

FOOD & WINE'S VINTAGE RATINGS 1981-1991

COMPILED BY ELIN McCOY & JOHN FREDERICK WALKER

	1981	1982	1983	1984	1985
Red Bordeaux	7½ Full, attractive wines. Drink now.	9½ Rich, massive. Start sampling now.	7½ Firm, powerful. Start drinking.	6 Small-scale, firm. Drink up.	8½ Soft, delicious, elegant. Start sampling.
Sauternes	7 Well-balanced wines. Start drinking.	6½ Variable. Best are big. Start drinking.	9 Rich, classic wines. Start drinking.	5½ Mixed quality. Few good. Drink now.	7½ Soft, full, good. Sample now.
Red Burgundy	6 Variable vintage. Thin. Drink up.	7 Big, soft wines. Drink now.	8 Variable. Some very good. Start drinking.	6 Variable, thin wines. Drink up.	9 Glorious, rich, round. Start drinking.
White Burgundy	7½ Attractive wines. Drink up.	8 Big, rich wines. Drink now.	7½ Good, rich wines. Drink up.	7 Crisp wines. Some fine. Drink up.	8 Big, but soft. Drink now.
Napa/Sonoma Cabernet Sauvignon	8 Variable. Many attractive. Drink now.	7½ Balanced, attractive. Drink now.	7 Good, but not great. Drink up.	8 Big, rich, powerful. Start drinking.	9½ Brilliant, firm & elegant. Start sampling.
Napa/Sonoma Chardonnay	7 Soft, ripe wines. Fading. Drink up.	7 Variable, light, fading. Drink up.	7 Good but fading year. Drink up.	7½ Good full wines. Fading. Drink up.	8 Good, but fading. Drink up.
Barolo & Barbaresco	6½ Firm, solid wines. Drink now.	8½ Big, powerful wines. Start drinking.	7 Lighter vintage. Drink up.	5½ Light, variable. Drink up.	9 Splendid, rich. Start sampling.
Chianti	7 Good, firm wines. Drink up.	7½ Attractive, early maturing. Drink up.	7 Attractive, lighter. Drink up.	5 Spotty. Avoid.	9½ Big, rich flavor. Start drinking.
Germany	7 Well-balanced, attractive. Drink up.	7 Soft, fruity. Drink up.	9 Excellent year. Marvelous late-harvest wines. Drink up.	6½ Lean & tart. Drink up.	8½ Excellent. Drink up.
Vintage Porto	No vintage declared.	7 Soft, well-balanced. Start drinking.	8 Firm, solid wines. Sample in 2-6 years.	No vintage declared.	9 Marvelous, deep & fruity. Wait 8 years.

The following ratings and comments reflect a variety of opinions, including our own, on the quality and character of various categories of wines from recent vintages. The ratings—0 for the worst, 10 for the best—are averages, and better or worse wine than indicated can be found in each vintage. Assessments of the most current vintages are more predictive and hence less exact than those of older vintages.

Scores are based on a wine's quality at maturity. A lower-rated but mature wine will often be superior to a higher-rated but immature wine. When-to-drink advice is based on how such wines seemed to be developing in mid-1992, and presumes good storage. The earliest date suggested for consumption applies to the lesser wines of the vintage, which will mature faster than the finest examples of the year.

1986	1987	1988	1989	1990	1991
9 Powerful, tannic wines. Try in 4 years.	7 Flavorsome, but lightweight. Start drinking.	7½ Good, but somewhat tannic. Wait.	9 Variable. Some big, fleshy wines. Wait.	8½ Promising, big, flavorsome.	7½ Average quality.
9 Luscious & rich. Sample now.	5½ Light, lean; few good wines.	9 Superlative, rich, concentrated. Start sampling.	8½ Rich & powerful. Start sampling.	8½ Rich, ripe wines.	7 Weak, variable.
7 Lean, light wines. Start drinking.	7½ Stylish wines. Start drinking.	9 Concentrated, fruity, classic. Start sampling.	8½ Big, fruity wines. Start sampling.	9½ Wonderful; very rich and round.	7½ Average to good quality.
8½ Crisp, balanced, classic. Drink now.	7 Light, round, soft. Drink up.	7½ Good; some very fine. Start drinking.	8 Big, full, fruity. Start drinking.	8½ Great balance, rich wines. Start sampling.	6½ Variable quality.
8 Deep, rich & powerful. Start sampling.	8½ Dark, firm, balanced. Start sampling.	7½ Mixed vintage; some concentrated. Sample.	7½ Variable quality. Start sampling.	8 Good, ripe vintage.	8½ Promising, concentrated.
9 Excellent. Crisp, leaner style. Drink up.	7½ Good & crisp. Drink up.	8½ Good, fruity. Drink now.	7 Uneven quality. Some good. Drink now.	9 Excellent, balanced.	8 Promising, fruity. Start sampling.
7½ Well-balanced & fruity. Start sampling.	8 Round, fruity. Start drinking.	8½ Rich, full wines. Wait.	9 Big, powerful, promising wines. Wait.	8½ Ripe & full. Wait.	7½ Average year.
7½ Good quality, firm. Start drinking.	7 Average quality. Drink now.	8½ Ripe, fruity, balanced. Sample now.	7 Fruity, pleasant wines.	8½ Deep & rich but early maturing.	7 Average year.
6 Light, crisp wines. Drink up.	7 Mostly lean, some fine. Drink now.	9 Outstanding, full-flavored, fruity. Start drinking.	9 Full, rich & fruity. Start drinking.	9 Excellent; ripe vintage. Start drinking.	8 Good quality.
No vintage declared.	No vintage declared.	No vintage declared.	No vintage declared.	———	———

A GUIDE TO SMART WINE BUYING

By Elin McCoy & John Frederick Walker

Every winelover knows how much a glass of good wine adds to the enjoyment of good food. But as anyone who's ever looked at the price tags in a well-stocked wine shop also knows, the best wines can be very expensive. As a result, many winelovers routinely settle for the most inexpensive (and often least interesting) bottlings to grace their dinner tables and accompany their favorite dishes. But that's not the best way to save money on wine.

In this comprehensive guide, we'll show you how you can drink better wine for less—a lot less.

How? First, by knowing how to find reliable retail sources and how to take advantage of available discounts. Second, by developing a buying strategy that maximizes your wine budget by focusing on your particular needs and interests. Third, by buying ahead for later enjoyment—in other words, starting a small wine cellar, even if it begins with a dozen bottles in a kitchen wine rack.

Opening an expensive famous wine is an extravagance that anyone willing to pay the price can indulge in, but only a smart wine buyer can regularly savor the pleasure of opening a first-rate wine for dinner that didn't cost a small fortune.

CHOOSING A WINE STORE

SHOPPING AND SAVING

Today's wine buyer can shop at a vast range of outlets, from neighborhood stores to gigantic wine supermarkets, or even, where regulations permit, order wine by catalog from out-of-state retailers. The selection available may be excellent or limited, prices may be bargain-basement or buyer-beware, and the staff may be woefully ignorant or knowledgeable and enthusiastic. These differences are important to any wine buyer: It makes sense to make your selections from a wide variety of choices, and no one wants to be stuck with an off-bottle, given bad advice or pay inflated prices.

It pays to shop around when buying wine, but price isn't everything. The discount outlets that offer the lowest prices aren't usually the best wine stores to patronize on a regular basis. A good wine store offers more than bargains. If you do most of your buying from a well-stocked store that takes a serious interest in wine—and wine-loving customers—you'll receive notice of special sales and limited offerings, services like free or discounted storage and delivery, the reassurance that the wine you buy has been properly stored, and most important, reliable advice. Consider the following when choosing a wine store in your area:

- Does it have a broad selection of wines in all price categories, not just the well advertised brands? If it doesn't have what you're looking for, will the store order it for you at the lowest price?
- Is the staff knowledgeable about wines in general? Are they familiar—through their own tastings—with the wines they sell? Are they happy to "talk wine" or are they only interested in making a sales pitch? Have you liked the wines they've recommended?
- Will the store take back spoiled wine for credit—without a quibble?
- Is there a descriptive catalog or a complete price list available?
- Will the store offer attractive discounts—say, 10% on a mixed case (1 case = 1 dozen bottles), larger discounts if you buy several cases of wine—and free delivery?
- Does the store have temperature-controlled storage for its own stock? Will it store case-lot purchases for free, or for a minimal charge?

SAVVY BUYING

Comparison shopping is the best way to avoid paying more than necessary for your favorite Chardonnay. The easiest way is to equip yourself with several sources of current information on wine prices.

Get on the mailing lists of several major retailers across the country who send out seasonal catalogs, as well as on those of local shops. (Look for their advertisements in the food section of major metropolitan newspapers.) That way you'll have an idea of the price spread for various fine wines (some of which can vary remarkably) and will be able to spot a genuine bargain when one comes along. But when shopping for wine, bear in mind these cautions:

- *Always taste a wine before you buy it in quantity.* No wine is a bargain if you end up not drinking it because it's not very good or turns out to be very different from what you expected—even if it only cost $4.99 a bottle. Most merchants will hold a case for you for a few days, which gives you time to try a bottle at home first.
- *Shop for quality, not just price.* An inexpensive wine isn't always a bargain, and a bargain wine isn't always inexpensive—it's just inexpensive for its quality. A superb Cabernet Sauvignon that costs $18 a bottle is no bargain compared to one that's nearly as good and costs only $12. Conversely, that $12 Cabernet is a much better buy than a $10 red that's not nearly as good.
- *Take advantage of seasonal sales.* Champagne and sparkling wines, for example, are often on sale from Thanksgiving through New Year's because that's when most are sold and consumed. Other good general buying opportunities are post-holiday sales and end-of-summer sales.
- *Don't be afraid to try something new.* Finding bargains also means searching out wines that are underpriced because they're unusual, unfashionable or little known. Examples include wines from new producers and unfamiliar regions and wines made from little-known grape varieties.

In the next section you'll find more detail on the types of wine that offer the best values.

A WINE-BUYING STRATEGY

CALCULATING YOUR WINE NEEDS

Most people purchase wines the way they purchase groceries: when they're just about to run out. But a last-minute dash to the local liquor store just before guests arrive is a good way to get stuck with a poor selection and high prices. It makes far more sense to plan ahead so that your wine purchases will both meet your needs and stretch your wine budget further.

The best way to buy wines is to have firm objectives in mind. Without a want-list in hand—of wine types, vintages or even specific labels—it's hard to make choices when you're standing among the bewildering array of possibilities in a large wine store, and to know when a good buy ought to be snapped up. While you're wondering if that bargain-priced 10-year-old tawny Port in the spring sale catalog is worth buying now to have on hand for next fall and winter, savvy buyers, having done their thinking previously, have already grabbed it.

Start by analyzing your pattern of consumption. Ask yourself the following questions.

- How often do you drink wine with meals at home? Figure per-bottle consumption per average week, then per month.
- How often do you entertain each month? How much wine do you serve?
- Do you splurge on special wines on special occasions? How often?

Multiply your monthly figure by 12 for an approximate yearly household consumption. It's surprising how fast it all adds up. A little over two bottles a week, for example, amounts to 10 cases of wine annually. If two people each have two glasses of wine with dinner at home on weekdays and give one dinner party per month for eight people (serving five bottles of wine per party), that's about 20 cases of wine a year.

Next, determine the types of wines you consume: Do you pour more reds than whites, or vice versa? How much sparkling wine and dessert wine? Do you have distinct geographical and varietal preferences? What are they? Estimate how much of various kinds of wine you use, then add up their cost. Let's say your annual wine consumption looks like this:

2 cases sparkling wine @ $150 each	$300
1 case Riesling @ $100	$100
1 case Sauvignon Blanc @ $100	$100
1 case Pinot Grigio @ $100	$100
1 case Beaujolais @ $100	$100
1 case Mâcon @ $100	$100
2 cases Chardonnay @ $150 each	$300
1 case Chianti @ $150	$150
2 cases Cabernet Sauvignon @ $150 each	$300
2 cases red Bordeaux @ $200 each	$400
1 case Port/sherry @ $150	$150
Total	$2100

Of course, your list may not look anything like this. You may even have a hard time finding any particular pattern in your purchases. But by determining—as closely as you can—what sorts of wines you'll probably drink and serve over the course of a year, you'll know your requirements so you can make planned purchases. At a minimum, aim to develop a list of wanted wines and take it with you on any buying forays and browsing trips. *Hint:* Even if you can spend an entire year's budget in a single shopping expedition, don't do it. Allow for worthwhile buying opportunities you may come across later. Quarterly buying gives you a chance to rethink your wine needs and buying priorities on a seasonal basis.

THE BEST WINE VALUES

It is difficult to make specific recommendations of bargains because the wines that fall into that category change so quickly. There are always special opportunities. For example: A wine shop may go out of business and liquidate its stock. A newly imported wine may appear on retail shelves initially at a reduced price to gain a share of the market. A California winery may change distributors in your state, and the previous distributor may "dump" some of its wines into retail channels at below-market prices.

Alert consumers are always on the lookout for such opportunities, whether they're interested in something new for an everyday table wine, or hoping for a once-in-a-lifetime chance to buy a scarce, prestigious bottling that's normally too expensive to consider.

However, there *are* certain categories of wines that consistently yield bargains.

• *Unfashionable wines*. Wines, like styles of clothes, go in and out of fashion. Currently, Chardonnay is all the rage among white wines worldwide. This means other superb white varietals, such as Riesling (also called Johannisberg, White and Rhine Riesling), don't sell as briskly and are often underpriced for their value. But Riesling from the U.S. and Germany (the grape's homeland) is also unfashionable for another reason: Many are made in a fruity-tart, slightly sweet style, which is widely (and wrongly) perceived as less compatible with food than drier wines. As a result, most wine drinkers think all Rieslings are on the sweet side, not realizing that bone-dry examples are made in Germany, the U.S., Alsace and elsewhere.

The upshot is that Rieslings (and similar fruity varietals such as Chenin Blanc) often represent excellent values.

• *Wines from unfamiliar regions*. In recent years, wines from Chile, Australia, New Zealand and South Africa have been joining the ranks of U.S., French, German and Italian wines on wine store shelves. Many of these wines are attractively priced in order to lure customers away from familiar labels. In addition, wines from less well-known wine-producing districts next door to famous ones—such as Fronsac, Canon-Fronsac, Côtes de Bourg and Blaye in Bordeaux—are also worth exploring. Consider, too, the wines of Oregon and Washington State, which do not yet have the cachet (or prices) of California wines—but whose quality is comparable.

• *Unfamiliar varietals*. The average wine drinker tends to shy away from wines made from unfamiliar grape varieties, not realizing that many offer as much character as the well-known varieties Chardonnay, Cabernet Sauvignon and Pinot Noir—and also offer a welcome change of flavor. Here are a dozen less-familiar grape varieties that appear on U.S. and imported wine labels.

WHITES

Gewürztraminer—flowery, spicy wine that stands up well to rich food and Asian cuisine

Muscat—perfumed, grapey wine, excellent with fruit

Pinot Gris—also known as Pinot Grigio, this spicy, full-bodied wine complements rich fish and many savory dishes

Sémillon—round-textured, crisp dry wine often blended with the more aromatic, herbaceous Sauvignon Blanc; good Chardonnay alternative—in fact, also blended with that popular grape

Seyval Blanc—best of hybrid grapes grown in Eastern U.S.; assertive, crisp and fruity; good with fish

Sylvaner—flavorful, clean wine, excellent with chicken and mild cheeses

REDS

Barbera—tart Northern Italian wine, great with tomato-based dishes

Dolcetto—soft, fruity, Northern Italian wine;

alternative to Beaujolais

Merlot—Soft, full-bodied cousin to Cabernet Sauvignon, similar in flavor, and often blended with it; excellent with meats, game, cheese

Sangiovese—principal grape of Italy's Tuscany region, sometimes blended with Cabernet Sauvignon. Very drinkable, medium-bodied, versatile wine with pointed flavors

Zinfandel—the "white" version is pink picnic fare; the red is spicy and berry-like, excellent with pizza and grilled meats

Syrah—known as Shiraz in Australia, this Rhône grape makes gutsy, deep-flavored wines ideal with casseroles and stews

• *"Off-vintages" of Red Bordeaux.* Don't let all the talk about great vintages trap you into thinking that only highly rated years are worth buying. In these days of modern wine-making techniques, it's more accurate to think of different vintage years as representing wines of different character rather than simply representing good and bad. Top châteaux often produce some fine, if lighter, wine even in poor-rated, so-called "off-years." And if they're priced accordingly, these can be excellent bargains for current drinking. The decade of the 1980s was remarkable for having so few "off-years," but châteaux-bottled wines from weaker vintages like 1987, for example, can sell for one-third to one-half less than they would in a highly regarded year like 1986 or 1989—and still offer much of the classic flavor and style of the wines of this region.

TRUST YOUR OWN TASTE

Because you're purchasing wine to drink yourself, no recommendation, no matter how authoritative, is as useful as a direct sample when it comes to deciding if you'd like to buy a particular wine. Anytime you can taste a wine other than at your own table—at a restaurant or dinner party, for example—is an opportunity to find new favorites. But these tasting experiences won't help unless you jot down the names of the bottles you like.

It's extremely annoying to find yourself standing in a wine shop desperately trying to remember the name of that great Pinot Blanc you had last week. Form the habit of writing down the type, producer, vintage and any special designations mentioned on the label of wines when you're enjoying them—so you won't forget the vital information necessary to add them to your "buy" list and readily track them down later.

You can increase your tasting experience by attending in-store tastings, taking a wine course, or—simplest of all—by buying and tasting a range of wines with like-minded friends. A single bottle will serve a dozen people a two-ounce "tasting pour" each, which means the shared cost of trying six or eight Chardonnays or Beaujolais is minimal. Best of all, your impressions will be based on direct comparisons. If there's a consensus on favorites at such a tasting, you can pool your purchases with friends to take advantage of quantity discounts.

Although smart wine buyers learn to sharpen—and trust—their own taste, it's not possible to preview every bottle you might buy. Recommendations from merchants, publications and critics as well as awards from tasting competitions can be helpful in narrowing choices, but remember no expert can tell you how good a wine will taste to you—and you're the one who's going to end up drinking it.

STARTING A WINE CELLAR

BUYING NOW FOR LATER

One of the best ways to drink better for less is to buy at least some wines for future consumption and store them yourself for enjoyment at some later date. We've all heard of wine collectors who can open a bottle of mature and pricey Bordeaux from a fine vintage—and feel smug rather than extravagant because they bought the wine years before when it was widely available and affordable.

Don't be put off by talk of wine cellars because you picture some vast cobwebbed, bottle-filled cave or room-sized temperature-controlled vault that bears no relation to your modest yearly requirements. This same money-saving strategy will work even if your "cellar" is a couple of cardboard cases in a hall closet. Think of a wine cellar as the vinous equivalent of a kitchen pantry where staples, preserves and canned goods are kept on hand.

The advantages are the same no matter what the size of your "cellar":

1) You always have a selection of wines available.

2) Because *you're* taking care of the wine, you know how it's been stored.

3) You can buy ahead, when the wines you want are available. Since there are only limited quantities of wine produced by any fine wine producer, many wines worth buying only appear in stores a month or two each year. Those that are relatively inexpensive don't remain on the shelves for long.

4) You can buy fine wines when they're least expensive. Fine wines, especially red Bordeaux, California Cabernet Sauvignon, Northern Italian reds and vintage Port, take years to mature properly. They're far cheaper when they first appear on the market than when they are fully mature and scarce. If you buy a case or so of fine reds when they're young and put them away, you'll be able to enjoy them later at a cost far below what you'd pay for them as mature wines.

A KITCHEN WINE RACK SELECTION

Think of this one-case wine cellar as the vinous equivalent of a spice rack: Whatever you're serving, there's probably a bottle here that will complement it. A mixed case of the following wines should cost about $100.

1 btl. Sparkling wine (aperitif)
1 btl. Sauvignon Blanc or Pinot Gris (shellfish)
2 btls. Chardonnay or Sémillon (salmon, chicken)
1 btl. Rosé or blush (Mexican, burgers)
2 btls. Beaujolais or Dolcetto (veal, turkey)
2 btls. Cabernet Sauvignon or Merlot (lamb, beef)
1 btl. Zinfandel or Côtes du Rhône (Italian, stews)
1 btl. Chenin Blanc or Riesling (Asian, ham)
1 btl. Amontillado sherry (aperitif, nuts)

FINDING THE RIGHT SPACE

Although many wine enthusiasts are convinced of the advantages of starting a wine cellar, they're daunted by what they've heard about space and storage requirements. Where do you store even a small amount of wine—say, 10 to 12 cases for current drinking and a small collection of bottles, perhaps accumulated over several years, for future drinking? Let's assume such a cache amounts to two dozen cases in all. Twenty-four cases will fill a small closet. Short of having a basement corner or fruit cellar that can be pressed into use, a closet may be the best choice, as it offers darkness and a place to keep the wine undisturbed.

But the right space isn't just a matter of cubic feet—it has to be relatively cool. Look for a cool spot away from hot pipes, heaters and furnaces and free from the vibration of washers or refrigerators. If possible, find a place with a constant temperature under 70° F (under 65° is better). Measure the temperature range with a minimum-maximum thermometer; this will show you the highest and lowest temperatures reached since you last set it. Around 55° F to 60° is considered perfect for long-term storage because it permits slow, gradual maturation, but steadiness of temperature is important as well. Ideally there should be no more than a few degrees variance during any 24-hour period, though a slow rise and fall of temperature in a slightly wider range from summer to winter won't harm wines.

The reason why temperature is so critical to the wine quality is that the warmer the temperature, the faster the evolution of the wines; wines stored at high temperatures (say 80° F or more) age rapidly, become fatigued and end up tasting flat and dull—or vinegary. Wines stored at constantly fluctuating temperatures also age prematurely. Of course excessive cold can be a danger as well: Bottles must be protected from freezing.

Don't ignore humidity either. An excessively dry environment will eventually dry out the corks in your bottles (even if the bottles are properly laid on their sides), thereby setting the stage for slow evaporation and spoilage.

About 50% to 75% relative humidity is a good range—above that and labels will begin to deteriorate from dampness (although the wine won't be harmed). You can check the humidity level by means of an inexpensive gauge called a hydrometer.

How close the conditions in your cupboard, closet or basement approximate ideal conditions will determine whether you can store wine in peak condition for decades or for six months to a year. A temperature-controlled unit works well but is very expensive—usually around $5 for each bottle stored.

If your storage conditions are inadequate or you simply lack the space, you can resort to splitting your cellar, storing wines for long-term aging either with friends or relatives who do have cool basement space or in a retailer's warehouse, and keeping only wines for current consumption on hand. This plan actually has one big advantage: You aren't tempted to drink up your better wines before they've reached maturity.

RACKS AND BINS

All wine bottles that have to be opened with a corkscrew should be stored in a horizontal position to keep the cork moist and insure the tight seal that keeps wines from spoiling. So, in your cellar, you need racks to hold the bottles on their sides. Bottles laid on flat shelves invariably roll around and assorted bottles stacked on top of each other are never in the right order.

Diamond-shaped bins that hold up to a dozen bottles are useful for quantity storage, but it's also essential to have some form of rack that will hold individual bottles. Then you can remove the wine you want without disturbing the others. There are plenty of well-designed racks on the market as well as a lot of decorative and expensive junk. If your racks are going to sit in a closet or cupboard out of sight anyway it's pointless to pay extra for decorative models when there are far cheaper and sturdier ones available, often for little more than $1 per bottle slot.

In looking for economical racks, remember that large wire metal racks, unless secured to a wall, are often unsteady. Wooden ones are more satisfactory in that respect, and if you have the space and your floor can take the weight, terra-cotta drain tiles—foot-long cylinders with a four-inch-diameter hole—stack easily in alcoves and provide rattle-free rest. If you're adept at carpentry, there are a number of designs that provide convenient bottle storage. Avoid designs that hold bottles with the neck slanting down.

Another advantage of buying in case lots, apart from the discounts offered, is the containers they come in. Cardboard boxes are difficult to stack securely, but wooden Bordeaux boxes make sturdy, stackable storage crates, especially for wines that should be stashed away for several years' aging anyway.

DIVIDE YOUR CELLAR

To get the most out of your cellar, use a twofold buying strategy. Look over your list of wine needs and divide it into two groups: wines that don't need further aging to be at their best—and those that do.

Among wines that don't need additional aging are your "everyday wines," simple, highly drinkable, modestly priced whites and reds such as Mâcon, Chardonnay, Beaujolais, Côtes du Rhône and the like. There are also some types of fine wines that don't need extended aging—Champagne, white Burgundy and lighter reds such as Pinot Noir—even though they will often keep their quality for several years in a cool cellar.

The key thing about all these wines is that there's no advantage to having any more on hand than you expect to consume within a year or two. With rare exceptions they won't get appreciably better as they get older even under excellent storage conditions and the everyday wines may lose their fresh fruity appeal. So your goal is simply to have an adequate supply of them on hand—and that means no more than one case of each type.

As you look over your pattern of wine consumption you'll probably note a certain amount of fine reds earmarked for dinner parties and special occasions—just the sort of bottles that are best with some additional age. Good vintages of California Cabernet Sauvignon, Red Bordeaux, Northern Rhônes, vintage Port, Barolo, Barbaresco, top Tuscan reds and other tannic reds are ideal for long-term cellaring, and you need to take a more thought-out approach with these.

A FINE WINE PIPELINE

Think of this portion of your cellar as a pipeline: You add a case or so of the latest (and least expensive) good vintages to one end and liquidate mature wines at the other.

Let's say you'd like to uncork a mature bottle of good California Cabernet Sauvignon a couple of times a month. To determine how much Cabernet you'd need in the pipeline, multiply your annual requirement (in this case 24 bottles) by the usual age at which that particular wine reaches maturity (8 years is about right for California Cabernet). That's about 16 cases. Because you'd be drinking up 2 cases' worth a year, you'd need to replenish that stock with a similar amount of Cabernet Sauvignon from a current good vintage. If you want to enjoy a mellow 12-year old vintage Port, say, 6 times a year, you'd need a 6-case Port pipeline to which you'd add a case every couple of years to make up for your inroads.

This cellar strategy is an easy way to ensure a steady supply of fine aged wine for your table when the occasion or dish demands it. To build up your stock initially, you either have to accumulate it over a period of years by making regular and systematic purchases over and above annual needs, or purchase a basic stock to start things off (see "Starter Cellars," page 17). At a minimum, buy one extra case per year of fine age-worthy reds that won't be touched until they've reached maturity. It's surprising how fast that cache builds up. If you'd started doing this a decade ago, you could be drinking your way through a case or two of expensive 1982 Bordeaux right now—and you'd have paid less than half the current price.

BUYING WINES TO AGE

You'll want some variety in your personal cellar, but remember: Cater to your own taste. If you don't like Port, for example, there's no reason to have it in your collection just to have a "balanced" cellar.

Many wine enthusiasts have a specialized wine collection whose emphasis reflects their tastes, interests and the kind of food they enjoy. You might decide to concentrate on the wines of small California producers, or Italian bottlings, or German vintages. But in the beginning there's no point in going overboard—even for a classic wine like Bordeaux—before trying Barbaresco or Zinfandel, or in ignoring Australian reds just because they aren't familiar.

We also recommend avoiding glamour wines that command a high premium simply because they're prestigious. In every wine category there are wines that compete with the best but aren't quite as trendy (or expensive) to collect, and your budget will go much farther if you concentrate on those. Some of your own discoveries will probably turn out to be among your best bottles. It's not necessary to buy famous labels, gold-medal winners and highly rated wines, even for the wines you're laying down for future enjoyment.

When you're buying for future drinking, there are two further guidelines to bear in mind:

- Whenever possible, buy one case of each wine you're laying down for later drinking. Having a dozen bottles of a given wine allows you the pleasure of sampling it through its aging cycle and to have on hand wines with whose taste you're familiar—a great help when it comes to selecting the right bottle to serve with a particular dish.
- Be cautious when it comes to buying wine futures. Many fine wines, including Bordeaux and some California reds, are now routinely offered by retailers on a "futures" basis: Customers pay in full for particular vintages of certain wines a year or more before they are delivered, presumably saving some money in the process. The main problem is that you're buying blind, and it's never a good idea to buy in quantity before trying a bottle. In addition, you've tied up that money for months. In some recent Bordeaux vintages, winelovers would have been better off getting interest on their money and paying full price later. In most cases, futures are only useful to secure wine of very limited availability.

WHEN TO DRINK YOUR WINES

The simplest answer: when they taste good. But how long it takes before a wine will taste its best depends on the kind of wine and on how the wine is stored. All wines change with time in the bottle, either for the worse or for the better. Many fine wines seem more harmonious and develop more bouquet with age. Here are some guidelines:

- Most wines, especially white wines, are ready to drink when you buy them. Muscadet, Mâcon, Sauvignon Blanc, Chenin Blanc, dry Riesling, Gewürztraminer, Pinot Grigio, lighter-style Chardonnay, sparkling wines and rosés are best when they're fresh and fruity and rarely improve with age. Dessert-sweet whites such as Sauternes can be enjoyed right away but will also age and improve for a decade or more after the vintage date. Fine dry white Graves from Bordeaux can last for 8 to 10 years and sometimes longer.

With red wines there's a lot of variation.

- Light reds, such as jug wines and Beaujolais, do not have the tannic structure to allow graceful aging and should be enjoyed within a year.
- More concentrated reds, such as Zinfandel and Chiantis, often seem rounder and more appealing at about 4 or 5 years of age, although they can be enjoyed young for their assertive flavors, especially with rich foods and many meat dishes.
- Pinot Noirs and red Burgundies can be drunk young, but develop extra nuances at about 5 years of age.
- Most Barolos, Brunellos, Cabernet Sauvignons, Merlots and many Bordeaux need 6 to 8 years to lose their initial harshness. A *cru classé* Bordeaux from a fine vintage often requires 10 to 12 years to develop smoothness of texture.
- Vintage Port can profit from 12 to 15 years and may continue to improve for 25.

Storage conditions make a big difference in when a wine will be ready to drink. If wines are kept at 70° F or higher, they will age more quickly than these guidelines suggest, and not always gracefully.

Keep a cellar log to monitor the development of your wines. It will help you keep track of the wines you have and what they taste like. Simply list the name, region, vintage and producer, and record the source (where bought), the date purchased, quantity and price.

In addition, keep a brief record of when you've enjoyed various bottles and what you thought of them. Three columns will do: dates served, quantity and comments. Under this last heading, note how it tasted, with whom you shared it, what dishes went particularly well with it and how it seems to be aging. It's amazing how useful this information is when it's time to pick out something for a special dinner party.

STARTER CELLARS

Because specific recommendations would be outdated by the next vintage, only broad categories are suggested here. Cellar #1 consists of a selection of wines for current drinking that will cover basic dining needs, as well as provide a range of tastes. Cellars #2 and #3 provide additional variety and a core selection of age-worthy wines. Prices given are approximate and based on 12 bottles per case. Of course, you'll want to vary the suggestions according to your needs and preferences and the wine's availability.

Cellar #1

1 case California sparkling wine $150
1 case Chilean Sauvignon Blanc $100
1 case Australian Chardonnay $150
1 case Washington State Merlot $150
1 case Chianti Classico $100
1 case Beaujolais-Villages $100

6 cases total: $750

Look to California for good-value sparkling wines, notably from producers affiliated with Champagne firms; alternatively, consider sparkling wines produced in France's Loire valley. Chile is an excellent source of crisp, inexpensive whites (as well as reds). For moderately priced Chardonnay, consider Australia; California is another good source, as is Bourgogne Blanc from France's Burgundy district. Washington State Merlot is an excellent value. Chianti Classico from Italy (or alternatively, red Rioja from Spain) is a fine choice for well-priced, medium-bodied red. Beaujolais-Villages is a particularly versatile light red; California Gamay is a good alternative.

Cellar #2

For an outlay of $2500, you can begin to lay away some fine wines for future enjoyment. (Code: **D** = drink over the next 2 years; **H** = hold for 5 years before starting to drink; **D/H** = drink over the next 5 or so years.)

6 cases from cellar #1 at left $750
1 case Chardonnay (D) $250
1 case Alsace Riesling (D) $150
1 case Pinot Noir (D/H) $250
1 case Rhône red (D/H) $150
1 case Italian Barbera (D/H) $150
2 cases Cabernet Sauvignon (H) $400
1 case Bordeaux red (H) $250
1 case late-harvest Riesling (D/H) $150

15 cases total: $2500

Look to California and Australia for rich, oak-aged Chardonnays. Alsace Riesling is dry and distinguished; alternatively, consider a dry *halbtrocken* German Riesling. Oregon and California are good sources of fine-value Pinot Noir. Among Rhône reds, consider the Syrah-based wines of Gigondas, Crozes-Hermitage or St.-Joseph; Zinfandel from California's Sonoma county offers much the same depth of flavor. Barbera from the Piedmont district of Northern Italy is a better value than better-known Barolo. Good Cabernet Sauvignon is produced worldwide, but California's Napa Valley remains a prime source; choose different producers and/or vintages to vary your stock. For Bordeaux red, look for a *cru classé* (classified growth) from the Médoc—possibly a fine château in an "off-year" or a fine vintage from a less prestigious *petit château*. A late-harvest Riesling from Australia or California is a versatile dessert wine; alternatively, consider Muscat de Beaumes de Venise from France's Rhône valley. For vintage guidance, see "Food & Wine's Vintage Ratings" chart on page 8.

Cellar #3

For an additional $2500, you could increase your stockpile of fine reds and add some additional categories of wine as well.

15 cases from cellar #2 at left $2500
3 cases Bordeaux red (H) $750
2 cases Cabernet Sauvignon (H) $500
2 cases Pinot Noir (D/H) $500
2 cases vintage Port (H) $750

24 cases total: $5000

Follow the buying advice on Bordeaux and Cabernet Sauvignon given above, but vary the vintages if possible. For vintage Port, stick with the traditional British-based firms; consider single-quinta vintage Ports that are produced in good but not great years and are excellent value. Alternatively, choose a classic dessert white, such as Sauternes from Bordeaux—bottlings from the Barsac district are often less expensive than the best-known Sauternes châteaux.

APPETIZERS & FIRST COURSES

SPICED PECANS

You'll enjoy these spicy and sweet nuts, which were first made at Chez Panisse by David Lebovitz. Serve them the same day you make them.

Makes About 1 Cup

1 cup pecan halves (about 4 ounces)
⅓ cup sugar
¼ teaspoon cinnamon
¼ teaspoon ground ginger
Pinch of nutmeg
Pinch of cream of tartar
Pinch of cayenne pepper

1. Preheat the oven to 375°. Spread the pecans on a baking sheet and toast for 4 to 5 minutes, until fragrant. Pour into a greased pie plate.

2. In a small saucepan, mix the remaining ingredients with 1 tablespoon plus 1 teaspoon of water. Cook undisturbed over moderate heat until the syrup reaches the soft-ball stage, about 5 minutes.

3. Immediately remove the pan from the heat and briskly stir the syrup into the pecans. Keep stirring until the syrup starts to crystallize and the nuts are thoroughly coated. Separate any nuts that are clumped together. Set aside.

—*Lindsey Shere*

• • •

OVEN-FRIED ALMONDS

Makes 2 Cups

2 cups whole blanched almonds
1 tablespoon extra-virgin olive oil
¼ teaspoon salt
¼ teaspoon sugar

1. Preheat the oven to 400°. Scatter the almonds on a baking sheet. Drizzle the oil on top and toss to coat completely. Roast the almonds for 15 to 20 minutes, tossing occasionally, until deep golden brown.

2. On the baking sheet, toss the almonds with the salt and sugar and set aside to cool. Spread the cooled almonds on several layers of paper towels and blot them to remove excess oil. *(The almonds will keep for about 2 weeks in a covered container.)*

Sally Schneider

• • •

MANCHEGO CHEESE IN OLIVE OIL

Manchego, a dry sheep's-milk cheese, is available at many cheese stores and at some Spanish food markets. Goat cheeses, such as Crottin de Chavignol, also work well with this marinade.

6 Servings

½ pound Manchego cheese, rind removed
About ¾ cup extra-virgin olive oil
2 teaspoons Spanish brandy
2 teaspoons fresh thyme or ¾ teaspoon dried
4 sprigs of fresh thyme
¼ to ½ teaspoon coarsely ground pepper

1. Slice the cheese ¼ inch thick. Cut each slice into 1-inch pieces.

2. In a medium jar or bowl, combine all the remaining ingredients. Add the cheese to the marinade and toss to coat. Add more olive oil if necessary to completely cover the cheese. Cover and refrigerate for at least 24 hours and up to 1 month. Serve at room temperature.

—*Sally Schneider*

• • •

MANCHEGO CHEESE STRAWS

Makes 64 Cheese Straws

¼ pound all-butter puff pastry, thawed if frozen
¼ cup grated aged Manchego cheese (about 1 ounce)
Sweet Spanish or Hungarian paprika

1. Preheat the oven to 500°. On a lightly floured work surface, roll the puff pastry to an 8-inch square, approximately ⅛ inch thick. Sprinkle evenly with the cheese and press it lightly into the dough. Sprinkle lightly with paprika.

2. Roll the dough into a cylinder and lightly sprinkle the work surface with flour. Roll the cylinder out into an 8-inch square again. Cut the square in half, then cut each half crosswise into ¼-inch strips. Place the strips on a lightly buttered heavy baking sheet.

3. Bake the cheese straws for about 5 minutes, or until puffed, cooked through and golden brown. Transfer to a rack to cool slightly. *(The straws can be made 1 day ahead and stored in an airtight container.)*

—*Colman Andrews*

• • •

CROSTINI WITH TUSCAN PESTO

We use kale in our version of the wonderful antipasto that Faith Heller Willinger, author of *Eating in Italy*, prepares with *cavolo nero*.

🍷 The oily, salty notes in these crostini call out for crisp, clean-flavored Italian whites with enough acidity to provide a palate-cleansing contrast, such as 1990 Ceretto Arneis del Piemonte Blangé or Santa Margherita Pinot Grigio.

6 Servings

1 pound fresh kale, ribs discarded, leaves coarsely chopped
¾ teaspoon coarse (kosher) salt
⅔ cup extra-virgin olive oil
2 teaspoons minced garlic
5 tablespoons unsalted butter
Eighteen ½-inch-thick diagonal slices cut from a long loaf of country bread

1. Bring a large saucepan of salted water to a boil over high heat. Add the kale, cover and cook until just tender, about 10 minutes. Drain and refresh under cold water. Using your hands, squeeze as much moisture as possible from the kale.

2. In a food processor, combine the kale, salt, olive oil and 1 teaspoon of the garlic. Process until smooth, scraping down the bowl once or twice. Season with more salt to taste if necessary. *(The pesto can be made several hours ahead and kept covered in the refrigerator. Bring to room temperature before serving.)*

3. Preheat the broiler. In a small saucepan, melt the butter with the remaining 1 teaspoon garlic over low heat. Brush the garlic butter on both sides of the bread slices and place on a baking sheet. Toast the bread under the broiler until lightly browned on both sides. Spread each toast with some of the kale pesto and serve immediately.

—*Johanne Killeen & George Germon*

• • •

TOASTED BREAD WITH TOMATO

This dish is best when made with a perfectly ripe tomato. It's particularly good when the bread is slightly smoky from being quickly grilled over hot coals, but you can get a similar flavor by smoking toasted bread in a pan as directed in Step 2 of the Wood-Roasted Sweet Peppers in Olive Oil (p. 24).

4 Servings

Four ½-inch-thick slices of peasant bread
1 medium garlic clove, halved lengthwise (optional)
1 large tomato, halved crosswise
Pinch of salt
About 1 tablespoon extra-virgin olive oil

1. In a toaster or under a broiler, lightly toast the bread slices.

2. If desired, rub each slice of bread with the cut garlic. Rub the cut side of a tomato half over 2 of the toasts, squeezing the tomato lightly to saturate the toast with its juices, seeds and a little pulp. Repeat with the remaining tomato half and 2 slices of toast.

3. Arrange the toast on a plate. Sprinkle the salt on top. Drizzle ¾ teaspoon of the olive oil, or more to taste, over each slice. Cut the toasts in half if large. Serve at once.

—*Sally Schneider*

• • •

TUNA CROSTINI WITH CAPERS

These crostini can be served as a passed hors d'oeuvre, or you can mound the tuna mixture in a pretty dish, surround it with the toasted bread and let guests help themselves. Grill the fish instead of sautéing it if you can.

Makes 5 Dozen Crostini

CROSTINI:
¾ cup extra-virgin olive oil
5 garlic cloves, peeled and minced
3 baguettes, cut into sixty ¼-inch slices

TUNA TOPPING:
½ cup olive oil
1 pound fresh tuna, sliced ½ inch thick
3 cups fresh bread crumbs, made from crustless country bread
1½ cups chopped flat-leaf parsley
6 garlic cloves
3 tablespoons drained capers
Juice of 1 lemon
½ teaspoon salt
½ teaspoon freshly ground pepper
Extra-virgin olive oil, for drizzling

1. *Make the crostini:* Preheat the oven to 400°. In a small bowl, combine the oil and minced garlic. Arrange the bread slices in a single layer on large baking sheets. Using a pastry brush, brush the oil and bits of garlic onto both sides of each slice of bread. Bake for 7 to 8 minutes until golden brown. Let cool. *(The crostini can be stored in a sealed paper bag for up to 2 days.)*

2. *Make the topping:* In a large skillet, heat 2 tablespoons of the olive oil over moderately high heat. Add the tuna and sauté, turning once, until cooked through, 3 to 4 minutes.

3. Transfer the tuna to a food processor. Add the remaining 6 tablespoons olive oil and the bread crumbs, parsley, garlic, capers, lemon juice, salt and pepper. Process for 30 seconds. If you wish a finely textured puree, scrape down the sides and process for an additional 30 seconds to 1 minute. Scrape the tuna mixture into a bowl.

4. To serve, spread the tuna on the crostini. Drizzle extra-virgin olive oil on top.

—Evan Kleiman

• • •

ONION AND ANCHOVY CROUTES

🍷 Salty bites such as these are well-suited to Champagne, since one of Champagne's virtues is moderate alcohol—and salty foods can taste harsh with high-alcohol wines. Serve a light, crisp, dry Champagne with these nibbles, such as Piper-Heidsieck's Brut Sauvage or Laurent-Perrier's Ultra Brut.

Makes 40 Croûtes

¼ cup fruity extra-virgin olive oil
1 large Spanish onion, very thinly sliced
1 tin (2 ounces) anchovies, drained and mashed
2 tablespoons finely chopped parsley plus more for garnish
2 tablespoons chicken stock or canned low-sodium broth
Pinch of nutmeg
1 baguette, preferably sourdough
Salt
About ¼ cup freshly grated Parmigiano-Reggiano cheese

1. In a large heavy skillet, heat 2 tablespoons of the olive oil over moderate heat. Add the onion, stir well to coat with oil and cook, stirring occasionally, until softened, about 25 minutes. Add the mashed anchovies and cook for 5 minutes. Stir in the 2 tablespoons chopped parsley, chicken stock and nutmeg and remove from the heat.

2. Meanwhile, preheat the oven to 400°. Slice the baguette into forty ¼-inch-thick rounds and place on a baking sheet. Brush the croûtes with the remaining 2 tablespoons olive oil and sprinkle with a little salt. Bake until just crisp and golden brown, about 2 minutes. Set aside to cool.

3. Preheat the broiler. Spread each croûte with 1 teaspoon of the onion-anchovy mixture and sprinkle with ¼ teaspoon of the grated Parmigiano-Reggiano. Broil the croûtes for about 1 minute, until the cheese has melted. Garnish each croûte with chopped parsley and serve at room temperature .

—David Rosengarten

• • •

SPRING BAGNA CAUDA

Bagna cauda literally means "hot bath." This dip is wonderful served with an assortment of fresh spring vegetables such as scallions, red radishes, slices of fennel and red bell pepper, tender spinach leaves, baby artichokes, whole mushrooms, carrot and celery sticks, fava beans and cooked new potatoes. The dip can be kept warm over a fondue-type burner. Do not overheat, or the butter will separate.

6 Servings

⅔ cup extra-virgin olive oil
3 garlic cloves, peeled and crushed
6 anchovy fillets—rinsed, patted dry and coarsely chopped
½ teaspoon fennel seeds
5 tablespoons unsalted butter, at room temperature
Platter of fresh spring vegetables

1. In a small saucepan, warm the oil with the garlic, anchovies and fennel seeds over low heat for 5 minutes. Remove from the heat and break up the anchovy pieces with a fork until they dissolve. *(The recipe can be made to this point up to 6 hours ahead of time; cover and refrigerate.)*

2. Just before serving, gently rewarm the *bagna cauda* over low heat. Whisk in the butter just until incorporated. Serve warm in a bowl placed in the center of the platter of vegetables.

—Johanne Killeen & George Germon

• • •

TOMATO TAPENADE

Though tapenade is most often made with olives, the vital ingredient is the caper (*tapéno* in Provençal) from which its name derives. This tapenade keeps well in the refrigerator and is best served at room temperature on crisp, thin toasts.

Makes About 1½ Cups

3 ounces sun-dried tomatoes
Boiling water
1 cup olive oil
1 rounded tablespoon drained capers
2 teaspoons minced garlic
1 teaspoon finely grated lemon zest
1 teaspoon fresh lemon juice
½ teaspoon herbes de Provence
Salt

1. Place the tomatoes in a heatproof

bowl and cover with boiling water. Set aside until softened, about 2 minutes. Drain the tomatoes and pat dry. When the tomatoes are cool, place them in a jar, cover with the olive oil and set aside at room temperature for about 1 week.

2. Pick the tomatoes out of the jar, leaving plenty of oil on them. Reserve the remaining oil.

3. In a food processor, combine the tomatoes with the capers, garlic, lemon zest, lemon juice and *herbes de Provence*. Pulse until a very coarse, rough puree forms, adding some of the reserved oil if necessary. Season to taste with salt.

—Ann Haskell

• • •

LOOKING-GLASS GUACAMOLE

This coarse puree of tomato with chunks of avocado is brightened with coriander and hot peppers. It is a lively, all-purpose salsa that's as good on grilled chicken as it is with tortilla chips.

Makes About 2¼ Cups

1 pound firm, ripe, thick-fleshed tomatoes, such as San Marzano, peeled
1 large garlic clove, lightly bruised
½ of a medium onion, finely grated
3 to 4 serrano or 2 to 3 jalapeño peppers, ribs and about half of the seeds removed, minced (3 tablespoons)
⅓ cup minced fresh coriander (cilantro)
Salt
½ of a very ripe Hass avocado, cut into ⅓-inch dice

1. Chop the tomatoes with a very sharp knife until you have a coarse puree with ¼-inch bits of tomato. Put the puree in a coarse sieve set over a bowl and let it drain for 20 minutes or so, tossing from time to time. (Save the juice for use in soups, sauces and stews.)

2. Rub a wide shallow serving bowl with the garlic, pressing on the clove to release as much juice as possible; leave the garlic in the bowl. Add the tomato puree to the bowl and stir in the grated onion, half of the peppers, half of the coriander and salt to taste. Let the mixture sit for 10 to 15 minutes, then remove the garlic clove.

3. Add additional minced peppers and coriander until you like the flavor balance, then stir in the avocado and serve.

—Leslie Land

• • •

CHOPPED LIVER

In this recipe the livers are sautéed but they can also be broiled. Chopped liver is most often served with crackers as an hors d'oeuvre, but it's also mighty good between two slices of rye bread with thinly sliced onions.

Makes About 2½ Cups

1 pound chicken livers
¼ cup rendered chicken fat (schmaltz)
3 medium onions, finely chopped
2 hard-cooked eggs, finely chopped
Salt and freshly ground pepper

1. Rinse the chicken livers under cold running water. Trim off any fat and discolored spots; pat dry.

2. In a large heavy skillet, heat 1 tablespoon of the chicken fat over moderately high heat. Add half the livers and cook, tossing, until firm but slightly pink in the center, about 5 minutes. Transfer to a plate and repeat with the remaining livers. Set aside to cool.

3. Add 1 tablespoon of the chicken fat to the skillet and reduce the heat to moderately low. Add the onions and cook, stirring occasionally, until softened and just beginning to brown, about 15 minutes. Set aside to cool slightly.

4. In a food processor, combine the livers and onions. Pulse just a few times; the mixture should not be pasty but should have a rough texture. Alternatively, pass the liver and onions through a meat grinder fitted with a coarse blade.

5. Transfer the liver to a medium bowl and stir in the eggs. Add the 2 remaining tablespoons chicken fat and season with salt and pepper to taste. Serve at room temperature.

—Susan R. Friedland

• • •

CARNITAS, GUADALAJARA STYLE

These little pieces of succulent browned pork can be served on their own as a snack or with warmed fresh tortillas and guacamole.

8 to 10 Servings

5 pounds boneless picnic pork shoulder roast, cut into 2-inch cubes
1 teaspoon salt
2½ pounds large tomatoes, seeded and chopped
5 serrano chiles, seeded and finely chopped
1 large white onion, coarsely chopped
½ cup chopped fresh coriander (cilantro) leaves

1. Pour ¼ inch of water into a large dutch oven. Add the meat and sprinkle the salt on top. Bring to a boil over high heat. Reduce the heat and simmer gently, stirring occasionally, until all the liquid has evaporated, the fat is rendered and the meat is tender, 1 to 1½ hours. Continue to cook, turning the pieces of pork in the rendered fat until evenly browned, about 15 minutes longer. Transfer the meat to paper towels to drain. Trim all the visible fat from the *carnitas*, if desired.

2. Pour off the fat in the dutch oven and return the *carnitas* to the casserole. Stir in most of the tomatoes, chiles, onion and coriander, reserving a little of each for garnish. Cover and cook over low heat until the tomatoes and onion soften slightly, 4 to 5 minutes. Season with salt to taste. Transfer the *carnitas* to a warmed serving platter and garnish with the reserved tomatoes, chiles, onion and coriander.

—*Chata DuBose*

• • •

WOOD-ROASTED SWEET PEPPERS IN OLIVE OIL

You can reproduce the smoky flavor of the Spanish *piquillo* pepper by smoking roasted bell peppers in a covered skillet.

If you don't want to roast the peppers yourself (Step 1), you can use a jar of imported *piquillo* peppers, available at specialty food shops, or you can use other good-quality commercially roasted peppers.

Serve this dish with baguette or peasant bread slices, toasted or not.

4 Servings

3 medium red bell peppers
One 1-inch piece of grapevine cutting or ½ teaspoon mesquite chips
5 medium garlic cloves, thinly sliced
⅓ cup extra-virgin olive oil
1 tablespoon boiling water
2 teaspoons sweet paprika
⅛ teaspoon salt
⅛ teaspoon sugar

1. Roast the red peppers directly over a gas flame or under the broiler as close to the heat as possible, turning frequently, until charred all over. Transfer the peppers to a paper bag and set aside to steam for 10 minutes. Scrape off the blackened skin and remove the cores, seeds and ribs. Rinse the peppers and pat dry.

2. Place the grapevine cutting on the bottom of a heavy skillet (preferably cast iron). Fit a rack into the skillet and heat over moderate heat until the grapevine starts smoking, about 3 minutes. Arrange the peppers on the rack, cover and smoke for 5 minutes. Transfer to a plate to cool slightly. Slice the peppers into ¾-inch-wide strips.

3. In a heavy medium skillet, cook the garlic in the olive oil over moderate heat, stirring occasionally, until slightly softened, about 2 minutes. Add the peppers, reduce the heat to moderately low and cook, tossing occasionally, for 15 minutes.

4. In a small bowl, combine the boiling water and paprika and set aside for 5 minutes. When the peppers are ready, stir in the paprika mixture, the salt and the sugar and cook, stirring, until the peppers are meltingly tender, about 15 minutes. Serve warm or at room temperature. *(The peppers will keep for up to 5 days; cover and refrigerate.)*

—*Sally Schneider*

• • •

VIETNAMESE BEEF BALLS

This favorite quick snack packs a great deal of pungent flavor.

Makes About 40 Beef Balls

1 pound beef round, trimmed of all fat
3 tablespoons plus 2 teaspoons fish sauce (nuoc mam)*
1 tablespoon fresh lime juice
1½ teaspoons tapioca or potato starch
½ teaspoon sugar
½ teaspoon baking powder
½ fresh cayenne or serrano chile, finely chopped
1¼ teaspoons whole black peppercorns
1 stalk of lemon grass,* white bulb only, thinly sliced, or 1 tablespoon dried lemon grass soaked in hot water for 30 minutes
1 medium onion, quartered
1 to 2 tablespoons Oriental sesame oil
Chile Paste (p. 263)
3 tablespoons chopped scallion greens
3 tablespoons fresh coriander (cilantro) leaves
Freshly ground pepper
****Available at Asian markets***

1. Slice the beef across the grain ¼ inch thick. In a nonreactive baking dish, combine 3 tablespoons of the fish sauce with the lime juice, tapioca, sugar, baking powder and 2 tablespoons of water. Add the beef slices and stir to coat thoroughly.

2. In a mortar, pound the chile with ¼ teaspoon of the whole black peppercorns. Add this to the marinating meat and stir well. Cover and refrigerate for at least 6 hours and up to 20 hours.

3. In a medium saucepan, bring 6

cups of water to a boil over high heat. Add the remaining 1 teaspoon whole black peppercorns, the fresh or reconstituted lemon grass and the onion and reduce the heat to moderately low. Cover and simmer to make a flavorful broth, about 20 minutes. Reserve until needed.

4. To prepare beef balls, place half of the meat in a food processor and process to a very smooth paste, about 1 minute. Transfer the meat to a medium bowl and repeat with the remainder.

5. Roll a small amount of the meat between your palms to form a ball about the size of a small walnut. Dab a little of the sesame oil on the palm of one hand and roll the beef ball in your palm to coat with the oil before setting on a plate. Repeat with the remaining meat and oil.

6. Bring the broth to a boil over high heat. Reduce the heat to moderate and add half of the beef balls; they will sink and then rise to the surface. Let them cook in the boiling broth for 3 minutes after they rise to the surface. Transfer the balls to a large plate and set aside. Repeat with the remaining beef balls.

7. For hors d'oeuvres, serve the beef balls with the Chile Paste for dipping. To serve as a more substantial soup or first course, stir the remaining 2 teaspoons fish sauce into the broth. Strain the broth; discard the solids. Serve the beef balls in small bowls with some broth, garnished with the scallion greens, coriander and freshly ground black pepper.

—Jeffrey Alford & Naomi Duguid

• • •

STIR-FRIED LAMB WITH LEMON-SOY VINAIGRETTE

6 First-Course Servings

LEMON-SOY VINAIGRETTE:
3 tablespoons rice wine vinegar
2 tablespoons peanut oil
2 tablespoons soy sauce
1 tablespoon Oriental sesame oil
1½ tablespoons fresh lemon juice
Salt and freshly ground pepper

4 shallots, minced
1 red jalapeño pepper, minced
2 green jalapeño peppers, minced
5 garlic cloves, minced
1 tablespoon plus 1 teaspoon peanut oil
1½ pounds lean ground lamb
½ cup chopped fresh coriander (cilantro) plus ¼ cup whole leaves, for garnish
¼ cup Chinese pickled or preserved cabbage
½ teaspoon soy sauce
¼ teaspoon salt
¼ teaspoon freshly ground black pepper
18 radicchio leaves
¼ of a small red onion, sliced crosswise ⅛ inch thick
¼ of a small white onion, sliced crosswise ⅛ inch thick

1. *Make the vinaigrette:* In a small bowl, whisk all the ingredients together until combined. Cover and refrigerate up to 1 day.

2. In a medium skillet, cook the shallots, red jalapeño, half of the green jalapeños and the garlic in 2 teaspoons of the peanut oil, stirring, over low heat until softened, about 5 minutes. Set aside to cool.

3. In a bowl, combine the cooled vegetable mixture with the ground lamb and mix thoroughly. Add the chopped fresh coriander, pickled cabbage, soy sauce, salt and black pepper.

4. In a large skillet, cook the lamb mixture in the remaining 2 teaspoons peanut oil over high heat, stirring well to break up clumps, until browned, about 4 minutes. Drain and set aside.

5. Place 3 radicchio leaves on each plate and fill with the lamb mixture. Combine the red onion, white onion, fresh coriander leaves and the remaining green jalapeños; sprinkle on top of the lamb. Serve drizzled with a few tablespoons of the vinaigrette; serve the remaining vinaigrette on the side.

—Kazuto Matsusaka,
Chinois on Main, Santa Monica

• • •

PORK SATAY

This South Thai version of the Southeast Asian classic is served with a choice of two sauces. Put a bowl of each on the table, or serve them in individual bowls.

4 to 6 First-Course Servings

MARINADE:
½ cup unsweetened coconut milk*
3 tablespoons fish sauce (nam pla)*
2 large garlic cloves, minced
2 tablespoons finely chopped fresh coriander (cilantro) roots
2 tablespoons peanut or vegetable oil
1 tablespoon brown sugar
1 tablespoon soy sauce
1 teaspoon freshly ground pepper

1 pound lean pork loin, sliced ¼ inch thick and cut into 3-by-¾-inch strips
Lettuce leaves and cucumber slices, for serving

Red Curry Sauce (p. 256)
Tangy Lime Sauce (p. 256)
****Available at Asian markets***

1. In a medium bowl, combine all the marinade ingredients. Mix well. Add the pork strips and toss to coat thoroughly. Cover and let marinate at room temperature for 1 hour. If using wooden skewers, soak 18 skewers in water for at least 30 minutes.

2. Light a grill or preheat the broiler. If using skewers, thread 1 or 2 pieces of the pork onto each skewer. Grill over hot coals for 2 to 3 minutes on each side, until the meat is cooked through. Alternatively, place the meat strips on an oiled broiling rack and broil 1 to 2 inches from the heat for about 5 minutes, turning once after 3 minutes, until browned and cooked through.

3. Arrange the lettuce leaves on a platter and place the pork on top. Put the cucumber slices on a plate and serve with the Red Curry Sauce and Tangy Lime Sauce.

—Jeffrey Alford & Naomi Duguid

• • •

SHRIMP WITH GARLIC

Soaking shrimp in salt water gives them a fresh briny flavor. Serve with lots of crusty bread.

4 Servings

1 tablespoon coarse sea salt
¾ pound medium shrimp (about 20), shelled and deveined
½ cup extra-virgin olive oil
1 tablespoon plus 1 teaspoon minced garlic
¼ teaspoon crushed hot red pepper
1 teaspoon dry sherry vinegar or white wine vinegar
¼ cup finely chopped flat-leaf parsley

1. In a medium bowl, stir the salt into 1 cup of water until dissolved. Add the shrimp and let soak for 5 minutes. Drain and pat dry.

2. In a heavy medium skillet, heat the oil over moderately high heat until hot but not smoking, about 4 minutes. Add the shrimp in 1 layer and sprinkle the garlic and red pepper on top. Cook the shrimp, turning once, until opaque, about 1 minute per side; do not overcook. Stir in the vinegar and parsley and serve.

—Sally Schneider

• • •

SAUTEED MUSHROOMS

Although white button mushrooms are traditionally used for this dish, portobello and cremini mushrooms are also delicious cooked this way, and they have an earthier flavor and slightly meatier texture.

6 Servings

½ cup extra-virgin olive oil
24 medium white or cremini mushrooms, stems removed, or 6 portobello mushrooms, stems removed and caps quartered
9 garlic cloves, thinly sliced
¾ teaspoon salt
Freshly ground pepper
Twelve 1-inch cubes of medium-textured French or Italian bread

1. In a large heavy skillet, heat the oil over moderate heat until hot but not smoking, about 3 minutes. Add the mushrooms, stemmed side down, and the garlic and cook for 2 minutes, shaking the pan occasionally. Flip the mushrooms over and place 1 or 2 slices of the cooked garlic in the cavity of each mushroom. Season with the salt and pepper to taste and cook until juices collect in the cavities, about 3 minutes.

2. Skewer 2 mushrooms with their garlic slivers and 1 bread cube onto each of 12 toothpicks. Serve at once.

—Sally Schneider

• • •

GRILLED SKEWERED SHRIMP AND COUNTRY BREAD

Makes 40

40 large shrimp, shelled and deveined
1 loaf of country bread, cut into forty 1½-inch cubes
40 fresh sage leaves
¾ cup extra-virgin olive oil
1 tablespoon finely chopped fresh rosemary
4 garlic cloves, minced
Juice of 1 to 2 lemons

1. Soak 40 wooden skewers in water for at least 15 minutes. Thread 1 shrimp, 1 cube of bread and 1 sage leaf onto each skewer. Arrange the skewers in a shallow baking dish.

2. In a small bowl, combine the olive oil, rosemary and garlic. Pour the herbed oil over the skewers and marinate at room temperature for at least 1 hour or refrigerate, covered, for up to 1 day.

3. Light a grill or preheat the broiler. Grill or broil the skewers, turning as necessary, for 3 to 4 minutes, until the shrimp are just warm and the bread is lightly toasted. Sprinkle with lemon juice and serve immediately.

—Evan Kleiman

• • •

MUSHROOM PAKORAS WITH FRESH MINT CHUTNEY

Street food in Singapore seems to include all the regional cuisines of India, but with a twist.

Makes About 20 Pakoras

3 cups peanut oil, for deep-frying
1⅓ cups chickpea flour (5 ounces)
1 teaspoon salt
1 teaspoon baking powder
½ teaspoon cayenne pepper
½ teaspoon garam masala (optional)
1 pound very fresh medium mushrooms, rinsed and dried
Fresh Mint Chutney (p. 261)

1. In a wok, heat the oil over moderately high heat to 375°. Meanwhile, in a small bowl, combine the chickpea flour, salt, baking powder, cayenne and *garam masala*. Make a well in the center of the flour and pour in 1 cup of warm water. Stirring from the center, incorporate the dry ingredients to make a smooth, thick batter. If the mixture is lumpy, pass it through a coarse strainer.

2. Drop 3 or 4 mushrooms into the batter and turn to coat well. Using chopsticks or tongs, lift out the mushrooms and gently place them in the hot oil. Fry, turning, until golden brown all over, 2 to 3 minutes. Transfer to paper towels to drain well. Repeat with the remaining mushrooms and batter. Serve hot, with the Fresh Mint Chutney.

—Jeffrey Alford & Naomi Duguid

• • •

SALT COD FRITTERS WITH ROMESCO SAUCE

Mildly salted salt cod is available in the freezer section of many supermarkets; it needs to be soaked for about 12 hours. The traditional stiff salt cod, with skin and bones, can be found at ethnic markets and at fish markets. Because it is more highly salted, it should be soaked for 24 to 36 hours. To test, taste a small piece—it should be faintly salty and quite tender. In some fish markets, you can also get presoaked, skinless, boneless *un*frozen cod, which is a very nice product.

Use the center-cut, rather than the tail-end, portion of the salt cod. It has a much better texture.

Makes About 2 Dozen Fritters

½ pound skinless, boneless center-cut salt cod
1 large or 2 medium boiling potatoes, peeled and sliced ¼ inch thick
1½ cups milk
⅛ teaspoon thyme
1 bay leaf
½ teaspoon minced garlic
1 egg yolk
1 tablespoon extra-virgin olive oil
2 tablespoons all-purpose flour
1 tablespoon minced flat-leaf parsley
½ teaspoon salt
½ teaspoon freshly ground pepper
Olive oil or peanut oil, for frying
Romesco Sauce (p. 257)

1. In a medium bowl, cover the salt cod with cold water. Refrigerate for at least 12 hours (see headnote), changing the water frequently.

2. Drain the salt cod. In a medium saucepan, combine the cod, potatoes, milk, thyme and bay leaf and bring just to a simmer over low heat, about 10 minutes. Simmer until the potatoes are tender, about 15 minutes longer. Remove from the heat and set aside for 10 minutes.

3. Strain the liquid and reserve. Break the cod into 1-inch pieces, discarding any membrane or bones, and place in a medium bowl. Add the potatoes and garlic to the cod. Discard the bay leaf. Using a hand-held electric mixer, beat the mixture until the cod is shredded and the potatoes are coarsely pureed, about 1 minute. Gradually beat in 1 tablespoon of the reserved cooking liquid, the egg yolk and the extra-virgin olive oil. Sprinkle the flour on top and beat it in with a spoon. Beat in the parsley, salt and pepper.

4. In a heavy medium saucepan, heat 1 inch of olive oil over moderate heat until very hot, about 375° on a deep-fat thermometer.

5. Meanwhile, using a tablespoon, form the cod mixture into 1-inch balls and place on a plate. When the oil is hot, fry the salt cod balls in batches, without crowding, until they are golden brown and crisp, about 2 minutes. Using a slotted spoon, transfer the fritters to paper towels to drain. Repeat with the remaining codfish balls. Serve at once with the Romesco Sauce.

—Sally Schneider

• • •

DEEP-FRIED PARMIGIANO-REGGIANO WITH SAFFRON

🍷 Deep-fried tidbits such as these love the refreshing bubbles of Champagne. Look for middle-of-the-road Champagnes, neither too heavy nor too light. Try a Brut from Louis Roederer or Charles Heidsieck.

Makes 40 to 45 Pieces

½ teaspoon (packed) saffron threads
½ pound young Parmigiano-Reggiano
8 cups sunflower oil, for deep-frying
½ cup all-purpose flour
2 eggs, beaten
4 cups fresh bread crumbs (from 4 slices of firm white bread)
Coarse (kosher) salt

1. In a small skillet, toast the saffron threads over moderately high heat, stirring until dry and brittle, about 3 minutes. Set aside to cool, then crumble.

2. In a small saucepan, bring ½ cup of water to a boil over high heat. Add the crumbled saffron and boil for 2 minutes. Remove from the heat and let the liquid cool to room temperature.

3. Cut the Parmigiano-Reggiano into long shards, no more than ¼-inch thick. Place in a large shallow dish and pour the cooled saffron liquid on top. Set aside at room temperature to marinate for at least 4 hours or overnight.

4. In a deep-fat fryer or deep, heavy saucepan with a fry basket, heat the oil to 375°.

5. Meanwhile, drain the cheese shards. Place the flour, beaten eggs and bread crumbs in separate shallow dishes. Piece by piece, dredge the cheese shards in the flour, shaking off the excess, then dip in the beaten egg and roll in the bread crumbs, pressing lightly so that the crumbs will adhere. Transfer the breaded pieces to a plate as you work.

6. Put half of the cheese into the fry basket and lower into the hot oil. Fry until golden and crisp, about 30 seconds. Transfer to paper towels to drain and sprinkle immediately with coarse salt. Fry the remaining cheese and serve immediately.

—David Rosengarten

• • •

EGG ROLLS

This is truly a creation of the Chinese-American restaurant. There is no such thing as an egg roll in China. There are spring rolls, delicate finger-size cylinders filled with bean sprouts, scallions, shrimp and pork, encased in a paper-thin skin. Egg rolls on the other hand are usually filled with a bewildering variety of ingredients, mostly chopped cabbage. It is, however, possible to create a fine egg roll, and here it is.

Makes 12 Egg Rolls

1-inch slice of fresh ginger, peeled
1 large garlic clove
1 tablespoon plus 1½ teaspoons sugar
2½ teaspoons salt
6 medium shrimp (¼ pound), shelled and deveined
2-pound head of green cabbage, tough outer leaves removed
1 medium onion, cut into ¼-inch dice
2 large celery ribs, cut into ¼-inch dice
¼ pound Chinese barbecued pork, cut into ¼-inch dice
12 egg roll wrappers
1 egg, beaten
4 cups peanut oil, for deep-frying
1 tablespoon dry mustard mixed with 1 tablespoon cold water

1. Fill a large saucepan with water. Add the ginger, garlic, sugar and salt and bring to a boil over high heat. Add the shrimp and cook until they curl and turn pink, about 1 minute. Discard the garlic and ginger and, using a slotted spoon, transfer the shrimp to a sieve to drain; let cool slightly, then cut into ¼-inch dice. Set aside.

2. Bring the water in the saucepan back to a boil over high heat. Halve, core and finely chop the cabbage. You should have 6 cups. Add the cabbage, onion and celery to the water and cook until the cabbage is bright green, about 1½ minutes. Drain thoroughly in a colander and set aside to cool slightly. Press down to extract any excess water from the vegetables.

3. In a large bowl, combine the reserved shrimp and the barbecued pork; season with salt to taste. Add the vegetables and mix well. Divide the filling into 12 equal portions.

4. Place an egg roll wrapper on a work surface like a diamond, with a tip facing you. Keep the remaining wrappers covered. Place one portion of the filling in a horizontal line across the bottom third of the wrapper, then fold the tip closest to you over the filling toward the center. Lightly brush the side tips of the wrapper with some of the beaten egg, then fold them into the center. Brush the surface with egg and roll up the wrapper from the bottom. Brush the top tip with egg; fold toward you to seal the cylinder. Repeat with remaining wrappers and filling.

5. Heat a wok over high heat for 45 seconds. Add the peanut oil and heat to 350°. Add 4 egg rolls to the wok and fry, turning frequently with tongs or chopsticks, until golden brown, 4 to 5 minutes. Transfer to a colander or large sieve set over a bowl to drain. Repeat with the remaining egg rolls, 4 at a time.

Serve immediately with the mustard sauce.

—*Eileen Yin-Fei Lo*

• • •

FRESH SARDINES IN PUFF PASTRY

Makes 12 Pastries

About ½ pound all-butter puff pastry, thawed if frozen
2 teaspoons Dijon mustard
1 teaspoon finely chopped fresh basil
3 fresh or thawed frozen sardines (about 7 inches long), filleted and halved crosswise
Egg wash: 1 egg yolk beaten with 1 teaspoon water

1. Preheat the oven to 400°. Roll out the puff pastry ⅛ inch thick and cut out three 5-inch squares. In a small bowl, mix the mustard and basil.

2. Work with 1 square of pastry at a time, keeping the others refrigerated. Using a sharp knife, halve the pastry to make two strips 2½ by 5 inches. Cut each strip crosswise into 4 equal strips, making 8 strips of pastry, 2½ by 1¼ inches each.

3. Place 1 piece of sardine on each of 4 strips of pastry and spread with some of the mustard and basil. Top with the remaining 4 pastry strips and crimp the edges to seal. Repeat with the 2 remaining pastry squares, sardines and mustard. Brush the tops with the egg wash.

4. Arrange the pastries on a baking sheet and bake for about 15 minutes, until golden brown. Serve hot.

—*Ann Haskell*

• • •

SHRIMP, WATERCRESS AND SUN-DRIED TOMATO WRAPS

Watercress and carrot give these cool shrimp wraps a fresh taste, and the pungent, minty dipping sauce lends an exotic edge.

Makes 8 Wraps

16 medium shrimp, shelled and deveined, shells reserved
1 garlic clove, minced
½ teaspoon crushed hot red pepper, chopped
½ teaspoon sugar
1½ tablespoons rice vinegar*
1 tablespoon chopped fresh spearmint
Eight 8-inch round rice paper wrappers*
1 bunch of watercress, large stems discarded
1 large carrot, halved crosswise and cut into ⅛-inch-thick sticks
8 oil-cured sun-dried tomato halves, cut in fine slivers
****Available at Asian markets***

1. In a small saucepan, cover the shrimp shells with 1½ cups of water and bring to a boil over high heat. Add the shrimp, packing them in among the shells. Cook until the shrimp begin to curl, about 1 minute. Remove the shrimp from the pan and let cool. Strain the broth and reserve 3 tablespoons. Halve each shrimp lengthwise.

2. In a small bowl, combine the garlic, crushed red pepper and sugar. Stir in the vinegar and the reserved shrimp broth until the sugar dissolves, then add the spearmint. Set aside.

3. Lay 4 of the rice paper wrappers on a work surface. Use a pastry brush to brush both sides of each wrapper with water. Let the wrappers absorb the water and soften, about 2 minutes. If the wrappers still feel firm, lightly moisten again.

4. Divide the watercress and carrot in 8 portions. Place a portion of watercress in a line across the lower third of each of the 4 moistened rice paper wrappers. Top each with a portion of carrot, 4 shrimp halves and 1 slivered sun-dried tomato. Pull the bottom flap of the rice paper up and over the filling to secure snugly. Tightly roll up each of the wraps, folding in the sides as you go. The wrappers should adhere to themselves when rolled. Repeat with the remaining 4 wrappers and fillings. Halve each wrap crosswise and serve with the mint-garlic dip.

—*Marcia Kiesel*

• • •

STEAMED SQUID WITH GINGER-GARLIC SAUCE

Wrap some squid in a lettuce leaf and pop the bundle in your mouth.

4 Servings

1 to 2 tablespoons grated or finely chopped fresh ginger
1 Thai, or bird, chile or 1 to 2 serrano chiles, finely chopped
2 small garlic cloves, minced, plus 4 medium garlic cloves, crushed
½ teaspoon sugar
5 tablespoons fish sauce (nuoc mam)*
5 tablespoons fresh lime juice
Freshly ground pepper
2 pounds cleaned small squid, bodies sliced into 1¾-inch rings
½ cup fresh coriander (cilantro) leaves
Lettuce leaves
1 lime, cut into wedges

Salt
**Available at Asian markets*

1. In a mortar, crush and blend together the ginger, chile, the 2 minced garlic cloves and the sugar. Alternatively, finely chop the ingredients together with a knife. Add 3 tablespoons of the fish sauce, 3 tablespoons of the lime juice and 1 tablespoon of water and blend well. Transfer the ginger-garlic sauce to a small serving bowl.

2. In a small bowl, combine the 4 crushed garlic cloves, the remaining 2 tablespoons fish sauce, 2 tablespoons lime juice and a few grindings of pepper. Add the squid pieces and mix well. Cover and marinate in the refrigerator for 1 to 2 hours.

3. Bring a large saucepan of water to a boil. Place the squid in a steamer basket and steam, tightly covered, until tender, about 20 minutes. Remove the squid from the steamer and toss with the coriander leaves.

4. Line a small platter with lettuce and mound the squid in the center. Serve with side dishes of lime wedges, salt, pepper and ginger-garlic sauce.

—*Jeffrey Alford & Naomi Duguid*

• • •

CHICKEN, ASPARAGUS AND SHIITAKE WRAPS

What makes these wraps utterly delicious is the rich sesame dip that brings all the flavors together.

Makes 8 Wraps

2 small garlic cloves, minced
1 teaspoon finely grated ginger plus a 1-inch piece of ginger, cut into ¼-inch slices
2 tablespoons tahini (sesame paste)
2 teaspoons soy sauce
1 teaspoon fresh lemon juice
16 asparagus spears, trimmed
1 whole skinless, boneless chicken breast (about 12 ounces)
2 teaspoons vegetable oil
48 medium shiitake mushrooms, stems discarded
Salt and freshly ground pepper
*Eight 8-inch round rice paper wrappers**
1 bunch of chives
**Available at Asian markets*

1. In a small bowl, combine the garlic, grated ginger and tahini. Stir in the soy sauce, lemon juice and 3 tablespoons of warm water. Set aside.

2. Bring a medium saucepan of water to a boil and add the ginger slices. Add the asparagus and cook until just tender, about 4 minutes. With tongs, remove the asparagus to a colander and cool them under cold running water. Add the chicken to the same pan and simmer over low heat until white throughout, about 10 minutes. Remove to a plate to cool. Cut the chicken into ¼-inch-thick strips. Separate into 8 equal piles.

3. In a large skillet, heat the vegetable oil over high heat. Add the shiitake mushrooms and cook for 1 minute. Spread the mushrooms in an even layer and reduce the heat to low. Cover and cook until tender, 3 to 4 minutes. Season the mushrooms with salt and pepper to taste and cut them in half.

4. Lay 4 of the rice paper wrappers on a work surface. Use a pastry brush to brush both sides of each wrapper with water. Let the wrappers absorb the water and soften, about 2 minutes. If parts of the wrappers still feel firm, lightly moisten them again.

5. Lay 2 asparagus spears across the lower third of each of the 4 moistened rice paper wrappers and arrange a portion of chicken and 12 mushroom halves evenly alongside. Top with 5 chives. Pull the bottom flap of the rice paper up and over the filling to secure snugly. Tightly roll up each of the wraps, bringing in the sides as you go. The rice paper should adhere to itself once rolled up. Repeat with the remaining 4 wrappers and fillings. To serve, cut each wrap in half crosswise and arrange on a platter. Serve the sesame dip on the side.

—*Marcia Kiesel*

• • •

CRISP SALMON-NORI HAND ROLLS

This is a heartier home-style version of my favorite Japanese restaurant snack. Salmon skin is delicious when it's flavored with soy sauce and sesame and cooked until crisp. The fish needs to marinate overnight in the refrigerator.

Makes 8 Rolls

2 tablespoons soy sauce
*1½ teaspoons Japanese mirin**
¼ teaspoon Oriental sesame oil
1 pound tail-end salmon fillet with skin, cut crosswise in eight ½-inch strips
1 teaspoon dry mustard
½ teaspoon sugar
1 teaspoon rice vinegar or white wine vinegar
½ cup medium grain or "sushi" rice, rinsed
1 tablespoon sesame seeds
2 teaspoons vegetable oil
4 square sheets of nori, cut in half on the diagonal*
2 scallions, halved crosswise, then thinly sliced lengthwise

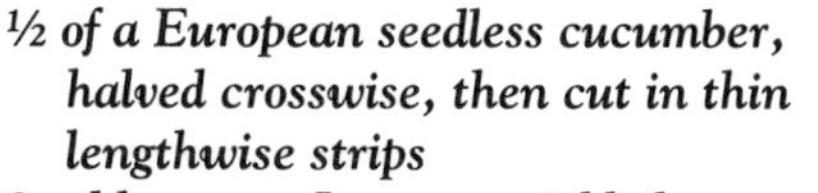

½ of a European seedless cucumber, halved crosswise, then cut in thin lengthwise strips
*2 tablespoons Japanese pickled ginger**
**Available at Japanese markets*

1. In a small bowl, mix 1 tablespoon of the soy sauce with the mirin and sesame oil. Put the salmon strips in a shallow dish, pour the marinade on top and turn to coat completely. Cover and refrigerate overnight.

2. The next day, make the dipping sauce. In a small bowl, combine the dry mustard and sugar. Stir in 2 tablespoons of hot water and then the vinegar and the remaining 1 tablespoon soy sauce. Set aside.

3. Put the rice in a small saucepan and cover with ¾ cup of water. Bring to a boil over high heat. Cover and reduce the heat to very low. Cook for 15 minutes without lifting the lid. Remove from the heat and let stand, covered, for 5 minutes.

4. In a small dry skillet, toast the sesame seeds over high heat, stirring occasionally, until golden brown, about 1½ minutes. Gently fold the sesame seeds into the rice.

5. In a large nonstick skillet, heat the vegetable oil over high heat until almost smoking. Carefully arrange the salmon pieces in the pan, placing them very close together, skin side down, so that they hold each other up. Cover the skillet, reduce the heat to moderately high and cook until the skin is dark and crisp, about 2 minutes. Uncover and sear the salmon pieces briefly on each side until cooked through, about 30 seconds per side. With a spatula, transfer the salmon to a plate.

6. To assemble the rolls, lay a nori triangle on a work surface with the long straight side to your left and the short point facing right. Arrange one-eighth of the scallion and cucumber strips crosswise in the center of the triangle. Top with 2 tablespoons of the sesame rice, a few pieces of pickled ginger and top with a piece of salmon. Form the hand roll by lifting the long tip nearest you up and over the filling, keeping the nori tight. Press the roll to keep the filling intact while rolling upward in a semicircle to make a horn-shaped roll. Repeat with the remaining ingredients. Serve with the mustard-soy dipping sauce.

—*Marcia Kiesel*

• • •

CHILE-ANISE BEEF WRAPS WITH ARUGULA AND RADISH

Chinese cabbage leaves and a light, tangy dressing make this wrap a cool beef salad to eat out of hand.

Makes 10 Wraps

2 teaspoons anise seeds, chopped
1 tablespoon pure chile powder
2 garlic cloves, minced
One 1-pound piece beef eye of round
2 teaspoons plus 3 tablespoons mild but fruity olive oil
2 tablespoons fresh lemon juice
10 Chinese cabbage leaves, lower third discarded
2 bunches of arugula, stemmed
1 bunch of radishes, cut in thin matchsticks
Coarse (kosher) salt, for serving

1. Combine the anise seeds, chile powder and garlic. Rub this mixture all over the beef. Cover and refrigerate overnight. Let return to room temperature before proceeding.

2. Preheat the oven to 450°. In a small ovenproof skillet, heat the 2 teaspoons olive oil over high heat until almost smoking. Reduce the heat to moderate and add the beef. Brown the meat all over, using a metal spatula when turning to keep the crust on the beef, about 2 minutes per side. Place the skillet in the oven and roast the beef for 15 minutes for rare to medium-rare, until an instant-read thermometer reaches 120° to 125°. Transfer the meat to a carving board and let rest for at least 10 minutes before slicing.

3. In a small bowl, combine the remaining 3 tablespoons olive oil with the lemon juice.

4. Cut the beef lengthwise in half. Slice the meat with the crusty side down crosswise against the grain into a total of 40 very thin slices.

5. To assemble the wraps, place the cabbage leaves on a large platter. Mound the arugula inside the leaves and top with the radish sticks. Arrange 4 slices of beef on each leaf. Have a small bowl of kosher salt next to the platter to sprinkle on the beef. To eat, roll up the wraps and dip in the dressing, or spoon the dressing on the meat before rolling up.

—*Marcia Kiesel*

• • •

FRUIT AND VEGETABLE WRAPS WITH CURRIED PEANUT DRESSING

Makes 10 Wraps

4 ounces dried rice noodles,* preferably medium width
2 teaspoons vegetable oil
1 medium onion, finely chopped
2 large garlic cloves, minced
⅛ to ¼ teaspoon cayenne pepper
1 tablespoon curry paste* or powder
1 teaspoon tomato paste
½ cup fresh orange juice
⅓ cup unsalted dry-roasted peanuts
½ teaspoon fresh lemon juice
Salt (optional)
10 large Boston lettuce leaves
1 large tart apple—peeled, cored and cut in ½-inch dice
2 cups fresh mung bean sprouts
10 large sprigs of fresh coriander (cilantro)
****Available at Asian markets***

1. Place the rice noodles in a large bowl and cover with cold water. Let sit for 20 minutes, until softened.

2. Meanwhile, in a small nonreactive skillet, heat the oil over moderate heat. Add the onion and garlic and stir well. Reduce the heat to low, cover and cook, stirring twice, until golden, about 7 minutes. Uncover and stir in the cayenne and curry paste until fragrant, about 1 minute. Add the tomato paste and cook for about 30 seconds. Pour in the orange juice and cook until reduced slightly, about 1 minute. Remove from the heat.

3. Place the peanuts in a food processor and chop very finely, almost to a paste. Add the curried onion mixture and process until a thick puree forms. Scrape the dressing into a small bowl and season with the lemon juice and salt to taste; set aside.

4. Bring a medium saucepan of water to a boil. Drain the rice noodles and cook them in the saucepan until translucent and chewy, about 1 minute. Drain well. Transfer the noodles to a work surface and quickly form them into a 10-by-6-inch rectangle. As the noodles cool, they will stick together. Cut the rectangle in half lengthwise and cut each half crosswise in 5 pieces.

5. To assemble the wraps, spread about 2 teaspoons of the curried peanut dressing on each lettuce leaf and top with a noodle cake. Cover with the apple, bean sprouts and a coriander sprig; roll up and eat.

—Marcia Kiesel

• • •

"EGG ROLL" WRAPS

Makes 12 Pieces

1 scallion, minced
1 tablespoon yellow miso*
1 teaspoon Chinese chile paste*
½ teaspoon tomato paste
¼ teaspoon fresh lemon juice
1 large orange sweet potato
2½ teaspoons vegetable oil
3 medium leeks, white and tender green, thinly sliced
6 eggs, beaten
Salt and freshly ground pepper
3 tablespoons fresh coriander (cilantro) leaves
****Available at Asian markets***

1. In a small bowl, combine the scallion, miso, chile paste, tomato paste and lemon juice. Stir in 2 tablespoons of hot water to blend. Cover and set aside.

2. In a saucepan, cover the sweet potato with water and bring to a boil over high heat. Reduce the heat and simmer until just tender, about 20 minutes. Drain and let cool to room temperature, then peel. Cut the sweet potato in half lengthwise. Cut each half in 6 lengthwise strips.

3. In a 9-inch nonstick skillet, heat 1 teaspoon of the oil over high heat. Add the leeks, stir and reduce the heat to low. Add 1 tablespoon of water, cover and cook, stirring a few times, until lightly browned. Scrape the leeks into a small bowl.

4. In the same skillet, heat ½ teaspoon of the oil over moderately high heat until very hot. Pour in one-third of the beaten eggs and with a spatula, quickly mix the eggs just until they begin to set, about 10 seconds. Smooth the eggs into a thin, flat cake the size of the pan, then carefully flip the egg cake over to briefly cook the other side, about 5 seconds. Turn the egg cake out on a work surface. Repeat this process, dividing the remaining eggs in half, to make 2 more cakes, using ½ teaspoon of oil each time. Season the cakes with salt and pepper.

5. To assemble the wraps, arrange 4 sticks of sweet potato in an even line across each egg cake, about 1 inch up from the bottom. Spread the cooked leeks alongside the potatoes and top with the coriander leaves. Pull the bottom flap of the egg cakes up over the filling and roll up tightly. Cut each roll crosswise in 4 pieces and stand them up on a platter. Serve with the miso-chile dip.

—Marcia Kiesel

• • •

Summer Ratatouille (p. 173).

Above, Looking-Glass Guacamole (p. 23). Right, Chimichangas (p. 107) with Salsa Ranchera (p. 259).

EGGPLANT NAPOLEON

Tom Colicchio of Mondrian in Manhattan serves crunchy disks of sautéed eggplant layered with an eggplant-mushroom caviar. A wilted parsley sauce surrounds this three-tiered ode to eggplant.

4 Servings

4 medium eggplants (about 4 pounds)
¼ cup plus 1 teaspoon extra-virgin olive oil
Salt and freshly ground pepper
2 teaspoons peanut oil
3 cups flat-leaf parsley leaves
½ teaspoon honey
½ teaspoon fresh lemon juice
¼ pound shittake mushrooms, stemmed
½ cup all-purpose flour
2 eggs, beaten
2 cups fresh bread crumbs
2 tablespoons vegetable oil, for frying

1. Preheat the oven to 350°. Cut 3 of the eggplants in half lengthwise. Brush the cut sides with 2 teaspoons of the olive oil and sprinkle with salt and pepper. Place cut sides down in a roasting pan, cover with foil and bake for 40 minutes. Uncover and bake for about 15 minutes longer, until the flesh is very soft. Remove the eggplants from the oven and let cool slightly.

2. Meanwhile, in a medium skillet, heat the peanut oil over high heat. Add the parsley and cook, stirring, until wilted, about 30 seconds. Transfer the parsley to a blender and add the honey and ¼ cup water. Puree until smooth. Transfer the parsley sauce to a small bowl, add the lemon juice and salt and pepper to taste.

3. When the eggplant is cool enough to handle, remove and discard as many seeds as possible, then scoop the pulp into a medium bowl. Mash well with a fork and set aside.

4. In a large skillet, heat 2 teaspoons of the olive oil over moderately high heat. Add the shiitakes and cook, stirring, until softened, about 4 minutes. Let cool slightly, then chop finely and add to the mashed eggplant pulp.

5. In a slow, steady stream, whisk the remaining 3 tablespoons olive oil into the eggplant mixture. Season with salt and pepper. Set the bowl over a pan of simmering water to keep warm.

6. Cut the remaining eggplant crosswise into twelve ⅛-inch-thick slices. Using your hands, dip the eggplant slices in the flour and dust off the excess. Then dip them into the beaten egg and, finally, coat with the bread crumbs, patting lightly to help the crumbs adhere. Be sure that each round is well coated with crumbs.

7. In a large skillet, heat 2 teaspoons of the vegetable oil over moderately high heat. When hot, add the eggplant rounds, 4 at a time, and fry, turning once, until deep golden and very crisp, about 3 minutes on the first side and 2 minutes on the second. Transfer to paper towels to drain. Reduce the heat to moderate and repeat with the remaining eggplant rounds, using 2 teaspoons of vegetable oil for each batch.

8. For each serving, spread 1 heaping tablespoon of the parsley sauce on a plate and place 1 fried eggplant round in the center. Top with 2 tablespoons of the eggplant puree and another eggplant round; press to flatten slightly. Top with 2 more tablespoons of the puree and another eggplant round. Serve immediately.

—*Baba S. Khalsa*

• • •

"Egg Roll" Wraps (p. 32).

SFINCIUNI PIZZA

🍷 This bready, salty hors-d'oeuvre pizza would be nicely contrasted by a crisp, light white. Two Italian choices are 1989 Anselmi Soave "Capitel Foscarino" or 1990 Ceretto Arneis del Piemonte Blangé.

Makes One 11-by-17-Inch Pizza

⅓ cup plus 1 tablespoon olive oil
1 can (2 ounces) anchovies in olive oil—drained, rinsed and chopped
6 medium garlic cloves, finely chopped
1 envelope (¼ ounce) active dry yeast
1 cup lukewarm water (105° to 115°)
2½ cups unbleached flour, plus more for dusting
1 teaspoon salt
¼ cup coarse semolina flour or yellow cornmeal
¾ cup freshly grated Pecorino or Romano cheese (about 3 ounces)
1 teaspoon oregano
Freshly ground pepper

1. In a small bowl, stir together ⅓ cup of the oil, the anchovies and garlic. Set aside to marinate while you prepare the dough.

2. In a large bowl, combine the yeast and lukewarm water; stir to dissolve. Stir in the flour, ½ cup at a time. Stir in the salt and 1½ teaspoons of the oil.

3. Turn the shaggy dough out onto a lightly floured surface and knead for 10 minutes, dusting lightly with flour as necessary, until smooth, soft and slightly sticky.

4. Rub a large clean bowl with the remaining 1½ teaspoons oil. Place the dough in the bowl and turn to coat with the oil. Cover the bowl and set in a warm place to rise until doubled in bulk, about 1 hour.

5. Punch down the dough and turn it out onto a floured work surface. Stretch it into an 11-by-17-inch rectangle. Sprinkle the semolina on an 11-by-17-inch baking sheet, then gently transfer the dough to the pan. Cover with a towel and let rest for 30 minutes.

6. Preheat the oven to 450°. Using a fork, spread the garlic-anchovy oil evenly over the dough, leaving a 1-inch border; press lightly with your fingertips to make slight indentations in the dough. Sprinkle the Pecorino, oregano and several generous grindings of pepper on top. Bake for about 20 minutes, or until the pizza is golden brown. Cut into squares and serve hot.

—Diane Darrow & Tom Maresca

• • •

TAMALE TART WITH ROAST GARLIC CUSTARD AND GULF COAST CRABMEAT

This dish combines the rustic flavors of tamales with the elegant silkiness of the roast garlic custard. Ancho chiles have a smoky flavor and the crabmeat is testimony to the rich diversity of Texan food.

🍷 1988 Chappellet Vineyard Chenin Blanc

8 to 10 First-Course Servings

3 tablespoons olive oil
6 large garlic cloves, peeled
2 ancho chiles (about 1½ ounces)
1 cup boiling water
2 cups heavy cream
1 egg
4 egg yolks
2 teaspoons salt
⅛ teaspoon white pepper
1 red bell pepper, cut into eighths
1¼ cups masa harina*
¾ cup yellow cornmeal
¼ teaspoon cayenne pepper
2 teaspoons cumin
½ cup plus 2 tablespoons vegetable shortening
½ small onion, finely chopped
10 ounces fresh lump crabmeat, preferably Gulf Coast
¼ cup peeled, seeded and diced red tomato
¼ cup peeled, seeded and diced yellow tomato
2 tablespoons chopped fresh coriander (cilantro)
1 serrano chile, seeded and minced
2 teaspoons fresh lime juice
****Available at Latin markets and many supermarkets***

1. Preheat the oven to 300°. In a small baking pan, heat 1 tablespoon of the olive oil in the oven. Add the garlic, toss to coat with oil and roast for about 25 minutes, until golden brown. Remove the garlic from the oven and let cool slightly.

2. Meanwhile, in a medium bowl, cover the ancho chiles with the boiling water. Set aside to soften for about 20 minutes. Pour off the soaking liquid, reserving 1 tablespoon. Stem and seed the chiles. In a food processor, combine the chiles with the reserved soaking liquid and process until a paste forms. Strain the paste through a coarse sieve set over a small bowl, pressing with a rubber spatula. Set the ancho paste aside.

3. In a medium saucepan, combine the roasted garlic with the cream and bring to a boil over moderate heat. Transfer to a food processor and puree until smooth. In a medium bowl, whisk the egg with the egg yolks, then gradually whisk in the garlic cream. Season with 1 teaspoon of the salt and the white pepper. Cover and set aside to cool.

4. In a steamer basket, steam the red bell pepper until soft, about 10 minutes. Puree the pepper in a food processor until smooth. Strain the puree and set aside.

5. In a medium bowl, combine the masa harina, cornmeal, cayenne, cumin and remaining 1 teaspoon salt. In a large bowl, using an electric mixer at medium speed, whip the shortening until light and fluffy. Gradually beat in the dry ingredients until smooth. Beat in the reserved ancho and red bell pepper purees. Form the dough into a disk. Using your fingers, pat the dough into a 9-inch tart pan with a removable bottom, pressing it evenly over the bottom and up the sides. Fill the tart pan with the reserved garlic custard and cover with plastic wrap.

6. Place a round metal cooling rack inside a wok and pour in about 2 cups water. The rack should fit at least 3 inches above the water. Bring the water to a boil over high heat, then turn off the heat. Place the wrapped tart on the cake rack and adjust the heat to moderate. When the water boils again, cover the wok and steam until the custard is set but still trembles slightly, 25 to 30 minutes. Using two kitchen mitts, carefully lift the tart off the rack; remove the plastic wrap and the sides of the tart ring. Transfer to a serving platter.

7. In a large nonreactive skillet, heat the remaining 2 tablespoons olive oil over high heat, until lightly smoking. Add the onion and cook, stirring, for 1 minute. Stir in the crabmeat, tomatoes, coriander, serrano chile and lime juice and cook until warmed through, about 2 minutes. Using a slotted spoon, cover the top of the tart with the crab mixture. Serve warm, cut into wedges.

—Stephan Pyles

• • •

BAKED STUFFED MUSSELS

Many of the mussels commercially available today are farmed. They are cleaner and more delicate than their wild counterparts and have a larger meat to shell ratio.

Makes 40 Stuffed Mussels

40 large black mussels (about 5 pounds), scrubbed and debearded
1½ cups dry white wine
2 tablespoons olive oil
3 tablespoons minced garlic
½ cup finely chopped flat-leaf parsley
1½ cups dry bread crumbs
12 imported large green olives, pitted and coarsely chopped
¼ cup freshly grated Parmesan cheese (1 ounce)
3 tablespoons drained capers
3 anchovy fillets, finely chopped
1 cup extra-virgin olive oil
Lemon wedges, for serving

1. Place the mussels in a large nonreactive casserole and add the wine, the 2 tablespoons olive oil, half the garlic and a handful of the parsley. Cover and bring to a simmer. Steam the mussels until opened completely, about 10 minutes. Transfer the mussels to a platter and set aside to cool; discard any that do not open. Strain the cooking liquid through a fine sieve and reserve. Leave the mussels attached to one shell half; pull off and discard the empty mussel shell halves.

2. In a medium bowl, combine the bread crumbs, olives, Parmesan cheese, capers, anchovies, the 1 cup extra-virgin olive oil and the remaining parsley and garlic. Add enough of the reserved mussel juice to moisten the filling so that it just holds together when squeezed. Mound a heaping tablespoon of the filling on top of each mussel in its shell and place on a large baking sheet. *(The mussels can be prepared to this point up to 1 day ahead and refrigerated, loosely covered. Let return to room temperature before proceeding.)*

3. Preheat the broiler. Broil the mussels for about 1 minute, until golden brown and heated through. Serve immediately, with lemon wedges.

—Evan Kleiman

• • •

DELMARVA CRAB CAKES

The crab makes the cake. Unless you're willing to settle for the shredded doormats that pass for crab cakes in most restaurants, use lump blue crabmeat from jumbo crabs. Handle the crab as little as possible and as gently as you can.

6 First-Course Servings

3 tablespoons unsalted butter
½ cup finely chopped onion
½ cup finely chopped celery
3 tablespoons low-fat mayonnaise
1 tablespoon plain nonfat yogurt
1 teaspoon Dijon mustard
1 teaspoon baking soda
1 teaspoon seafood seasoning, such as Old Bay Seasoning
1 tablespoon finely chopped parsley
1 tablespoon drained capers
¼ teaspoon salt
¼ teaspoon freshly ground black pepper
Pinch of cayenne pepper
1 pound lump blue crabmeat, picked over
1 cup finely crushed Ritz crackers
Lemon wedges, for serving

1. In a medium skillet, melt the butter over moderately low heat. Add the onion and celery and cook, stirring occasionally, until softened, about 8 minutes. Remove from the heat and let cool.

2. In a large bowl, stir together the mayonnaise, yogurt, mustard, baking soda, seafood seasoning, parsley, capers, salt, black pepper and cayenne. Add the cooled onion and celery and the crabmeat and toss gently but thoroughly to combine.

3. Preheat the oven to 450°. Lightly

grease a large baking sheet. Place the cracker crumbs in a shallow dish. With a ¼-cup measure, scoop the crab mixture into 12 mounds. Dusting your hands liberally with the cracker crumbs, shape the crab mounds into 2½-inch patties. Thoroughly coat the patties with crumbs and arrange them on the prepared baking sheet.

4. Bake the crab cakes in the middle of the oven for 20 minutes, turning once, until golden brown all over. Serve warm, with lemon wedges.

—Mary Anne Dolan

• • •

LOBSTER WITH WHITE TRUFFLE OIL

4 First-Course Servings

2 live lobsters (1½ pounds each)
About 1 tablespoon plus 1 teaspoon white truffle oil*
Table salt and freshly ground pepper
Rock salt, for serving
Chervil sprigs, for garnish
****Available at specialty food shops***

1. In a large stockpot of boiling salted water, boil the lobsters for 12 minutes until red all over. Using tongs, transfer the lobsters to a work surface.

2. Twist the lobster bodies to separate the tail sections. Place the sections upside down and, using a large sharp knife, halve the tails lengthwise, cutting through the shell. Remove the tail meat from the shells and place in a stainless steel bowl. Set the bowl over the hot lobster cooking water to keep the meat warm. Reserve the tail shells. Crack the claws and remove the meat in one piece.

3. Using a large sharp knife, cut all the lobster meat in broad, thin slices. Return to the bowl, pour in 1 tablespoon of the truffle oil and toss to coat thoroughly. Season with table salt and pepper to taste and another teaspoon of truffle oil if desired.

4. Pour enough rock salt on each salad plate to hold a lobster tail shell. Nestle 1 tail-shell half on each plate and stuff with the lobster meat. Garnish with chervil sprigs and serve at once.

—David Rosengarten

• • •

OYSTER SACKS

These crisp bundles are made by filling crêpes with a savory oyster filling and then deep-frying them.

A fruity, round-textured, simple white, such as 1989 Mirasol "White Burgundy" Pinot Blanc, or even an off-dry white, such as 1989 Simi Chenin Blanc, would provide a refreshing foil to the briny taste of these crêpes.

Makes 8 Sacks

1 stick (4 ounces) unsalted butter, melted
½ cup chopped onions
½ cup diced celery
½ teaspoon thyme
½ teaspoon granulated garlic
¼ teaspoon crushed hot red pepper
¼ teaspoon salt
2 cups oyster liquor or clam juice
1 teaspoon Worcestershire sauce
1 bay leaf
½ cup finely chopped scallions, plus 8 whole scallions
2 cups freshly shucked oysters, liquor reserved
2 tablespoons cornstarch
8 Crêpes (recipe follows)
Vegetable oil, for frying
1 cup heavy cream

1. In a large skillet, melt the butter over moderate heat. Add the onions and celery and cook, stirring, until softened. Add the thyme, garlic, crushed red pepper and salt. Stir in all of the oyster liquor and 1 cup of cold water. Cook the mixture over moderately high heat for 10 minutes.

2. Add the Worcestershire sauce, bay leaf and ¼ cup of the chopped scallions and cook over moderate heat for 10 minutes. Stir in the oysters and bring to a boil.

3. Whisk the cornstarch with 2 tablespoons water until smooth. Whisk it into the boiling mixture until thickened. Discard the bay leaf. Remove from the heat and let cool, then refrigerate until cold.

4. Cut the prettiest, longest scallion greens into 8-inch lengths and blanch in scalding water just until limp. Dry on paper towels.

5. To assemble the sacks, spoon about 1½ tablespoons of the chilled oyster mixture in the center of each crêpe. Gather the crêpes up around the stuffing to form sacks and tie each one gently but securely with a scallion green.

6. In a medium saucepan, heat 4 inches of oil to 350°. Meanwhile, make the sauce. Transfer all the remaining oyster mixture to a medium saucepan and stir in the heavy cream. Cook until warmed through.

7. Fry the oyster sacks in the hot oil in batches until golden brown all over. Drain on paper towels. Stir the remaining ¼ cup chopped scallions into the sauce and ladle it onto warmed plates. Set the sacks on the sauce and serve immediately.

—Tim Patton

• • •

CREPES

These crêpes can be cooked up to three days in advance and refrigerated, well wrapped in plastic.

Makes One Dozen 6-Inch Crêpes

4 eggs
1 cup cold milk
½ teaspoon salt
2 cups sifted all-purpose flour
4 tablespoons unsalted butter, melted and cooled

1. In a blender, combine the eggs, milk, salt and 1 cup of cold water. Blend until smooth. Add the flour and blend. Add the butter and blend at high speed for 1 minute. Cover and refrigerate the batter for at least 2 hours or overnight.

2. Heat a 6- or 7-inch crêpe pan over moderate heat until hot. Lightly butter the pan. Ladle in some of the batter and swirl to lightly coat the bottom of the pan; pour out the excess batter. Cook the crêpe until the edges look golden and slightly dry, then flip and cook until brown spots appear on the second side. Transfer the crêpe to a plate and repeat with the remaining batter. (Stack the crêpes with strips of wax paper between them.)

—*Tim Patton*

• • •

PAN-ROASTED QUAIL WITH RED ONION-BELL PEPPER COMPOTE AND PARSLEY PESTO

🍷 The flavors of this dish point to a wine that will echo its herbal bite while balancing the sweetness of the pepper and onions. A California Sauvignon (Fumé) Blanc has the requisite character and enough depth of flavor for quail.

8 First-Course Servings

¼ cup olive oil
1 large sweet red onion, thinly sliced
1 small red or yellow bell pepper, thinly sliced
2 tablespoons unsalted butter
2 shallots, finely chopped
2 large white mushrooms, thinly sliced
1 cup canned chicken broth
⅓ cup dry white wine
½ cup heavy cream
1½ tablespoons Dijon mustard
1 tablespoon chopped fresh tarragon or 1 teaspoon dried
Salt and freshly ground black pepper
8 partially boned whole quail (4 to 5 ounces each)
Parsley Pesto (p. 263)

1. In a medium nonreactive saucepan, heat 2 tablespoons of the oil. Add the onion and bell pepper and cook over moderate heat, stirring, until the onion is translucent but not browned, about 5 minutes. Transfer the vegetables to a plate and keep warm.

2. Preheat the oven to 500°. In the same saucepan, combine the butter, shallots and mushrooms and cook over moderately high heat, stirring occasionally, until lightly browned, about 3 minutes. Add the chicken broth and wine and cook until reduced by half, about 6 minutes. Add the cream and mustard and cook until slightly thickened, about 4 minutes. Strain the sauce through a coarse sieve set over a small nonreactive saucepan. Stir in the tarragon and season to taste with salt and black pepper. Keep warm.

3. In a large ovenproof skillet, preferably cast iron, heat the remaining 2 tablespoons oil over high heat. Season the quail with salt and pepper, add to the skillet and cook, turning once, until browned on both sides, about 5 minutes. Transfer the skillet to the oven and roast the quail for 4 to 5 minutes, or until the meat is pink and the juices run clear when the thigh is pierced.

4. To serve, place the reserved onion and pepper compote on warm plates. Spoon the mustard sauce around the compote. Place the quail on top and drizzle the Parsley Pesto over the quail.

—*John Ash & Sid Goldstein*

• • •

FENNEL-CURED SALMON WITH FENNEL-MUSTARD DRESSING

This is definitely not a traditional dish —it's an Italianate take on gravlax that uses ouzo and fennel tops for flavoring.

Makes About 2¼ Pounds

One 3-pound Norwegian salmon, filleted, skin on
2 tablespoons ouzo
Juice of 1 lemon
1 cup sugar
⅔ cup coarse (kosher) salt
2 tablespoons crushed white peppercorns
1 bunch of fennel fronds, rinsed and dried

Extra-virgin olive oil
Fennel-Mustard Dressing (p. 257)
1 cup thinly sliced peeled cucumber
1 medium red onion, finely diced

1. Lay the salmon fillets on a work surface and sprinkle the ouzo over the flesh side of each fillet. Let sit for 2 minutes. Pour the lemon juice over the fillets and let sit for another 2 minutes.

2. In a small bowl, combine the sugar, salt and white peppercorns. Pat the salmon dry. Sprinkle half of the salt mixture evenly over both fillets. Spread half of the fennel fronds evenly over one fillet and top with the other fillet to reform the fish (flesh sides touching). Wrap the salmon in parchment or wax paper and place in a pan that is at least 1 inch deep. Weigh down the salmon with a large heavy casserole and refrigerate for 24 hours.

3. The next day, drain the liquid from the pan and unwrap the salmon. Discard the old fennel fronds and pat the salmon dry. Spread the remaining salt mixture over the fillets and place the remaining fennel fronds on one fillet. Reform the fish as before, wrap in fresh parchment or wax paper and refrigerate for 3 more days. Turn the salmon, drain the liquid from the pan and rewrap the fish once each day.

4. On the final day, unwrap the salmon and discard the fennel fronds. Brush the salmon lightly to remove excess peppercorns. Oil the salmon lightly. To serve, place the fillets on a work surface, skin side down. Use a thin sharp knife to slice the salmon very thin on a slight angle, beginning at the tail ends. Do not cut through the skin. Serve with the Fennel-Mustard Dressing, cucumber and red onion.

—*Evan Kleiman*

• • •

SMOKED SALMON WITH STIR-FRIED CABBAGE AND CLOVE OIL

6 First-Course Servings

1 teaspoon whole cloves
5 tablespoons safflower oil
5 cups finely shredded green or Savoy cabbage
Salt and freshly ground pepper
12 ounces thinly sliced mild smoked salmon
Thinly sliced French bread, toasted

1. In a mortar, crush the cloves to a coarse powder. Alternatively, grind the cloves in a spice grinder. In a small jar, combine the ground cloves with 3 tablespoons of the oil. Cover tightly and set aside at room temperature overnight or for up to 4 days.

2. In a large skillet or wok, heat the remaining 2 tablespoons oil over high heat. Add the cabbage and stir-fry until crisp-tender, about 3 minutes. Season lightly with salt and pepper and mound the cabbage on 6 small plates.

3. Arrange the smoked salmon slices around the cabbage. Drizzle 1½ teaspoons of the clove oil over the salmon on each plate and a few drops on the cabbage. Serve immediately with the toasts.

—*David Rosengarten*

• • •

SOUPS & CHOWDERS

TORTILLA SOUP

Epazote is a pungent herb with pointed serrated leaves.

6 to 8 Servings

12 corn tortillas, cut into ¼-inch strips
3 dried pasilla chiles
½ cup plus 1 tablespoon corn or canola oil
½ pound tomatoes
½ of a medium onion
1 garlic clove
5 cups Caldo Pollo (recipe follows)
1 sprig of epazote*
1 cup shredded mild white Cheddar cheese (about 3½ ounces)
2 to 3 Hass avocados, diced
Sour cream, for serving
****Available at Mexican markets***

1. Preheat the oven to 200°. Spread the tortilla strips on a large baking sheet and bake, tossing occasionally, for 20 minutes, or until dried. Turn the oven off and leave the strips in the oven overnight to finish drying.

2. Heat a large cast-iron skillet over moderately high heat. Add the pasilla chiles and roast, turning frequently, until softened, about 5 minutes. With a sharp paring knife, split the chiles and remove and discard the seeds and veins.

3. In the same skillet, heat ½ cup of the oil over moderately high heat. Add the tortilla strips in batches and fry until light golden, about 3 minutes. Drain on paper towels.

4. Add the roasted chiles to the oil and fry for 30 seconds. Remove from the oil and drain well. Cut the chiles into thin strips and set aside.

5. In a blender, combine the tomatoes, onion and garlic and puree until smooth. In a medium nonreactive saucepan, heat the remaining 1 tablespoon oil over moderate heat. Add the puree and cook for 5 minutes. Add the Caldo Pollo and epazote and bring to a simmer. Cook for 5 minutes. Add the tortilla strips and cook until softened slightly, about 3 minutes.

6. To serve, ladle the soup into bowls and garnish with the reserved pasilla strips and the Cheddar cheese, avocados and sour cream.

—Chata DuBose

• • •

CALDO POLLO

This chicken stock is lightly flavored with fresh mint.

Makes About 5 Cups

One 3-pound frying chicken, cut up
½ of a medium white onion, quartered
1 celery rib, thickly sliced
1 garlic clove, crushed
10 fresh mint leaves
1 teaspoon salt
½ teaspoon cracked black pepper

1. Combine all of the ingredients in a large saucepan and add 6 cups of water. Bring to a boil over moderately high heat, skimming occasionally. Reduce the heat and simmer gently until the broth is flavorful, 1 to 1½ hours.

2. Remove the chicken and reserve it for another use. Strain the broth through a fine sieve into a bowl and let cool to room temperature. Refrigerate until chilled; skim the fat from the surface before using.

—Chata DuBose

• • •

BUTTERNUT SQUASH CONSOMME WITH LEEK RAVIOLI

Tom Colicchio of Mondrian in Manhattan makes a stock with squash and onion, which he refrigerates overnight and skims of fat before clarifying with egg white and leek. The clear consommé is served garnished with creamy leek ravioli.

4 Servings

2 medium butternut squash (about 3½ pounds total)
2 tablespoons unsalted butter
1 medium onion, halved and thinly sliced
4 medium leeks
2 egg whites
2 teaspoons vegetable oil
⅓ cup heavy cream
Pinch of cinnamon
Pinch of ground cardamom
Salt and freshly ground pepper
Twelve 3-inch round gyoza or won ton skins*
****Available at Asian markets***

1. Slice off the narrow neck portion of both squash, about the top 5 inches. Halve the neck portions crosswise, peel and cut into 1-inch cubes. Set all but 2 of the cubes aside. Cut the 2 reserved cubes into ¼-inch dice for garnish and set aside separately.

2. Trim the ends from the remaining bulbous portions of the squash. Peel and coarsely chop.

3. In a large saucepan, heat 1 tablespoon of the butter over low heat. Add the onion and cook, stirring occasionally, until translucent, about 10 minutes; set aside.

4. In a large saucepan, heat the remaining 1 tablespoon butter over moderate heat. Add the large squash cubes and cook, stirring occasionally, until lightly browned, about 5 minutes. Stir in the onion and add 8 cups of water. Bring just to a simmer, carefully ladling the scum from the surface of the liquid. Reduce the heat to low and cook for 1 hour. Strain the stock into a large bowl and discard the solids; you should have about 4 cups. Let cool, cover and refrigerate overnight.

5. Using a slotted spoon, remove the solidified fat from the surface of the stock. Transfer the stock to a medium saucepan and set aside.

6. In a food processor, finely chop 1 of the leeks. Add the reserved coarsely chopped squash and pulse until finely chopped. Add the egg whites and pulse to mix. Whisk this mixture into the cold stock in the saucepan and bring to a simmer over low heat, whisking occasionally. Once the egg whites begin to coagulate on the surface of the stock, stop whisking. Simmer the stock very gently for 20 minutes from the time it starts to boil lightly. Carefully strain the consommé through fine-mesh cheesecloth or a clean piece of muslin into another large saucepan. You should have about 2¼ cups.

7. While the stock is being clarified, cut the 3 remaining leeks into ¼-inch dice. Reserve 2 tablespoons for garnish. In a large skillet, heat the oil over low heat. Add the diced leeks, cover and cook, stirring occasionally, until tender, about 10 minutes. Add the cream and cook until thickened, about 4 minutes. Set aside to cool. Add the cinnamon and cardamom; season to taste with salt and pepper.

8. Lay out the gyoza skins on a work surface. Moisten the edges with water and put 1 teaspoon of the leek filling in the center of each. Fold the skins over the filling to make half circles; press the edges to seal.

9. In a large saucepan of boiling water, blanch the reserved diced squash and leek garnishes over high heat until tender, about 3 minutes. Using a slotted spoon, transfer to a small bowl. Reduce the heat to moderately high and add the ravioli. Cook, stirring gently, until tender, about 5 minutes. Drain well.

10. Meanwhile, gently reheat the consommé over moderate heat; do not let it boil. Season to taste with salt. To serve, place 3 ravioli in each of 4 large, shallow soup bowls. Ladle the hot consommé into the bowls and garnish each serving with the blanched diced leek and squash.

—Baba S. Khalsa

• • •

UDON WITH CHICKEN AND LEEKS IN GINGER BROTH

Noodles in broth, a typical workday lunch, is the Japanese take on Chinese soup noodles. The only way to eat *udon* is to lift them with chopsticks or a fork and slurp them from the bowl. The cooking times given for *udon* may seem long, but these thick chewy noodles are served soft.

🍷 The flavors of this subtle, perfumed soup can be attractively underscored by a relatively delicate but assertively tart Riesling, such as 1988 Bürklin-Wolf Ruppertsberger Kabinett or 1989 Sichel Rheinpfalz QbA.

4 Servings

¾ cup chicken stock or canned broth
¼ cup sake
¼ cup plus ½ teaspoon Japanese soy sauce
1 whole chicken breast (about 1 pound), split and skinned
Dashi (recipe follows)
2 tablespoons plus 1 teaspoon sugar
1 tablespoon plus 1 teaspoon minced fresh ginger
1 medium leek, chopped
1 pound fresh udon, preferably Nabeyaki udon, or 12 ounces dried
2 medium scallions, minced
Marinated Fresh Ginger (p. 264)
Shichimi togarashi (see Note)

1. In a medium saucepan, combine the chicken stock, 1 tablespoon of the sake and 2 teaspoons of the soy sauce and bring to a simmer over high heat. Add the chicken breast and reduce the heat to moderately low. Cover and simmer, turning occasionally, until the chicken is cooked through, about 25 minutes. Let the chicken cool slightly in the broth. Then remove from the broth, shred the meat and set aside; discard the bones. Reserve the broth.

2. Add enough Dashi to the chicken broth to make 5 cups. Stir in the sugar and the remaining 3 tablespoons sake and 3½ tablespoons soy sauce and bring to a boil over high heat. Reduce the heat to moderate, cover and simmer for 4 minutes. Remove from the heat and stir in the fresh ginger. Add more soy sauce to taste.

3. Pour 1 cup of the ginger broth into a small saucepan and bring to a boil over high heat. Add the leek, reduce the heat to moderate and simmer until tender but still slightly crisp, about 8 minutes. Using a slotted spoon, transfer the leek to a small bowl and set aside. Return the cup of broth to the rest of the broth.

4. Bring a large pot of water to a boil over high heat. Add the fresh *udon* and simmer until soft, about 25 minutes.

Drain well. Alternatively, if using dried *udon*, add them to the pan, and when the water returns to a boil, add ¾ cup cold water and bring to a boil again. Repeat 3 more times for a total of 12 minutes cooking time. Remove the noodles from the heat, cover and set aside until softened, about 15 minutes; then drain.

5. To serve, add the noodles to the broth and heat through. Transfer the noodles to 4 bowls, top with the reserved chicken and leek and add some broth. Sprinkle with scallions and Marinated Fresh Ginger. Serve with *shichimi togarashi* as a table condiment.

NOTE: *Available at Japanese markets, or combine 2 tablespoons toasted sesame seeds with 1 minced small, dried Asian chile.*

—*Linda Burum*

• • •

DASHI

Dashi can be made from scratch or purchased in small packets. Just follow the package directions.

Makes About 5 Cups

Two 6-by-2-inch pieces of dried kelp*
½ cup (loosely packed) bonito flakes* (about ¼ ounce)
****Available at Japanese markets***

1. In a medium saucepan, cover the kelp with 5 cups of water and bring to a simmer over low heat. Immediately remove from the heat and test the kelp with a fork. If it doesn't feel tender, set aside for up to 15 minutes, until tender.

2. Remove and discard the kelp. Add the bonito flakes to the broth and cook over low heat for 5 minutes. Strain the *dashi* through a fine strainer.

—*Linda Burum*

• • •

GAZPACHO

This version of the Spanish classic is a smooth tomato soup served with an assortment of garnishes.

6 Servings

8 juicy medium tomatoes (2 pounds)
3 garlic cloves, crushed
2 medium cucumbers—peeled, halved and seeded
1 Spanish onion or 1 large red onion (about 8 ounces)
1 large green bell pepper, seeded and deribbed
2 cups bottled tomato juice
½ cup extra-virgin olive oil
¼ cup fresh lemon juice
¼ teaspoon cayenne pepper
¾ teaspoon salt
1 tablespoon unsalted butter
1 small loaf of Italian bread, crust removed, bread cut into ¼-inch dice

1. Core 5 of the tomatoes and coarsely chop them. In a blender, combine the chopped tomatoes with 1 garlic clove and puree until smooth. Strain the puree into a large nonreactive bowl.

2. Coarsely chop 1 of the cucumbers, ½ of the onion and ½ of the green pepper. Add the chopped vegetables to the blender with ½ cup of the tomato juice. Blend until liquefied; strain into the large bowl.

3. In the blender, combine the remaining 1½ cups tomato juice with 6 tablespoons of the olive oil, 1 garlic clove, the lemon juice, cayenne and salt. Blend until smooth and strain into the large bowl. Cover and refrigerate for at least 4 hours or overnight.

4. Finely dice the remaining 3 tomatoes, ½ onion, ½ green pepper and 1 cucumber and place them in separate small bowls.

5. In a medium skillet, combine the remaining 2 tablespoons olive oil and 1 garlic clove with the butter and cook over moderate heat until the butter stops foaming, about 1 minute. Discard the garlic. Add the diced bread and sauté until crisp and golden, about 5 minutes. Drain on paper towels and place in a small bowl. Serve the chilled gazpacho in bowls, with the diced vegetables and croutons alongside.

—*Diana Sturgis*

• • •

SORREL, SPINACH AND TOMATO SOUP

The spinach and tomato in this soup clearly reflect an Italian influence. Its Polish spirit is revealed in the tanginess of the sorrel and sour cream. If you are trying to limit egg yolks in your diet, add just the whites in Step 3. Unlike many soups, this one is at its best when freshly made.

8 Servings

4 tablespoons unsalted butter or vegetable oil
1 large onion, cut into ¼-inch dice
½ pound fresh sorrel, stemmed, leaves cut into 1-inch pieces (see Note)
2 tablespoons all-purpose flour
1½ quarts chicken stock or canned low-sodium broth
1 pound ripe tomatoes, seeded and cut into ½-inch dice
½ pound fresh spinach, stemmed, leaves sliced into ½-inch strips
3 eggs, at room temperature

1 cup sour cream, light sour cream or crème fraîche, at room temperature
Salt and freshly ground pepper

1. In a heavy 4-quart nonreactive stockpot, melt the butter over moderate heat. Add the onion and cook, stirring, until tender and lightly golden, 8 to 10 minutes. Add the sorrel and cook, stirring occasionally, until wilted, about 4 minutes; the sorrel will turn olive-green. Add the flour, stir well and cook for 3 minutes.

2. Gradually add 1 cup of the stock, stirring constantly with a wooden spoon to beat out any lumps. Gradually stir in the remaining stock and bring to a boil over high heat. Reduce the heat and simmer the soup for 10 minutes. Add the tomatoes and spinach and return to a simmer.

3. One at a time, break each egg into a small dish and slip it into the simmering soup without stirring. Simmer until the egg whites are set, about 2 minutes. Then, with a large metal spoon, break up the eggs, stirring the yolks into the soup. Cook for 1 minute.

4. Place the sour cream in a small bowl and whisk until smooth. Gradually whisk in ½ cup of the hot soup. Add the sour cream mixture to the soup, stirring well until incorporated. Bring the soup just to a simmer; do not let it boil or it will curdle. Season the soup with salt and pepper and serve immediately.

NOTE: *If sorrel is unavailable, use ½ pound spinach and 2 tablespoons lemon juice in its place. Add them in Step 1 and increase the cooking time to 7 minutes to soften the spinach.*

—*Andrew Ziobro*

• • •

MINESTRA OF SWISS CHARD, POTATOES AND TOMATOES

Use the full quantity of chicken broth to make a main-dish *minestra,* less (to taste) to make a side-dish accompaniment to a meat course.

6 Main-Course or 8 Side-Dish Servings

2½ pounds Swiss chard, trimmed
5 medium waxy potatoes (1½ pounds), peeled
3 tablespoons olive oil
½ teaspoon crushed red pepper
3 garlic cloves, minced
1 can (28 ounces) Italian peeled tomatoes, drained and finely chopped
½ teaspoon oregano
½ cup freshly grated Pecorino or Romano cheese (2 ounces)
¼ to 1 cup canned chicken broth diluted with an equal amount of water (see headnote)
Salt and freshly ground black pepper
Extra-virgin olive oil, for serving

1. Bring a large pot of salted water to a boil. Add the Swiss chard and blanch for 10 minutes; drain and chop into 2-inch pieces; set aside.

2. Place the potatoes in a medium saucepan and add enough water to cover by 1 inch. Bring to a boil over moderately high heat and cook just until tender, 10 to 12 minutes. Drain and cut into 1½-inch chunks.

3. In a medium nonreactive casserole, heat the olive oil and crushed red pepper over moderately high heat until very hot, about 1 minute. Add the garlic and cook, stirring, until very lightly colored, about 1 minute. Stir in the tomatoes and oregano and cook until thickened, about 5 minutes. Add the reserved Swiss chard and potatoes; sprinkle the Pecorino on top. Pour in the chicken broth as desired. Cover and simmer over moderate heat until heated through and the flavors are blended, about 10 minutes. Season to taste with salt and black pepper.

4. To serve, spoon the *minestra* into individual bowls. Pass extra-virgin olive oil and additional crushed red pepper alongside.

—*Diane Darrow & Tom Maresca*

• • •

POTATO-SPINACH SOUP WITH ARTICHOKES

4 to 6 Servings

2 tablespoons unsalted butter
1 tablespoon olive oil
3 medium leeks, white and tender green, thinly sliced crosswise
1 medium onion, coarsely chopped
1 cup dry white wine
1 pound Idaho potatoes, peeled and quartered
2 large artichokes, stems removed
1 pound fresh spinach, large stems removed
2 cups milk
1 tablespoon fresh lemon juice
½ teaspoon finely grated lemon zest
1½ teaspoons salt
½ teaspoon freshly ground pepper
¼ teaspoon ground mace
¼ cup ½-inch strips of chive

1. In a heavy medium casserole or large nonreactive saucepan, melt the butter in the olive oil over moderate heat. Add the leeks and onion and reduce the heat to low. Cover and cook, stirring occasionally, until softened, about 10 minutes. Add the wine and boil over high heat until reduced to ¼ cup, about 4 minutes. Add the potatoes and 4 cups of water and bring to a boil. Reduce the heat to moderately low and simmer the potatoes until very tender, about 30 minutes.

2. Meanwhile, in a medium saucepan, bring 4 cups of water to a boil. Place the artichokes in a steamer in the pan, cover and steam until the bottoms are tender when pierced with a knife, about 50 minutes. Remove all the leaves and scoop out the hairy chokes with a spoon. Set the artichoke bottoms aside.

3. Working in batches, transfer some of the potatoes from the casserole to a food processor. Process just until smooth; do not overprocess or the potatoes will become gluey. Transfer the puree to a large bowl. Repeat with the remaining potatoes. Transfer the leeks with some of the cooking liquid to the food processor and puree until as smooth as possible; add to the potatoes.

4. Add the remaining cooking liquid to the leek-potato puree. Strain the soup through a coarse sieve, pressing hard with a rubber spatula to extract as much liquid as possible. Discard the solids. Pour the soup back into the casserole.

5. In the medium saucepan, bring 1 inch of water to a boil over high heat. Place the spinach in a steamer in the pan, cover and steam, stirring once, until wilted, about 2 minutes. When the spinach is cool enough to handle, squeeze it to extract as much water as possible, then coarsely chop. *(The recipe can be made to this point up to 1 day ahead. Cover and refrigerate the soup, artichoke bottoms and spinach separately.)*

6. Place the soup over moderate heat, stir in the milk and heat until warmed through. Halve the reserved artichoke bottoms and slice crosswise ¼ inch thick. Stir the artichokes and the chopped spinach into the soup. Stir in the lemon juice, lemon zest, salt, pepper and mace. Just before serving, stir in the chives.

—Marcia Kiesel

• • •

OKRA SOUP

This hearty beef-and-vegetable soup from South Carolina is sometimes called Charleston Gumbo, but it is a much simpler preparation than its Louisiana relative.

8 Servings

2 to 3 pounds meaty beef soup bones, such as shank or chuck
1 large onion, coarsely chopped
2 pounds fresh okra, finely chopped
4 large tomatoes—peeled, seeded and coarsely chopped
¼ pound slab bacon, cut into ¼-inch dice
1 large bay leaf
2½ teaspoons salt
1 teaspoon freshly ground pepper

1. In a large stockpot, combine the soup bones, onion and 2 quarts of water and bring to a boil over high heat. Reduce the heat to moderate, cover and simmer for 2 hours.

2. Remove the soup bones, dice the meat and return the meat to the pot. Discard the bones.

3. Stir in the okra, tomatoes, bacon, bay leaf, salt and pepper. Bring to a boil over high heat. Reduce the heat to moderate, cover and simmer for 2 hours. Discard the bay leaf.

—Jessica B. Harris

• • •

EGG DROP SOUP

In China this simple, but excellent, family soup is made from the freshest and most honest of ingredients: fine chicken stock or broth, fresh eggs and freshly pulled scallions.

6 Servings

6 cups Chicken Stock (recipe follows)
Salt
6 eggs at room temperature, beaten
½ cup thinly sliced scallions

In a large pot, bring the Chicken Stock to a boil over high heat. Season to taste with salt. Gradually pour in the beaten eggs, whisking constantly with a large cooking fork until soft threads of egg form, about 1 minute. Pour the soup into a warm tureen. Serve hot with the scallions mounded in the center.

—Eileen Yin-Fei Lo

• • •

CHICKEN STOCK

Makes About 2 Quarts

7 pounds chicken backbones and wings
1½-inch slice of fresh ginger, smashed
4 garlic cloves
4 to 5 scallions, halved crosswise
2 medium onions, quartered
3 celery ribs, halved lengthwise

1. In a stockpot, bring 3 quarts of water to a boil. Add the chicken parts and boil for 1 minute. Pour off the water and run cold water over the chicken; drain well.

2. Return the chicken to the stockpot. Add 3 quarts of cold water and the ginger, garlic, scallions, onions and celery. Cover and bring to a boil over high heat. Reduce the heat to moderately low, cover partially and simmer for 4 hours.

3. Strain the broth through a colander set over a large bowl; discard the chicken and vegetables. Refrigerate the stock for up to 3 days. Skim off the fat before using. *(The stock can be frozen for up to 1 month.)*

—*Eileen Yin-Fei Lo*

• • •

POTATO, ONION AND ROQUEFORT SOUP

This substantial soup can be the centerpiece of a summer meal, served either cold, like vichyssoise, or hot. Serve the soup with something simple, such as breadsticks.

🍷 With its pungent overtones of onion and Roquefort, this creamy soup would be best shown off by a contrastingly acidic wine with some herbaceousness. Try a California Sauvignon Blanc, such as 1990 Cain Musqué or 1990 Estancia Estates.

Makes About 5 Cups

3 tablespoons unsalted butter
2 medium-large onions, thinly sliced
½ teaspoon minced garlic
3 medium all-purpose potatoes, peeled and cut into 1-inch chunks
About 2 cups light chicken stock or canned low-sodium broth
1 cup light cream
⅓ cup heavy cream
½ cup plus 2 tablespoons crumbled Roquefort cheese (3½ ounces)
Salt and freshly ground pepper

1. In a large, heavy, nonreactive saucepan, melt the butter over moderately high heat. Add the onions and garlic and cook until the onions are soft but not brown. Add the potatoes, stirring to coat with butter, and cook for 5 minutes.

2. Add 2 cups of chicken stock and bring to a boil. Reduce the heat to moderately low, cover and simmer until the potatoes are tender, about 30 minutes. Let cool.

3. Add the light and heavy creams and gently reheat the soup; do not let it boil. Stir in the ½ cup Roquefort cheese. Transfer the soup to a blender and puree in batches until smooth. Season with salt and pepper to taste. Thin with additional stock if necessary. Serve hot or cold, garnished with the remaining crumbled Roquefort cheese.

—*Ann Haskell*

• • •

FRESH CORN CHOWDER WITH ROASTED POBLANO PEPPERS

Look in Latin-American markets for the dark green, bell-shaped poblano chile (called ancho chile when dried) or the long, skinny green chile called Anaheim. *Queso fresco*, a term that covers any number of fresh white cheeses made in the Mexican or Spanish style, is also available at some Latin-American markets or at cheese stores.

🍷 An off-dry, fruity white, such as a California Gewürztraminer, would best balance the soup's sweetness and heat. Look for 1990 Parducci or 1990 Clos du Bois Early Harvest.

4 Servings

4 to 6 large ears of corn
4 tablespoons unsalted butter
½ of a medium onion, finely chopped
2 medium garlic cloves, minced
2 cups milk
2 poblano or 3 Anaheim chiles
1 cup crème fraîche or milk
Salt
½ cup crumbled queso fresco, feta cheese or farmer cheese
2 tablespoons chopped flat-leaf parsley, for garnish

1. Using a thin sharp knife, slice the corn kernels from each cob into a large measuring cup, scraping the cobs with the knife to extract any juices, until you have 3 cups. Transfer to a blender or food processor.

2. In a small skillet, melt 2 tablespoons of the butter over moderate heat. Add the onion and cook until soft, about 5 minutes; stir in the garlic and cook for 1 minute longer. Scrape the mixture into the corn and add ¼ cup of the milk. Blend until smooth.

3. In a medium saucepan, melt the remaining 2 tablespoons butter over moderate heat. Add the corn puree and cook, stirring constantly, until quite thick, about 3 minutes. Whisk in the remaining 1¾ cups milk. Cover partially and simmer, stirring occasionally, for about 15 minutes.

4. Meanwhile, roast the poblanos directly over a gas flame or under the broiler as close to the heat as possible, turning frequently, until charred all over. Transfer the chiles to a bag and set aside to steam for 10 minutes. Scrape off the blackened skin and remove the core, seeds and ribs. Rinse the chiles, pat dry and cut into ¼-inch dice.

5. Strain the soup through a sieve. Rinse out the saucepan and return the soup to it. Stir in the chiles and crème fraîche, season with salt to taste and cook over moderately low heat for 10 minutes, stirring. *(The soup can be made* *up to 2 days ahead; cover and refrigerate. Reheat over moderately low heat; do not boil.)*

6. To serve, ladle the chowder into small warm bowls. Garnish with the cheese and parsley and serve.

—*Rick Bayless, Frontera Grill, Chicago*

• • •

MATZO BALLS

Matzo balls generate a great deal of conversation among the makers and the eaters. Are they heavy or light? Small or large? Do you use seltzer or water? In fact, matzo balls are mainly about texture, and most people do prefer them light rather than heavy. A good texture is insured by refrigerating the mixture for several hours before boiling them.

Makes 16 Matzo Balls

4 eggs
½ cup water or seltzer
6 tablespoons rendered chicken fat (schmaltz), melted
1 teaspoon salt
¼ teaspoon freshly ground white pepper
1½ cups unsalted matzo meal
2 quarts water or chicken stock

1. In a medium bowl, beat the eggs until the whites and yolks are just combined. Stir in the water, chicken fat, salt and white pepper. Gradually stir in the matzo meal until well combined. Cover and refrigerate for at least 3 hours or overnight.

2. Bring a pot of salted water or chicken stock to a boil over high heat. Meanwhile, between moistened palms, roll the matzo meal mixture, 2 tablespoonfuls at a time, into balls. Drop the matzo balls into the boiling liquid, reduce the heat to moderately low and simmer, covered, until cooked through, about 25 minutes. Using a slotted spoon, transfer the matzo balls to a plate. *(The matzo balls can be kept at room temperature, loosely covered, for several hours.)* Serve in chicken soup or Chicken in the Pot (p. 87).

—*Susan R. Friedland*

• • •

BOURBON-RUTABAGA BISQUE

4 to 6 Servings

2 tablespoons unsalted butter
2 medium onions, sliced
1½ pounds rutabaga, peeled and cut into ½-inch chunks
1 large carrot, sliced
3 cups chicken stock or canned broth
Pinch of celery seed
1 cup light cream
2 to 3 tablespoons bourbon
Salt and freshly ground white pepper
Freshly grated nutmeg

1. In a large saucepan, melt the butter. Add the onions and cook until translucent. Add the rutabaga, carrot, stock and celery seed and bring to a boil. Reduce the heat, cover and simmer until the rutabaga is tender, about 30 minutes.

2. In a food processor, puree half of the contents of the pan at a time until smooth. Return the puree to the pan and add the cream and bourbon. Warm the soup over moderate heat, stirring frequently; do not let it boil. Season with salt and white pepper. Ladle the soup into warm bowls, and dust lightly with nutmeg.

—*Barbara Lee Hanson*

• • •

MINESTRONE

Makes About 4 Quarts

½ pound dried pinto beans
2 tablespoons olive oil
¼ pound lean slab bacon, finely chopped
¼ pound salt pork, finely chopped
2 tablespoons finely chopped garlic
2 tablespoons chopped parsley
1 tablespoon basil
½ teaspoon thyme
½ teaspoon oregano
½ teaspoon rosemary
⅛ teaspoon crushed red pepper
½ pound Savoy cabbage, shredded
½ pound Swiss chard, coarsely chopped
1 medium leek, white part only, halved lengthwise and sliced crosswise ¼ inch thick
1 celery rib, sliced crosswise ⅜ inch thick
4 canned Italian peeled tomatoes, coarsely chopped
½ pound all-purpose potatoes, peeled and cut into ½-inch pieces
1 medium carrot, sliced crosswise ¼ inch thick
1 medium zucchini, halved lengthwise and sliced crosswise ½ inch thick
2 teaspoons salt
Freshly grated Parmesan cheese
Freshly cracked black pepper

1. Place the beans in a large bowl and pour in enough cold water to cover by 2 inches. Let soak overnight. (Alternatively, place the beans in a large saucepan with cold water to cover, bring to a boil, boil for 2 minutes and then let sit for 1 hour before proceeding.) Drain and rinse well.

2. In a 6- to 8-quart stockpot, warm

the olive oil over moderate heat. Add the bacon and salt pork and cook until the fat is rendered, 7 to 8 minutes. Add the garlic, parsley, basil, thyme, oregano, rosemary and crushed red pepper. Cook, stirring occasionally, for 2 minutes. Stir in the cabbage, Swiss chard, leek and celery. Cover and cook until soft, about 5 minutes.

3. Stir in the drained beans, tomatoes and 2 quarts of water. Bring to a boil over high heat. Reduce the heat to moderately low, cover and simmer for 30 minutes. Stir in the potatoes and carrot, cover and cook until tender, about 30 minutes. Stir in the zucchini and salt and cook for 15 minutes longer. *(The soup will keep for up to 1 week; cover and refrigerate. Reheat before serving.)* Serve in bowls with a sprinkling of Parmesan and black pepper.

—Diane Darrow & Tom Maresca

• • •

CRAYFISH SOUP

This is an elegant, distinctive soup that would make a lovely first course for a special occasion. If live crayfish are hard to come by, lobster is a fine substitute (see Note).

🍷 This elegant bisque points to a crisp white for contrast. A California Chardonnay, such as 1990 Freemark Abbey "Carpy Ranch" or 1989 Matanzas Creek, would have the necessary subtlety and depth of flavor.

8 Servings

1 bunch of dill, rinsed, plus ½ cup chopped dill
1 bunch of parsley, rinsed, plus 1 tablespoon chopped parsley
1 lemon, sliced
Salt
3 pounds live crayfish
1 stick (4 ounces) unsalted butter
3 quarts Veal Stock (recipe follows)
½ cup cooked rice
2 tablespoons fine dry bread crumbs
1 egg, separated
Freshly ground pepper
2 tablespoons all-purpose flour
1 cup heavy cream

1. In a 2½-gallon stockpot, combine the bunches of dill and parsley, the lemon, 2 tablespoons of salt and 6 quarts of water. Bring to a simmer over high heat and simmer for 15 minutes.

2. Meanwhile, wash the crayfish in at least 4 changes of cold water to remove all sand and silt. Discard any crayfish that are not alive.

3. Drop the crayfish into the stockpot, cover and bring to a boil. Simmer, stirring occasionally, for 8 minutes. Drain the crayfish and rinse briefly under cold water. Refrigerate until cool enough to handle.

4. Twist off the crayfish tails and remove the meat from the shells; reserve the tails and all the shells in separate bowls. If any of the tail meat has any mustard-colored fat attached, remove it and add it to the shells. Make a shallow slit down the middle of the tails and pull out the veins, beginning at the head ends. You should have about ½ pound of crayfish tails. Cover and refrigerate.

5. Choose 16 of the largest crayfish bodies. Pull off the legs and empty out the chest cavities into the shell bowl. Rinse these 16 shells thoroughly and set aside for stuffing.

6. In a food processor, working in batches, chop all the crayfish body and tail shells as fine as possible.

7. In a large heavy saucepan, melt the butter over moderate heat and add the ground shells. Cook, stirring frequently, until most of the liquid has evaporated and a coral-colored butter remains. Stir in 1 quart of the Veal Stock and simmer very slowly, without stirring, to allow the butter to rise to the surface. Using a large spoon, skim off the butter and strain it through a fine-mesh sieve into a small bowl. Add the remaining 2 quarts Veal Stock to the saucepan, stir once and repeat the process until you have collected most of the crayfish butter. Refrigerate the butter until firm. Simmer the stock over low heat, skimming once or twice, for 1 hour longer. Strain the stock through the fine-mesh sieve, pressing hard on the solids.

8. Meanwhile, in a bowl, combine the cooked rice, bread crumbs, egg yolk, chopped parsley, 2 tablespoons of the chopped dill, 2 tablespoons of the crayfish butter and ⅛ teaspoon each of salt and pepper. Chop ¼ cup of the crayfish tails and add them. Beat the egg white until stiff and fold it into the stuffing. Stuff the 16 reserved crayfish bodies.

9. Return the stock to a simmer over low heat. Add the stuffed shells and poach for 10 minutes, keeping the stock at a slow simmer. Remove the stuffed shells and any loosened filling and cover to keep warm.

10. Place the flour in a small bowl and gradually whisk in the cream until smooth. Gradually whisk the cream into the simmering stock and return to a simmer. Skim off any foam. Add the remaining crayfish tails and 3 tablespoons of the chopped dill. Season with salt and pepper and simmer for 2 minutes.

11. Place 2 stuffed crayfish shells in each serving bowl and ladle the soup on top. Garnish with the remaining 3 tablespoons chopped dill. Float 1 teaspoon of the crayfish butter in each bowl and serve.

NOTE: *Use a 2-pound live lobster. In Step 3, boil the lobster for 12 minutes. In*

Step 4, remove the claw and tail meat and cut into ½-inch pieces. For the butter and stock, use all of the legs, shells, body, roe and tomalley, discarding only the head sac behind the eyes. Smash and chop the shells with a hammer. In Step 8, make the stuffing with ¼ cup of the claw meat and shape it into 16 dumplings with a spoon. Poach as directed.

—*Andrew Ziobro*

• • •

VEAL STOCK

In the Polish kitchen, clear broth-like meat stock, *rosol*, is generally made with meat and bones. These broths are served on their own with various garnishes or used as the basis for a compound soup.

The following recipe for veal stock can be used as a guide for chicken and beef stocks as well. Veal stock has the special quality of being the most neutral, but it contributes rich body and subtle enhancement to any soup it's used in.

Makes About 3½ Quarts

5 pounds veal bones and/or meat
3 carrots, cut into 1-inch pieces
3 parsnips, cut into 1-inch pieces
2 celery ribs, cut into 1-inch pieces
1 pound onions, quartered
2 leeks, cut into 1-inch pieces
4 garlic cloves, crushed
2 bay leaves
1 tablespoon whole black peppercorns
12 juniper berries, lightly crushed
1 tablespoon fennel seeds
1 tablespoon thyme
1 bunch of flat-leaf parsley, rinsed

1. In a 3-gallon stockpot, cover the bones with 5 quarts of cold water and bring to a simmer over high heat. Cook for 5 minutes. Drain the bones and rinse with cold water.

2. Return the bones to a clean stockpot and cover with 5 quarts of cold water. Bring to a simmer and skim the foam from the surface as it rises. Never let the stock boil. Once the foam stops surfacing, add all of the remaining ingredients. Simmer the stock for 3 hours, skimming as necessary.

3. Strain the stock through a fine-mesh sieve. Let cool, then refrigerate for up to 3 days. Skim off the congealed fat before using. *(The stock can be frozen for up to 6 months.)*

—*Andrew Ziobro*

• • •

SEAFOOD CONSOMME WITH MANCHEGO CHEESE STRAWS

Dry fino sherry is classic with consommé and fried seafood in Andalusia. This recipe adds a bit of seafood (though not fried) to the soup. Manchego cheese from La Mancha adds richness and a hint of pungency to the cheese straws.

6 Servings

2½ pounds halibut steaks
½ pound medium shrimp in their shells
2 medium onions, unpeeled and halved
2 leeks, white and tender green, halved lengthwise
1 celery rib, cut into 3 pieces
1 bay leaf
1 egg white
Salt
Good-quality dry sherry
1 sprig of parsley, minced
Manchego Cheese Straws (p. 20)

1. Remove the skin from the halibut steaks and cut the flesh from the bones; reserve the bones. Place 1 pound of the fish in a large saucepan; cover and refrigerate the remaining halibut. Add the fish bones, shrimp, onions, leeks, celery, bay leaf and 2 quarts of water to the saucepan. Cover and bring to a boil over moderately high heat, then reduce the heat to low and simmer, uncovered, for about 30 minutes. Skim the foam from the surface occasionally.

2. Strain the stock through a sieve set over a large bowl, then return the strained stock to the pan; discard the halibut, shrimp and vegetables. Boil the stock over high heat until reduced by one-third, about 5 minutes. Let cool slightly, then refrigerate until chilled, about 1 hour.

3. Chop the reserved halibut in small pieces. In a medium bowl, combine the halibut with the egg white and mash with a fork; transfer to a clean large saucepan and add the cold stock. Cover and bring to a simmer over moderately high heat, stirring constantly. Reduce the heat to low and simmer undisturbed, for about 20 minutes. Strain the stock through a cheesecloth-lined sieve set over a medium saucepan. *(The recipe can be prepared to this point 1 day ahead and refrigerated, covered.)*

4. To serve, reheat the consommé over low heat. Do not boil. Season with salt to taste and ladle into bowls or cups. Stir in a drop or two of sherry and garnish with a pinch of parsley. Pass the Manchego Cheese Straws separately.

—*Colman Andrews*

• • •

Butternut Squash Consommé with Leek Ravioli (p. 44).

Crayfish Soup (p. 51).

Sorrel, Spinach and Tomato Soup (p. 46).

CREAM OF FENNEL SOUP WITH OYSTERS

🍷 The bubbles of Champagne supply a perfect textural foil for soup. With creamy fish soups, the flavors of aged Champagne are delicious. With lighter soups such as this one, light Blanc de Blancs Champagnes work well. For a really special match, serve a 1979 Dom Ruinart Blanc de Blancs or a 1982 Salon Blanc de Blancs.

4 Servings

4 tablespoons unsalted butter
3 large fennel bulbs (about 2½ pounds), cored and finely chopped
2 tablespoons fennel seeds, crushed
3 medium leeks, thinly sliced
3 Idaho potatoes (about 1½ pounds), peeled and cut into 2-inch pieces
6 cups chicken stock or canned low-sodium broth
3¼ cups dry white wine
¼ cup heavy cream
24 freshly shucked medium oysters, liquor reserved
Salt and freshly ground pepper
Fresh tarragon or fennel fronds, for garnish

1. In a large casserole, melt the butter over high heat. Add the fennel, fennel seeds and leeks. Reduce the heat to moderate, cover and cook, stirring occasionally, until the vegetables soften, about 15 minutes. Add the potatoes, stock and wine and bring to a boil over high heat. Reduce the heat to moderately low and cook until the potatoes are tender, about 25 minutes.

2. Transfer the potatoes to a coarse sieve set over a large bowl. With a rubber spatula, push the potatoes through the sieve. Strain the liquid through the sieve, pushing on the vegetables to extract as much liquid as possible. Discard the vegetables. Return the soup to the saucepan. *(The recipe can be prepared to this point up to 1 day ahead and refrigerated, covered.)*

3. Stir the cream into the soup and bring to a simmer over moderately high heat. Strain the reserved oyster liquor through cheesecloth into the soup and season with salt and pepper. Add the oysters and cook until just heated through, 1 minute or less. Ladle the soup into bowls and garnish with the tarragon leaves or fennel fronds.

—David Rosengarten

• • •

Okra Soup (p. 48).

LOBSTER CHOWDER

I like the unorthodox contrast of rich lobster and cream with the down-home gusto of this traditional potato-and-onion stew. Make the chowder ahead to allow the flavors time to develop.

6 to 8 Servings

Two live 1½-pound lobsters
1 tablespoon unsalted butter
¼ cup diced meaty salt pork (2 ounces)
1 large onion, minced (2 cups)
¾ pound potatoes, peeled and cut into ¾-inch dice
1 cup fresh corn kernels, cut from 2 cobs
2 Anaheim peppers
1 quart milk
18 smoked mussels (optional)
1 cup heavy cream
Salt and freshly ground black pepper

1. In a large pot, bring about 2 inches of heavily salted water to a rolling boil. Plunge the lobsters in head first, cover the pan and return to a boil. Cook the lobsters for about 12 minutes. To test for doneness, give one of the tentacles a sharp tug. If it pulls away from the head easily, the lobster is done. Drain immediately and set the lobsters aside until cool enough to handle.

2. Shell the lobsters and cut the tail and claw meat in bite-size chunks, discarding the intestinal vein that runs down the tail. If there is green tomalley (liver) in the lobster cavity, scoop it out and reserve.

3. In a medium flameproof casserole, melt the butter over moderate heat. Add the salt pork and cook, stirring, until the fat is rendered and the meat begins to brown. Add the onion and cook, stirring, until softened and golden, about 10 minutes.

4. Add the potatoes and stir to coat. Add any reserved tomalley and 1 cup of water and bring to a gentle simmer. When the potatoes begin to soften, after about 10 minutes, add the corn kernels and ¾ cup of water. Cover partially and simmer until the vegetables are tender, about 8 minutes longer.

5. Meanwhile, roast the peppers directly over a gas flame or under the broiler, turning frequently with tongs, until the skins are blackened and blistered all over. Hold the peppers under running water and peel off the skins. Cut the peppers in half and discard the cores, seeds and white membranes; pat dry. Slice the peppers crosswise in ¼-inch strips.

6. Drain the reserved lobster meat and add it to the casserole along with the milk, pepper strips and the smoked mussels. Bring to a very gentle simmer over low heat, stirring occasionally. Do not let the chowder boil. Remove from the heat and let cool to room temperature. Then cover and refrigerate for several hours or overnight.

7. Shortly before serving, stir the cream into the chowder and bring to a gentle simmer over moderately low heat. Season with salt and black pepper to taste and serve hot.

—Nancy Harmon Jenkins

• • •

CHILLED SHRIMP AND JICAMA SOUP

You can duplicate the goat buttermilk by adding cultured buttermilk to goat milk and allowing it to sit for several hours or overnight.

🍷 1988 Pheasant Ridge Sauvignon Blanc

6 *Servings*

1 medium red bell pepper
1 medium yellow bell pepper
1 medium cucumber, peeled and seeded
1 large jicama (about 1½ pounds), peeled and cut into ¼-inch dice
¼ cup raspberry vinegar
2 teaspoons sugar
Salt
½ pound small shrimp (about 15), shelled and deveined
¼ teaspoon cayenne pepper
2 tablespoons olive oil
2 cups goat buttermilk or cultured buttermilk
1 cup heavy cream
1 cup sour cream
1 cup (packed) chopped fresh basil

1. Roast the red and yellow bell peppers directly over a gas flame or under a broiler as close to the heat as possible, turning frequently until charred all over. Put the peppers in a paper or plastic bag, seal and let steam until cool. Peel the peppers and discard the cores, seeds and ribs. Cut the peppers into 1-by-¼-inch strips and set aside.

2. In a food processor, puree the cucumber until smooth. Pour the puree into a large bowl and add the jicama. Mix in the vinegar, sugar and 1 teaspoon salt; set aside.

3. Sprinkle the shrimp with 1 teaspoon salt and the cayenne. In a large skillet, heat the olive oil over high heat until lightly smoking. Add the shrimp and sauté until they turn pink, about 2 minutes. Remove from the pan and set aside.

4. In a large bowl, combine the buttermilk and heavy cream, then whisk in the sour cream. Add the reserved peppers and jicama and cucumber mixture, the shrimp and the basil. Combine thoroughly. Season with additional salt to taste. Serve immediately or cover and refrigerate for up to 4 hours.

—Stephan Pyles

• • •

MALAY RICE NOODLES WITH SEAFOOD AND COCONUT

This is a seafood soup-stew served over noodles.

8 *Servings*

½ pound firm white fish fillets, such as cod or halibut, cut into 1-inch squares
½ pound medium shrimp, shelled and deveined
1 pound dried rice vermicelli*
2 quarts boiling water
2 cups fresh bean sprouts
3 small red serrano chiles, seeded and quartered
7 medium shallots, quartered
4 garlic cloves
One 3-by-1-inch piece of fresh ginger, peeled and quartered
¼ cup macadamia nuts
3 tablespoons peanut oil
1 medium tomato, peeled and coarsely chopped
2 tablespoons minced lemon grass* (white bulb only) or the grated zest of ½ lemon
1 teaspoon sugar
1 teaspoon dried shrimp paste*
1 teaspoon turmeric
1 teaspoon ground coriander
1¼ teaspoons salt
¾ teaspoon freshly ground white pepper
5 cups fresh coconut milk (see Note) or 3 cans (14 ounces each) unsweetened coconut milk*
6 ounces lump crabmeat, picked over
1 small European seedless cucumber, unpeeled, grated
3 scallions, thinly sliced
½ cup fresh mint leaves, coarsely chopped
****Available at Asian markets***

1. In a small saucepan, bring 1 cup of water to a boil over moderately high heat. Add the fish and return to a boil. Reduce the heat to moderately low and simmer for 2 minutes. Add the shrimp and cook until firm and opaque, about 3 minutes. Drain the fish, reserving the liquid; set aside to cool.

2. Place the rice vermicelli in a large heatproof bowl and pour the boiling water on top. Stir with tongs to separate the strands and set aside to soak until softened, about 20 minutes. Drain and set aside.

3. In a medium saucepan, bring ½ cup of water to a boil. Add the bean sprouts and stir for 1 minute. Drain and refresh under cold water. Set aside. *(The recipe can be prepared to this point up to 1 day ahead. Cover the noodles and keep at room temperature. Cover and refrigerate the seafood, reserved liquid and the bean sprouts separately; return to room temperature before proceeding.)*

4. In a food processor or blender, combine the serranos, shallots, garlic, ginger and macadamia nuts and process to a coarse paste, scraping down the sides of the bowl as necessary with a rubber spatula. Add 1 tablespoon of the oil and process briefly to incorporate.

5. Heat a wok over moderately high heat for 3 minutes. Add the remaining 2 tablespoons peanut oil. Scrape the paste from the food processor into the wok and stir-fry until the mixture begins to darken slightly, about 1 minute.

6. Stir in the tomato, lemon grass, sugar, shrimp paste, turmeric and coriander and cook, stirring often, until the fragrances mellow and the tomato has softened, about 3 minutes. Add the salt, white pepper, reserved seafood cooking liquid and the coconut milk. Increase the heat to high and bring to a boil. Immediately reduce the heat to moderate and stir in the reserved cooked seafood and the crabmeat. Cook, stirring occasionally, until heated through, about 4 minutes.

7. To serve, transfer the rice vermicelli to 8 bowls. Ladle about 1 cup of the sauce and seafood over the noodles in each bowl. Sprinkle the grated cucumber and reserved bean sprouts on top and garnish with the scallions and mint. Serve at once.

NOTE: *Here's a quick and inexpensive method for making coconut milk. Combine a generous 1¼ cups of unsweetened, desiccated coconut (available at health food stores and Asian markets) with 5 cups of water; heat the mixture to just under a boil, then let cool to lukewarm. Strain the mixture through a cheesecloth-lined sieve, then gather up the edges of the cloth and squeeze hard until the last drop of liquid has been extracted. You will have about 5 cups of coconut milk.*

—Jennifer Brennan

• • •

FISH SOUP WITH GARLICKY CROUTONS

Makes 4½ Quarts

½ cup plus 2 tablespoons extra-virgin olive oil
2 large onions, coarsely chopped
5 cups coarsely chopped celery ribs with leaves (½ bunch)
10 garlic cloves, chopped
Fish Stock (recipe follows)
2 cups dry white wine
1 cup chopped flat-leaf parsley
2 tablespoons fresh rosemary, minced
2 pounds skinless white fish fillets, such as tilefish, halibut or sea bass, cut into 1-inch pieces

CROUTONS:
2½ sticks (10 ounces) unsalted butter
¼ cup minced garlic
Ten ¾-inch-thick slices cut from a small loaf of country bread, halved

1. In a large flameproof casserole or stockpot, heat the olive oil over moderate heat. Add the onions and celery and cook, stirring occasionally, until softened, about 15 minutes. Stir in the garlic and cook until fragrant, about 3 minutes. Add the Fish Stock, wine, parsley and rosemary and bring to a boil. Reduce the heat and simmer for 10 minutes.

2. Add the fish fillets to the casserole and poach just until firm and opaque, 6 to 8 minutes. Pass the soup through a food mill or puree in a food processor. *(The soup can be prepared up to 2 days ahead. Let cool, then cover and refrigerate. Reheat before proceeding.)*

3. *Make the croutons:* Preheat the oven to 400°. In a saucepan, melt the butter over low heat. Add the garlic and cook for 30 seconds. Remove from the heat.

4. Dip both sides of each piece of bread in the garlic butter and place on a baking sheet. Toast in the oven for about 5 minutes or until golden.

5. Ladle the piping hot soup into shallow bowls and float the croutons on top.

—Evan Kleiman

• • •

FISH STOCK

Makes 3½ Quarts

4 pounds non-oily fish bones and trimmings
2 medium onions, chopped
2 leeks, white and tender green, chopped
2 carrots, chopped
2 sprigs of parsley
2 sprigs of thyme
1 bay leaf
2 teaspoons salt
8 whole black peppercorns
1 bottle (750 ml) dry white wine

Place all the ingredients in a nonreactive stockpot and add 3½ quarts of water. Bring to a boil and skim the surface. Simmer the stock over moderate heat for 30 minutes, skimming occasionally. Strain through a fine sieve and let cool. *(The stock can be made up to 2 days ahead; cover and refrigerate.)*

—*Evan Kleiman*

• • •

ROAST DUCK AND SOUR CHERRY SOUP

This festive soup is usually served during the holiday season. *Czarnina* translates as "black soup," so called because it's traditionally made with the blood from the freshly killed duck, which darkens it. This tamer version is only slightly less authentic. Pass extra vinegar at the table.

Folklore has it that when a young man was invited to the home of the girl he wanted to marry, the serving of this soup was a clear sign of her parents' disapproval.

8 Servings

4½-pound duck, rinsed and dried, neck and giblets reserved
Salt and freshly ground pepper
¼ cup vegetable oil or duck fat
5 medium carrots—3 sliced 1 inch thick, 2 cut into ½-inch dice
2 large onions, peeled but with root bases intact, quartered and stuck with 8 whole cloves
2 leeks, whites halved and sliced crosswise ½ inch thick, greens coarsely chopped
3 garlic cloves, lightly crushed
2 tablespoons red wine vinegar
2 cans (13¾ ounces each) beef broth, plus more if necessary
1 bay leaf
1 tablespoon juniper berries, crushed
1 teaspoon allspice berries
1 teaspoon whole black peppercorns
Three 3-inch sprigs of thyme
2 small parsnips, cut into ½-inch pieces
3 tablespoons all-purpose flour
1 cup dried sour cherries* (3 ounces)
1 cup heavy cream
6 ounces broad flat or curly egg noodles (2½ cups)
¼ cup thinly sliced scallion greens cut on the diagonal
¼ cup chopped flat-leaf parsley
****Available at specialty food shops***

1. Preheat the oven to 400°. Cut out the backbone of the duck and quarter the bird. Season the duck with salt and pepper.

2. Set a 12-by-16-inch heavy-duty roasting pan or 14-inch ovenproof nonreactive skillet over 2 burners over high heat. Add 2 tablespoons of the oil and heat briefly, then add the duck pieces, skin side down. Add the reserved neck, giblets and backbone along with the sliced carrots, onions, leek greens and garlic to the pan. Cook the duck until browned, about 5 minutes, then turn the pieces over. Place the pan in the oven and reduce the temperature to 375°. Roast for 30 minutes.

3. Remove the duck breasts from the pan and set aside. Return the pan to the oven and roast the legs for about 30 to 40 minutes longer, or until cooked through. Turn the legs and vegetables after 15 minutes to prevent sticking. Add the duck legs to the breasts, and use a slotted spoon to set the vegetables, giblets and bones aside. Drain all fat from the roasting pan.

4. Set the pan over moderate heat and add the vinegar and 2 cups of water. Scrape the bottom of the pan to loosen all the flavorful browned bits. Pour the liquid into an 8-quart stockpot. Add the reserved roasted vegetables, giblets and bones along with the beef broth, bay leaf, juniper berries, allspice berries, peppercorns, thyme and 2½ quarts of water. Bring to a simmer over moderate heat, skimming the foam as necessary.

5. Remove all the meat from the duck breasts and legs and cut into ½-inch cubes; reserve. Add the skin and bones to the stockpot.

6. Simmer the stock for 2 hours, skimming frequently. Never let the stock boil or it will remain fatty and cloudy. Strain the stock through a cheesecloth-lined colander, pressing hard on the solids. When the stock settles, skim the fat from the surface. You should have 10 cups of stock; if not, supplement with beef broth. Pull the meat from the neck and add it to the diced duck.

7. In a heavy 4-quart stockpot, heat the remaining 2 tablespoons oil over high heat. Add the diced carrots, parsnips and leek whites and cook for 3 minutes. Stir in the flour and cook for 2 minutes. Gradually add the duck stock, stirring constantly. Bring to a simmer and skim the surface. Add the reserved duck and the sour cherries and reduce the heat to moderately low. Simmer until all the vegetables are tender, 10 to 12 minutes.

8. In a small bowl, stir a little of the hot soup into the cream. Stir into the soup and remove from the heat. Season with salt and pepper.

9. Cook the noodles in a pot of boiling salted water until al dente. Drain and rinse with hot water.

10. Place the noodles in 8 serving bowls and ladle the soup on top. Garnish generously with the scallion greens and parsley.

—*Andrew Ziobro*

• • •

CHICKEN CONGEE

Congee can be a thin watery rice gruel or a thick, comforting rice porridge; the rice can be cooked to a smooth paste or only until soft. The real differences lie in the range and variety of the condiments used to dress up and enliven an essentially uncomplicated dish.

6 to 8 Servings

One 1½-by-½-inch piece of fresh ginger, peeled and cut into small chunks, plus ¼ cup slivered fresh ginger
2½ pounds chicken legs and breasts
2 cups Thai or jasmine rice*
½ teaspoon salt
Boiling water, if necessary
2 teaspoons peanut oil
8 garlic cloves, finely chopped
Light soy sauce
Chinese chile paste*
Chinese hot chile oil (la yu)*
3 tablespoons dried shrimp*
3 tablespoons Chinese preserved vegetables,* finely chopped
¼ cup fresh coriander (cilantro) leaves
3 shallots, finely chopped
¼ cup raw shelled and skinned peanuts, roasted (see Note) and coarsely chopped
***Available at Asian markets**

1. In a large pot, combine the chunks of ginger with 3 quarts of water and bring to a boil over high heat. Add the chicken pieces and reduce the heat to moderate. Simmer until the chicken is cooked through, 30 to 40 minutes; the breasts will be done before the legs.

2. Remove the chicken from the broth. When the pieces are cool enough to handle, remove and discard the skin and bones and shred the meat with your fingers. Cover and refrigerate the broth until the fat congeals on the surface. *(The recipe can be prepared to this point up to 1 day ahead. Refrigerate the chicken overnight, but bring to room temperature before proceeding.)*

3. Skim the fat off the cooled chicken broth and discard the ginger pieces. Return the broth to the pot and bring to a boil over high heat. Add the rice and stir until the broth returns to a boil. Add the salt, reduce the heat to moderately low and cover. Simmer until the rice is cooked, about 15 minutes. Stir in the reserved shredded chicken and heat through, about 2 minutes; the congee should be somewhat soupy. If the rice has absorbed all the broth, add boiling water, 1 cup at a time, until the desired consistency is achieved.

4. While the rice cooks, heat the peanut oil in a small skillet, over moderate heat until hot. Reduce the heat to moderately low and add the garlic. Fry until golden brown, about 5 minutes.

5. Put the fried garlic, soy sauce, chile paste, chile oil, dried shrimp, preserved vegetables, coriander leaves, slivered ginger, shallots and peanuts into separate bowls. Serve the congee in soup bowls accompanied with the bowls of condiments.

NOTE: *Freshly roasted peanuts have a wonderful flavor. Follow this method: In a small cast iron skillet, roast the peanuts over moderately high heat, stirring constantly, until browned, about 5 minutes. Set aside to cool.*

—Jeffrey Alford & Naomi Duguid

• • •

PHEASANT CHOWDER WITH WILD RICE AND LEEKS

You can ask your butcher to cut up the pheasant as described in Step 1.

🍷 The variety of flavors in this savory broth would be underscored by a crisp, clean, rounded California Chardonnay. Another good strategy would be to serve a Pinot Noir, whose pungent, dried-fruit flavors would provide a nice contrast to the chowder.

4 Servings

One 2½- to 3-pound pheasant
2 tablespoons olive oil
Freshly ground pepper
¼ pound bacon or pancetta, cut into ¼-inch dice
3 medium leeks, white and tender green, thinly sliced
1 large carrot, finely diced
1 celery rib, finely diced
3½ cups canned chicken broth diluted with 2½ cups water
1 can (14 ounces) Italian peeled tomatoes
1 cup hearty red wine
2 bay leaves
2 teaspoons minced fresh rosemary or 1 teaspoon dried
1 teaspoon fennel seeds
½ cup wild rice, rinsed thoroughly
1 tablespoon unsalted butter
¼ pound shiitake or other fresh wild mushrooms, stemmed and sliced ¼ inch thick
1½ teaspoons balsamic vinegar
Salt
Chopped fresh basil or flat-leaf parsley, for garnish

1. Using a small sharp knife, carefully remove the pheasant breasts from the bone; remove and discard the skin. Rub the breasts with the oil and season with pepper; set aside. Chop the remaining pheasant into 6 pieces.

2. In a nonreactive stockpot, cook the bacon over low heat until crisp, about 10 minutes. Using a slotted spoon, transfer the bacon to paper towels to drain. Add the 6 pheasant pieces to the pot, increase the heat to moderately high and cook, turning, until lightly browned all over, about 8 minutes. Transfer the pheasant pieces to a plate.

3. Reduce the heat to low, add the leeks to the pot and cook just until soft, about 4 minutes. Add the carrot and celery and cook for 3 minutes longer. Add the diluted chicken broth, tomatoes, wine, bay leaves, rosemary and fennel seeds. Return the pheasant pieces to the pot and bring to a boil over high heat. Reduce the heat to low and simmer the stock for 35 minutes, skimming any fat or scum that rises to the surface.

4. Add the wild rice and simmer until tender, about 30 minutes longer. Remove from the heat.

5. Meanwhile, in a medium skillet, heat the butter over moderate heat. Add the mushrooms and cook until tender, about 4 minutes.

6. Remove the pheasant pieces from the stockpot and pull off any remaining meat; discard the skin and bones. Return the pheasant meat to the pot. Stir in the vinegar and season with salt and pepper to taste.

7. Preheat a grill or broiler. Season the pheasant breasts with salt and grill or broil to medium rare, 3 to 4 minutes per side. Do not overcook. Let sit for a minute or two, then slice thinly on the diagonal.

8. To serve, ladle the warm chowder into warm bowls. Then add the sliced breasts, the reserved bacon and mushrooms and the basil.

—*John Ash & Sid Goldstein*

• • •

SOUR RYE SOUP WITH KIELBASA

This old-style Polish soup is flavored with *kwas*, a fermented liquid made from rye or oat flour, garlic and water. You will need to start the *kwas* four to five days before you make the soup. Ready-made *kwas*, called *zur naturalny*, is available at food shops that carry Polish specialties.

8 Servings

Boiling water
1 cup whole-grain rye or oat flour
3 cups boiled water, cooled to lukewarm
2 garlic cloves—1 crushed, 1 chopped
1 teaspoon oil
¼ pound thick-sliced smoked bacon, cut into ½-inch dice
1 medium onion, cut into ½-inch dice
½ pound cremini or white mushrooms, sliced ¼ inch thick
2 tablespoons all-purpose flour
1½ quarts Veal Stock (p. 52) or chicken stock
¾ pound yellow potatoes, such as Yellow Finnish or Yukon Gold
1 tablespoon fresh marjoram, or 1 teaspoon dried
½ pound kielbasa (smoked Polish sausage), sliced ¼ inch thick
½ cup heavy cream
Salt and freshly ground pepper
4 hard-cooked eggs, quartered (optional)
¼ cup chopped chives

1. With boiling water, sterilize a 2-quart glass jar or crock and a spoon. In the jar, combine the whole-grain flour and 1½ cups of the lukewarm water. Mix with the spoon until smooth. Add the crushed garlic clove and pour the remaining 1½ cups lukewarm water on top. Seal the jar with plastic wrap and pierce with a knife tip. Set aside in a warm place for 4 to 5 days. When the *kwas* has fermented sufficiently, it will have a sour aroma and there will be a clear separation of flour and liquid. Discard any floury foam floating on the surface. Strain the *kwas* through a fine sieve, leaving behind most of the settled flour. Refrigerate until ready to use.

2. In a large heavy stockpot, heat the oil over moderate heat. Add the bacon and cook, stirring frequently, until golden, about 10 minutes. Pour off all but 2 tablespoons of the fat and add the onion and chopped garlic. Cook until translucent, 4 to 5 minutes. Add the mushrooms and cook for 5 minutes longer.

3. Stir in the flour and cook for 2 minutes. Gradually add the Veal Stock, stirring. Bring to a simmer and cook over low heat for 15 minutes, skimming as necessary.

4. Meanwhile, peel the potatoes and cut them into ¾-inch cubes. Boil them in a small saucepan of salted water until slightly underdone, about 7 minutes. Drain and set aside.

5. Add 1½ cups of the *kwas* to the stockpot and bring to a simmer. Skim and add the marjoram, potatoes and kielbasa. Simmer until the potatoes are tender, about 5 minutes. Add the cream and season to taste with salt and pepper. Do not let the soup boil once the cream has been added.

6. To serve, ladle the soup into bowls and garnish with the hard-cooked eggs and chives.

—Andrew Ziobro

• • •

SAVOY CABBAGE, PARSNIP AND SMOKED HAM SOUP

Smoked kielbasa, ham hocks or bacon can be substituted for the ham.

🍷 The full, sweet taste of the root vegetables, the pungent cabbage and salty ham require a tart, fruity wine to bridge these flavors. Look for either a Beaujolais, such as 1990 Château de la Chaize Brouilly, or an Alsace Gewürztraminer, such as 1989 Willm Clos Gaensbroennel or 1989 Trimbach Réserve.

8 Servings

¼ cup vegetable oil or unsalted butter
1 small head of Savoy cabbage (1¼ pounds)—quartered, cored and cut into 1-by-¼-inch strips
Salt and freshly ground pepper
2 medium onions, cut into ½-inch pieces
3 to 4 medium parsnips—peeled, quartered and cut into ½-inch pieces
2 garlic cloves, thinly sliced
1 tablespoon tomato paste
2 teaspoons caraway seeds, coarsely chopped
2 quarts chicken stock or canned low-sodium broth
1 bay leaf
¾ pound smoked ham, such as Black Forest, cut into ½-inch cubes
2 medium carrots, coarsely shredded
2 to 3 teaspoons cider vinegar
⅓ cup finely chopped flat-leaf parsley
⅓ cup snipped chives

1. In a large nonstick skillet, heat 1 tablespoon of the oil over high heat. Add half the cabbage and season lightly with salt and pepper. Reduce the heat to moderately high and cook, tossing frequently, until the cabbage is evenly wilted and lightly browned on the edges, about 5 minutes. Transfer to a bowl and repeat with another tablespoon of oil and the remaining cabbage.

2. In a large heavy stockpot, heat the remaining 2 tablespoons oil over moderately high heat. Add the onions and cook, stirring frequently, until just translucent, about 5 minutes. Add the parsnips and continue to cook, stirring, until the vegetables are a light golden brown, 8 to 10 minutes.

3. Add the garlic, tomato paste and caraway seeds and cook for 2 minutes, stirring to coat the vegetables. Add the stock, bay leaf and ham and bring to a simmer over high heat, skimming. Reduce the heat to moderate and cook for 8 minutes. Add the reserved cabbage and the carrots and cook until all the vegetables are tender, about 8 minutes longer.

4. Stir in the vinegar and half of the parsley and chives. Season the soup with salt and pepper. Ladle the soup into bowls and garnish with the remaining parsley and chives.

—Andrew Ziobro

• • •

SPLIT PEA SOUP WITH BACON AND MARJORAM

This version of the ubiquitous central European split pea soup is made with dried mushrooms. It's an aromatic and hearty blend, enhanced with the smokiness of the bacon, the pungency of the garlic and the zesty note of marjoram. Traditionally yellow split peas are used, but green split peas result in an equally flavorful rendition.

8 Servings

1½ ounces dried Polish mushrooms or cèpes
2 cups boiling water
½ pound thick-sliced smoked bacon, sliced crosswise ½ inch thick
4 large garlic cloves, lightly crushed
1 large onion, cut into ¼-inch dice
2 leeks, white part only, halved and sliced crosswise ½ inch thick
1 cup yellow or green split peas (½ pound), rinsed
2 quarts chicken stock or low-sodium broth
1 cup cubed sourdough or rye bread (½-inch pieces)
1 large carrot, cut into ½-inch dice
1 tablespoon fresh marjoram, chopped, or 1½ teaspoons dried
Salt and freshly ground pepper
1 tablespoon fresh lemon juice
3 tablespoons chopped flat-leaf parsley

1. In a sieve or colander, rinse the dried mushrooms under cold running water to remove any loose sand. Place in a medium bowl and pour the boiling water on top. Set aside to soak for at least 30 minutes, tossing occasionally.

2. Meanwhile, cook the bacon and garlic in a small heavy skillet over moderately low heat, stirring frequently, until the bacon is crisp and the garlic is golden, about 10 minutes. Pour the contents of the skillet into a small sieve set over a bowl. Reserve the fat. Separate the bacon and garlic; coarsely chop the garlic and set aside.

3. Using a slotted spoon, remove the mushrooms from the soaking liquid; squeeze any excess liquid back into the bowl. Rinse the mushrooms in a colander under cold running water to remove any remaining sand. Chop the mushrooms into ¼-inch pieces. Strain the soaking liquid through a paper coffee filter and reserve.

4. In a heavy 4-quart stockpot, heat 3 tablespoons of the bacon fat (or vegetable oil, if you prefer). Add the onion and leeks and cook over moderate heat until tender and lightly colored, about 8 minutes. Stir in the split peas and cook for 2 minutes. Add the chicken stock and the mushrooms and their liquid and bring to a simmer. Adjust the heat to maintain a simmer and cook for 30 minutes.

5. While the soup is cooking, toss the bread cubes with 2 tablespoons of the reserved bacon fat and place on a small baking tray. Toast in a toaster oven or broil until crisp and golden; set aside.

6. Add the carrot, marjoram, reserved garlic and half of the bacon to the soup. Season with salt and pepper. Simmer until the split peas are tender, about 15 minutes longer.

7. Stir the lemon juice and half the parsley into the soup. Ladle the soup into bowls and garnish with the reserved croutons and the remaining bacon and parsley.

—*Andrew Ziobro*

JAPANESE ONE-POT STEW

6 Servings

4 cups canned chicken broth
4 cups Dashi (p. 46) or bottled clam juice
1 pound medium all-purpose potatoes, peeled and cut into 1-inch cubes
One 6-inch piece of daikon*—peeled, halved lengthwise and sliced crosswise ¾ inch thick
½ cup mirin* or ⅓ cup sake
¼ cup soy sauce
1 large skinless, boneless chicken breast (about 12 ounces), cut into 1-inch cubes
Pork and Beef Meatballs (recipe follows)
6 hard-cooked eggs
6 small rectangles of deep-fried bean curd* or two 2-ounce cakes of pressed bean curd (see Note), cut into 1-inch cubes
Salt
1 tablespoon plus 1 teaspoon Japanese or American ground mustard, mixed with about 1 tablespoon water
****Available at Asian markets***

1. In a medium flameproof casserole, combine the chicken broth and Dashi and bring to a simmer over moderately high heat. Immediately reduce the heat to moderate and add the potatoes, daikon, mirin and soy sauce. Return to a simmer and cook for 15 minutes.

2. Add the chicken, Pork and Beef Meatballs, hard-cooked eggs and deep-fried bean curd and return to a simmer. Cook until the liquid has reduced by about one-quarter and all the vegetables are tender, about 45 minutes. If you are using fresh bean curd, add it 5 minutes before the cooking time is up. Season to taste with salt.

3. To serve, ladle the soup into 6 large bowls. Place an equal amount of mustard in 6 little dishes and serve alongside for dipping.

NOTE: *To make pressed bean curd, place two 2-ounce cakes of tofu between two towels and weigh down with a cast iron skillet for two to three hours.*

—*Jennifer Brennan*

• • •

PORK AND BEEF MEATBALLS

Makes 12 Meatballs

¼ pound lean ground beef
¼ pound ground pork
1 egg, beaten
1 teaspoon all-purpose flour
¼ teaspoon salt
1½ cups vegetable oil

1. In a medium bowl, combine the beef, pork, egg, flour and salt. Knead together thoroughly. Roll a small amount of the mixture between your palms to form a ¾-inch ball. Repeat with the remaining mixture.

2. Heat a medium skillet over moderately high heat for 4 to 5 minutes. Add the oil and heat until shimmering. Add half of the meatballs to the hot oil and fry, turning once, until well browned and cooked through, about 3 minutes. Using a slotted spoon, transfer the meatballs to paper towels to drain. Repeat with the remaining meatballs. *(The meatballs can be made up to 4 hours ahead; cover and refrigerate.)*

—*Jennifer Brennan*

• • •

FISH & SHELLFISH

BRANDADA ENCHILADAS IN RED PEPPER SAUCE

There is virtually no connection between the Spanish and Mexican cuisines in practice. In Spain a tortilla is an omelet, and a taco is (among other things) a pool cue. These enchiladas, then, are not truly Spanish, but if you were to replace the (Mexican) tortillas with rolled pasta sheets—*canalones*—you'd end up with exactly the sort of dish you might find in a contemporary Catalan restaurant.

🍷 Serve with a Penedès Chardonnay, such as Jean León Chardonnay 1990.

6 Servings

1 pound skinless, boneless salt cod
5 medium red bell peppers
1 pound Idaho potatoes, peeled and cut into 2-inch pieces
1 bay leaf
4 garlic cloves, minced
1 tablespoon minced fresh parsley
1 tablespoon sour cream
1 cup extra-virgin olive oil
½ teaspoon salt
¼ teaspoon freshly ground black pepper
1 cup heavy cream
Spicy Spanish paprika or hot Hungarian paprika
Vegetable oil, for frying
Twelve 8- to 10-inch flour tortillas
1 cup frozen peas
3 ounces Danish Blue, Maytag Blue or other young blue cheese, crumbled

1. Place the salt cod in a large bowl and cover with cold water. Set aside in the refrigerator to soak for at least 24 and up to 48 hours, changing the water at least three times a day.

2. Preheat the oven to 450°. Place the red peppers on a baking sheet and roast on the top rack of the oven until blistered and somewhat blackened on top, about 20 minutes. Turn and roast until very soft, about 10 minutes longer. Set aside to cool slightly, then peel, core and discard the seeds. Cut the peppers into large pieces. Transfer the peppers to a food processor and puree. Set aside.

3. Meanwhile, in a large saucepan, cover the potatoes with cold water and bring the water to a boil over high heat. Cook the potatoes until just tender, about 20 minutes. Drain and set aside.

4. In a medium saucepan, cover the salt cod and bay leaf with cold water. Bring almost to a boil over high heat, then remove from the heat, cover and set aside for 10 minutes. Drain carefully and remove any bones, skin or dark flesh.

5. Place the potatoes in a large bowl and mash them with a potato masher or a fork. Add the salt cod and mash together well. Stir in the garlic, parsley and sour cream.

6. Pour in the olive oil in a slow, steady stream, stirring constantly with a wooden spoon, until all the oil is incorporated. Season with the salt and pepper and set the *brandada* aside.

7. In a medium saucepan, bring the cream to a boil over high heat. Reduce the heat to low and stir in the pepper puree, a little at a time. Continue cooking, stirring constantly, until the mixture returns to a simmer. Remove from the heat and season to taste with paprika and salt. Transfer the red pepper sauce to a large shallow bowl.

8. In a large nonstick skillet, heat a small quantity of oil over high heat. Add the tortillas, one by one, and fry for a few seconds on each side, turning with wooden tongs until softened. Drain the tortillas on paper towels and stack them between pieces of paper towel as they are fried. Add more oil to the pan as needed and reduce the heat to moderate if the tortillas cook too quickly.

9. Preheat the oven to 350°. Lightly oil a 9-by-13-inch baking dish. Using a pastry brush, lightly brush both sides of a tortilla with the red pepper sauce. Place a heaping ¼ cup of the *brandada* down the center of the tortilla; bring one side of the tortilla up over the filling and roll like a cigar. Place seam side down in the oiled baking dish. Repeat with the remaining tortillas, sauce and *brandada*, arranging the enchiladas side by side in the baking dish. Spoon the remaining sauce over the enchiladas, cover the baking dish loosely with foil and bake for about 15 minutes, or until heated through and bubbling around the edges.

10. Meanwhile, in a medium saucepan, cook the peas in boiling salted water until heated through, about 1 minute. Drain immediately and set aside.

11. Sprinkle the blue cheese over the enchiladas and bake until the cheese is just melted, 2 to 3 minutes. To serve, center 2 enchiladas on each plate, top with any additional sauce and garnish with the peas.

—Colman Andrews

• • •

DINNER ON THE EASTERN SHORE

Delmarva Crab Cakes (p. 39)

Pan-Fried Indian River Inlet Flounder (below)

Anne Ogletree Noble's Fried Green Tomatoes (p. 168)

Fresh Corn Soufflé (p. 161)

Cherry Tomato Salad with Fresh Herbs (p. 142)

Less-Cream, No-Egg Ice Cream of the Peach Variety (p. 250)

Ga's Sunday Night Cake (p. 221)

—Mary Anne Dolan

PAN-FRIED INDIAN RIVER INLET FLOUNDER

The commercial fishermen who unload their daily hauls of Atlantic flounder and bluefish at the dock at Indian River Inlet are experts at filleting and do it on site after weighing their customers' choice of the catch. Great flounder is thick, juicy and white with a platinum-pink cast.

6 Generous Servings

1½ cups cracker meal
¾ teaspoon salt
½ teaspoon freshly ground pepper
6 large flounder fillets (about 8 ounces each)
3 tablespoons unsalted butter
3 tablespoons vegetable oil
Lemon wedges, for serving

1. In a paper bag, combine the cracker meal, salt and pepper. Place one fillet at a time in the bag and shake to coat thoroughly. Lay the coated fillets on a baking sheet.

2. In a large heavy skillet, melt 1 tablespoon of the butter in 1 tablespoon of the oil over moderately high heat until hot. Place 2 fillets in the pan and fry, turning once, until golden brown outside and just flaky, about 3 minutes per side. Transfer the fillets to a platter and blot with paper towels to remove excess oil. Keep warm in a low oven.

3. Wipe out the skillet. Fry the remaining flounder in 2 batches in the remaining butter and oil. Serve with lemon wedges.

—Mary Anne Dolan

• • •

ROAST MONKFISH WITH ROSEMARY

With its substantial flesh and strong rosemary flavor, this monkfish dish acts almost as a meat course. Although the dish is designed to serve a crowd, it is easily scaled down.

16 Servings

7 pounds monkfish fillets
3 eggs
¾ cup milk
2 cups fine dry bread crumbs
2 tablespoons minced fresh rosemary
2 cups all-purpose flour
Salt and freshly ground pepper
1 cup extra-virgin olive oil
Sprigs of fresh herb, for garnish
Lemon wedges

1. Preheat the oven to 400°. Thoroughly clean the monkfish fillets by trimming off all of the purplish membrane. In a shallow bowl, beat the eggs with the milk. In another shallow bowl, combine the bread crumbs and rosemary. Place the flour in a third shallow bowl.

2. Season the monkfish with salt and pepper. Roll the fillets in the flour until thoroughly coated; shake off the excess. Dip the floured fish in the eggs and then in the bread crumbs until coated.

3. Divide the oil between 2 large shallow roasting pans set over moderate heat. When the oil is hot, place the fish in the pan; be careful not to splash the oil. Cook on one side until golden brown, about 4 minutes. Turn the fillets over with 2 spatulas. Place the pans in the oven and bake for 12 minutes, or until the fish is cooked through; large pieces can take up to 6 minutes longer. Remove from oven and let rest for 6 minutes.

4. Beginning at the tail ends, thinly slice the fish on a slight diagonal. Overlap the slices on a serving platter. Decorate with fresh herb sprigs and lemon wedges.

—Evan Kleiman

• • •

GRILLED RED SNAPPER WITH BLACK BEAN SALSA AND JICAMA-MELON RELISH

Some of the best red snapper in the world comes from the Texas Gulf Coast. Black beans are a southwestern staple and the salsa gets an added dimension from ingredients that are indigenous to Mexico. Catfish can be substituted.

🍷 1989 Fall Creek Emerald Riesling

8 to 12 Servings

1½ cups dried black beans (12 ounces), rinsed and picked over

2 tablespoons olive oil
6 garlic cloves, diced
1 medium onion, chopped
1 medium carrot, chopped
1 celery rib, chopped
2 serrano chiles, seeded
8 cups chicken stock or canned low-sodium broth
1 small red bell pepper, cut into ¼-inch dice
1 small yellow bell pepper, cut into ¼-inch dice
2 tablespoons chopped fresh coriander (cilantro), plus whole leaves for garnish
1 tablespoon chopped fresh basil
2 teaspoons finely diced mango (optional)
2 teaspoons finely diced pineapple (optional)
Salt
Eight 4-ounce red snapper fillets
½ teaspoon chopped fresh oregano
1 tablespoon fresh lime juice
Jicama-Melon Relish (p. 261)

1. In a large bowl, cover the beans with water and set aside to soak overnight. Drain and set aside.

2. In a large saucepan, heat the olive oil over moderately low heat. Add the garlic, onion, carrot, celery and serrano chiles and cook, stirring frequently, until softened but not browned, about 7 minutes. Add the chicken stock and bring to a boil over high heat. Add the black beans, reduce the heat to low and simmer, skimming the surface a few times and stirring once or twice, until the beans are tender, about 2½ hours.

3. Scoop out 1 cup of the cooked black beans and set aside. Place the remaining beans, with their cooking liquid and vegetables, in a blender or food processor and puree until smooth. Combine with the reserved whole beans. *(The recipe can be prepared to this point up to 1 day ahead. Cover and refrigerate.)*

4. Preheat the broiler. In a medium saucepan, combine the beans with the red and yellow bell peppers, chopped coriander, basil and the mango and pineapple if using. Season with salt to taste and place over low heat to warm.

5. Prepare a medium-hot charcoal fire. Lightly brush both sides of the snapper fillets with oil and sprinkle lightly with salt. Grill, turning once until just cooked through, about 3 minutes per side. Alternatively, place the fillets on a broiling pan, skin side down, and broil for about 2 minutes, until the fish is almost cooked through. Rotate the pan and, using a large metal spatula, carefully flip the fillets without disturbing the skin. Broil for about 1 minute longer, until the skin is crisp.

6. Stir the oregano and lime juice into the warm bean salsa. Serve the fish fillets skin-side up, on top of the salsa with some of the Jicama-Melon Relish spooned on top. Garnish with the fresh coriander leaves.

—*Stephan Pyles*

• • •

SEARED RED SNAPPER WITH SZECHUAN SHRIMP AND SNOW PEAS

Serve this dish with white rice.

4 Servings

1 pound large shrimp (about 15)—shelled, deveined and cut into ½-inch dice
½ teaspoon Chinese chili paste with garlic*
½ teaspoon mushroom soy sauce*
White Butter Sauce (p. 258)
2 tablespoons peanut oil
4 red snapper fillets with skin (about 6 ounces each)
Salt and freshly ground white pepper
1 pound snow peas
½ of a medium green bell pepper, cut into ⅓-inch dice
½ of a medium red bell pepper, cut into ⅓-inch dice
½ of a medium yellow bell pepper, cut into ⅓-inch dice
3 medium scallions, white and green, cut into ½-inch pieces
1 small onion, cut into ¼-inch dice
1 teaspoon Oriental sesame oil
****Available at Asian markets***

1. In a medium bowl, toss together the shrimp, chili paste and soy sauce and set aside for 30 minutes. Place the White Butter Sauce in a double boiler over warm water. Bring a large saucepan of salted water to a boil over moderately high heat.

2. Heat a large heavy skillet over moderately high heat until very hot. Add 1 tablespoon of the peanut oil to the skillet and tilt the pan to coat. Season the snapper fillets lightly with salt and white pepper and add them to the skillet, skin side down. Cook, turning once, until firm and cooked through, 6 to 7 minutes. Transfer to an ovenproof platter and set aside in a warm oven.

3. Meanwhile, add the snow peas to the boiling water and cook until crisp-tender, about 1 minute. Drain and cover to keep warm.

4. Increase the heat under the skillet to high. Add the remaining 1 tablespoon peanut oil and the green, red and yellow bell peppers, the scallions and the onion. Stir-fry for 30 seconds. Add the shrimp and stir-fry until opaque throughout, about 2 minutes. Remove from the heat and stir in the sesame oil.

5. Arrange the snow peas in small mounds on 4 warm dinner plates. Ladle about ¼ cup of the warm White Butter Sauce around each mound of snow peas. Spoon the shrimp and vegetables on top of each mound and arrange a fish fillet, skin side up, on top. Serve immediately with any extra sauce.

—Roy Yamaguchi, Roy's, Honolulu, Hawaii

• • •

OVEN-ROASTED SNAPPER WITH VEGETABLES

Besugo, or sea bream, is the fish of choice in Galicia for this classic dish, but any large fish with firm-textured white flesh will do. Red snapper is an ideal choice. The fish should be cooked whole for the best flavor. This recipe came from the grandmother of Maria del Carmen Pérez, a Santiago housewife. 🍷 A light, crisp, refreshing white is all that's required to match this dish: Try a light white Spanish Rioja, such as 1989 Bodegas Montecillo Viña Cumbrero; or light Washington State white, such as 1990 Columbia Crest Sémillon.

6 Servings

One 4-pound red snapper, cleaned and scaled
Sea salt or kosher salt
1 lemon, sliced crosswise ¼ inch thick
½ cup plus 2 tablespoons olive oil
2 medium onions, coarsely chopped
2 pounds small new potatoes, peeled and sliced ¼ inch thick
1 large red bell pepper, sliced into ¼-inch strips
1 large green bell pepper, sliced into ¼-inch strips
1 medium tomato, sliced crosswise ⅓ inch thick
1 teaspoon saffron threads, crumbled and dissolved in ¾ cup dry white wine
2 tablespoons fine dry bread crumbs

1. Rinse the fish inside and out and pat dry with paper towels. With a sharp knife, make 3 deep vertical slashes, almost to the bone, on both sides of the fish. Sprinkle a little salt over each lemon slice and press a slice into each of the slashes. Tuck the remaining lemon slices into the belly cavity.

2. In a large skillet, heat 2 tablespoons of the olive oil over moderately low heat. Add the onions and cook, stirring occasionally, until softened, about 12 minutes. Using a slotted spoon, remove the onions from the oil and spread them on a large, rimmed baking sheet or roasting pan large enough to hold the fish.

3. Preheat the oven to 400°. Add ¼ cup of the remaining oil to the skillet and heat over moderately high heat. Add the potatoes and fry, turning once or twice, until golden brown, about 15 minutes. Drain the potatoes on paper towels, then scatter them in the baking dish. Add the red and green pepper strips to the skillet and cook, stirring occasionally, until softened, about 5 minutes. Set the fish on top of the potatoes and distribute the softened pepper strips and tomato slices around it.

4. In a small bowl, whisk the remaining ¼ cup of oil with the saffron and white wine until blended. Pour over the fish and vegetables and sprinkle the bread crumbs and 1 teaspoon salt on top.

5. Bake for 35 to 40 minutes, until the fish is firm and cooked through. Remove from the oven, cover, and set aside for 5 to 10 minutes before serving.

—Maria del Carmen Pérez

• • •

MAINE SEAFOOD DINNER

Lobster Chowder (p. 57)

Broiled Salmon with Herb Butter (below)

Marjorie Mosser's Potato Pancakes (p. 165)

A Mess of Peas (p. 165)

Salad with Hard-Boiled Egg Dressing (p. 142)

Maine Wild Blueberry Slump (p. 240)

—Nancy Harmon Jenkins

BROILED SALMON WITH HERB BUTTER

For the herb butter, you can use fresh basil or thyme, if you prefer, instead of the dill.

8 to 10 Servings

One 5-pound salmon, filleted, with the skin on
1 stick (4 ounces) unsalted butter, at room temperature
1 tablespoon fresh lemon juice
¼ cup minced fresh chives
¼ cup minced fresh dill
Coarse sea salt
Freshly cracked black pepper

1. Preheat the broiler. Place a broiler pan in the broiler for about 5 minutes to heat, then brush it lightly with oil.

2. Place the salmon on the hot broiler pan, skin side down. Broil about 3 inches from the heat for about 10 minutes, just until opaque but still slightly rare in the center. (The salmon can be cooked through, if you prefer.)

3. While the salmon cooks, place the butter in a small bowl. Using the back of a spoon, cream the butter with the lemon juice. Gradually blend in the chives and dill.

4. Transfer the salmon to a warmed platter and dot liberally with the herbed butter. Sprinkle with sea salt and cracked pepper and serve immediately. Pass additional salt and pepper separately in little saucers.

—*Nancy Harmon Jenkins*

• • •

POACHED SALMON WITH SORREL MAYONNAISE

This simply prepared dish is a showcase for the best salmon you can find. Ask your fishmonger to gut and clean the fish for you but to leave the head and tail intact.

8 Servings

One 4½-pound salmon, cleaned
1 bunch of fresh dill, stemmed
1 medium red onion, very thinly sliced crosswise, with the rings intact
2 lemons, very thinly sliced crosswise
2 tablespoons corn oil
1 bottle dry white wine
Young mustard greens or leaf lettuce, for garnish
1 slice of pimiento-stuffed green olive, for garnish
Sorrel Mayonnaise (p. 258)

1. Preheat the oven to 350°. Dip 1 large double-thick piece of cheesecloth (about 2 by 3 feet) in water and squeeze out the excess water. Spread the dampened cheesecloth on a work surface.

2. Rinse the salmon under cold running water and pat dry with paper towels. Lay the fish on its side on top of the damp cheesecloth. Place half of the dill in the cavity. Arrange the onion slices in a single layer over the dill, then top with half the lemon slices. Rub the head and tail of the fish with the oil, then wrap them in aluminum foil. Place the remaining dill under and on top of the salmon. Wrap up the entire fish in the cheesecloth and tie the ends with kitchen string; trim off any excess cheesecloth.

3. Place the fish in a 17-by-11-inch glass or enamel baking dish (the head and tail will probably not lie flat in the dish). Pour the wine over the fish, completely soaking the cheesecloth, and bake, basting every 20 minutes to keep the cheesecloth moist, for about 1 hour, or until an instant-read thermometer reads 140°.

4. Using 2 large metal spatulas, carefully transfer the salmon to a platter and set aside to cool for about 30 minutes. Refrigerate for about 3 hours until chilled. *(The salmon can be prepared to this point up to 3 days ahead; keep wrapped in the cheesecloth, cover securely with plastic wrap and refrigerate.)*

5. To serve, line a large oval platter with the mustard greens or lettuce. Remove the cheesecloth from the salmon and discard. Using your fingers, peel off all the skin gently but thoroughly. Discard the contents of the cavity. Remove the aluminum foil from the head and tail. Carefully transfer the fish to the prepared platter. Cover the eye with the olive slice and tuck the remaining lemon slices into the cavity. Serve the salmon at room temperature or chilled, with the Sorrel Mayonnaise.

—*Janie Hibler*

• • •

SALMON CORN CAKES

It is essential to prepare these patties with a light touch; overworking the ingredients will create a dense texture. Serve these fish cakes with a vegetable salsa or tartar sauce.

🍷 A full-bodied Chardonnay, such as 1989 Acacia "Marina Vineyard," 1990 Beringer Private Reserve, or 1990 Benziger, would stand up to these rich cakes and have enough crispness to underscore their flavor.

6 Main-Course or
12 First-Course Servings

2 large ears of fresh corn
1 cup dry white wine
1 bay leaf, preferably fresh
4 whole black peppercorns
2 sprigs of flat-leaf parsley
A few celery leaves
Two 8-ounce salmon steaks
1½ cups cracker meal
3 large shallots, finely chopped
½ of a large red bell pepper, diced
1 large celery rib, finely diced
¼ cup chopped fresh coriander (cilantro)
½ cup mayonnaise
1 egg, lightly beaten
½ teaspoon dry mustard
½ teaspoon salt
¼ teaspoon freshly ground black pepper
Dash of hot pepper sauce
¼ cup olive oil
Lime wedges, for serving

1. Using a thin sharp knife, slice the corn kernels from each cob into a bowl. In a small saucepan of boiling water, boil the corn kernels until crisp-tender, about 2 minutes. Drain, refresh under cold water, drain again and set aside.

ITALIAN CHRISTMAS SEAFOOD FEAST

Tuna Crostini with Capers (p. 21)

Grilled Skewered Shrimp and Country Bread (p. 26)

Fennel-Cured Salmon with Fennel-Mustard Dressing (p. 41)

Baked Stuffed Mussels (p. 39)

Fish Soup with Garlicky Croutons (p. 59)

Linguine with Tomato Clam Sauce (p. 129)

Roast Monkfish with Rosemary (p. 67)

Grilled Salmon Fillet with Parsley Pesto (at right)

Sicilian Orange Salad (p. 145)

Roasted Beets

Green Salad with Olive Oil and Coarse Salt

Almond Cookies (p. 231)

Panforte

Espresso

—Evan Kleiman

2. In a medium nonreactive skillet, bring the wine, bay leaf, peppercorns, parsley, celery leaves and 2 cups of water to a simmer over moderate heat. Add the salmon steaks and poach, basting occasionally with the liquid, until just cooked through, 7 to 10 minutes. Transfer the salmon to paper towels to drain.

3. Flake the salmon in large pieces into a large bowl, discarding all skin and bones. Add ¼ cup of the cracker meal, the shallots, red bell pepper, celery, coriander and the reserved corn. Using a rubber spatula, gently fold the ingredients to combine.

4. In a small bowl, whisk the mayonnaise, egg, mustard, salt, black pepper and hot pepper sauce. Gently fold into the salmon mixture.

5. Using a ⅓-cup measure, form the salmon mixture into twelve 3-inch round patties. Coat the patties well on both sides with as much of the remaining 1¼ cups cracker meal as needed. Cover and refrigerate for up to 1 hour.

6. In a nonstick skillet, heat 2 tablespoons of the oil over moderate heat. Add 6 cakes and cook, turning once, until crisp and golden brown, about 3 minutes per side. Transfer to paper towels to drain. Wipe out the skillet and repeat with the remaining 2 tablespoons oil and 6 cakes. Serve with lime wedges.

—Sheila Lukins

• • •

SALMON WITH GARLIC SAUCE

2 Servings

2 tablespoons vegetable oil
4 garlic cloves, minced
¼ teaspoon freshly ground white pepper
1 teaspoon sugar
2 tablespoons soy sauce
½ pound asparagus, trimmed 5 inches long
½ pound broccoli, cut into florets
Two 8-ounce salmon fillets, skinned

1. In a small skillet, heat 1½ teaspoons of the oil over moderate heat until hot. Add the garlic and cook, stirring, until light brown, about 2 minutes. Reduce the heat to low and add the white pepper, sugar and soy sauce; cook the mixture, stirring, for about 30 seconds. Remove from the heat and set aside.

2. In a steamer over boiling water, steam the asparagus and broccoli until bright green and tender, about 2 minutes. Drain and cover to keep warm.

3. Preheat the broiler. Place the salmon on a broiler pan and brush with the remaining 1½ tablespoons oil. Broil the salmon fillets on one side only until brown and crusty on the outside and slightly translucent in the center, 4 to 5 minutes.

4. Place the grilled salmon on warm dinner plates and top with the garlic sauce. Serve with the warm asparagus and broccoli.

—Talesai, West Hollywood

• • •

GRILLED SALMON FILLET WITH PARSLEY PESTO

14 Servings

½ cup plus 2 tablespoons pine nuts
6 cups flat-leaf parsley leaves
6 tablespoons freshly grated Parmesan cheese
2 teaspoons chopped garlic
Juice of 2 lemons
1½ teaspoons salt
1 teaspoon freshly ground pepper
1½ cups extra-virgin olive oil, plus more for brushing
One 7- to 8-pound Norwegian salmon, filleted and skinned
Sprigs of fresh herbs, for garnish

1. Preheat the oven to 400°. Place the pine nuts on a small baking sheet and roast until golden brown, about 4 minutes. Let cool. Set aside ¼ cup of the pine nuts for garnish.

2. In a food processor, combine the remaining pine nuts with the parsley, Parmesan, garlic, lemon juice, salt, pepper and the 1½ cups oil and process until smooth. Set the parsley pesto aside.

3. Light the grill or preheat the broiler. Season the salmon fillets with salt and pepper and brush with olive oil. Place the fillets on the grill and cook for 4 minutes. Using 2 long spatulas, turn the fillets and grill for 4 to 5 minutes longer, until the fish is firm to the touch and cooked to medium. Alternatively, place the fillets, skinned side up, on a large baking sheet and fold the tail ends under to ensure even cooking. Broil the fillets for 4 minutes, rotating the pan to cook evenly. Using two large spatulas, flip the fillets and broil, rotating, for about 4 minutes longer, until there is just a trace of translucency in the thickest part.

4. Transfer the salmon fillets to a serving platter and sprinkle with the reserved pine nuts. Decorate the platter with sprigs of fresh herbs. Serve the parsley pesto on the side.

—*Evan Kleiman*

• • •

GRILLED SWORDFISH WITH SWEET RED PEPPER-PAPAYA-CORN SALSA

4 Servings

1 large red bell pepper
¼ cup fresh corn kernels (from 1 small ear)
¼ cup finely diced papaya (from 1 small papaya)
1 tablespoon minced fresh coriander (cilantro), plus whole leaves
2 tablespoons extra-virgin olive oil
Salt and freshly ground black pepper
Four 8-ounce swordfish steaks, about 1 inch thick

1. Roast the red bell pepper directly over a gas flame or under the broiler as close to the heat as possible, turning frequently, until charred. Transfer the pepper to a bag and set aside to steam for 10 minutes. Peel off the blackened skin and remove the core, seeds and ribs. Cut the pepper into ¼-inch dice and place in a bowl.

2. Place a steamer basket in a small saucepan and bring ½ inch of water to a boil. Add the corn kernels, cover and steam until almost tender, about 3 minutes. Drain and set aside to cool.

3. Add the corn, papaya, minced coriander and 1 teaspoon of the olive oil to the bell pepper in the bowl. Mix well and season with salt and black pepper to taste. Set the salsa aside. *(The salsa can be made up to 3 hours ahead; cover and refrigerate.)*

4. Light a grill or preheat the broiler. Rub the swordfish on both sides with 1 tablespoon of the olive oil and season lightly with salt and black pepper. When the coals are very hot, grill the fish, turning once and brushing with the remaining 2 teaspoons olive oil, until just cooked through, 4 to 5 minutes. (Alternatively, broil the swordfish without turning for 3 to 4 minutes, until just cooked through.) Transfer the fish to plates, and garnish with the salsa and coriander leaves.

—*David Rosengarten*

• • •

SEA BASS WITH WHITE WINE AND LEMON GRASS

4 Servings

1½ tablespoons unsalted butter
1 medium shallot, minced
1 stalk of fresh lemon grass, white bulb only, pounded flat and minced
4 sea bass or red snapper fillets with skin (about 6 ounces each)
Salt and freshly ground pepper
¼ cup dry white wine
1 tablespoon finely chopped parsley

1. Preheat the oven to 425°. Rub 1 tablespoon of the butter over the bottom of a nonreactive flameproof baking dish just large enough to hold the fish in 1 layer. Sprinkle the shallot and lemon grass into the dish.

2. Slash the skin of each fillet in 2 or 3 places. Season the fillets with salt and pepper and place skin side down in the prepared dish. Pour the wine and ¼ cup of water around the fillets and bring to a simmer over moderately low heat. Cover the dish with aluminum foil and bake for 8 to 9 minutes, until the fish is barely cooked through; do not overcook.

3. Transfer the fillets to plates and keep warm. Place the baking dish over moderately high heat and boil the sauce until reduced by half, adding any liquid from the fish plate. Remove from the heat and whisk in the remaining ½ tablespoon butter and the parsley. Season with salt and pepper and spoon the sauce over the fish.

—*Stephanie Lyness*

• • •

Pan-Fried Indian River Inlet Flounder *(p. 67).*

Above, Grilled Scallops with Black and White Beans (p. 80).
Right, Roast Monkfish with Rosemary (p. 67).

GRILLED SWORDFISH WITH THREE SAUCES

🍷 The dense, meaty texture of grilled swordfish pairs well with flavorful whites. The accompanying piquant sauces, particularly the wasabi, add a bite best met with a full-bodied white, such as 1989 deLorimier "Spectrum" (a Sauvignon Blanc-Sémillon blend from California) or 1989 Domaine Ostertag Pinot Gris "Barrique" from Alsace.

4 Servings

Four 8-ounce swordfish steaks, about 1 inch thick
Salt
Yellow Miso Sauce (recipe follows)
Pickled Ginger Sauce (recipe follows)
Wasabi Sauce (recipe follows)
Stir-fried eggplant, broccoli and mushrooms, at room temperature, as accompaniments

1. Preheat a grill or the broiler. Sprinkle the swordfish steaks lightly with salt on both sides and grill on an oiled grill rack over ashen coals, turning once, for 1½ to 2 minutes per side, until the flesh is firm and no longer translucent. Alternatively, place the swordfish on a broiler pan and broil, turning once, for about 2 to 3 minutes per side.

2. Snip the tip off a bottom corner of 3 sturdy plastic sandwich bags and fill each bag with one of the sauces. Alternatively, use a plastic squirt-type applicator bottle. Squeeze patterns of the sauces on 4 large serving plates. Place the swordfish steaks on top; serve with stir-fried eggplant, mushrooms and broccoli.

—Dean Fearing, The Mansion on Turtle Creek, Dallas

• • •

Clams and Mussels in Black Bean Sauce (p. 79).

YELLOW MISO SAUCE

Makes 1¼ Cups

2 tablespoons Oriental sesame oil
3 medium shallots, minced
4 medium garlic cloves, minced
1½ tablespoons finely grated fresh ginger
1 cup chicken stock or canned low-sodium broth
2 tablespoons seasoned rice vinegar
1 medium yellow bell pepper—cored, seeded and cut into 1-inch squares
1½ tablespoons yellow miso*
2 teaspoons fresh lime juice
Salt
****Available at Asian markets and health food stores***

1. Heat a small heavy saucepan over moderately high heat until hot. Add the sesame oil, shallots, garlic and ginger. Cook, stirring constantly, for 1 minute; do not brown. Add the chicken stock, vinegar and yellow bell pepper and bring to a boil. Reduce the heat to moderately low and simmer gently until the pepper is soft, about 20 minutes.

2. Transfer the mixture to a blender and puree until smooth. Add the miso and lime juice and blend well. Strain through a fine sieve into a small bowl; season with salt to taste. *(The recipe can be made up to 1 day ahead; cover and refrigerate. Serve at room temperature.)*

—Dean Fearing, The Mansion on Turtle Creek, Dallas

• • •

PICKLED GINGER SAUCE

Makes 1¼ Cups

2 tablespoons Oriental sesame oil
3 medium shallots, minced
3 medium garlic cloves, minced
1 tablespoon finely grated fresh ginger
1 cup chicken stock or canned low-sodium chicken broth
1 medium red bell pepper—cored, seeded and cut into 1-inch squares
2 tablespoons pickled ginger,* drained and liquid reserved
Salt
****Available at Asian markets***

1. Heat a small heavy saucepan over moderately high heat until hot. Add the sesame oil, shallots, garlic and ginger and cook, stirring constantly, for 1 minute; do not brown. Add the chicken stock and red bell pepper; bring the mixture to a boil, then reduce the heat to moderately low. Simmer gently until the pepper is soft, about 20 minutes.

2. Transfer to a blender, add the pickled ginger and puree until smooth. Strain through a fine sieve into a small bowl. Add salt and a few drops of the reserved pickling liquid to taste. *(The recipe can be made up to 1 day ahead; cover and refrigerate. Return to room temperature before serving.)*

—Dean Fearing, The Mansion on Turtle Creek, Dallas

• • •

WASABI SAUCE

Makes 1½ Cups

1 tablespoon wasabi powder*
2 tablespoons vegetable oil
3 medium shallots, minced
3 medium garlic cloves, minced
2 serrano chiles, seeded and minced (2 teaspoons)
2 tablespoons seasoned rice vinegar
1 cup chicken stock or low-sodium chicken broth
2 large green bell peppers—cored, seeded and cut into 1-inch squares
1 tablespoon chopped fresh coriander (cilantro)
Salt
****Available at Asian markets***

1. In a small bowl, mix the wasabi powder with 1 tablespoon of water to form a paste; set aside.

2. Heat a small heavy saucepan over moderately high heat until hot. Add the oil, shallots, garlic and chiles and cook, stirring constantly, for 1 minute; do not brown. Add the vinegar, stock and bell peppers; bring the mixture to a boil, then reduce the heat to moderately low. Simmer gently until the peppers are soft, about 20 minutes.

3. Transfer to a blender, add the reserved wasabi paste and fresh coriander and blend until smooth. Strain the mixture through a fine sieve into a small bowl; season to taste with salt and more wasabi if desired. *(The recipe can be made up to 1 day ahead; cover and refrigerate. Serve at room temperature.)*

—Dean Fearing, The Mansion on Turtle Creek, Dallas

• • •

FRESH TUNA DAUBE PROVENCALE

This intensely flavored daube is also delicious served cold.

Serve with a hearty but uncomplicated red Côtes du Rhône wine, such as Vacqueyras.

6 to 8 Servings

10 olive oil-packed anchovy fillets, drained
½ teaspoon whole black peppercorns
5 large garlic cloves, halved
¼ cup extra-virgin olive oil
1 large Spanish onion, minced
½ teaspoon finely grated lemon zest
One 2-pound tuna steak, cut about 2 inches thick
1 large green bell pepper
1 large red bell pepper
5 medium tomatoes—peeled, seeded and chopped—or 1 can (14 ounces) Italian peeled tomatoes, drained and chopped
Bouquet garni: 5 flat-leaf parsley sprigs, 3 thyme sprigs and 2 bay leaves tied in cheesecloth
⅛ teaspoon cayenne pepper
2 cups dry white wine, such as Aligoté
1 tablespoon drained capers
Salt and freshly ground black pepper

1. Rinse the anchovies briefly in cold water if they are very salty. Using the back of a fork, mash 4 of the anchovies to a paste.

2. In a mortar, crush the peppercorns with a pestle. Add the garlic and pound to form a paste. Add the mashed anchovies and pound to incorporate. Alternatively, use the back of a knife to crush the peppercorns and garlic, then mash with the anchovies.

3. Drizzle 1 tablespoon of the oil in a nonreactive flameproof baking dish just slightly larger than the tuna. Add the garlic paste, onion and lemon zest and mix well. Place the tuna on top and drizzle in 1 more tablespoon of the oil. Rub the garlic paste mixture all over the tuna. Cover and marinate at room temperature for several hours, turning the tuna twice, or refrigerate overnight.

4. Meanwhile, roast the green and red bell peppers directly over a gas flame or under the broiler, turning, until charred all over. Enclose the peppers in a paper bag and set aside to steam for 10 minutes. Peel the peppers and discard the cores, seeds and ribs; reserve as much juice as possible. Rinse the peppers well, then drain and slice lengthwise into wide strips. Set aside.

5. Preheat the oven to 350°. Remove the tuna from the marinade and scrape clean; reserve the marinade and onion. In a large nonreactive skillet, heat the remaining 2 tablespoons oil over high heat until hot. Add the tuna and sear for 2 minutes on each side. Transfer the tuna to a platter.

6. Add the reserved marinade and onion to the skillet and cook, stirring occasionally, until the onion is speckled with brown, about 5 minutes. Add the tomatoes, bouquet garni and cayenne and cook, stirring, for 1 minute. Add the wine and boil for 3 minutes.

7. Spoon the sauce into the baking dish and place the tuna on top. Scatter the roasted pepper strips and their juice and the capers around the tuna. Cover and bake for about 40 minutes, or until the tuna is just cooked through. Meanwhile, mash the 6 remaining anchovies.

8. Using a spatula, transfer the tuna to a platter. Set the baking dish over high heat, stir in the mashed anchovies, bring to a boil and boil for 3 minutes to concentrate the flavors. Season with salt

and black pepper to taste. Discard the bouquet garni. Cut the tuna in thick slices and arrange on warmed plates. Spoon the sauce alongside.

—Patricia Wells

• • •

CLAMS AND MUSSELS IN BLACK BEAN SAUCE

3 Servings

1 pound small fresh clams, scrubbed
1 pound small fresh mussels, scrubbed and debearded

AROMATICS:
1 tablespoon Chinese fermented black beans* (do not rinse them), minced
3 scallions, thinly sliced crosswise
1½ tablespoons finely minced fresh ginger
1 tablespoon finely minced garlic
½ to 1 teaspoon dried red chili flakes or seasonings drained from Chili-Lemon Oil or Chili-Orange Oil (p. 263)

SAUCE:
1 cup chicken or vegetable stock
3 tablespoons Chinese rice wine* or dry sherry
1 tablespoon plus 1 teaspoon mushroom soy sauce or 2 tablespoons regular soy sauce*
1 teaspoon cider vinegar or balsamic vinegar
1 teaspoon sugar

4 ounces red pearl onions or 1 small red onion, cut into 1-inch dice
Ice water
2 cups (loosely packed) stemmed spinach or wide ribbons of red chard (4 ounces)
½ cup fresh peas, asparagus tips or corn kernels
½ teaspoon corn or peanut oil
1 ounce bacon or Chinese or andouille sausage, cut into small dice (optional; see Note)
1 medium red bell pepper, cut into 1-inch dice
Cooked rice or fettuccine, for serving
****Available at Asian markets***

MEDITERRANEAN DINNER PARTY

Oven-Fried Almonds (p. 20)

Wood-Roasted Sweet Peppers in Olive Oil (p. 24) with Peasant Bread Toasts

Sweet Vermouth

Fresh Tuna Daube Provençale (p. 78)

Buttered Pastina

Côtes du Rhône

Frisée, Mâche and Arugula Tossed with Olive Oil and Sea Salt

Cherry-Frangipane Tart (p. 216)

Café Filtre

1. Discard any clams or mussels that are broken or do not clamp shut under water. Cover with a wet towel and refrigerate until ready to use.

2. Set aside 1 teaspoon of the black beans and 2 tablespoons of the scallions from the aromatics for garnish, then combine the remaining aromatics. In a bowl, combine the sauce ingredients.

3. If using pearl onions, blanch them in unsalted boiling water for 1½ to 2 minutes to loosen their skins, then plunge into ice water to chill. Peel the onions, trim the roots and halve them lengthwise through the root ends.

4. In another pot of boiling water, blanch the spinach for several seconds just to wilt the leaves, then remove with a slotted spoon and chill in ice water. Squeeze dry, then shake the leaves to loosen. Blanch the peas until crisp-tender, then plunge them in ice water and drain well.

5. Heat a wok or a large heavy skillet over high heat until hot enough to evaporate a bead of water on contact. Add the oil and bacon and stir-fry briskly until the fat is mostly rendered and the meat is crisp, about 1 minute. Reduce the heat if necessary to prevent scorching. Remove the bacon and reserve; leave behind the fat.

6. Add the aromatics and stir until fully fragrant, about 1 minute; adjust the heat as necessary to prevent scorching. Add the onions and bell pepper and stir-fry until crisp-tender, 2 to 3 minutes. Add the reserved spinach, peas and bacon and toss to combine. Remove from the heat.

7. About 10 minutes before serving, place the clams in a medium cast-iron casserole. Spread the vegetables over the clams and arrange the mussels on top. Stir the sauce and add it to the pot. Cover and bring to a lively simmer over high heat. Cook until the clams and mussels open, 4 to 5 minutes; discard any that do not open.

8. Taste the sauce and if it is not sufficiently salty, add a sprinkle of the reserved black beans for flavor. Serve at once in bowls with rice or fettuccine, garnished with the reserved scallions.

NOTE: *If not using the bacon, use a total of 2 tablespoons of oil in Step 5).*

—Barbara Tropp

• • •

GRILLED SCALLOPS WITH BLACK AND WHITE BEANS

The scallop is practically the heraldic emblem of Galicia, and white beans are an essential ingredient of the regional standard *caldo gallego*, a hearty bean and ham hock soup. The black beans are less traditional but add an attractive contrast of both color and flavor.

🍷 Serve with an Albariño, such as Martin Códax Albariño 1990.

6 Servings

4 tablespoons unsalted butter
2 tablespoons olive oil
1 large Spanish onion, chopped
2 garlic cloves, minced
1 celery rib, chopped
1 bay leaf
2 cups drained chopped tomatoes, from a 28-ounce can
2 pounds kale, trimmed and finely chopped
2 cups drained, canned black beans, from a 19-ounce can
2 cups drained, canned white beans (cannellini or navy), from a 19-ounce can
Salt
1½ tablespoons fresh lemon juice
24 large sea scallops (about 2 pounds)
Sweet Spanish or Hungarian paprika

1. In a large nonreactive saucepan, melt 2 tablespoons of the butter in the olive oil over low heat. Add the onion, garlic, celery and bay leaf and cook, stirring frequently, until the onion is very soft and the mixture begins to brown, about 30 minutes. Add the tomatoes. Reserve a small handful of the kale for garnish and add the rest to the saucepan. Cook, stirring frequently, for 10 minutes. Stir in the beans and season to taste with salt; remove from the heat and set aside.

2. Preheat the broiler. In a small saucepan, melt the remaining 2 tablespoons butter over moderate heat. Stir in the lemon juice and set aside.

3. Thread 4 scallops on each of six 8-inch metal or bamboo skewers, then brush with the lemon butter. Broil close to the heat, turning once, until the scallops are browned on the outside but still moist within, about 2 minutes on each side.

4. To serve, spoon the room-temperature bean mixture onto 6 serving plates and top with a skewer of scallops. Sprinkle the scallops lightly with paprika and salt. Finely chop the reserved kale and scatter over the beans.

—Colman Andrews

• • •

SPRING SEAFOOD SUPPER

Grilled Shrimp and Scallops (at right)

Orzo with Saffron (p. 124)

Asparagus with Lemon Vinaigrette (p. 158)

🍷 *1988 Gauer Estate Chardonnay or 1988 Elk Cove Chardonnay*

Fresh Strawberries

—Stephanie Lyness

GRILLED SHRIMP AND SCALLOPS

The simplicity of this recipe demands the freshest shrimp and scallops. Serve the seafood on a bed of orzo.

🍷 This grilled main course is well matched by a rich, fleshy oak-aged Chardonnay, such as 1988 Gauer Estate from California or 1988 Elk Cove from Oregon.

4 Servings

¾ pound large shrimp (16 to 20), shelled and deveined
¾ pound large sea scallops (16 to 20), membrane removed
Olive oil, for brushing
Salt and freshly ground pepper

1. Preheat a grill or the broiler. Thread about 5 shrimp on each of four 8-inch skewers. Thread about 5 scallops on each of 4 more skewers. Brush the seafood with olive oil and season lightly with salt and pepper.

2. Grill or broil the seafood, turning the skewers once, until just cooked through, about 2 minutes on each side for the shrimp and 3 minutes on each side for the scallops.

—Stephanie Lyness

• • •

SHRIMP ETOUFFEE

This recipe is from Billy and Tracy Fava, who run Mayers Catering company and a restaurant, Mayers Famous Plate Lunches, in Lafayette, Louisiana.

🍷 Shrimp indicates a white wine; tomato sauce calls for a crisp one to match, and the scallions and parsley require an equally herbaceous example. All of which narrows the likely good partners to crisp Sauvignon Blancs, such as 1990 Flora Springs or 1990 Kenwood.

6 Servings

1 stick (4 ounces) unsalted butter
2 medium onions, chopped
1 celery rib, finely chopped
3 garlic cloves, minced
1½ teaspoons minced jalapeño pepper
2 tablespoons all-purpose flour
1 can (14 ounces) Italian peeled tomatoes, chopped, juices reserved
1 tablespoon sweet paprika
½ teaspoon salt
½ teaspoon freshly ground black pepper
Pinch of cayenne pepper
2 pounds medium shrimp, shelled and deveined
4 scallions, chopped
½ cup chopped parsley
Cooked white rice, for serving

1. In a heavy nonreactive 14-inch skillet, melt the butter. Add the onions and celery and cook over moderate heat until translucent, about 5 minutes. Add the garlic and jalapeño and cook for 2 minutes. Add the flour and cook, stirring constantly, for 5 minutes.

2. Stir in the tomatoes and their juice, the paprika, salt, black pepper and cayenne. Bring to a simmer, cover and cook for 5 minutes. Add the shrimp and stir until they curl and turn pink, 2 to 3 minutes. Stir in the scallions and parsley and serve over rice.

—*Billy & Tracy Fava*

• • •

SAUTEED SHRIMP WITH SPICY WINE SAUCE

🍷 The spiciness and the heat of this dish, along with the sweetness of the corn, is best balanced by a crisp white with off-dry, fruity flavors, such as a dry Chenin Blanc from California. A 1990 Hacienda or 1990 Pine Ridge are top choices.

4 Servings

1 pound large shrimp (about 18), shelled and deveined, shells reserved
2 tablespoons vodka
1 egg white
5 garlic cloves, minced
1 tablespoon finely chopped Chinese dried shrimp*
3 tablespoons vegetable oil
¼ cup sake
3 large plum tomatoes—peeled, seeded and finely chopped
1½ cups chicken or fish stock or low-sodium chicken broth
1 teaspoon coarse (kosher) salt
½ teaspoon freshly ground white pepper
1 teaspoon cornstarch mixed with 1 tablespoon of water
1 tablespoon finely grated fresh ginger
¼ of a medium red bell pepper—cored, seeded and finely chopped
1 large jalapeño pepper, most seeds removed, minced
½ cup fresh white corn kernels (from 1 small ear), or thawed frozen
3 scallions, thinly sliced crosswise
****Available at Asian markets***

1. In a medium bowl, combine the fresh shrimp, vodka and egg white; set aside for 30 minutes.

2. Meanwhile, in a small saucepan, cook the garlic and dried shrimp in 1 tablespoon of the oil over high heat until fragrant, about 1 minute. Add the reserved shrimp shells, the sake, and ½ cup of the chopped tomato. Reduce the heat to moderately low and cook, stirring, until the liquid has reduced slightly, about 3 minutes. Add the stock, salt, white pepper and cornstarch mixture and simmer until the liquid is reduced to ¾ cup, about 20 minutes. Strain through a fine sieve into a bowl and cover.

3. In a large heavy skillet or wok, heat 1 tablespoon of the oil over moderately high heat until hot but not smoking. Stir-fry the marinated fresh shrimp until half cooked, about 1 minute. Using a slotted spoon, transfer to a medium bowl.

4. Add the remaining 1 tablespoon oil to the skillet and stir-fry the ginger, red bell pepper, jalapeño pepper, remaining chopped tomato and the corn for 2 minutes. Reduce the heat to moderate, add the reserved sake sauce and cook until the mixture thickens and reduces slightly, about 3 minutes. Return the shrimp to the skillet, add the scallions and cook until the shrimp are cooked and the mixture is heated through, about 1 minute. Transfer to a serving platter and serve immediately.

—*Susanna Foo*

• • •

SHRIMP EGG FOO YUNG

True egg foo yung, made with fresh shrimp and well-beaten eggs, is a dish of great delicacy and elegance.

6 Servings

8 eggs
1 cup peanut oil
¼ teaspoon salt
Pinch of freshly ground white pepper
¼ cup thinly sliced scallion greens
½ pound medium shrimp—shelled, deveined and halved lengthwise
Cooked rice, for serving

1. In a large bowl, whisk the eggs with 1½ tablespoons of the oil until frothy. Mix in the salt and white pepper; then stir in the scallion greens. Set aside.

2. Heat a wok over high heat for 30 seconds, add the remaining oil and heat to 350°. Add the shrimp and fry, turning, until the shrimp begin to curl and turn pink, about 30 seconds. Transfer the shrimp to a strainer and set aside to cool slightly. Add the shrimp to the beaten eggs and stir gently to combine.

3. Pour off all but 2 tablespoons of the oil from the wok. Return the wok to high heat. When a wisp of white smoke appears, pour in the eggs and cook, stirring gently with a spatula, until the eggs are softly scrambled but not runny, about 3 minutes. Transfer to a warm platter and serve immediately with the cooked rice.

—Eileen Yin-Fei Lo

• • •

POULTRY

HONEY-PEPPER POUSSINS

The use of both a marinade and a glaze gives these tender baby chickens flavor that's more than skin deep. Elegant enough for company and easy enough for family, this is one of my favorite recipes—especially during the hectic holiday season.

Poussins, increasingly available at quality supermarkets, are worth looking for. If you can't find them, fresh Cornish hens are also delicious when prepared this way. Serve with a nutty grain, such as wild rice or the wonderful wild pecan rice of Louisiana.

🍷 The taste of these sweet glazed chickens would be supported by the full-bodied, enveloping flavors of an oak-aged Chardonnay, such as 1989 Jekel from California or 1990 Rothbury Estate from Australia.

4 Servings

¼ cup plus 2 tablespoons mild olive oil
½ cup plus 2 tablespoons red wine vinegar
2 large sprigs of thyme
2 large garlic cloves, smashed
Four 1-pound poussins
¼ cup plus 2 tablespoons honey, preferably the Greek thyme-flavored Mount Hymettus honey
½ teaspoon coarsely ground black pepper
Coarse (kosher) salt

1. In a shallow nonreactive dish just large enough to hold the poussins in a single layer, combine the olive oil, ¼ cup of the vinegar, the thyme and garlic to make a marinade. Let stand for 30 minutes, then discard the garlic.

SUMMER BARBECUE

Barbecued Chicken (p. 84)

Warm Potato Salad with Thyme (p. 145)

Gingered Ice Cream with Berries (p. 241)

—Stephanie Lyness

2. Meanwhile, rinse the birds inside and out and pat dry with paper towels. Using poultry shears or heavy kitchen scissors, cut each poussin along both sides of the backbone from tail to neck; discard the backbones (or reserve them for stockmaking). Spread the birds open on a work surface, breast sides up. With the heel of your hand, press down hard on the breast bones to crack them and to flatten the birds. Fold the wings back and tuck the wing tips behind the shoulders. Add the poussins to the marinade and let sit at room temperature for 30 minutes, turning once.

3. Meanwhile, preheat the broiler. Pour the honey into a bowl and gradually stir in the remaining 6 tablespoons vinegar until blended. Just before cooking, stir in the pepper.

4. Remove the poussins from the marinade and place them on a broiler pan breast sides down. Broil 6 inches from the heat for 6 minutes. Turn and broil for 6 minutes longer.

5. Turn the poussins again and sprinkle lightly with coarse salt. Brush with the honey-pepper glaze and broil for 3 minutes. Turn the birds over, salt lightly, and brush the skin generously with the glaze. Broil for 2 minutes. Brush with the glaze and broil for about 1 minute longer, until the poussins are nicely browned, the flesh is moist and tender and the juices run clear when a thigh is pierced. Serve immediately.

—Leslie Newman

• • •

BARBECUED CHICKEN

4 to 6 Servings

1 tablespoon vegetable oil
½ medium onion, finely chopped
1 garlic clove, minced
1 can (6 ounces) tomato paste
⅓ cup molasses
¼ cup plus 2 tablespoons distilled white vinegar
2 tablespoons Dijon mustard
1½ teaspoons sugar
1½ teaspoons hot pepper sauce
1 teaspoon paprika
1 teaspoon salt
½ teaspoon ground ginger
Two 3-pound chickens, each cut into 8 pieces

1. Light a grill or preheat the broiler. In a medium nonreactive saucepan, heat the oil over moderately low heat. Add the onion and cook, stirring, until softened, about 3 minutes. Add the garlic and cook for 1 minute longer. Stir in the tomato paste, molasses, vinegar, mustard, sugar, hot pepper sauce, paprika, salt, ginger and 1¼ cups of water. Cover partially, increase the heat to moderate and simmer until thickened, about 20 minutes. (*The sauce can be made up to 1 week ahead. Pour into an airtight container and refrigerate.*)

2. Place the chicken pieces away from the hottest part of the grill, cover and grill, turning 2 or 3 times, until almost cooked through, about 30 minutes. (Alternatively, broil the chicken, turning, for about 25 minutes.) Brush on the

sauce and grill or broil the chicken, turning and basting with the sauce 2 or 3 more times, until the juices run clear, 10 to 15 minutes longer.

—*Stephanie Lyness*

• • •

ROASTED CHICKEN WITH POTATOES AND CHORIZO

The classic Rioja dish *patatas a la riojanas* is the inspiration for the garnish with this roasted chicken.

🍷 Serve with a white Rioja, such as Marqués de Murrieta Rioja Blanco Reserva 1986.

4 to 6 Servings

1 tablespoon unsalted butter, at room temperature
One 4- to 5-pound roasting chicken
1½ teaspoons salt
1½ teaspoons freshly ground black pepper
½ cup plus 1 tablespoon olive oil
2 pounds small red potatoes, peeled and halved (or quartered if large)
2 onions, coarsely chopped
2 red bell peppers, cut into 1-inch squares
½ pound chorizo or other firm paprika-flavored pork sausage, cut into ⅓-inch pieces
2 cups chicken stock or canned low-sodium broth

1. Preheat the oven to 375°. Rub the butter all over the chicken; sprinkle 1 teaspoon each of salt and pepper on the skin and inside the cavity. Truss the chicken and roast in a roasting pan, breast up, until the skin is golden brown and the juices run clear when a thigh is pierced, 1¼ to 1½ hours.

2. Meanwhile, heat ½ cup of the olive oil in a large heavy skillet over moderately high heat. Add the potatoes and cook, turning occasionally, until golden brown all over, about 20 minutes. Pour off the oil and set the potatoes aside in the skillet.

3. Heat the remaining 1 tablespoon oil in a medium skillet over moderate heat. Add the onions and peppers and cook, stirring occasionally, until softened and starting to brown, 12 to 15 minutes; add the chorizo and cook for 5 minutes more.

4. Transfer the mixture to the pan of potatoes. Add the chicken stock and bring to a simmer over moderate heat. Cook until the potatoes are tender and the stock has reduced by half, about 10 minutes. Season with the remaining ½ teaspoon each of salt and pepper. Serve immediately with the roasted chicken.

—*Colman Andrews*

• • •

UN-FRIED CHICKEN

4 Servings

Two 2½-pound chickens, cut into 8 pieces, wings and backs reserved for another use
½ cup fine dry bread crumbs
¼ cup unbleached flour
1 tablespoon freshly ground pepper
¾ teaspoon salt
3 tablespoons olive oil

1. Preheat the oven to 400°. Using your hands, a knife and a paper towel (to facilitate your grip), skin the chicken pieces.

2. In a paper or plastic bag, combine the bread crumbs, flour, pepper and salt and shake to mix. Rinse the chicken in cold water. Place several pieces in the bag and shake until well coated; set aside. Repeat with the remaining chicken.

3. In a low-sided, 3-quart casserole or large heavy skillet, heat the oil over moderately high heat until hot. Add all the chicken pieces, skinned sides down, and cook until beginning to brown, 1 to 2 minutes. Place the casserole on the bottom rack of the oven and bake for about 15 minutes, until the chicken is golden brown on the underside.

4. Remove the casserole from the oven and turn the pieces over with tongs. Return the chicken to the oven and cook for about 20 minutes longer, until the breasts are no longer pink at the bone. Transfer the breasts to a platter. Cook the thighs and legs for 5 more minutes. Transfer to the platter. Serve immediately.

—*Susan Shapiro Jaslove*

• • •

TERIYAKI CHICKEN

4 Servings

¼ cup dry sherry
¼ cup soy sauce
2 tablespoons honey
1 medium garlic clove, chopped
4 skinless, boneless chicken breast halves (about 1 pound)
1½ tablespoons vegetable oil

1. In a medium nonreactive bowl, whisk the sherry, soy sauce, honey and garlic. Add the chicken, turning to coat, and set aside to marinate for 30 minutes.

2. Heat a large heavy skillet over high heat until very hot, about 2 minutes. Meanwhile, remove the chicken from the marinade, shake off any excess marinade and discard any clinging bits of garlic. Add the oil to the skillet and tilt the pan to coat evenly. Reduce the heat to moderately high. Place the chicken in the skillet with the small fillet of the breast halves pushed to the side so that as much of the meat's surface as possible is exposed to direct heat. Cook, turning once, until browned, 6 to 7 minutes. Transfer to a platter to serve.

—Susan Shapiro Jaslove

• • •

KEDJENOU

This dish hails from the Ivory Coast where it is cooked in a clay pot, or *canari,* which is sealed with a banana leaf. Use a flameproof, heavy-lidded enameled or cast-iron casserole. The *kedjenou* can be served with white rice instead of the traditional *attieké,* a fermented starch.

🍷 This stew calls for a simple, dry white, such as 1990 Columbia Crest Sémillon from Washington State.

4 Servings

One 2½- to 3-pound chicken, cut into 8 pieces
2 medium onions, sliced
2 tablespoons minced fresh ginger
1 garlic clove, minced
1 bay leaf
Salt and freshly ground pepper

Place the chicken, onions, ginger, garlic and bay leaf in a heavy flameproof casserole and season with salt and pepper. Cover tightly and cook over moderately low heat for about 40 minutes, shaking the casserole every 5 minutes to prevent sticking and to mix the ingredients. Do not uncover the casserole during cooking. Discard the bay leaf.

—Jessica B. Harris

• • •

SPICY TROPICAL DINNER

Jamaican Jerk Chicken (below)

Red Banana-Curry Ketchup (p. 261)

Grilled Green Onions (p. 164)

Fried Green Plantains (p. 166)

Tropical Fruit Cocktail with Chile Peppers (p. 144)

—Chris Schlesinger & John Willoughby

JAMAICAN JERK CHICKEN

The "jerk" method of cooking meat and fowl—a combination of slow grilling and smoking—was developed by the Arawak Indians and perfected by escaped slaves on the island of Jamaica. The spice rubs that are applied to "jerk" foods vary as greatly as barbecue sauces do in the States. The only common ingredient is the Scotch Bonnet, known as the hottest chile pepper in the world.

4 to 6 Servings

10 large Scotch Bonnet chiles or other fresh chiles (5 ounces), stemmed
¼ cup fresh lime juice
¼ cup yellow mustard
2 tablespoons orange juice
2 tablespoons white vinegar
3 scallions, finely chopped
2 tablespoons chopped fresh rosemary
2 tablespoons chopped fresh basil
2 tablespoons chopped fresh thyme
2 tablespoons chopped fresh parsley
2 tablespoons mustard seeds
1 teaspoon salt
1 teaspoon freshly ground pepper
6 large whole chicken legs (with thighs)

1. Puree the chiles in a food processor. Add all of the remaining ingredients except for the chicken and puree to a paste. Transfer the paste to a small bowl, cover and refrigerate for at least 2 hours.

2. Light a grill or preheat the oven to 350°. Rub the chicken liberally with the paste and grill over very low heat for about 40 minutes, turning once, until dark brown and crusty. If you have a covered grill, put the coals on one side, the chicken on the other, cover and cook for 40 to 50 minutes. Alternatively, bake the chicken for 50 minutes, then broil it for 2 to 3 minutes on each side for a nice crust. Separate the drumsticks from the thighs and serve.

—Chris Schlesinger & John Willoughby

• • •

GRILLED SPICY CHICKEN WITH TWO SAUCES

6 Servings

3 tablespoons raw sugar*
2 teaspoons rubbed sage
2 teaspoons cumin
2 teaspoons thyme
1 teaspoon salt
½ teaspoon cayenne pepper
6 whole chicken legs, split into legs and thighs
Peanut Dipping Sauce (p. 256)
Pineapple Salsa (p. 259)
****Available at supermarkets***

1. In a medium bowl, toss the sugar, sage, cumin, thyme, salt and cayenne until well mixed.

2. Preheat the oven to 350°. Rinse the chicken pieces and pat dry. Rub the spice mixture all over. Place on a broiler pan and bake for 40 minutes, until the juices run clear when pierced with a knife.

3. Preheat the broiler or light a grill. Broil or grill the chicken, turning once, for 5 to 10 minutes, until browned and crisp. Serve hot, with the Peanut Dipping Sauce and Pineapple Salsa.

—Peter Merriman, Merriman's, Waimea, Hawaii

• • •

CHICKEN IN THE POT

If you make Chicken in the Pot with a rich homemade chicken stock, the dish will be sublime. If you use canned chicken broth diluted with water, it will still be delicious and satisfying.

🍷 This deeply flavored chicken dish would be best matched with a big, round, fruity Chardonnay. A 1988 Zaca Mesa Reserve or, for a kosher choice, 1988 Gan Eden from California would fit the bill.

8 to 10 Servings

One 4- to 5-pound chicken, neck and giblets reserved
3 medium celery ribs, quartered
6 medium carrots, quartered
3 small turnips, peeled and quartered
4 parsnips, quartered
6 medium leeks, white and tender green, coarsely chopped
1 bunch of parsley, tied with string
3 to 3½ quarts chicken stock or 2 quarts canned low-sodium chicken broth diluted with 1 to 1½ quarts water
Salt and freshly ground pepper
4 ounces dried egg noodles
8 Matzo Balls (p. 50)
8 Cheese and Potato Kreplach (p. 132)
¼ cup chopped fresh dill

1. Rinse the chicken under cold water and remove all visible fat (save the fat for rendering, if desired). In a stockpot, place the chicken, neck and giblets, celery, carrots, turnips, parsnips, leeks, parsley and 3 quarts of the chicken stock. If the liquid does not just barely cover the chicken, add the remaining 2 cups stock. Bring to a simmer over moderately high heat and skim off any foam. Reduce the heat to moderately low. Cover partially and simmer until the chicken is just cooked but not falling off the bone, about 1 hour.

2. Transfer the chicken to a cutting board and cut it into 8 to 10 pieces. Skim the fat from the surface of the soup and discard the parsley. Season with salt and pepper.

3. Bring a medium saucepan of salted water to a boil over high heat. Add the egg noodles and cook until al dente, about 7 minutes. Transfer to a colander to drain.

4. To serve, fill each shallow soup bowl with a ladleful of soup, a piece of chicken, some of the vegetables, a Matzo Ball and a Kreplach, some of the cooked noodles and a sprinkling of dill. Serve immediately.

—Susan R. Friedland

• • •

CHICKEN AND CHORIZO SAUTE WITH ANCHO-TOMATO SAUCE

🍷 This spicy dish with its coarse textures would overwhelm any delicate Champagne. In fact, it's a good idea to avoid sparklers from Champagne, France. But some of the world's not-quite-so-elegant sparkling wines provide ideal refreshment next to this dish. Try a sparkling wine from S. Anderson in the Napa Valley or from Codorníu in Catalonia.

4 Servings

Eight 4- to 5-ounce boneless chicken thighs, skin on
2 medium garlic cloves, minced, plus 8 unpeeled whole cloves
1½ teaspoons cumin seeds, freshly ground
Heaping ¼ teaspoon cayenne pepper
1 teaspoon salt
¼ teaspoon freshly ground black pepper
1 cup instant polenta
1 large ancho chile
1 can (20 ounces) Italian peeled tomatoes, chopped and drained, liquid reserved
2 tablespoons dried currants
1 tablespoon unsalted butter
2 tablespoons olive oil
¼ pound chorizo or other hot pepper sausage, sliced ¼ inch thick
¼ cup minced fresh coriander (cilantro) plus extra for garnish

1. Cut each chicken thigh in quarters. In a shallow dish, combine the minced garlic, ground cumin, cayenne pepper and ¼ teaspoon each of salt and black pepper. Toss the chicken pieces in the mixture, cover and refrigerate for at least 2 hours or overnight.

2. Meanwhile, lightly grease an 8-inch square pan. In a medium saucepan, stir the remaining ¾ teaspoon salt into 3 cups of water and bring to a boil over high heat. Reduce the heat to moderate. Gradually sprinkle in the polenta and cook, stirring constantly until very thick, about 5 minutes. Scrape the polenta into the prepared dish and spread in an even layer. Set aside until firm. *(The polenta can be made 1 day ahead and refrigerated, covered.)*

3. Preheat the oven to 375°. Place the remaining 8 garlic cloves on a heavy baking sheet and bake for about 25 minutes, until brown outside and soft inside. Remove from the oven and let cool slightly. Pinch the garlic skins and squeeze the soft pulp into a small bowl.

4. Place a small heavy skillet over high heat until hot. Add the ancho chile and cook, pressing the chile down with the back of a spoon until it softens, about 3 minutes per side. Remove from the pan and let cool slightly. Remove the core and seeds, then cut the chile into fine shreds.

5. In a medium nonreactive saucepan, combine the tomatoes and their liquid with the currants and cook over moderate heat until warmed through. Stir in the roasted garlic pulp and the ancho chile and simmer for 5 minutes. Season with salt and pepper to taste.

6. Cut the polenta into 16 squares. In a large skillet, heat 1½ teaspoons each of the butter and oil over moderately high heat. Add half of the polenta squares and fry until golden and crisp, about 3 minutes per side. Set aside to drain on paper towels. Repeat with another 1½ teaspoons each of butter and oil and the remaining polenta.

7. Wipe out the skillet and increase the heat to high. Add the chorizo and fry until browned on both sides, about 2 minutes. Drain on paper towels.

8. In the same skillet, heat 1½ teaspoons of the oil over moderately high heat. Add half of the chicken, skin side down, and fry until browned, crisp and cooked through, 6 to 7 minutes. Repeat with the remaining 1½ teaspoons oil and chicken.

9. Reheat the tomato sauce and add the coriander. Place 4 polenta squares on each warmed plate and spoon the chicken and sausage on top. Spoon the sauce over the chicken and garnish with coriander leaves. Serve immediately.

—David Rosengarten

• • •

UNA CENA ITALIANA

Campari and Soda

Antipasto

Breadsticks

Maresca Family Chicken Cacciatore (at left)

Polenta

🍷 *Chianti Classico, such as 1988 Fontodi or 1988 Nozzole*

Arugula Salad (p. 142)

Peaches in Prosecco (p. 236)

Espresso

MARESCA FAMILY CHICKEN CACCIATORE

4 Servings

One 3½-pound chicken, cut into 8 pieces
1 cup all-purpose flour
¾ teaspoon salt
½ teaspoon freshly ground black pepper
3 tablespoons olive oil
½ pound medium, white mushrooms, sliced ¼ inch thick
2 large green bell peppers, cut into ¾-inch-wide strips
½ of a large onion, sliced ¼ inch thick
2 garlic cloves, minced
One can (35 ounces) Italian peeled tomatoes, lightly drained and chopped
3 tablespoons chopped parsley

1. Rinse the chicken and pat dry. In a medium bowl, toss together the flour, ½ teaspoon of the salt and ¼ teaspoon of the pepper. Dredge the chicken in the seasoned flour and set aside on a plate.

2. In a large nonreactive skillet, heat 2 tablespoons of the olive oil over moderately high heat. Place the chicken breasts and wings in the pan, skin side down, and cook, turning occasionally, until well browned, about 6 minutes. Transfer to a plate. Repeat the procedure with the thighs and legs. Pour off the fat from the skillet and wipe it dry.

3. Add the mushrooms to the dry skillet and stir-fry over moderately high heat until some of the juices are exuded, about 2 minutes. Add the remaining 1 tablespoon oil and the bell peppers, onion and garlic and stir-fry until crisp-tender, about 5 minutes. Stir in the tomatoes, parsley and the remaining ¼ teaspoon each of salt and black pepper. Bring to a simmer over moderately high heat, then reduce the heat to moderate and return the chicken pieces to the skillet.

4. Cover and cook the chicken until tender, turning the pieces occasionally and adjusting the heat, if necessary, to maintain a slow simmer, about 30 minutes. If the sauce appears too thin, remove the cover for the last 10 minutes of cooking.

—Diane Darrow & Tom Maresca

• • •

MALAYSIAN COCONUT-CHICKEN CURRY WITH TWO NOODLES

The Indian influence on Malay cooking is evident in the way this dish is served. Diners adorn the noodle curry to their tastes with condiments served on the side. Do not shake the coconut milk as directed on most cans. Refrigerate it upright for at least four hours before using.

6 Servings

1½ cups chicken stock or canned broth
6 dried or 4 fresh kaffir lime leaves*
Four ¼-inch-thick slices fresh galangal or 7 slices dried (kha or laos)*
1½ tablespoons seedless tamarind pulp*
1½ teaspoons coriander seeds
6 dried red Asian chiles*
¼ teaspoon whole white or black peppercorns
2 tablespoons dried shrimp*
¾ teaspoon ground turmeric
3 stalks fresh lemon grass*
2 medium garlic cloves
2 red or green serrano chiles
1 cup minced shallots (about 8 medium)
¼ cup peanut or vegetable oil
2 cans (13½ ounces each) unsweetened coconut milk*
1 tablespoon plus 1 teaspoon fish sauce (nam pla or nuoc mam)*
¾ teaspoon sugar
4 chicken thighs (about 1¼ pounds), trimmed of fat
1¼ pounds skinless, boneless chicken breasts
1 teaspoon salt
3 ounces bean thread noodles*
1⅓ pounds fresh flat Chinese egg noodles*
1 tablespoon fresh lime juice
Cayenne pepper or hot pepper sauce (optional)
2 tablespoons fresh coriander (cilantro) leaves, plus additional sprigs for garnish

GARNISH:
2 limes, cut into wedges
Fresh basil leaves, preferably Asian
Sliced fresh red and green chiles, such as jalapeños
Crispy Shallots (recipe follows)
Shrimp chips,* fried
Asian hot sauce, such as Indonesian sambal olek, Thai sriracha sauce or Vietnamese chile and garlic sauce*
****Available at Asian markets***

1. In a medium saucepan, bring the chicken stock to a boil. Remove from the heat, add the kaffir lime leaves (and dried galangal, if using) and set aside to soak until needed. In a small bowl, combine the tamarind pulp with ⅓ cup of water and break it up with a fork. Set aside to soak.

2. In a small heavy skillet, roast the coriander seeds over moderately high heat, shaking the pan occasionally, until toasted, about 1½ minutes. Using scissors, cut the dried red chiles in half lengthwise and shake out and discard one-third of the seeds. Snip the chiles into small pieces.

3. In a mortar or spice grinder, combine the coriander seeds, dried chiles, peppercorns and dried shrimp, and pound or grind until completely pulverized. Stir in the turmeric.

4. Remove the tough outer leaves from the lemon grass and thinly slice the stalks. In a food processor, combine the lemon grass, fresh galangal (or reconstituted dried), garlic, serrano chiles and shallots and process until almost pureed, about 40 seconds. Mix in the ground spice mixture and the oil.

5. In a large skillet, cook the spiced lemon grass mixture over moderate heat, stirring frequently, until very fragrant, about 10 minutes. Set aside.

6. Remove the lime leaves from the stock and set aside. Open the cans of coconut milk and pour off the thick milk at the top; set aside. Blend the thin coconut milk at the bottom with enough of the infused chicken stock to make 3½ cups of liquid.

7. In a large deep pot, combine the coconut stock with the fried seasonings, reserved lime leaves, fish sauce and sugar. Add the reserved tamarind to the pot. Stir the stock mixture well.

8. Add the chicken thighs and bring to a boil over high heat. Reduce the heat to moderate and simmer for 15 minutes. Add the chicken breasts and simmer until the chicken is cooked through and the meat comes away from the thigh bones easily, about 30 minutes. Using tongs, transfer the chicken to a plate. When cool enough to handle, skin and bone the thighs and shred all the chicken meat. Stir the reserved thick coconut milk into the stock, then return the shredded chicken. Simmer gently over moderate heat until thickened slightly, about 15 minutes. Do not let it boil. Stir in the salt. *(The recipe can be prepared to this point up to 3 days ahead. Let cool to room temperature, then cover and refrigerate.)*

9. Shortly before serving, soak the bean threads in warm water to cover for

20 minutes. Bring a large pot of water to a boil over high heat. Drain the bean threads in a medium strainer. Dip the bean threads in the strainer into the boiling water until translucent, about 30 seconds. Immediately rinse under cold water and drain well. Place the bean threads in a bowl and stir in about ¼ cup of the coconut gravy.

10. Return the water to a boil and add the egg noodles. Cook until tender, about 2 minutes. Drain, rinse immediately under cold water and drain well.

11. Reheat the chicken in its sauce over moderate heat until hot. Remove the lime leaves. Add the lime juice and season with additional salt and cayenne pepper. Transfer the chicken and most of the sauce to a bowl and set aside.

12. Mix the bean threads with the egg noodles and add them to the remaining sauce in the pot. Stir occasionally until heated through, about 2 minutes.

13. Transfer the noodle mixture to a large serving platter or 6 large bowls. Spoon the remaining sauce and the chicken on top. Garnish with the fresh coriander and pass the garnishes in individual bowls.

—Linda Burum

• • •

CRISPY SHALLOTS

Makes ⅔ Cup

About ⅓ cup peanut or vegetable oil
6 medium shallots, very thinly sliced crosswise

1. In a medium skillet, heat the oil over moderate heat. Add half the shallots and fry, shaking the pan almost constantly, until they are evenly golden, about 4 minutes. Do not let them darken. Remove the shallots with a slotted spoon. Spread in a single layer on paper towels to drain and cool.

2. Reheat the oil, adding more, if necessary, and repeat with the remaining shallots. If the shallots are not crisp, bake them in a 225° oven until crisp. *(The shallots can be refrigerated, covered, for at least 1 week.)*

—Linda Burum

• • •

MOO GOO GAI PAN

6 Servings

MARINADE:
1 tablespoon finely grated fresh ginger
1½ teaspoons Oriental sesame oil
1 teaspoon white wine
½ teaspoon sugar
¼ teaspoon salt
1½ teaspoons oyster sauce
½ teaspoon light soy sauce
1 teaspoon cornstarch
Pinch of freshly ground white pepper

½ pound skinless, boneless chicken breasts, cut into 2-by-1½-inch strips

SAUCE:
½ teaspoon sugar
2 teaspoons oyster sauce
1 teaspoon light soy sauce
½ teaspoon Oriental sesame oil
2 teaspoons cornstarch
Pinch of freshly ground white pepper
5 tablespoons chicken stock or canned low-sodium broth

3½ tablespoons peanut oil
1 tablespoon minced fresh ginger
¼ teaspoon salt
¼ pound small button mushrooms, stemmed, caps sliced ¼ inch thick
6 ounces fresh snow peas, sliced diagonally ½ inch wide
¼ cup bamboo shoots, cut into 1-by-1½-inch slices
4 water chestnuts, sliced ¼ inch thick
1 large garlic clove, minced
1 tablespoon white wine

1. *Make the marinade:* Place the grated ginger in a small strainer set over a medium bowl. Press hard with the back of a spoon to extract 1 teaspoon of juice; discard the ginger pulp. Stir in the remaining marinade ingredients. Add the chicken and toss to coat well. Cover and set aside to marinate for 30 minutes.

CHINESE-AMERICAN SUPPER

Egg Drop Soup (p. 48)

Barbecued Spareribs (p. 112)

Moo Goo Gai Pan (at left)

Steamed Rice

Stir-Fried Broccoli and Red Peppers

🍷 Light fruity white, such as 1990 Dry Creek Chenin Blanc or 1991 Rosemount Traminer Riesling

Starfruit

Almond Cookies

Tea

2. *Make the sauce:* In a large bowl, combine all the sauce ingredients and reserve.

3. Heat a wok over high heat for 30 seconds. Add 2 tablespoons of the peanut oil and turn the wok to coat with oil. When a wisp of white smoke appears, add the ginger and salt. Stir, using a large metal spatula, for 10 seconds. Add the mushrooms and stir-fry for 10 seconds. Add the snow peas, bamboo shoots and water chestnuts; sprinkle with a little water and stir-fry for 2 minutes. Transfer the vegetables to a bowl and set aside. Wipe out the wok with paper towels.

4. Heat the wok over high heat for 20 seconds and add the remaining 1½ tablespoons peanut oil. Turn the wok to coat with oil. When a wisp of white smoke appears, add the garlic. When it begins to brown, add the chicken with the marinade. Spread the chicken out in a single layer and cook undisturbed for 2 minutes. Turn the chicken pieces over and cook for 1 more minute. Drizzle the wine down the inside rim of the wok and stir it into the chicken. Continue to cook until the chicken is cooked through, about 1 minute longer.

5. Add the reserved vegetables and stir-fry for 2 minutes. Make a well in the center of the mixture. Stir the sauce to combine and pour it into the well. Mix all the ingredients together, bring the sauce to a boil and cook until thickened, about 30 seconds. Transfer to a warm platter and serve immediately.

—*Eileen Yin-Fei Lo*

• • •

CHICKEN STEW WITH CORNMEAL DUMPLINGS

🍷 This homey dish would be nicely complemented by a satisfying but modest red Bordeaux, such as 1989 B&G Bordeaux Rouge or 1988 Château St-Georges St-Emilion.

4 Servings

One 3½- to 4-pound chicken, cut into 8 pieces
4 cups chicken stock or canned low-sodium broth, skimmed of fat
1 bay leaf
2 medium celery ribs, thinly sliced crosswise
4 medium carrots, sliced on the diagonal 1 inch thick
6 small white onions, peeled but with root end left intact, halved lengthwise
4 large sprigs of thyme
1 small bunch of kale, stems trimmed and leaves coarsely chopped (2 firmly packed cups)
Salt and freshly ground pepper

CORNMEAL DUMPLINGS:
1 cup unbleached flour
½ cup cornmeal
2 teaspoons baking powder
½ teaspoon salt
2 tablespoons cold unsalted butter, cut into pieces
⅔ cup milk

1. Using your hands and a towel to facilitate your grip, pull the skin off all the chicken parts except the wings; discard the skin.

2. In a medium flameproof casserole, combine the chicken, chicken stock and bay leaf and bring to a boil over high heat. Reduce the heat to moderate, turn the chicken over, cover and simmer for 15 minutes.

3. Skim the broth of any fat. Stir in the celery, carrots, onions and thyme sprigs. Continue to simmer over moderate heat, partially covered, until the carrots and onions are just tender, about 15 minutes. Stir in the kale. Season to taste with salt and pepper.

4. *Prepare the dumplings:* In a medium bowl, toss together the flour, cornmeal, baking powder and salt. With your fingertips, work the butter into the flour until the mixture is crumbly. Using a fork, stir in the milk until blended.

5. Drop tablespoons of the dumpling batter in 16 clumps over the top of the stew. Reduce the heat to moderately low, cover and simmer until the dumplings are cooked through, about 10 minutes. Discard the bay leaf and thyme sprigs and serve the stew immediately in shallow soup bowls.

—*Susan Shapiro Jaslove*

• • •

ENCHILADAS SUIZAS

These simple chicken enchiladas are baked under a blanket of creamy tomatillo-coriander sauce and topped with Swiss cheese.

4 to 6 Servings

2 small whole chicken breasts on the bone (about 1 pound)
1 large celery rib, quartered
3 garlic cloves
1½ teaspoons salt
1 pound fresh tomatillos—husked, rinsed and quartered
1 small onion, coarsely chopped
1 to 2 serrano chiles, cut into pieces
1 teaspoon sugar
½ cup plus 2 tablespoons corn oil

1 cup sour cream
¾ cup fresh coriander (cilantro) leaves
12 fresh corn tortillas
2 cups grated Swiss cheese (½ pound)

1. In a large saucepan, combine the chicken breasts, celery, 1 garlic clove and ½ teaspoon of the salt. Add 3 cups of water and bring to a boil over moderately high heat. Reduce the heat slightly and simmer, skimming occasionally, until the chicken is cooked through, about 45 minutes. Transfer the chicken to a plate and let cool. Strain the broth into a 2-cup measure and skim the fat from the surface. Remove and discard the chicken skin. Pull the meat into shreds and set aside in a bowl.

2. In a food processor, combine the tomatillos, onion, chiles, sugar and the remaining 2 garlic cloves and 1 teaspoon salt. Process until a coarse puree forms.

3. In a medium nonreactive saucepan, heat the 2 tablespoons oil over moderately high heat. Add the tomatillo puree and bring to a boil. Reduce the heat and simmer, stirring occasionally, for 10 minutes. Remove from the heat and let cool slightly, then stir in the sour cream.

4. In a food processor, finely chop the coriander leaves. Add the reserved 2 cups chicken broth and process for 1 minute. Stir the coriander broth into the tomatillo sauce.

5. Preheat the oven to 350°. In a medium skillet, heat the remaining ½ cup oil over moderately high heat until shimmering. One at a time, add the tortillas to the hot oil and fry briefly to soften, about 10 seconds per tortilla. Drain well.

6. Lightly grease an 11-by-8-by-2½-inch ovenproof serving dish. Ladle enough of the tomatillo sauce into the dish to cover the bottom. Fill each softened tortilla with about 2½ tablespoons of the shredded chicken. Roll up the tortillas and arrange them in the baking dish, seams down. Pour the remaining sauce over the enchiladas and sprinkle the grated Swiss cheese on top.

7. Bake the enchiladas for 20 to 25 minutes, until the sauce is bubbling and the cheese is thoroughly melted. Broil briefly to brown the cheese. Serve hot.

—*Chata DuBose*

• • •

CHICKEN FLAUTAS WITH GUACAMOLE AND SALSA VERDE CRUDA

The smooth guacamole and uncooked tomatillo sauce are perfect accompaniments for these crisp, fried tortillas filled with chicken.

4 to 6 Servings

2 small whole chicken breasts on the bone (about 1 pound)
1 large celery rib, quartered
3 garlic cloves
1½ teaspoons salt
½ pound fresh tomatillos—husked, rinsed and quartered
¾ cup fresh coriander (cilantro) leaves
2 to 3 serrano chiles, cut into pieces
3 large Hass avocados, peeled and pitted
12 fresh corn tortillas
1 cup corn oil, for frying
6 cups finely shredded, crisp romaine lettuce
Salsa Verde Cruda (p. 259)

1. In a large saucepan, combine the chicken breasts, celery, 1 garlic clove and ½ teaspoon of the salt. Add 3 cups of water and bring to a boil over moderately high heat. Reduce the heat and simmer, skimming occasionally, until the chicken is cooked through, about 45 minutes.

2. Meanwhile, in a food processor, combine the tomatillos, fresh coriander, chiles and the remaining 2 garlic cloves and 1 teaspoon salt. Add the avocados and puree until smooth and creamy. Set the guacamole aside.

3. When the chicken is done, transfer it to a plate and let cool. Strain the broth and reserve for another use. Remove and discard the chicken skin. Pull the meat into shreds and set aside in a bowl.

4. Place about 2½ tablespoons of the shredded chicken across each tortilla then roll them up tightly like a cigar and place, seams down, on a plate. Line the *flautas* up next to each other to hold their shape.

5. In a medium skillet, heat the oil over moderately high heat until very hot. Using tongs, place 2 of the *flautas* in the oil, seam side down, and hold them there until they hold their shape and are golden brown on the bottom. Turn and cook until browned on the other side. Hold the *flautas* over the pan to release any excess oil, then transfer to paper towels to drain. Repeat with the remaining *flautas*.

6. Spread the lettuce on a large serving platter and arrange the *flautas* on top. Spoon some of the guacamole in a line over the *flautas* and serve immediately, passing the remaining guacamole and the Salsa Verde Cruda separately.

—*Chata DuBose*

• • •

Chicken Flautas with Guacamole and Salsa Verde Cruda (recipe at left).

Left, Maresca Family Chicken Cacciatore (p. 88). Above, Chicken and Chorizo Sauté with Ancho-Tomato Sauce (p. 87).

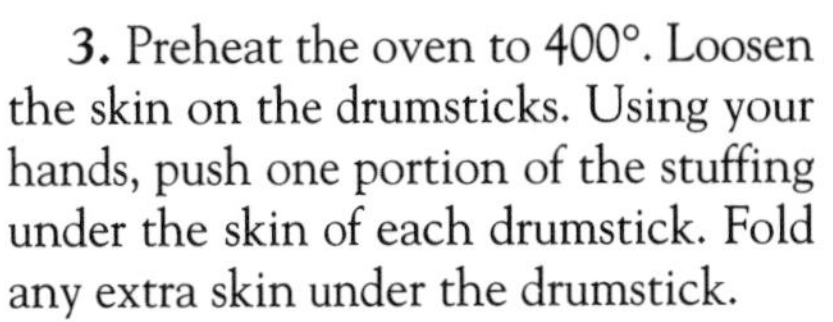

CHICKEN SAUSAGE PATTIES

This recipe can easily be doubled for a crowd. Partially freeze the meat before processing to prevent it from getting mushy in the food processor.

6 Servings

12 ounces skinless, boneless chicken breast and thigh meat, cut into 1-inch cubes
6 ounces boneless pork shoulder, cut into 1-inch cubes
2 teaspoons light brown sugar
1 teaspoon salt
½ teaspoon freshly ground black pepper
½ teaspoon whole white peppercorns, crushed in a mortar
¼ teaspoon rubbed sage
¼ teaspoon ground allspice
¼ teaspoon crushed red pepper

1. Spread the chicken and pork cubes on opposite ends of a small baking sheet. Freeze until firm on the outside, about 30 minutes.

2. In a food processor, grind the pork until very coarsely chopped. Add the chicken, brown sugar, salt, black pepper, white pepper, sage, allspice and crushed red pepper and process for 5 seconds to combine.

3. Using lightly floured hands, form the mixture into six ½-inch-thick patties. Heat a large skillet, preferably cast iron, over moderately high heat for 5 minutes. Add the sausage patties to the pan and cook, turning once, until crisp and cooked through, about 10 minutes. Serve hot.

—*Lee Bailey*

• • •

STUFFED TURKEY DRUMSTICKS

6 Servings

6 slices of bacon, chopped
½ pound ground pork
3 eggs, beaten
1½ cups fresh bread crumbs
1 tablespoon brandy
1½ teaspoons thyme
¾ teaspoon minced garlic
¾ teaspoon salt
¾ teaspoon freshly ground pepper
Generous pinch of allspice
Six 12-ounce turkey drumsticks, boned, with skin on
2 tablespoons unsalted butter, softened, plus 3 tablespoons chilled
½ cup dry red wine
2 tablespoons finely chopped parsley

1. In a large skillet, cook the bacon over moderate heat, stirring, until lightly browned, about 3 minutes. Transfer to paper towels.

2. In a large bowl, thoroughly combine the reserved bacon, the pork, eggs, bread crumbs, brandy, thyme, garlic, salt, pepper and allspice. Divide into 6 portions; set aside.

3. Preheat the oven to 400°. Loosen the skin on the drumsticks. Using your hands, push one portion of the stuffing under the skin of each drumstick. Fold any extra skin under the drumstick.

4. Rub the drumsticks with the softened butter and sprinkle generously with salt and pepper. Place in a roasting pan, skin side up. Bake on the upper rack of the oven for 30 to 35 minutes, basting the drumsticks halfway through until puffed and golden brown and an instant-reading thermometer registers 145° in the stuffing and 165° in the meat. Transfer to a large platter and cover with foil to keep warm.

5. Place the roasting pan directly on two burners. Add the red wine and boil over high heat, scraping up the browned bits, until reduced by half, about 2 minutes. Add ⅔ cup water and boil until reduced slightly and the flavor is concentrated, about 4 minutes longer. Pour the sauce into a small nonreactive saucepan and whisk in the chilled butter, 1 tablespoon at a time. Season with salt and pepper.

6. Slice the drumsticks crosswise ½ inch thick and arrange on plates. Spoon the sauce over and around the turkey and garnish with the parsley.

—*David Rosengarten*

• • •

Honey-Pepper Poussins (p. 84).

SIMPLE QUAIL SUPPER

Pan-Fried Quail (at right)

Pastina with Roasted Red Bell Peppers and Sweet Corn (p. 124)

Steamed Buttered Broccoli

Merlot or Chardonnay

Peanut Butter, White Chocolate and Macadamia Nut Cookies (p. 230)

—Lee Bailey

GRILLED CURRY-AND-PEPPER-RUBBED BREAST OF SQUAB

A subtle, older Bordeaux would flatter this flavorsome, meaty bird.

6 Servings

1 teaspoon cumin
1 teaspoon ground coriander
1 medium jalapeño pepper, minced, or ½ teaspoon crushed red pepper
1 large garlic clove, minced
1 tablespoon minced red onion
1 teaspoon turmeric
1 teaspoon coarse (kosher) salt
¼ teaspoon cinnamon
2 teaspoons peanut oil
6 whole boneless squab breasts
2 tablespoons olive oil or softened unsalted butter

1. In a small skillet, toast the cumin and coriander over high heat, stirring, until fragrant, about 1 minute. Transfer the spices to a small bowl and let cool.

2. Stir the jalapeño, garlic, onion, turmeric, salt and cinnamon into the spices. Stir in the peanut oil. Rub the marinade all over the squab breasts and set aside to marinate for at least 2 hours.

3. Prepare a grill or preheat the broiler. Brush the squab breasts with the olive oil or rub with the softened butter, then grill or broil, skin side down, for 2 to 3 minutes. Turn and grill or broil for 2 to 3 minutes on the other side, or until the meat is juicy and pink. Do not overcook. Slice the breasts on the diagonal.

—John Ash & Sid Goldstein

• • •

PAN-FRIED QUAIL

Ask your butcher to partially bone the quail (snipping off the wings and leaving the legs intact) and to give you the bones; they are used to enhance the flavor of the sauce.

4 Servings

2 tablespoons vegetable oil
8 partially boned quail, bones reserved
½ cup dry white wine
5 medium shallots, finely chopped
3 medium carrots, finely chopped
1 large celery rib, finely chopped
2 sprigs of flat-leaf parsley
5 whole black peppercorns
2 cups canned low-sodium chicken broth
½ cup all-purpose flour
¼ teaspoon freshly ground white pepper
Salt
2 tablespoons unsalted butter
¼ teaspoon freshly ground black pepper

1. In a medium saucepan, heat 1 tablespoon of the oil over moderately high heat until hot, about 2 minutes. Add the quail bones and cook, turning occasionally, until well browned, about 4 minutes. Pour in ¼ cup of the wine. Stir in two-thirds of the shallots and the carrots, celery, parsley, peppercorns and chicken broth. Bring to a boil, reduce the heat to moderate and boil gently until the liquid is reduced by half, about 10 minutes. Strain the liquid into a measuring cup; you should have about 1 cup. If you have more, boil again to reduce the liquid; if you have less, add enough water to compensate. Set aside. *(The quail stock can be made up to 1 day ahead; cover and refrigerate. Return to room temperature before using.)*

2. In a medium bowl, toss together the flour, white pepper and a pinch of salt. Dredge the quail in the seasoned flour, shake off the excess and set aside.

3. In a large heavy skillet big enough to hold all the quail, heat the remaining 1 tablespoon oil over moderately high heat until hot, about 1 minute. Place the quail in the pan, breast side down, and cook until well browned on the bottom, about 5 minutes. Turn and cook another 5 minutes on the other side. Transfer the quail to a platter and cover loosely to keep warm.

4. Pour off any fat from the skillet, add the remaining shallots and ¼ cup white wine and cook over moderately high heat, scraping the bottom of the pan with a wooden spoon to loosen any browned bits. Stir in the reserved quail stock and bring to a boil; boil until slightly reduced, about 2 minutes. Remove the skillet from the heat and swirl in the butter. Season with the black pepper and salt to taste.

5. To serve, place 2 quail on each dinner plate. Pour the sauce on top.

—Lee Bailey

• • •

MEAT

VEAL CHOPS WITH DANDELION GREENS AND PANCETTA DRESSING

Marinating veal in buttermilk for at least eight hours tenderizes the meat and produces a juicy chop. Chilled rice flour gives the veal a crisp crust.

🍷 These savory chops, enhanced by the dressed greens, would pair perfectly with a deep red with pointed flavors to match, such as Barbaresco. Look for 1987 Prunotto or 1985 Marchesi di Gresy.

6 Servings

Six 2-inch-thick rib veal chops (about 12 ounces each)
1 quart buttermilk
¾ cup light pure olive oil
1 cup unbleached flour
½ cup well-chilled rice flour* (see Note)
1 teaspoon coarse (kosher) salt
½ teaspoon freshly ground pepper
3 ounces pancetta, cut into ¼-inch dice
6 cups dandelion greens—picked over, washed and dried
¼ cup fruity extra-virgin olive oil
2 tablespoons red wine vinegar
****Available at health food stores***

1. Place the veal chops in a large nonreactive bowl and add the buttermilk; the chops should be submerged. Cover and refrigerate for at least 8 hours or overnight.

2. Preheat the oven to 375°. In a large heavy skillet, heat the ¾ cup pure olive oil over high heat.

3. In a large paper bag, combine the unbleached flour, rice flour, salt and pepper. Remove a chop from the buttermilk and drop it into the bag with the flour mixture; shake the bag to coat the chop completely. Immediately place in the hot oil. Repeat quickly with as many chops as will fit in the skillet at one time. Fry the chops, turning once, until a light brown crust forms, about 3 minutes per side.

4. Transfer the chops to a rack set over a baking sheet. Stand them up on their bones and keep them about 2 inches apart. (To secure the chops, make a loose roll of foil to run the length of the baking sheet, then prop the chops up against the foil.) Roast in the oven for 30 to 35 minutes, until the chops are golden brown and cooked to medium.

5. Meanwhile, spread the pancetta in the bottom of a 9-inch pie tin and roast until most of the fat has been rendered, 12 to 15 minutes.

6. In a large bowl, toss the dandelion greens with the extra-virgin olive oil and a pinch of coarse salt. Pour off any excess fat from the pancetta. Add the vinegar to the pie tin, swirl it around and pour over the greens. Toss again and arrange on 6 large plates. Top each salad with a veal chop and serve hot.

NOTE: *Rice flour yields the crispest results when it is very well chilled.*

—Johanne Killeen & George Germon

• • •

SPRING CELEBRATION, ITALIAN STYLE

Crostini with Tuscan Pesto (p. 21)

Spring Bagna Cauda (p. 22)

Roasted Asparagus Lasagna (p. 133)

Veal Chops with Dandelion Greens and Pancetta Dressing (at left)

Strawberry-Rhubarb Crostata (p. 216) with Mint Crème Anglaise (p. 217)

—Johanne Killeen & George Germon

BRAISED VEAL SHANKS WITH ARTICHOKES AND BREAD DUMPLINGS

When Spanish cook Pilar Plana prepares this dish, she adds the little spineless artichokes that are a feature of Aragonese markets in the springtime.

🍷 This satisfying dish needs an equally satisfying, straightforward red—try a Penedès red, such as 1988 Torres Coronas from Spain, or an Australian Cabernet/Shiraz, such as 1987 Seaview.

6 Servings

¼ cup plus 2 tablespoons olive oil
6 pounds meaty pieces of veal shank, cut crosswise 1½ to 2 inches thick
6 garlic cloves, thinly sliced
½ teaspoon freshly ground black pepper
½ teaspoon freshly ground white pepper
1 teaspoon sweet Spanish or Hungarian paprika
Pinch of cinnamon

4 large artichokes
1 loaf of day-old French or Italian bread (14 ounces), crust removed
1½ cups milk
2 eggs, lightly beaten
1 teaspoon salt
1 cup dry bread crumbs

1. In a very large flameproof casserole or dutch oven, heat 3 tablespoons of the oil over moderately high heat. Working in batches, add the veal in a single layer and cook, turning occasionally, until well browned on all sides. (Regulate the heat if necessary.) Transfer the veal to a platter.

2. Reduce the heat to low and add the remaining 3 tablespoons oil to the casserole. Add the garlic and cook, stirring, until lightly browned. Be careful not to burn the garlic. Remove the casserole from the heat and stir in the black and white pepper, paprika and cinnamon and any meat juices. Return the veal to the casserole and stir to coat with the spices.

3. Increase the heat to moderate and when the meat begins to sizzle, add enough water to submerge the veal halfway. Reduce the heat to low, cover and bring to a simmer. Cook, turning the veal once or twice, until the meat is very tender and falling off the bone, about 2 hours. Remove from the heat and let cool to room temperature. Transfer the shanks to a large bowl. Cover both the shanks and the casserole separately and refrigerate overnight.

4. Remove fat from the liquid and return the shanks to the casserole. Bring to a simmer over low heat.

5. Meanwhile, bring a medium saucepan of salted water to a boil over high heat. Trim the artichokes by first snapping off the tough outer leaves near the base. Using a sharp, stainless steel knife, cut off the stems; cut the crowns to within 1½ inches of the base. Scoop out the hairy chokes with a spoon and trim carefully to remove all of the leaves. Quarter the artichoke bottoms, add them to the saucepan and cook until just tender, about 8 minutes. Drain in a colander set over a bowl; reserve the cooking liquid.

6. Increase the heat under the casserole to moderate and add the artichokes and ½ cup of their cooking liquid. Simmer until the artichokes are tender, about 5 minutes.

7. Meanwhile, tear or cut the bread into large pieces (you should have about 2 packed cups) and place in a medium bowl. Add the milk and toss the bread gently until thoroughly moistened. Squeeze the bread to extract about 1 cup of the milk; discard the milk. Place the soaked bread and the eggs in a medium bowl, add the salt and beat well to form a dense paste. Beat in ½ cup of the dry bread crumbs. The dumpling mixture should be sticky enough to just hold together. Sprinkle 1 tablespoon of the bread crumbs on a large plate. Form the dumpling mixture into small egg shapes using a tablespoon and bread crumb-dusted hands and set aside on the plate.

8. Transfer the veal shanks and the artichokes to a large warmed serving platter and cover with foil to keep warm. Bring the sauce to a boil over moderate heat. If it is very thick, add more of the reserved artichoke liquid; you should have about 2 cups of sauce. Carefully lower the dumplings into the boiling sauce and poach until firm, turning once, about 15 minutes. Place the dumplings on the platter with the veal and artichokes and ladle the sauce over all. Serve immediately.

—Pilar Plana

• • •

SAUSECEDES

The Perrone family, of the Progress Grocery in New Orleans, describes this dish as little veal rolls, or *braciole*. They don't know where the name "sausecedes" comes from. Mrs. John J. Perrone bakes them in quantity and reheats them in batches as needed. We find them more tender and fresh flavored if they're broiled and served at once.

🍷 The stuffing in these veal rolls calls for a red, and the subtle preparation points to an elegant wine as the best match. A 1989 Poggio Antico Rosso di Montalcino or 1985 Tignanello are the top Tuscan choices.

6 to 8 Servings

6 tablespoons unsalted butter
About 3 tablespoons olive oil
1 medium onion, minced
2 garlic cloves, minced
¼ pound boiled ham, minced
¾ cup fine dry bread crumbs
¼ cup freshly grated Pecorino or Romano cheese (about 1 ounce)
1 hard-cooked egg, minced
1 small tomato, minced
¼ cup minced parsley
¼ cup red wine vinegar
2 tablespoons pine nuts, minced

½ teaspoon salt
¾ teaspoon freshly ground pepper
¼ teaspoon oregano
2 pounds veal scallops
2 lemons, quartered

1. In a medium nonreactive skillet, melt 2 tablespoons of the butter in 2 tablespoons of the olive oil over moderate heat. Add the onion and garlic and cook, stirring constantly, until softened, about 3 minutes. Add the ham and cook, stirring, for 1 minute. Stir in the bread crumbs, Pecorino, hard-cooked egg, tomato, parsley, vinegar, pine nuts, salt, pepper and oregano. Cook, stirring, for 2 minutes, adding the remaining 1 tablespoon olive oil if necessary to moisten and bind the stuffing.

2. Pound the veal scallops thin. Cut into twenty-four 3-inch squares. Pound each piece lightly to flatten. Lightly season with salt and pepper. Place 1½ tablespoons of the stuffing at one edge of each of 6 veal pieces and roll up the meat around it. Line up the rolls and join them together with two 8-inch-long wooden skewers, in a log-raft fashion. Repeat 3 more times with the remaining veal and stuffing. Refrigerate until ready to cook. *(The recipe can be prepared to this point up to 4 hours ahead.)*

3. Preheat the broiler. In a small saucepan, melt the remaining 4 tablespoons butter over moderate heat. Use 1 tablespoon to grease a shallow baking sheet. Position the four veal "rafts" on the sheet. Season with salt and pepper and brush with half of the remaining melted butter. Broil for 4 minutes, or until lightly browned. Turn over, brush with the remaining melted butter and broil for 3 to 4 minutes longer.

4. To serve, carefully remove the skewers and place the "sausecedes" on a warm platter. Squeeze the lemon on top and serve at once.

—*Diane Darrow & Tom Maresca*

• • •

VEAL DAUBE WITH GREEN OLIVES AND SUMMER SAVORY

In France this daube is usually made with *tendron*, one of the most popular cuts of veal for long, slow cooking. It's the part of the breast that contains the cartilaginous ribs that are full of flavor and body; they are slightly gelatinous and chewy when cooked. For this recipe, however, you can choose from any number of good cuts of stewing veal, including the short ribs, shoulder or the meaty shanks used here.

This is the sort of dish that reminds you that it is always better to cook meat on the bone, for it will be tastier. Thorough browning of the meat is essential for flavor.

🍷 Drink the same wine you use for cooking; a light, fresh and lemony Mâcon-Villages would be a good choice.

6 Servings

3 tablespoons extra-virgin olive oil
6 meaty pieces of veal shank, cut 2 inches thick (about 11 ounces each)
Salt and freshly ground pepper
3 medium onions, halved and thinly sliced
3 large carrots, thinly sliced
2 tablespoons minced fresh summer savory or 1 tablespoon dried
2 cups dry white wine, such as a Mâcon-Villages
1 can (28 ounces) Italian peeled tomatoes with their liquid
½ pound green Moroccan or picholine olives, drained and pitted

1. In a large dutch oven or flameproof casserole, heat the oil over moderately high heat until hot. Add the veal shank pieces in 2 batches and cook until well browned on all sides. Regulate the heat to avoid scorching the meat. Transfer the veal to a large plate and season with salt and pepper.

2. Add the onions and carrots to the casserole and cook over moderate heat until the onions are soft and translucent, about 10 minutes. Sprinkle the savory over the vegetables. Add the wine and tomatoes, and crush the tomatoes with a wooden spoon. Bring to a boil and cook for 2 to 3 minutes.

3. Return the veal and any accumulated juices to the casserole and bring to a boil over moderate heat. Reduce the heat to very low, cover and simmer gently, turning the shanks occasionally to coat with the sauce, until the meat is almost falling off the bone and the sauce is thick, about 2 hours.

4. In a medium saucepan of boiling water, blanch the olives for 4 minutes. Drain well and add them to the casserole. Simmer the daube over very low heat for 30 minutes longer.

5. Transfer the veal shanks to warm plates. Boil the sauce over high heat until slightly reduced, about 5 minutes. Season the sauce with salt and pepper to taste and spoon it over and around the meat.

—*Patricia Wells*

• • •

TENDERLOIN OF BEEF WITH CASCABEL CHILE AIOLI

The cascabel is a dried chile named from the Spanish word for jingle bells, because of the rattling sound the seeds make inside the dried pod.

🍷 1986 Llano Estacado Winery, Cellar Select Cabernet Sauvignon

10 to 12 Servings

1 cascabel chile, stemmed and broken into large pieces, seeds discarded
¾ cup mayonnaise
1 small garlic clove, minced
1 small shallot, minced
2 teaspoons red wine vinegar
1 teaspoon fresh lime juice
¼ teaspoon paprika
¼ teaspoon pure chili powder
¼ teaspoon cayenne pepper
Salt
2 tablespoons vegetable oil
1 whole trimmed beef tenderloin (about 3¾ pounds)
Freshly ground black pepper

1. In a small skillet, toast the cascabel chile pieces over high heat, turning once with tongs, until blistered and fragrant, about 30 seconds per side. Transfer to a mortar and let cool until brittle, about 5 minutes. Using a pestle, pound the chile pieces to a powder.

2. In a small bowl, combine the mayonnaise, garlic, shallot, vinegar, lime juice, paprika, chili powder, cayenne, cascabel powder and ¼ teaspoon salt. Whisk to blend, then set the aioli aside. *(The aioli can be made up to 2 days ahead. Cover and refrigerate.)*

3. Preheat the oven to 450°. In a heavy roasting pan, heat the oil over moderately high heat. Pat the beef dry and sprinkle all over with salt and black pepper. Add the meat to the roasting pan and brown well all over, about 5 minutes. Roast the tenderloin in the oven for 25 to 35 minutes, until an instant-reading thermometer inserted in the middle registers 130° for rare or 150° for medium. Let the meat rest loosely covered with foil for about 10 minutes before slicing. Serve the aioli on the side.

—Stephan Pyles

• • •

SOUTHWESTERN SUMMER BUFFET

Red Tomato Salsa (p. 260), Tomatillo Salsa (p. 260) and Yellow Tomato Salsa (p. 260)

Arugula and Fried Okra Salad with Roasted-Corn Vinaigrette (p. 145)

Grilled Red Snapper with Black Bean Salsa and Jicama-Melon Relish (p. 67)

Tenderloin of Beef with Cascabel Chile Aioli (at left)

Exotic Fruit Salad

—Stephan Pyles

PEPPER STEAK

This Cantonese classic was always known as Black Beans and Garlic with Peppers and Beef because the emphasis was on the intense flavor of the fermented black beans mashed with garlic. In its transition to the West, this emphasis changed to bell peppers and beef, ingredients more familiar to Western palates.

🍷 The salty, garlicky accents here would overwhelm a subtle wine. Look for a forthright but fruity red of equal intensity, such as 1988 Guigal Côtes du Rhône from France or 1989 Ravenswood Vintner's Blend Zinfandel from California.

6 Servings

MARINADE:
1½ teaspoons finely grated fresh ginger
1 teaspoon Oriental sesame oil
2 teaspoons oyster sauce*
1½ teaspoons Shao-Hsing wine (Chinese rice wine)* or medium-dry sherry
¾ teaspoon dark soy sauce*
½ teaspoon salt
1½ teaspoons cornstarch
1 teaspoon sugar
Pinch of freshly ground white pepper

¾ pound lean beef, such as top round or London broil, sliced across the grain ¼ inch thick and cut into 2-inch pieces

SAUCE:
2 teaspoons oyster sauce*
1 teaspoon Oriental sesame oil

1 teaspoon dark soy sauce*
1 teaspoon sugar
2 teaspoons cornstarch
Pinch of freshly ground white pepper
½ cup chicken stock or low-sodium chicken broth

2 large garlic cloves, minced
1 tablespoon fermented black beans,* rinsed and finely chopped

3 tablespoons peanut oil
½ inch slice of fresh ginger, peeled
1 green bell pepper, cut into 2-by-1-inch pieces
1 red bell pepper, cut into 2-by-1-inch pieces
****Available at Asian markets***

1. *Make the marinade:* Place the grated ginger in a small strainer set over a medium bowl. Press hard with the back of a spoon to extract ½ teaspoon of juice; discard the ginger pulp. Stir in the remaining marinade ingredients. Add the beef slices and toss to coat well. Cover and set aside to marinate for 30 minutes.

2. *Make the sauce:* In a large bowl, combine all the sauce ingredients and set aside.

3. Place the garlic and black beans in a bowl and mash together with a fork. Set aside.

4. Heat a wok over high heat for 30 seconds. Add 1 tablespoon of the peanut oil and turn the wok to coat with oil. When a wisp of white smoke appears, add the slice of ginger. When the ginger turns light brown, add the green and red bell peppers and stir-fry with a large spatula for 1 minute. Sprinkle 1 tablespoon of water into the wok, cover and cook for 2 minutes. Remove from the heat and transfer the peppers to a small bowl; set aside. Using paper towels, wipe out the wok and the spatula.

5. Heat the wok over high heat for 30 seconds and add the remaining 2 tablespoons peanut oil. When a wisp of white smoke appears, stir in the reserved black bean and garlic paste. When the garlic turns light brown, add the beef with the marinade and spread in one layer. Cook undisturbed for 1 minute, tipping the wok from side to side for even cooking. When the beef is cooked, add the reserved peppers and stir-fry for 2 minutes.

6. Make a well in the center of the ingredients. Stir the sauce to combine and pour it into the well. Mix all the ingredients with the sauce and cook until the sauce thickens and turns dark brown, about 1 minute. Transfer to a warm platter and serve immediately.

—Eileen Yin-Fei Lo

• • •

SPEEDY MEXICAN MEAL

Steak Burritos (at right)

Garden Salad Salsa (p. 260)

Lemon Sorbet with Raspberries and Cassis (p. 239)

—Susan Shapiro Jaslove

STEAK BURRITOS

The steak can also be grilled outdoors. Wrap the tortillas in foil and place them on the grill while the steak is cooking. You'll find flour tortillas in the refrigerator section of most supermarkets and at Hispanic markets.

4 Servings

One 1-pound skirt steak, halved crosswise
2 tablespoons fresh lime juice
Four 10-inch or eight 6-inch flour tortillas
Salt
1 bunch of watercress, large stems removed
2 medium Hass avocados, halved and thinly sliced lengthwise
Garden Salad Salsa (p. 260)
About ½ cup sour cream or plain yogurt

1. In a shallow, nonreactive dish, place the steak and lime juice; turn to coat. Set aside at room temperature for at least 15 minutes and up to 1 hour, turning once.

2. Preheat the broiler. Wrap the tortillas in aluminum foil and warm in the oven. Broil the steak about 3 inches from the heat, turning once, until rare, about 2 minutes per side. Thinly slice the steak on the diagonal. Season lightly with salt.

3. Line a platter with the watercress and arrange the steak and avocado slices on top. Serve the Garden Salad Salsa, sour cream and warm tortillas alongside.

—Susan Shapiro Jaslove

• • •

BEEF DAUBE WITH MUSTARD, HERBS AND WHITE WINE

The beef juices, white wine, mustard and fresh herbs combine to make a nicely acidic sauce that balances well with the heartiness of the beef. This daube should be made the day before you plan to serve it. If you have any leftovers, shred the beef and layer it in a small terrine with sliced cornichons and rinsed capers. Strain the cooking juices over the terrine, then cover and refrigerate. Slice the terrine and serve with additional cornichons, a cabbage salad and buttered fresh pasta, with or without a sprinkling of cheese.

🍷 This dish will go well with a dry white wine, either an earthy Graves from Bordeaux or a tangy, more elegant Meursault from Burgundy.

6 to 8 Servings

3 tablespoons extra-virgin olive oil
3 pounds boneless beef chuck, cut into 4-ounce cubes
Salt and freshly ground pepper
1 bottle (750 ml) dry white wine, such as a Graves
2 tablespoons Dijon mustard
3 large tomatoes—peeled, seeded and chopped—or 1 can (14 ounces) crushed Italian tomatoes
3 medium onions, quartered
3 garlic cloves, halved
Bouquet garni: 5 flat-leaf parsley sprigs, 3 thyme sprigs, 2 bay leaves and 2 leek greens tied in cheesecloth
Pinch of sugar

1. In a large flameproof casserole or dutch oven, heat the oil over moderately high heat until hot. Add the beef in batches, without crowding, and cook until well browned on all sides. Regulate the heat to avoid scorching the meat. As each batch is browned, transfer the meat to a large plate and season generously with salt and pepper.

2. Pour off any excess oil from the casserole. Add the wine and cook over moderate heat, scraping up any browned bits from the bottom of the pan. Stir in the mustard until blended.

3. Return the beef and any accumulated juices to the casserole and stir in the tomatoes and their liquid, the onions, garlic, bouquet garni and sugar. Cover and bring to a boil over moderate heat. Reduce the heat to low and simmer until the meat is very tender, about 3½ hours. Let the daube cool for several hours, then cover and refrigerate overnight.

4. Scrape off and discard all the fat that has solidified on the surface of the daube. Reheat the daube over moderate heat until warmed through. Discard the bouquet garni. Transfer the beef to a platter. Boil the sauce over high heat until reduced by about one-third, about 10 minutes. Season with salt and pepper to taste. Return the beef to the sauce and serve immediately.

—*Patricia Wells*

• • •

TANTE YVONNE'S CLASSIC PROVENÇALE DAUBE

This recipe comes from Yvonne Soliva, better known as Tante Yvonne. A native of Marseilles, Tante Yvonne was a restaurateur in Paris and a radio personality in Provence.

This is only one of many versions of the classic *daube provençale*. A simple dish, it uses a medley of everyday ingredients. Yvonne's secret is to cook and cool the daube over several days; it could be served after the second cooking, but the flavor really does improve if it's cooled and cooked once more.

6 to 8 Servings

3 tablespoons extra-virgin olive oil
3 pounds boneless beef chuck, cut into 4-ounce cubes
Salt and freshly ground pepper
16 large garlic cloves—4 minced, 12 halved
3 large onions—2 minced, 1 stuck with 4 whole cloves
2 large carrots, diced
3 large tomatoes—peeled, seeded and chopped—or 1 can (14 ounces) crushed Italian tomatoes
1 bottle (750 ml) red wine, such as Côtes du Rhône
¼ cup sherry wine vinegar
Bouquet garni: 5 flat-leaf parsley sprigs, 3 thyme sprigs, 2 bay leaves and 2 leek greens tied in cheesecloth

1. In a large flameproof casserole or dutch oven, heat the oil over moderately high heat until hot. Add the beef in batches, without crowding, and cook until well browned on all sides. Regulate the heat to avoid scorching the meat. As each batch is browned, transfer the meat to a large plate and season generously with salt and pepper.

2. In the remaining fat in the casserole, cook the minced garlic, minced onions and carrots over moderate heat, stirring occasionally, until soft and fragrant, about 8 minutes. Add the tomatoes and their liquid and cook for 3 minutes longer. Add the wine and vinegar and bring to a boil over high heat; boil for 3 minutes. Add the beef and any accumulated juices, the halved garlic cloves, the onion stuck with cloves and the bouquet garni. Let cool completely,

SPANISH SUPPER

Toasted Bread with Tomato (p. 21)

Sherry

Seafood Consommé with Manchego Cheese Straws (p. 52)

Herb-and-Garlic-Rubbed Pork Roast (p. 107)

Artichoke Hearts Sautéed in Olive Oil

Crusty Peasant Bread

Baked Quinces with Crema Catalana (p. 242)

then cover and refrigerate for 24 hours.

3. Let the meat and vegetables return to room temperature. Cover and bring to a boil over moderate heat. Reduce the heat to very low and simmer very gently until the meat is fairly tender, about 2 hours. Let cool completely, then cover and refrigerate for 24 hours.

4. Scrape off any fat that has solidified on the surface of the daube. Bring to a boil over moderate heat, stirring occasionally. Reduce the heat to low, cover and simmer gently for 1 hour. The daube is ready to serve at this point, but for even better flavor, repeat the cooling, overnight chilling and cooking one more time.

5. Discard the bouquet garni. Remove the meat from the casserole and boil the liquid until thickened, about 10 minutes. Season to taste with salt and pepper. Return the meat to the casserole and serve.

—*Patricia Wells*

• • •

STIR-FRIED ORANGE BEEF WITH WILD MUSHROOMS

4 Servings

MARINADE:
1 tablespoon soy sauce
¾ teaspoon Chili-Orange Oil (p. 263)
½ teaspoon (packed) brown sugar
½ teaspoon dried red chili flakes*
2 teaspoons cornstarch

½ pound trimmed flank steak, sliced crosswise ⅛ inch thick

AROMATICS:
2 scallions, thinly sliced crosswise
2 tablespoons finely minced fresh ginger
1 tablespoon finely minced garlic
1½ teaspoons dried red chili flakes*
Zest of 1 orange, finely minced

SAUCE:
1¼ cups chicken or vegetable stock
⅓ cup strained fresh orange juice
2½ tablespoons soy sauce
2 tablespoons cider vinegar
1½ to 2 teaspoons granulated sugar

¼ cup corn or peanut oil
3 tablespoons Chinese rice wine*
1 small red onion, cut into 1-inch dice
1 large red bell pepper or 1 small red plus 1 small yellow bell pepper, cut into 1-inch dice
½ of a small fennel bulb, cored and sliced crosswise ⅛ inch thick
½ pound wild mushrooms, such as stemmed shiitakes, oyster mushrooms or a combination, halved or quartered if large
½ pound stemmed fresh spinach and/or red chard, chard cut into 1½-inch ribbons (8 packed cups)
1 tablespoon cornstarch dissolved in 2 tablespoons cold stock or water
Scallions, thinly sliced on the diagonal, for garnish
***Available at Asian markets**

1. In a medium bowl, combine the marinade ingredients and stir to blend. Add the beef and toss to coat thoroughly. Set aside for several hours at room temperature or overnight in the refrigerator. Bring to room temperature before cooking.

2. In a small dish, combine the aromatics. In a bowl, combine the sauce ingredients.

3. Heat a wok or a very large heavy skillet over high heat until hot enough to evaporate a bead of water on contact. Add 1 tablespoon of the corn oil and swirl to coat the pan. Reduce the heat to moderately high. Toss the beef to separate the pieces. When the oil is hot enough to sizzle a ribbon of beef on contact, add all the meat to the wok and stir-fry to sear, about 1 minute. Add 1 tablespoon of the rice wine, toss briskly and scrape the wok to deglaze it, then transfer the beef to a shallow dish. It should still be very rare.

4. Return the wok to high heat. Add the remaining 3 tablespoons corn oil, then reduce the heat to moderately high. Add the aromatics and stir gently until fully fragrant, 2 to 3 minutes. Add the onion and bell pepper, increase the heat to high and stir-fry until half-cooked, about 2 minutes. Don't worry if the vegetables scorch a bit.

5. Add the fennel and stir-fry for 1 minute, sprinkling in 1 to 2 tablespoons of the rice wine if needed to prevent sticking. Add the mushrooms and stir-fry to sear and heat through, about 1 minute more, then add any remaining rice wine. Stir the sauce, add it to the wok and bring almost to a boil. Add the spinach and toss several times to mix.

6. Stir the cornstarch mixture to recombine and add it to the wok, then stir briefly until the sauce turns glossy, about 1 minute. Quickly fold in the beef. Immediately transfer the stir-fry to a heated serving platter and garnish with the scallions. Serve hot.

—*Barbara Tropp*

• • •

CHIMICHANGAS

When you stuff a large flour tortilla, then roll it up and fry it, you end up with a *chimichanga*. These are filled with beef and potatoes.

12 Servings

2 pounds chuck roast, coarsely chopped
2 medium potatoes, peeled and halved
1 large tomato, diced, plus 2 tomatoes, each cut into 12 wedges
2 garlic cloves, finely chopped
1 large onion, finely chopped
1 teaspoon salt
1 teaspoon oregano
¼ teaspoon sugar
¼ teaspoon cumin
Twelve 8- to 9-inch flour tortillas
Safflower oil, for frying
2 cups sour cream
Salsa Ranchera (p. 259)
2 cups shredded romaine lettuce

1. In a large saucepan, combine the meat, potatoes, diced tomato, garlic, onion, salt, oregano, sugar and cumin. Add water just to cover and bring to a boil over high heat. Reduce the heat and simmer until soupy, about 1¼ hours. Break up the potatoes and simmer until thick, about 30 minutes longer. Let cool slightly. Season with salt to taste.

2. Preheat the oven to 325°. Wrap the tortillas in foil and place in the oven for 10 minutes to soften.

3. Spoon a scant ½ cup of the meat and potato filling in the middle of each tortilla. Fold one side of the tortilla over the filling, then fold in the two adjacent sides. Finally, fold over the fourth side and secure with a toothpick.

4. In a large heavy skillet, heat 2 inches of the oil to 360° over moderately high heat. Place 3 of the filled tortillas in the skillet, seam side down, and fry, turning, until evenly golden brown all over, about 3 minutes. Drain on paper towels. Repeat with the remaining filled tortillas. Remove the toothpicks.

5. Arrange the *chimichangas* on a warm platter. Top each one with sour cream, Salsa Ranchera and shredded lettuce. Arrange the tomato wedges around the platter and serve.

—*Chata DuBose*

• • •

HERB-AND-GARLIC-RUBBED PORK ROAST

Variations of this hearty dish exist all over Spain. Araceli Filguiera, a food writer from Santiago de Compostela, makes it with a red pepper garnish and potatoes, which mark it as Galician, since the *gallegos*, like their Celtic cousins in Brittany and Ireland, are great potato lovers.

🍷 This garlicky pork dish needs a firm, somewhat tannic red to cut across the oily, rich tastes here. A California Cabernet Sauvignon, such as 1985 Foppiano Fox Mountain Reserve, would be ideal.

6 Servings

6 garlic cloves, peeled
2 teaspoons salt
2 tablespoons finely chopped parsley
1 tablespoon sweet Spanish or Hungarian paprika
½ teaspoon oregano
¼ cup olive oil
One 3-pound boneless pork loin, tied
2 pounds small red potatoes, peeled

1. In a mortar, pound the garlic with the salt to form a smooth paste. Add the parsley and pound until incorporated. Stir in the paprika and oregano, then gradually stir in the olive oil to form a thick, oily, but not homogeneous mixture. Rub the mixture all over the pork loin, then cover and refrigerate at least overnight or for up to 2 days, turning the loin from time to time. Bring to room temperature before roasting.

2. Preheat the oven to 450°. Place the potatoes in a medium saucepan with water to cover and ½ teaspoon of salt. Bring to a boil over moderately high heat and continue to boil for 10 minutes. Drain and set aside.

3. Place the pork in a roasting pan and pour over any excess marinade. Roast the pork for 15 minutes, then reduce the temperature to 350°. Add the partially cooked potatoes to the pan and roast for about 45 minutes longer, until the juices run clear when the meat is deeply pierced and the potatoes are browned.

4. Transfer the pork to a cutting board, cover loosely with foil and let rest for 10 minutes. Slice ¼ inch thick and serve with the potatoes.

—*Araceli Filguiera*

• • •

TAMARIND-GLAZED PORK CHOPS

Tamarind is the fruit of an evergreen tree. The pods contain a bittersweet pulp, which is used extensively in Mexico as a flavoring.
🍷 1982 Calera Zinfandel, Doe Mill Vineyard

8 Servings

½ cup red wine vinegar
½ cup dark brown sugar
½ cup chicken stock or canned low-sodium broth
2 plum tomatoes, chopped
2 tablespoons tamarind pulp*
8 center-cut pork chops, about ¾-inch thick
Salt
****Available at Asian, Indian and Latin markets***

1. In a medium nonreactive saucepan, combine the vinegar, brown sugar, chicken stock, tomatoes and tamarind pulp. Cook over moderate heat, stirring occasionally, until thickened, about 15 minutes. Strain through a coarse strainer set over a medium bowl and let cool.

2. Preheat the broiler. Sprinkle the pork chops on both sides with salt and brush generously with the tamarind glaze. Put the chops on a broiler pan and broil for 6 to 8 minutes per side, rotating the pan as necessary, until deep brown, crusty and just cooked through but still moist. Serve immediately.

—Stephan Pyles

• • •

BIG-TIME TEXAS DINNER

Tamale Tart with Roast Garlic Custard and Gulf Coast Crabmeat (p. 38)

Tamarind-Glazed Pork Chops (at left)

Papaya-Tomatillo Chutney (p. 261)

Green-Chile Spoon Bread (p. 214)

Chocolate-Pecan Cake with Cherimoya Custard Sauce (p. 224)

—Stephan Pyles

PORK CHOPS WITH PICKLED PEPPERS

This Neapolitan-American dish comes in many versions, from simple to elaborate. This one, from Tom Verdillo of Tommaso's restaurant in Brooklyn, is an exuberant example. Double the amount of hot pickled peppers if desired.
🍷 Choose a soft, fruity red, such as Italy's Dolcetto d'Alba (1989 Bruno Giacosa or 1989 Mauro Molino) to underscore the flavorsome chops and the assertive caponata.

4 Servings

Four 1-inch-thick loin pork chops
¼ cup red wine vinegar or cider vinegar
¼ cup dry Marsala or red wine
1 tablespoon sugar
2 garlic cloves, minced
1 small eggplant (¾ pound), cut into 1-inch cubes
1 teaspoon salt
1 large celery rib, cut crosswise into ½-inch pieces
3 tablespoons olive oil
2 green bell peppers, cut into 1-inch squares
3 scallions, white and tender green, cut into 1-inch lengths
2 hot pickled peppers—cored, seeded and cut into eighths
20 Gaeta olives, pitted
1 tablespoon drained capers
1 tablespoon tomato paste dissolved in 2 tablespoons red wine vinegar
¼ teaspoon oregano
Freshly ground black pepper

1. Place the pork chops in an 8-inch square nonreactive dish. Whisk together the vinegar, Marsala, sugar and garlic and pour on top. Cover and set aside at room temperature to marinate for 4 to 8 hours, turning the chops occasionally.

2. In a large colander, toss the eggplant cubes with the salt and let drain for 30 minutes. Sprinkle water over the eggplant, squeeze in a towel to dry and set aside.

3. Meanwhile, bring a small pot of salted water to a boil. Drop in the celery and blanch for 3 minutes. Drain, refresh and drain again.

4. In a large nonreactive skillet, heat 2 tablespoons of the oil over moderately high heat. Remove the pork chops from their marinade and pat dry; reserve the marinade. Add the chops to the skillet and cook, turning once, until browned all over, about 10 minutes. Transfer to a plate and set aside.

5. Wipe out the skillet and heat the remaining 1 tablespoon oil over moderately high heat. Add the reserved eggplant and celery, the bell peppers, scallions, hot pickled peppers, olives and capers and cook, stirring frequently, for 10 minutes. Pour in the reserved marinade and stir in the tomato paste mixture. Return the pork chops to the pan, nestling them down among the vegetables. Season lightly with a pinch of salt, the oregano and black pepper to taste. Cover and cook for 20 minutes, turning after 10 minutes. Serve at once.

—*Diane Darrow & Tom Maresca*

• • •

PAN-FRIED PORK CHOPS WITH BLACK BEANS AND KALE

This dish is a variation on a Brazilian specialty, *tutu a mineira*, which is made with black beans that are creamed with cassava flour.

🍷 A red with forthright flavors, such as 1988 Round Hill or 1989 Franciscan California Zinfandel, would be an appropriate selection.

4 Servings

Eight ½-inch-thick pork chops
¼ cup fresh lemon juice
2 tablespoons minced garlic
1 habañero chile or other small fresh chile, seeded and minced
Salt and freshly ground black pepper
¼ pound slab bacon, cut into thin 1-inch squares
2 medium onions, finely chopped
3 cups freshly cooked black beans or 2 cans (16 ounces each) black beans, rinsed and drained
3 tablespoons olive oil
1½ to 2 pounds fresh young kale, thinly sliced crosswise

1. Rinse the pork chops under cool water and pat dry. Place the chops on a platter in a single layer and rub with the lemon juice and 2 teaspoons of the garlic. Sprinkle the chile on top and season lightly with salt and black pepper. Set aside to marinate while you proceed.

2. Heat a heavy medium skillet over moderate heat. Add the bacon and cook, stirring occasionally, until the fat is rendered and the bacon is crisp, about 8 minutes. Using a slotted spoon, transfer the bacon to paper towels to drain.

3. Add half of the onions to the skillet and cook, stirring occasionally, until soft and golden, about 6 minutes. Stir in 2 teaspoons of the garlic and cook until fragrant, 1 to 2 minutes. Add the black beans and ½ teaspoon each of salt and black pepper and cook, stirring, until hot, about 5 minutes. Set aside.

4. In a large heavy saucepan, heat 2 tablespoons of the olive oil over moderate heat. Add the remaining onions and 2 teaspoons garlic and cook, stirring occasionally, until softened, about 5 minutes. Add the kale and cook, stirring, until just tender, about 5 minutes. Remove from the heat and season with salt and black pepper to taste. Set aside.

5. While the kale is cooking, heat the oven to 200°. Heat a large heavy skillet, preferably cast iron, over moderately high heat. Add the remaining 1 tablespoon olive oil and tilt to coat the pan. Add 4 of the pork chops and fry, turning once, until browned on the outside and barely pink on the inside, 5 to 6 minutes. Arrange the chops on an ovenproof platter and keep warm in the oven. Repeat with the remaining chops.

6. Return the black beans and the kale to moderately low heat and cook, stirring, until heated through. To serve, place a mound of black beans on each dinner plate, sprinkle some of the reserved bacon bits over the beans, top with 2 pork chops and surround with the kale.

—*Jessica B. Harris*

• • •

STIR-FRIED SPICY PORK RIBBONS WITH SUMMER BEANS

Serve this summery stir-fry over rice or noodles drizzled with Chili-Lemon Oil or Chili-Orange Oil.

4 Servings

1 pound boneless pork loin

MARINADE:
2 tablespoons soy sauce
2 tablespoons Chinese rice wine* or dry sherry
1 tablespoon cornstarch
1 teaspoon Chili-Orange Oil or Chili-Lemon Oil (p. 263)
½ teaspoon sugar
½ teaspoon minced garlic

AROMATICS:
2 tablespoons finely minced fresh ginger
2 tablespoons thinly sliced scallions
1 tablespoon finely minced garlic
1½ teaspoons seasonings drained from Chili-Orange Oil or Chili-Lemon Oil

SAUCE:
1½ cups chicken stock
2 tablespoons soy sauce
2 tablespoons unseasoned Japanese rice vinegar* or juice from Homemade Pickled Ginger (p. 264)
1 teaspoon sugar (or less if using pickled ginger juice)
½ to 1 teaspoon Chili-Orange Oil or Chili-Lemon Oil

½ pound baby squash (with blossoms intact, if available)

8 ears of fresh baby corn, cleaned, or ½ cup freshly shucked corn kernels
¼ pound tender young yellow and/or green beans
Ice water
¼ cup corn or peanut oil
1 small onion, halved lengthwise and sliced ½ inch thick
1 small red bell pepper, cut lengthwise into ¼-inch strips
1 tablespoon tiny basil leaves, plus finely shredded basil, for garnish
1 tablespoon cornstarch dissolved in 2 tablespoons cold stock or water
Cooked rice or noodles, for serving
****Available at Asian markets***

1. Thinly slice the pork against the grain ¼ inch thick, then cut each slice crosswise into 2-inch ribbons. In a bowl, whisk the marinade ingredients to combine. Add the pork and toss well to coat. Cover and set aside at room temperature for several hours or refrigerate overnight. Let return to room temperature and toss before cooking.

2. In a small bowl, combine the aromatics. In another bowl, stir together the sauce ingredients.

3. Bring a medium saucepan of water to a boil. Meanwhile, cut the squash and baby corn lengthwise in half if they are thicker than your finger. Slice the beans in finger lengths on the diagonal if they are long. Separately blanch the squash, baby corn and beans in the water until crisp-tender, then plunge in ice water to chill; drain well.

4. About 10 minutes before serving, in a wok or a large heavy skillet, heat 2 tablespoons of the corn oil over moderately high heat until hot enough to slowly sizzle a pork ribbon. Add the pork and stir-fry briskly to sear, about 2 minutes. Transfer the meat to a plate; it will be rare.

5. Return the wok to moderately high heat and add the remaining 2 tablespoons corn oil. When the pan is hot enough to slowly sizzle a pinch of the aromatics, add them and stir gently until fully fragrant, 2 to 3 minutes; adjust the heat so that they won't scorch. Add the onion and stir-fry until half-cooked, about 2 minutes, then add the bell pepper and stir-fry for 2 minutes longer. Add the blanched squash, beans and baby corn (if using corn kernels, they get added in the next step) and the whole basil leaves. Toss to mix well and heat through.

6. Stir the sauce, add it to the wok and bring to a simmer over high heat. Stir the cornstarch mixture to recombine, then add it to the wok and stir until the sauce turns glossy, 10 to 20 seconds. Turn off the heat and stir in the pork (add the corn kernels here if using). Serve hot over rice or noodles, garnished with the shredded basil.

—Barbara Tropp

• • •

WARMING WINTER SUPPER

Pan-Fried Pork Medallions with Rosemary and Scallions (at right)

Winter Fruit Compote with Mustard Syrup (p. 262)

Boiled Potatoes with Shallot-Garlic Butter (p. 166)

Red Bordeaux

Gingersnap Honey Custard (p. 243)

Coffee

—Lee Bailey

PAN-FRIED PORK MEDALLIONS WITH ROSEMARY AND SCALLIONS

The smooth, rich flavors in this sauce provide an ideal showcase for an elegant red Bordeaux, such as 1988 Château Poujeaux or 1985 Château Meyney.

6 Servings

½ cup all-purpose flour
¼ teaspoon freshly ground white pepper
2 pounds well-trimmed boneless pork loin, sliced ¼ inch thick
¼ cup olive oil
1¼ cups canned chicken broth
¼ cup dry white wine
1 tablespoon white wine vinegar
2 medium scallions, white and green, thinly sliced
1 tablespoon minced fresh rosemary
2 tablespoons unsalted butter
½ teaspoon freshly ground black pepper

1. In a medium bowl, toss together the flour and white pepper. Lightly dredge the pork slices in the flour, shaking off the excess.

2. Heat a large, heavy, nonreactive skillet over moderately high heat. Add 2 tablespoons of the oil. Add one-third of the pork to the pan and fry until the bottom edges begin to brown, about 2 minutes. Turn and fry until just cooked through, 2 to 3 minutes longer. Transfer with tongs to a large platter, arranging the slices in a single layer. Fry the remaining pork in the same way, using 1 more tablespoon of oil for each batch. Set the pork aside.

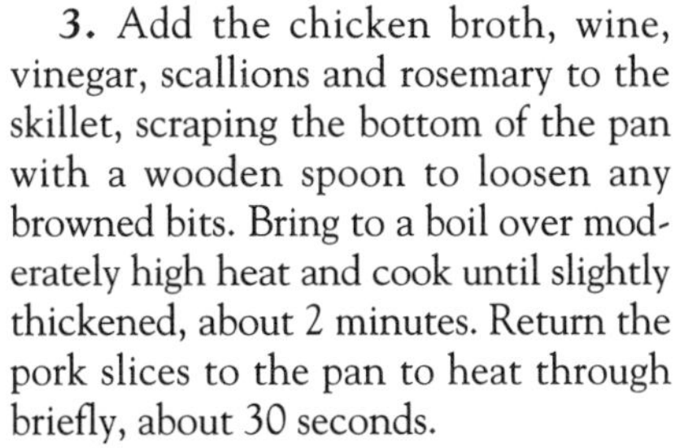

3. Add the chicken broth, wine, vinegar, scallions and rosemary to the skillet, scraping the bottom of the pan with a wooden spoon to loosen any browned bits. Bring to a boil over moderately high heat and cook until slightly thickened, about 2 minutes. Return the pork slices to the pan to heat through briefly, about 30 seconds.

4. Transfer the pork to a serving platter or individual dinner plates. Swirl the butter into the sauce until incorporated and stir in the black pepper. Spoon the sauce over the pork. Serve immediately.

—Lee Bailey

• • •

SWEET-AND-SOUR PORK

Sweet-and-Sour Pork is a Chinese-American universal. It does exist in China, but as it evolved in the United States, it became overly sweet, with a thick, gluey sauce in which canned pineapple became a prime ingredient.

6 Servings

BATTER:

¾ cup all-purpose flour
¾ cup cornstarch
1½ tablespoons baking powder
¼ teaspoon salt
1½ tablespoons peanut oil

SAUCE:

¾ cup white vinegar
½ teaspoon salt
6 tablespoons tomato sauce or 1 tablespoon tomato paste diluted with 5 tablespoons water
1 tablespoon Worcestershire sauce
¾ cup sugar
1 tablespoon cornstarch

4 cups peanut oil, for deep-frying
¾ pound boneless pork loin, cut into 1-inch cubes
1 tablespoon all-purpose flour
1 large garlic clove, minced
4 scallions, white part only, sliced ½ inch thick on the diagonal
½ cup bamboo shoots, cut into ¾-by-1-inch pieces
1 medium red bell pepper, cut into ¾-inch cubes

1. *Make the batter:* In a large bowl, combine the flour, cornstarch, baking powder and salt. Slowly add 1 cup of cold water, stirring with a fork until the batter is smooth. Stir in the peanut oil until thoroughly combined. The batter should be the consistency of pancake batter. If the batter is too thick, add up to 2 more tablespoons of water, 1 tablespoon at a time. Set aside.

2. *Make the sauce:* In a large bowl, combine all the sauce ingredients. Set aside.

3. Preheat the oven to 250°. Heat a wok over high heat for 40 seconds. Add the peanut oil and heat to between 350° and 375°. Meanwhile, in a shallow pan, dust the pork cubes with the flour. Working with one-third of the pork at a time, place the cubes in the batter, then use tongs to transfer them to the hot oil. Fry for 5 seconds, then turn over the pork pieces. Fry for a total of 3 minutes, turning several times, until light brown. Using a slotted spoon, transfer the pork to a strainer set over a large bowl to drain. Remove any bits of fried batter from the oil with a skimmer or slotted spoon. Repeat with the remaining 2 batches of pork.

4. Skim the oil of all pieces of batter. Return the oil to 350° to 375°. Place all the pork cubes in the oil and fry until deep golden brown, about 3 minutes longer. Using a slotted spoon, transfer the pork to a warm platter and place in the oven.

5. Pour off all the oil from the wok and return the wok to high heat. When a wisp of white smoke appears, stir in the garlic, then add the scallions and stir-fry for 30 seconds. Add the bamboo shoots and red pepper and stir-fry for 30 seconds. Stir the sauce to combine, pour it into the wok and continue to stir. Bring the liquid to a boil, then turn off the heat. Pour the sauce over the pork and serve immediately.

—Eileen Yin-Fei Lo

• • •

CHILES RELLENOS

In this version of the classic dish, the roasted poblano chiles are stuffed with ground pork, olives, raisins, pine nuts and almonds.

12 to 14 Servings

12 to 14 large poblano chiles

SAUCE:

¼ cup vegetable oil
½ of a medium onion, chopped
4 medium garlic cloves, finely chopped
4 pounds tomatoes, seeded and pureed in blender, or 42 ounces canned Italian peeled tomatoes, pureed
1 cup beef stock or canned broth
1 teaspoon sugar
1 teaspoon salt
¾ teaspoon cinnamon
1½ teaspoons finely chopped parsley

STUFFING:

2 tablespoons olive oil
¾ cup finely chopped onion
1 garlic clove, chopped

1 pound tomatoes, seeded and diced
2 pounds lean ground pork
1 cup blanched slivered almonds, chopped (4 ounces)
⅓ cup raisins
⅓ cup sliced green olives
¼ cup pine nuts (1 ounce)
1 teaspoon salt
1 teaspoon freshly ground black pepper

½ to ¾ cup all-purpose flour, for dredging
3 cups corn or other vegetable oil, for frying
7 eggs, separated

1. Roast the poblanos directly over a gas flame or under a broiler, turning, until blistered and slightly charred all over. Put them in a heavy paper bag and set aside to steam for 30 minutes.

2. *Meanwhile, prepare the sauce:* In a large nonreactive saucepan, heat the oil over moderate heat. Add the onion and garlic and cook until slightly softened. Stir in the pureed tomatoes, stock, sugar, salt and cinnamon and cook until thickened and reduced to 4½ cups, about 20 minutes. Stir in the parsley and set aside.

3. *Prepare the stuffing:* In a large nonreactive skillet, heat the oil. Add the onion, garlic and tomatoes and cook over moderately high heat, stirring occasionally, until the onion is softened. Add the pork and cook, stirring frequently, until it loses all trace of pink. Add the almonds, raisins, olives, pine nuts, salt and black pepper and stir constantly until the mixture is dry, about 10 minutes. Set aside to cool.

4. Peel the poblanos. Make a lengthwise slit in the side of each one. Using small scissors, carefully snip out the seedy cores, keeping the stems intact. Remove and discard the veins and any remaining seeds, then rinse the chiles and dry well on paper towels. *(The recipe can be prepared to this point up to 1 day ahead. Cover and refrigerate all the prepared ingredients. Let return to room temperature before proceeding.)*

5. Stuff the poblanos with the pork mixture. Using toothpicks, thread the seams of the chiles together to seal. Dredge the chiles in the flour until lightly coated.

6. In a deep-fat fryer or large deep skillet, heat the oil to 360°. Reheat the tomato sauce.

7. Meanwhile, lightly beat the egg yolks. In a large bowl, beat the egg whites until stiff, then fold in the beaten yolks. One by one and working in batches of three, dip the dredged chiles into the eggs to coat, then fry them in the hot oil, turning, until golden, about 4 minutes. Drain on paper towels.

8. Remove the toothpicks from the chiles. Spoon 2 tablespoons of tomato sauce onto each plate. Place the *chiles rellenos* on the sauce and spoon more sauce on top to cover. Serve hot.

—*Chata DuBose*

• • •

BARBECUED SPARERIBS

In China most households did not—and still do not—have ovens, so barbecued meats were usually cooked commercially and at restaurants in large brick ovens, fired with wood or charcoal. Here's the real thing.

6 Servings

1 whole rack pork spareribs (3½ pounds)
3½ tablespoons honey
2½ tablespoons Chinese rice wine or medium-dry sherry
2 tablespoons oyster sauce
2½ tablespoons hoisin sauce
1½ tablespoons light soy sauce
2 tablespoons double dark soy sauce
⅛ teaspoon freshly ground white pepper

1. Trim the spareribs by cutting off the flap and extra fat; score the meat with the tip of a sharp knife.

2. In a small bowl, combine the remaining ingredients; set aside.

3. Line the inside of a roasting pan with heavy aluminum foil and place the rack of ribs in it. Pour the marinade over the ribs and rub it into both sides. Cover and set aside to marinate for at least 4 hours or refrigerate overnight. Turn the ribs occasionally and spoon the marinade over them. Bring to room temperature before cooking.

4. Preheat the oven to 500°. Bake the ribs in the upper third of the oven, meat side up, for 10 minutes. Add ½ cup water to the pan and baste the ribs. Bake for 10 minutes, then add ¼ cup water, baste again and bake for 10 minutes. Add another ¼ cup water and turn the ribs over to brown the underside, about 10 minutes. Then turn the ribs right side up, baste and bake for 5 to 10 minutes longer, until browned. The ribs are done when the meat is no longer pink. To check, insert a small knife into the thick portion of the rib meat.

5. Transfer the rack of ribs to a cutting board. Using a cleaver, cut between the bones to separate the ribs. Place the ribs on a warm platter and serve hot.

—*Eileen Yin-Fei Lo*

• • •

Loin of Venison with Dried Cherries, Walnuts and Shiitake Mushrooms (p. 122).

Left, Veal Daube with Green Olives and Summer Savory (p. 102). Above, Stir-Fried Orange Beef with Wild Mushrooms (p. 106).

BABY BACK RIBS WITH HOISIN BARBECUE SAUCE

The recipe for hoisin barbecue sauce makes more than you will need for the ribs. Store the remainder in an airtight container and refrigerate it for up to one month. This is a great sauce for meat or chicken.

Start this recipe one day in advance so that the ribs can marinate overnight. If you like, garnish this dish with slices of fresh fruit.

4 Servings

¼ cup plus 2 tablespoons hoisin sauce
¼ cup honey
2½ tablespoons double black soy sauce*
2½ tablespoons dry sherry
1 cup ketchup
2½ tablespoons distilled white vinegar
1 tablespoon plus 1 teaspoon curry powder
1 tablespoon plus 1 teaspoon Oriental sesame oil
1 tablespoon minced garlic
1 tablespoon finely grated orange zest
1 tablespoon fermented black beans,* rinsed and finely chopped
1½ teaspoons Oriental chili sauce*
4 pounds baby back pork ribs, cut into 3-rib segments
Sesame seeds, for garnish
****Available at Asian markets***

1. In a medium nonreactive bowl, whisk the hoisin sauce, honey, soy sauce and sherry until blended. Stir in the ketchup, vinegar, curry powder, sesame oil, garlic, orange zest, black beans and chili sauce. Cover and refrigerate the hoisin barbecue sauce until ready to use.

2. In a large flameproof casserole, combine the ribs and enough water to cover and bring to a boil over moderately high heat. Reduce the heat to moderate and simmer until the meat is tender and nearly falls off the bones, about 1½ hours. Drain the ribs and set aside to cool to room temperature, about 1 hour.

3. Brush about 1 cup of the hoisin barbecue sauce over the ribs and place in a nonreactive bowl. Cover and refrigerate the ribs and the remaining sauce for 24 hours.

4. Preheat the broiler or light a grill. Place the ribs on a broiler pan or on the grill and cook, turning and brushing with extra sauce as necessary, until nicely charred, about 15 minutes. Serve hot or cold, sprinkled with sesame seeds.

—Alan Wong, Canoe House, Kohala Coast, Hawaii

• • •

Spinach Pappardelle with Smoked Duck and Red Lentils (p. 128).

STIR-FRIED BEAN CURD WITH GROUND PORK

4 Servings

½ pound ground pork
1 egg, beaten
1 tablespoon plus 2 teaspoons cornstarch
½ teaspoon five-spice powder
½ cup minced scallions
1 tablespoon sugar
¾ teaspoon Oriental sesame oil
¼ teaspoon salt
1½ tablespoons vegetable oil
½ cup minced red bell pepper
½ teaspoon minced jalapeño pepper
1 tablespoon minced garlic
1 tablespoon minced fresh ginger
1 cup chicken stock or low-sodium chicken broth
2 tablespoons soy sauce
2 tablespoons oyster sauce
1 pound fresh bean curd, cut into ¾-inch cubes, at room temperature
Cooked rice, for serving

1. In a medium bowl, combine the pork, egg, 1 tablespoon of the cornstarch, the five-spice powder, 1 tablespoon of the scallions, ½ teaspoon of the sugar, ¼ teaspoon of the sesame oil and the salt. In a wok, heat 1 tablespoon of the vegetable oil over very high heat until shimmering, then add the pork mixture in small clumps. Stir-fry the pork until brown and cooked through, about 2 minutes. Transfer to a bowl.

2. Lower the heat to moderate and heat the remaining 1½ teaspoons vegetable oil until hot. Stir in 6 more tablespoons of the scallions, the red bell pepper, jalapeño, garlic and ginger. Stir-fry until fragrant, about 30 seconds. Add the pork and the remaining 2½ teaspoons sugar; mix well. Increase the heat to high, stir in the chicken stock, soy sauce and oyster sauce and bring to a boil.

3. Meanwhile, dissolve the remaining 2 teaspoons cornstarch in 2 teaspoons of water, add to the pork mixture and bring back to a boil. Gently stir in the bean curd and cook until heated through. Spoon onto a serving platter and sprinkle the remaining scallions on top. Drizzle the remaining ½ teaspoon sesame oil over the mixture. Serve hot with rice.

—David Rosengarten

• • •

SEVEN-HOUR LEG OF LAMB

Traditionally, this dish was prepared with mutton, but any size leg of lamb can be used. The one called for here actually cooks in about five hours. According to the French, the lamb is done when it is so tender you can eat it with a spoon.

🍷 Serve a sturdy, rich and spicy red Côtes du Rhône, such as Gigondas.

10 to 12 Servings

6 medium onions, quartered
6 carrots, quartered
1 whole head of garlic, cloves peeled and halved
6 bay leaves
1 large sprig of fresh thyme or 1 teaspoon dried
One 7- to 8-pound leg of lamb, trimmed of visible fat
Salt and freshly ground pepper
2 bottles (750 ml each) dry white wine, such as Aligoté
4½ pounds large boiling potatoes, peeled and cut into 1½-inch chunks
5 large tomatoes—peeled, seeded and chopped—or 1 can (28 ounces) crushed Italian tomatoes

1. Preheat the oven to 425°. Layer the onions, carrots, garlic, bay leaves and thyme in a roasting pan large enough to hold the lamb. Place the lamb on top and roast for 30 minutes. Remove the pan from the oven and generously season the lamb with salt and pepper. Return it to the oven and roast for 30 minutes longer.

2. Remove the roasting pan from the oven and set it over 2 burners. Leave the oven on. Slowly pour the wine over the lamb and bring to a boil over high heat. Cover the lamb and return it to the oven. Roast for about 4 hours longer, or until the meat is moist and falling off the bone. (Timing will vary depending on the size and age of the lamb and the type of roasting pan used. Check the lamb periodically, reducing the oven temperature if the lamb begins to burn or the liquid begins to evaporate too quickly.)

3. About 1½ hours before the lamb is done, add the potatoes and the tomatoes with their liquid and submerge them in the liquid in the roasting pan.

4. Transfer the lamb and vegetables to a carving board. Pour the pan juices into a bowl and skim all the fat from the surface. If necessary, pour the pan juices into a small nonreactive saucepan and boil over high heat for a few minutes to intensify the flavors. Season with salt and pepper. Carve the lamb in thick slices, place on warmed dinner plates and surround with the vegetables. Pass the pan juices separately.

—*Patricia Wells*

• • •

CELEBRATORY FRENCH DINNER

Onion and Anchovy Croûtes (p. 22)

🍷 *Champagne*

Seven-Hour Leg of Lamb (at left)

🍷 *Côtes du Rhône*

Bitter Greens with Toasted Walnuts and Roquefort Cheese (p. 142)

Individual Warm Chocolate Tortes (p. 226) with Roasted Hazelnut Ice Cream (p. 250)

Coffee

Armagnac

ROAST LEG OF LAMB WITH CHICKPEAS

The Ribera del Duero is famous for its roasted meats, and chickpeas and garlic are well loved in almost every corner of Spain.

🍷 Serve with a Ribera del Duero, such as Pesquera Reserva 1986.

6 Servings

One 5- to 6-pound leg of lamb, trimmed of excess fat
3 tablespoons olive oil
Sea salt
Freshly ground pepper
2 large heads of garlic, separated into cloves and peeled
1 tablespoon Spanish Málaga or medium-dry sherry, such as amontillado
3 cups drained, canned chickpeas, from two 19-ounce cans
1 tablespoon minced parsley
2 teaspoons chopped fresh marjoram
2 cups Toro or other reasonably priced dry Spanish red wine

1. Preheat the oven to 500°. Rub the leg of lamb on all sides with 1 tablespoon of the oil, then sprinkle generously all over with sea salt and pepper. Place in a shallow roasting pan and roast for 10 minutes. Reduce the temperature to 300° and continue to roast, basting occasionally with the pan juices, until medium-rare, about 1 hour and 10 minutes. An instant-read thermometer inserted in the thickest part of the meat should register 125°.

2. Meanwhile, bring a small saucepan of salted water to a boil over high heat. Add the garlic cloves. Reduce the heat to moderate and cook until the cloves can be easily pierced with the tip of a sharp knife, about 10 minutes. Drain the garlic cloves and pat dry. Transfer to a medium bowl and toss with the Málaga.

3. In a large skillet, heat the remaining 2 tablespoons olive oil over low heat. Add the garlic and Málaga and cook, stirring frequently, until the garlic browns lightly, about 10 minutes. Stir in the chickpeas, parsley and marjoram. Remove from the heat and set aside.

4. Transfer the lamb to a platter to rest and cover lightly with foil to keep warm; set the roasting pan over 2 burners on high heat; pour in the wine. Cook, scraping the bottom of the pan to dislodge the browned bits, until the liquid reduces to 1 cup, about 4 minutes. Transfer the sauce to a small pan and keep warm.

5. Add ⅓ cup of the sauce to the chickpeas and rewarm over moderate heat, stirring. Add a little water if necessary. Season to taste with sea salt and keep warm.

6. To serve, carve the lamb and arrange the slices around the outer rim of a large warm oval platter. Pour any accumulated juices from the lamb into the wine sauce and boil the sauce over high heat to reduce slightly, 2 to 3 minutes. Season to taste with salt and pepper and strain the sauce through a fine sieve set over a sauceboat. Spoon the chickpeas into the middle of the platter and drizzle the sauce over the meat.

—Colman Andrews

• • •

BRAISED LAMB SHANKS WITH HONEY

Pepe Marin, who developed this recipe at his restaurant, El Caballo Rojo in Córdoba, traces the food of his native Andalusia back to the Moors who held the territory for some 700 years.

🍷 The sauce's sweet-sour flavor adds intensity to this rich lamb dish and suggests a red with equally assertive flavors, such as 1987 Pesquera Ribera del Duero from Spain or 1988 Arrowood Merlot from California.

6 Servings

¼ cup olive oil
5 pounds meaty lamb shanks, cut crosswise into 2½-inch pieces
2 medium onions, finely chopped
½ medium green bell pepper, finely chopped
One .2 gram tube of saffron filaments (about 1½ teaspoons), crumbled and dissolved in 3 tablespoons water
1 tablespoon sweet Spanish or Hungarian paprika
1 cup dry white wine
¼ cup Spanish brandy
2 tablespoons mild honey
3 tablespoons sherry vinegar
½ teaspoon salt

1. In a large flameproof casserole or dutch oven, heat 2 tablespoons of the oil over moderately high heat until hot. Add a single layer of lamb pieces and cook, turning occasionally, until browned on all sides, 8 to 10 minutes. Transfer to a platter and repeat with the remaining lamb. Pour out the fat from the casserole and wipe clean.

2. In the same casserole, warm the remaining 2 tablespoons oil over moderately low heat. Stir in the onions and bell pepper and cook, stirring occasionally, until softened, about 8 minutes. Stir in the dissolved saffron, paprika, wine and brandy. Bring to a boil and cook until the liquid is reduced by half.

3. Return the lamb to the casserole and add enough water to halfway submerge the lamb. Cover and cook over moderately low heat, stirring occasionally, until the meat is very tender and falling off the bone, about 2¼ hours. Remove from the heat and let cool to room temperature.

4. Using tongs, transfer the lamb pieces to a bowl. Cover the lamb and the liquid in the casserole separately and refrigerate until completely chilled, at least 3 hours or overnight.

5. Remove any congealed fat from the surface of the cooking liquid and return the shanks to the casserole. Cover and cook over moderate heat until heated through, about 20 minutes. Transfer the lamb to a large, rimmed platter and cover lightly with foil to keep warm.

6. Increase the heat under the casserole to moderately high and stir in the honey, vinegar and salt. Boil until the sauce is reduced to 2 cups, about 10 minutes. Season with salt to taste. Pour the sauce over the shanks and serve hot.

—Pepe Marin

• • •

SKEWERED LAMB AND PEPPERS

This dish displays a range of African ingredients, flavors and techniques. Skewered lamb is popular throughout northern Africa. It is often served with *harissa*, a hot chile-based condiment.

4 Servings

2 pounds lean boneless leg of lamb, cut into 1-inch cubes
¼ cup olive oil
2 teaspoons minced garlic
2 large red bell peppers—cored, seeded and each cut into 8 squares
Salt and freshly ground black pepper

1. Prepare a medium hot grill or preheat the broiler. Place the lamb in a shallow dish. Combine the olive oil and garlic and pour over the lamb. Toss to coat well.

2. Skewer the lamb and red pepper pieces alternately on 4 long metal skewers. Season with salt and black pepper. Grill or broil the lamb, turning the skewers once, about 10 minutes for medium-rare. Serve hot.

—Chris Schlesinger & John Willoughby

• • •

GRILLED LAMB DINNER

Skewered Lamb and Peppers (at left)

Harissa (p. 263)

Apricot-Fig Blatjang (p. 262)

Baked Sweet Potatoes

Hot and Sweet Cucumber Salad (p. 143)

Sliced Mangoes with Lime and Ginger (p. 236)

—Chris Schlesinger & John Willoughby

LOIN LAMB CHOPS WITH LEMON THYME AND SEARED SHALLOTS

This simple dish of mine can be prepared and put on the table in less than an hour. I prefer to infuse the lamb with the subtle flavor of lemon thyme, but regular English or German thyme will provide an equally delicious though different taste.

🍷 Bordeaux is the classic match with lamb, never more so than when the meat is prepared with herbs that find flavor echoes in the wine. A youthful example, such as 1988 Château Larose Trintaudon or 1989 Mouton-Cadet, would have just enough tannic astringency to cut the fattiness of the chop.

4 Servings

¼ cup olive oil
6 tablespoons plus 1 teaspoon fresh lemon thyme
8 loin lamb chops, cut about 1¼ inches thick
½ teaspoon salt
2 large shallots, minced
Freshly ground pepper

1. In a small saucepan, heat the oil over moderately low heat until hot. Stir in 3 tablespoons of the thyme and set aside for 30 minutes.

2. Preheat the broiler. Mince the remaining 3 tablespoons plus 1 teaspoon thyme and set aside ½ teaspoon. Rub the remaining minced thyme on both sides of the chops.

3. Pour all but 2 teaspoons of the infused thyme oil into a metal baking dish or roasting pan just large enough to hold the lamb chops. Place the chops in the pan and turn to coat on both sides with the oil. Sprinkle ¼ teaspoon of the salt over the chops and broil, turning once and sprinkling with the remaining ¼ teaspoon salt, about 4 minutes per side for medium-rare. Cover loosely with foil and let rest for 5 minutes.

4. Meanwhile, heat a small skillet over moderately high heat until hot, about 4 minutes. Add the reserved 2 teaspoons thyme oil and reduce the heat to moderate. Add the shallots and cook, stirring frequently, until golden and beginning to crisp. Remove from the heat and stir in the reserved ½ teaspoon minced thyme.

5. Arrange the lamb chops on 4 warmed plates, drizzle with any pan juices, dust them with pepper and top with the shallot mixture. Serve at once.

—Susan Herrmann Loomis

• • •

LAMB CHOPS WITH RED WINE AND THYME

🍷 Lamb has a distinct affinity for red wines made from Cabernet Sauvignon and related grapes. Their somewhat herbaceous flavors accent the meat's taste while their intrinsic tannins cut the fattiness. Youthful *petits châteaux* Bordeaux would be ideal. Look for 1988s, such as Château Larose-Trintaudon or Château La Tour de By.

4 Servings

1 tablespoon vegetable oil
Eight 1¼- to 1½-inch-thick loin lamb chops
Salt and freshly ground pepper
⅓ cup dry red wine
1 teaspoon chopped fresh thyme
1 tablespoon unsalted butter

1. Heat a large nonreactive skillet over moderately high heat for 5 minutes. Add the oil. Season the lamb chops on both sides with salt and pepper, add them to the skillet and cook until lightly browned, about 3 minutes per side. Reduce the heat to moderate and cook until medium-rare, 2 minutes longer on each side.

2. Transfer the lamb chops to a warmed platter and cover loosely with foil. Pour off the fat from the skillet, add the wine and scrape the bottom of the pan to loosen the browned bits. Stir in the thyme. Cook the sauce until thickened, about 1 minute. Pour in any accumulated lamb juices. Remove the skillet from the heat and swirl in the butter. Pour the sauce over the chops.

—*Stephanie Lyness*

• • •

FAMILY LAMB STEW

Meat without bones makes a stew without soul. Serve with Real-Good Southern Biscuits (p. 213) or crusty French bread.

🍷 This thick, hearty meat stew needs a full-textured red, such as a California Merlot, to match. 1988 Matanzas Creek or 1986 Robert Keenan are excellent choices.

6 to 8 Servings

¼ cup plus 2 tablespoons safflower or peanut oil
2 medium onions, finely chopped
1½ teaspoons finely chopped garlic
½ cup all-purpose flour
1 teaspoon coarse (kosher) salt
¼ teaspoon freshly ground pepper
6 lamb shanks (¾ to 1 pound each), sawed crosswise into thirds
½ cup full-bodied dry red wine
1 cup beef stock or canned broth
2 tablespoons tomato paste
½ teaspoon sugar
Bouquet garni: 4 flat-leaf parsley sprigs, 2 fresh thyme sprigs and 1 bay leaf, enclosed in 2 strips of leek greens and tied with string
18 small white boiling onions (¾ pound)
6 medium carrots, cut into 2-inch lengths
12 small turnips (1½ inches in diameter), peeled, or larger turnips, peeled and cut into wedges
12 small red potatoes (1½ to 2 inches in diameter), peeled, or larger potatoes, peeled and cut into wedges
½ pound fresh green beans, cut into 2-inch lengths
1 cup frozen baby peas, thawed

1. In a large, heavy, nonreactive skillet, heat 2 tablespoons of the oil over moderately high heat. Add the chopped onions and cook, stirring, until golden, about 10 minutes. Add the garlic and cook until softened but not browned, about 3 minutes. Scrape the onions and garlic into a large, heavy, flameproof casserole; set aside. Set the skillet aside.

2. In a paper bag, combine the flour, salt and pepper and shake well. Pat the lamb pieces dry with paper towels and toss in the paper bag, a few pieces at a time, to coat with the flour; shake off any excess.

3. Set the skillet over moderately high heat, add 3 tablespoons of the oil and heat until hot but not smoking. Add as many pieces of meat as will fit without crowding and brown on all sides, turning with tongs and regulating the heat to prevent burning. Transfer the meat to the casserole and repeat until all the lamb has been browned. Pour off the fat from the skillet.

4. Add the wine to the skillet and scrape up any browned bits from the bottom of the pan. Pour this liquid into the casserole. Add the stock and 3 cups of water to the casserole. Stir in the tomato paste and ¼ teaspoon of the sugar and push the bouquet garni down into the liquid. Bring to a simmer over moderately high heat. Cover tightly, reduce the heat to low and simmer gently until the lamb is just tender, 1 to 1½ hours. Remove from the heat.

5. Using tongs or a slotted spoon, transfer the lamb pieces to a large bowl. Remove and discard the bouquet garni and any loose bones and pour the sauce into another large bowl. Wash and dry the casserole and set aside. *(The recipe* can be prepared to this point up to 1 day ahead. Cover and refrigerate the meat and sauce separately.)* Skim all fat from the surface of the sauce before proceeding.

6. In a large heavy skillet, heat the remaining 1 tablespoon oil. Add the white boiling onions and sauté over moderately high heat until lightly browned all over, about 10 minutes; remove and set aside. Add the carrots and turnips to the skillet and sprinkle with the remaining ¼ teaspoon sugar. Sauté, stirring, until lightly browned on all sides, about 10 minutes. Remove from the heat.

7. Place the onions, carrots, turnips and potatoes in the casserole. Return the pieces of meat and pour the degreased sauce over all. Bring to a simmer over moderate heat. Cover and cook gently, stirring and basting once or twice, until the meat and vegetables are fork-tender, about 35 minutes.

8. In a medium saucepan of rapidly boiling salted water, blanch the green beans just until crisp-tender, 3 to 5 minutes. Drain and refresh under cool running water. Drain again. Add the beans and the peas to the simmering stew and cook for 5 minutes longer. Season with additional salt if necessary. Serve the stew directly from the casserole.

—Leslie Newman

• • •

LOIN OF VENISON WITH DRIED CHERRIES, WALNUTS AND SHIITAKE MUSHROOMS

The sheer richness of the elements in this dish demands a full-throttle but not overly subtle red to provide a dry but fruity contrast.

6 Servings

¼ cup plus 2 tablespoons walnut oil
1 cup plus 3 tablespoons dry red wine
1 tablespoon plus 2 teaspoons chopped fresh thyme or 2½ teaspoons dried
1 teaspoon freshly ground pepper
Six 6-ounce boneless venison loin steaks
⅓ cup walnut halves
2 tablespoons olive oil
3 medium shallots, thinly sliced
4 ounces shiitake mushrooms, stems discarded, caps thinly sliced
2 cups beef stock or canned broth
¼ cup finely chopped flat-leaf parsley
⅓ cup dried sour cherries*
1 tablespoon wild honey
2 tablespoons vegetable oil
Coarse (kosher) salt
6 sprigs of thyme, for garnish
****Available at specialty food stores***

1. Whisk the walnut oil with 3 tablespoons of the wine, 1 tablespoon of the chopped thyme (or 1½ teaspoons dried) and the pepper. Pour the marinade over the venison and refrigerate for 4 to 6 hours, turning occasionally.

2. Preheat the oven to 400°. Spread the walnuts on a baking sheet and toast in the oven until fragrant, about 4 minutes; set aside.

3. In a medium nonreactive saucepan, heat the olive oil. Add the shallots and mushrooms and cook over moderately high heat until very lightly browned, about 5 minutes. Transfer half of the mushroom mixture to a plate and keep warm. Add the beef stock and the remaining 2 teaspoons chopped thyme (or 1 teaspoon dried) and 1 cup wine to the saucepan and bring to a boil over high heat. Boil until slightly reduced, about 5 minutes. Strain the sauce, pressing on the solids. Stir in the parsley, dried cherries and honey.

4. Pat the venison dry with paper towels. In a large skillet, heat the vegetable oil over high heat. Add the venison steaks and cook until rare, about 3 minutes per side. Do not overcook.

5. Meanwhile, drain the oil from the skillet. Pour in the reserved sauce and cook over high heat, scraping the bottom of the pan, until reduced slightly, about 3 minutes. Season with coarse salt and pepper.

6. To serve, pour the warm sauce in the middle of 6 warm plates and arrange the venison on top. Scatter the toasted walnuts and mushroom mixture over the meat and garnish with the thyme sprigs.

—John Ash & Sid Goldstein

• • •

PASTA & NOODLES

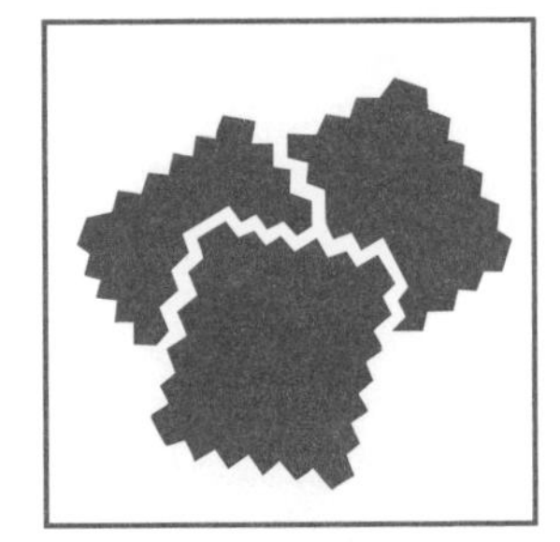

PASTINA WITH ROASTED RED BELL PEPPERS AND SWEET CORN

4 to 6 servings

2 medium red bell peppers
3 tablespoons unsalted butter
1 medium onion, chopped
2 cups fresh or frozen sweet white or yellow corn kernels
2½ cups canned low-sodium chicken broth
¾ cup pastina
⅓ cup minced fresh chives
½ teaspoon salt
½ teaspoon freshly ground black pepper

1. Roast the red bell peppers directly over a gas flame or under the broiler as close to the heat as possible, turning frequently, until charred all over. Transfer the peppers to a paper bag and set aside to steam for 10 minutes. Using a small sharp knife, scrape off the blackened skin and remove the core, seeds and ribs. Rinse the peppers and pat dry. Cut the peppers into ¼-inch dice, place in a bowl and set aside.

2. In a medium skillet, melt 2 tablespoons of the butter over moderate heat. Add the onion and cook, stirring, until translucent, about 5 minutes. Stir in the corn and cook until heated through, about 2 minutes. Remove the pan from the heat and cover to keep warm.

3. In a medium saucepan, bring the chicken broth to a boil over moderately high heat. Stir in the pastina, reduce the heat to maintain a steady simmer and cook until tender, about 6 minutes.

4. Stir the corn mixture into the pastina. Add the remaining 1 tablespoon butter, the reserved diced red bell peppers with the chives, salt and black pepper and toss gently to blend. Serve warm.

—Lee Bailey

• • •

ORZO WITH SAFFRON

Although the dish as is does not lack flavor or richness, you can substitute chicken stock or canned broth for the water, in which case the amount of salt should be decreased.

4 Servings

1 tablespoon olive oil
1¼ cups orzo (8 ounces)
2½ cups boiling water
1½ teaspoons unsalted butter
½ teaspoon salt
Generous pinch of saffron threads
Freshly ground pepper

1. In a medium saucepan, heat the oil over moderate heat. Add the orzo and cook, stirring, until well coated with the oil, 1 to 2 minutes.

2. Stir in the water, butter, salt and saffron and bring to a boil. Reduce the heat to moderately low, cover and simmer until the pasta is tender, most of the water has been absorbed and the mixture is creamy, about 15 minutes. If necessary, stir in additional hot water in small increments and cook a little bit longer, stirring occasionally, to achieve the right consistency. Season to taste with pepper and serve immediately.

—Stephanie Lyness

• • •

KASHA VARNISHKES

Kasha and bow-tie egg noodles are a classic Jewish side dish.

4 to 6 Servings

2 cups chicken stock or canned low-sodium broth
1 cup kasha
1 egg, lightly beaten
¼ teaspoon salt
4 tablespoons rendered chicken fat (schmaltz) or butter
1 medium onion, coarsely chopped
2 cups bow-tie egg noodles

1. In a medium casserole, bring the chicken stock to a boil over high heat. Reduce the heat to moderate and cover to keep at a boil. Meanwhile, in a medium bowl, combine the kasha and the egg, stirring until the grains are coated.

2. Heat a large heavy skillet over moderately high heat until hot. Add the kasha and cook, stirring constantly, until the grains have separated and have a nutty aroma, about 2 minutes. Add to the boiling chicken stock, stirring constantly. Add the salt and 2 tablespoons of the chicken fat. Reduce the heat to low, cover and cook until the kasha is tender and the liquid is absorbed, about 20 minutes. Set aside.

3. Meanwhile, in a small skillet, heat the remaining 2 tablespoons chicken fat over moderately low heat. Add the onion and cook until softened and very lightly browned, about 15 minutes. Set aside.

4. Bring a large pot of salted water to a boil over high heat. Add the noodles and cook until tender, about 10 minutes. Drain thoroughly.

5. In a large serving bowl, combine

the kasha, onions and bow-ties. Season to taste with salt. Serve immediately. *(The recipe can be made several hours ahead and kept, covered, at room temperature in a buttered dish. Reheat, covered, in a 300° oven for 15 to 20 minutes before serving.)*

—*Susan R. Friedland*

• • •

BOW-TIES WITH VEAL SAUCE

6 Servings

½ cup dried porcini mushrooms (1½ ounces)
2 cups hot chicken stock or canned broth
¼ cup olive oil
2 pounds veal shank meat, trimmed and cut into 1-inch cubes
1 medium onion, chopped
1 cup dry white wine
4 bay leaves
Salt and freshly ground pepper
1 celery rib, finely chopped
1 carrot, shredded
2 tablespoons finely chopped flat-leaf parsley
1 tablespoon tomato paste
1 cup drained canned Italian peeled tomatoes, chopped
1 pound bow-ties (farfalle)
½ cup freshly grated Parmigiano-Reggiano cheese

1. Soak the porcini in 1 cup of the stock until softened, about 30 minutes. Drain the mushrooms, reserving the liquid. Rinse and chop the mushrooms, discarding any tough bits. Strain the liquid through a sieve lined with cheesecloth and reserve.

2. Meanwhile, heat the oil in a large nonreactive casserole. Add the veal in a single layer and cook over moderately high heat, turning once, until browned, about 5 minutes. Add the onion and cook until golden. Add the wine and bay leaves, sprinkle with salt and pepper and cook, stirring, until the wine evaporates, about 10 minutes.

3. Reduce the heat to moderate, stir in the celery, carrot, parsley and tomato paste and cook for 3 minutes. Stir in the tomatoes, the chopped porcini and their liquid and the remaining 1 cup stock. Cover partially and cook over low heat, stirring occasionally, until the veal is very tender, about 1 hour. *(The veal sauce can be made up to 4 days ahead. Cover and refrigerate. Reheat before proceeding.)*

4. Cook the bow-ties in a large pot of boiling salted water until al dente. Drain well. Toss the pasta with half of the liquid sauce and the Parmigiano. Transfer to a serving bowl or plates, spoon the veal and remaining sauce on top and serve.

—*Lidia Bastianich*

• • •

FUSILLI WITH CHERRY TOMATOES

6 Servings

3 cups halved cherry tomatoes
⅓ cup extra-virgin olive oil
½ teaspoon crushed red pepper
¼ teaspoon salt
1 pound fusilli
10 fresh basil leaves, finely shredded
1 cup freshly grated Pecorino cheese (4 ounces)

1. In a large serving bowl, toss the tomatoes with the oil, crushed red pepper and salt. Let marinate at room temperature for 20 minutes.

2. Cook the fusilli in a large pot of boiling salted water until al dente. Drain the pasta, reserving ½ cup of the cooking water. Stir the hot pasta water into the tomatoes and add the basil. Add the pasta and toss. Add the Pecorino, toss again and serve.

—*Lidia Bastianich*

• • •

ROTINI WITH BACON, SWEET PEPPERS AND PEAS

4 Servings

½ pound sliced bacon, cut into 1-inch-wide pieces
1 tablespoon olive oil
1 medium onion, thinly sliced
3 bell peppers—1 red, 1 green and 1 yellow—cut into thin lengthwise strips
Salt
1 cup half-and-half
Freshly ground black pepper
1 pound rotini or other short corkscrew pasta
1 cup frozen peas

1. Bring a large pot of lightly salted water to a boil.

2. In a large skillet, fry the bacon over moderately high heat, spooning off the fat as it collects in the pan, until all the fat is rendered and the bacon is lightly browned, 5 to 7 minutes. Using a slotted spoon, transfer the bacon to paper towels to drain. Discard all but 1 tablespoon bacon fat from the pan.

3. Add the olive oil to the skillet, then add the onion, bell peppers and ¼ teaspoon salt. Cover and cook over moderate heat, stirring often, until the vegetables are softened, about 10 minutes. Reduce the heat to low and stir in the reserved bacon. Pour in the half-and-half and cook until reduced and slightly thickened, about 1 minute. Season to taste with salt and black pepper.

4. Meanwhile, cook the pasta in the boiling water until just al dente. Add the peas and cook for 2 minutes longer. Drain and toss with the sauce. Serve hot.

—Stephanie Lyness

• • •

TRIPLE CHEESE PASTA WITH GREEN PEAS

6 to 8 Servings

4 ounces Gorgonzola, at room temperature
3 tablespoons unsalted butter, softened
5 ounces mozzarella, cut into ½-inch cubes
5 ounces Italian Fontina, cut into ½-inch cubes
1 tablespoon olive oil
¼ teaspoon freshly ground pepper
2 cups fresh peas or 1 package (10 ounces) frozen baby peas
¾ pound rotelle pasta
3 tablespoons minced fresh chives
Salt

1. In a small bowl, mash the Gorgonzola and butter. In a medium bowl, combine the mozzarella, Fontina, olive oil and pepper.

2. Using a steamer rack, steam the peas over moderate heat until tender, 5 to 7 minutes.

3. In a large pot of boiling salted water, cook the rotelle until tender but still firm to the bite, 5 to 7 minutes; drain well.

4. Meanwhile, place the Gorgonzola and butter mixture in a large warmed bowl and let melt. Add the pasta and peas to the bowl. Toss to coat well. Sprinkle with the chives, add the mozzarella and Fontina mixture and toss again. Season with salt and additional pepper to taste.

—Lee Bailey

• • •

FUZI WITH PHEASANT

6 Servings

½ cup dried porcini mushrooms (1½ ounces)
¼ cup olive oil
One 2½-pound pheasant, cut into 14 pieces
Salt and freshly ground pepper
3 medium onions, chopped
⅓ cup finely chopped pancetta or bacon (1½ ounces)
½ cup chicken livers, trimmed and coarsely chopped (6 ounces)
4 whole cloves
2 bay leaves
1 sprig of fresh rosemary or 1 teaspoon dried
1 cup dry white wine
3 tablespoons tomato paste
3 cups chicken stock or canned broth
Fuzi (recipe follows)
½ cup freshly grated Parmigiano-Reggiano, plus more for serving

1. Soak the porcini in 2 cups of warm water until softened, about 30 minutes. Drain the porcini, reserving the liquid. Rinse the mushrooms and chop coarsely, discarding any tough bits. Strain the liquid through a sieve lined with cheesecloth and reserve.

2. Meanwhile, in a large nonreactive casserole, heat the oil over high heat. Add the pheasant pieces and sprinkle lightly with salt and pepper. Reduce the heat to moderately high and cook, turning, until lightly browned, about 10 minutes. Pour off all but 2 tablespoons of the fat.

3. Add the onions and pancetta to the casserole, season lightly with salt and pepper and sauté until golden, about 5 minutes. Add the chicken livers and cook, stirring, for 2 minutes. Add the chopped porcini, cloves, bay leaves and rosemary and cook, stirring, for 5 minutes. Add the wine and cook, stirring, until nearly evaporated, about 3 minutes.

4. Stir in the tomato paste. Add the reserved porcini liquid and the chicken stock and bring to a boil. Reduce the heat to low, cover partially and simmer gently for 1 hour. Remove and discard the cloves, bay leaves and rosemary sprig. *(The pheasant stew can be made up to 2 days ahead and refrigerated, covered.)*

5. Skim the fat from the surface of the stew. Remove all the meat from the bones and return the meat to the sauce. Reheat until simmering.

6. Meanwhile, drop the Fuzi into a large pot of boiling salted water, a handful at a time, stirring. Mix well and cook until the water returns to a full boil and the pasta rises to the surface, 3 to 5 minutes. Drain the Fuzi and place in a bowl. Add half of the liquid part of the sauce and Parmigiano and mix well. Spoon the remaining pheasant sauce and Parmigiano on top and serve with the extra cheese passed separately.

—Lidia Bastianich

• • •

FUZI

Makes 2 Pounds

4 cups unbleached flour
½ teaspoon salt
2 eggs, beaten
1 teaspoon olive oil
½ to ¾ cup warm water

1. In a food processor, combine the flour and salt and pulse a few times to blend. Mix the eggs with the oil and add to the processor. Turn the machine on and gradually drizzle in the water, beginning with the smaller amount. Stop and feel the dough; it should adhere when squeezed together between your fingers, but it shouldn't feel sticky. Continue to knead the dough in the processor until satiny-smooth. Transfer the dough to a bowl, cover and let rest for 1 hour before rolling out.

2. Cut the dough into 4 parts. Working with one part at a time and keeping the rest covered, roll the dough through successively narrower settings on a manual pasta machine, ending at the next to the last setting.

3. Cut the rolled out dough crosswise into 1½-inch wide strips. Lightly flour the strips and arrange them in 6 stacks. Cut the stacked strips on the diagonal at 2-inch intervals to form 3 triangular lozenges.

4. Roll each pasta lozenge around the tip of a finger, a thin spoon handle or a wooden dowel, pressing lightly where the pasta corners overlap to help them adhere. The *fuzi* should look like large, free-form quills. Arrange the *fuzi* on a lightly floured kitchen towel in a single layer as they are formed. The pasta can be cooked immediately.

—Lidia Bastianich

• • •

PAPPARDELLE WITH FRESH PORCINI

4 Servings

¼ cup olive oil
1 pound fresh porcini mushrooms, trimmed and sliced
4 garlic cloves, lightly crushed
Salt and freshly ground pepper
2 tablespoons unsalted butter
3 tablespoons chopped flat-leaf parsley
¾ cup chicken stock or canned broth
Egg Pasta (recipe follows), cut into pappardelle
½ cup freshly grated Parmigiano-Reggiano cheese

1. In a large skillet, heat 2 tablespoons of the oil. Add half the porcini and garlic, season with salt and pepper and cook over high heat, turning the porcini gently with a spatula, until lightly browned, 2 to 3 minutes. Transfer the porcini to a plate and repeat with the remaining oil, garlic and porcini. Discard the garlic.

2. Return all the porcini to the pan and add the butter and the parsley. Add the stock and simmer over moderate heat for 1 minute. Season with salt and pepper to taste.

3. Meanwhile, cook the Egg Pasta pappardelle in a large pot of boiling salted water until al dente. Drain well. Add the pappardelle to the porcini and toss gently, adding half the Parmigiano. Serve immediately, with the remaining Parmigiano passed separately.

—Lidia Bastianich

• • •

EGG PASTA

Makes 1 Pound

2 cups unbleached flour, sifted
¼ teaspoon salt
3 eggs, beaten
½ teaspoon olive oil
1 to 1½ tablespoons warm water, or more if necessary

1. In a food processor, combine the flour and salt and pulse a few times to blend. Mix the eggs with the oil and add to the processor. Turn the machine on and gradually drizzle in the water, beginning with the smaller amount. Stop and feel the dough; it should adhere when squeezed together between your fingers, but it shouldn't feel sticky. Continue to knead the dough in the processor until satiny-smooth. Transfer the dough to a bowl, cover and let rest for 1 hour before rolling out.

2. Cut the dough into 4 parts. Working with one part at a time and keeping the rest covered, roll the dough through successively narrower settings on a manual pasta machine, ending at the next to the last setting.

For pappardelle: Using a knife, cut the rolled dough crosswise in 1½-inch-wide strips. Let the pappardelle dry slightly, either on a work surface, a large baking sheet or a rack, for about 30 minutes.

For tagliatelle: Cut the rolled out dough into 12-inch lengths. Roll up each piece, beginning with a short end, then cut crosswise with a very sharp knife into ¼- to ⅓-inch-wide strips. Unravel the strips and spread them out on a clean kitchen towel to dry for about 30 minutes.

—Lidia Bastianich

• • •

GARDEN-STYLE WHOLE WHEAT PAPPARDELLE

6 Servings

2 small zucchini, cut into 1½-inch long sticks
6 asparagus spears, cut into 1-inch lengths
1 cup sliced green beans (1 inch long)
1 cup peas
1 cup small broccoli florets
⅓ cup olive oil
½ cup slivered onions
4 garlic cloves, minced
1 cup sliced shiitake mushroom caps
2 cups sliced peeled plum tomatoes
½ teaspoon crushed red pepper
Salt and freshly ground black pepper
½ cup hot chicken stock or canned broth
¼ cup chopped fresh basil
Whole Wheat Pappardelle (recipe follows)
1½ cups freshly grated Parmigiano-Reggiano cheese

1. Bring a large saucepan of salted water to a boil. One by one, cook the zucchini, asparagus, beans, peas and broccoli in the water just until al dente. Remove each vegetable with a slotted spoon, refresh under cold running water and set aside.

2. In a large nonreactive skillet, heat the oil. Add the onions and garlic and sauté over moderately high heat until golden. Add the shiitakes and sauté for 3 minutes, then add the tomatoes, crushed red pepper and salt and black pepper to taste. Reduce the heat to moderate and cook for 10 minutes, stirring frequently. Add the stock and the reserved green vegetables and cook for 5 minutes, stirring. Stir in the basil and keep warm.

3. In a large pot of boiling salted water, cook the Whole Wheat Pappardelle until al dente, 3 to 4 minutes. Drain well and return the pasta to the pot. Add half of the liquid portion of the sauce, leaving most of the vegetables behind, and toss lightly. Add half of the Parmigiano and toss again. Transfer the pappardelle to a platter or plates and spoon the remaining sauce and vegetables on top. Sprinkle with the remaining cheese and serve.

—Lidia Bastianich

• • •

WHOLE WHEAT PAPPARDELLE

Makes 2 Pounds

4 cups whole wheat flour
½ teaspoon salt
2 eggs, beaten
1 teaspoon olive oil
½ to ¾ cup warm water

1. In a food processor, combine the flour and salt and pulse a few times to blend. Mix the eggs with the oil and add to the processor. Turn the machine on and gradually drizzle in the water, beginning with the smaller amount. Stop and feel the dough; it should adhere when squeezed together between your fingers, but it shouldn't feel sticky. Continue to knead the dough in the processor until satiny-smooth. Transfer the dough to a bowl, cover and let rest for 1 hour before rolling out.

2. Cut the dough into 4 parts. Working with one part at a time and keeping the rest covered, roll the dough through successively narrower settings on a manual pasta machine, ending at the next to the last setting.

3. Using a knife, cut the rolled dough crosswise in 1½-inch-wide strips. Let the pappardelle dry slightly, either on a work surface, a large baking sheet or a rack, for about 30 minutes.

—Lidia Bastianich

• • •

SPINACH PAPPARDELLE WITH SMOKED DUCK AND RED LENTILS

🍷 The welter of tastes here point to a solid, forthright red with some tannic assertiveness, such as a California Cabernet Sauvignon.

4 Servings

3 cups chicken stock or canned broth
1 cup red lentils (7 ounces), rinsed
1 pound fresh spinach pappardelle
½ pound Swiss chard, leafy portion only, finely shredded
2 tablespoons olive oil
½ pound boneless smoked duck, skinned and cut into thick strips
½ cup slivered, oil-packed sun-dried tomatoes
Coarse (kosher) salt and freshly ground pepper
4 ounces goat cheese, such as Montrachet, crumbled
Fresh basil sprigs, for garnish

1. In a saucepan, bring the stock to a boil over high heat. Reduce the heat to moderately high, add the lentils and cook just until tender, 6 to 7 minutes. Drain the lentils, reserving 1 cup of the stock. Save the remaining stock for another use.

2. In a large pot of boiling water, cook the pappardelle until al dente. Drain and keep warm.

3. In a medium saucepan of boiling

water, blanch the Swiss chard for 1 minute; drain. In a large skillet, heat the olive oil over moderately high heat, add the Swiss chard and cook for 1 to 2 minutes. Add the drained lentils, smoked duck, sun-dried tomatoes, pappardelle and the reserved 1 cup of stock and toss. Season with coarse salt and pepper.

4. Mound the pasta on 4 warm dinner plates. Sprinkle the goat cheese over the pasta and top with basil sprigs and a grinding of pepper; serve immediately.

—John Ash & Sid Goldstein

• • •

WIDE PASTA WITH GRILLED TOMATOES

6 First-Course Servings

4 pounds large tomatoes, cored and sliced crosswise ⅓ inch thick
2 tablespoons minced garlic
3 tablespoons extra-virgin olive oil
1 teaspoon red wine vinegar
¼ cup minced fresh basil plus whole leaves, for garnish
Salt and freshly ground pepper
12 strips of dried lasagna, broken into 1-by-3-inch pieces
Freshly grated Parmesan cheese

1. Preheat the broiler. On a large heavy baking sheet, broil the tomatoes, turning once, until charred on both sides. Alternatively, grill the tomato slices over hot coals. Transfer to a large serving bowl.

2. In a medium skillet, cook the garlic in 1 tablespoon of the olive oil over low heat, stirring frequently until beginning to brown, about 5 minutes. Add to the tomatoes and gently stir in 1 tablespoon of the olive oil, the vinegar and the minced basil. Season to taste with salt and pepper.

3. In a large pot of boiling salted water, cook the lasagna just until al dente, about 8 minutes. Add 2 tablespoons of the pasta cooking water to the tomatoes, then drain the pasta.

4. Stir the remaining 1 tablespoon olive oil into the pasta, then add to the tomatoes. Season with salt and pepper. Sprinkle with cheese, then garnish with the basil leaves and serve immediately.

—David Rosengarten

• • •

LINGUINE WITH TOMATO CLAM SAUCE

The key to good clam sauce is cleaning the clams thoroughly to remove all traces of grit. This recipe is easily scaled down to serve 4 or 8.

16 Servings

12 pounds littleneck clams (about 9 dozen), scrubbed
1½ cups extra-virgin olive oil
20 garlic cloves, minced
2 teaspoons crushed red pepper
4 cups dry white wine
4 cans (16 ounces each) tomato puree
4 pounds imported linguine
2 cups chopped flat-leaf parsley

1. Soak the clams in cold salted water for 30 minutes. Remove the clams from the water, a few at a time, and rinse under cold running water. Place in a large bowl. Repeat the soaking process for another 30 minutes. Discard any clams that are open and do not close to the touch or any that seem exceedingly heavy.

2. Bring a large pot of salted water to a boil over high heat. Meanwhile, heat the oil in 2 large, heavy, nonreactive casseroles over low heat. Add half of the garlic and red pepper to each and cook until the garlic releases its aroma, about 4 minutes. Increase the heat to high and add half the wine to each casserole. Boil over high heat for 3 minutes. Stir half the tomato puree into each and bring to a boil.

3. Add the linguine to the boiling water and cook until al dente. Drain.

4. Meanwhile, add the clams to the casseroles, cover and cook over moderately high heat until the clams open, about 8 minutes. Remove the clams as they open; discard any that do not open. Stir the parsley into the sauce in the casseroles. Add the pasta and toss until well coated.

5. Transfer the pasta to 2 large platters. Arrange the clams in their shells on the pasta and top with any remaining sauce. Serve immediately.

—Evan Kleiman

• • •

IŠTRIAN-STYLE VERMICELLI WITH SHELLFISH

6 Servings

6 garlic cloves, crushed
¼ cup olive oil
2 cups peeled and crushed fresh tomatoes
1 teaspoon crushed red pepper
18 littleneck clams, scrubbed and rinsed
1 pound vermicelli
1 pound small shrimp, shelled and deveined
½ pound sea scallops, quartered
1 tablespoon chopped flat-leaf parsley

1. In a medium nonreactive skillet, cook the garlic in 2 tablespoons of the oil until lightly browned. Add the toma-

toes and crushed red pepper and simmer over moderate heat for 20 minutes. Discard the garlic.

2. Meanwhile, place the clams in a medium saucepan with ½ inch of water. Cover and steam over moderately high heat until the clams open. (Discard any that do not open.) Remove and chop the clams. Strain the liquid in the saucepan and reserve.

3. Cook the vermicelli in a large pot of boiling salted water until al dente. Drain well.

4. Meanwhile, in a large nonreactive skillet, heat the remaining 2 tablespoons oil over high heat. Add the shrimp and scallops and sauté for 2 minutes. Add the chopped clams and their liquid and the tomato sauce and cook until slightly reduced, about 3 minutes. Stir in the parsley.

5. In a large bowl, toss the pasta with half the sauce and spoon the remainder on top.

—Lidia Bastianich

• • •

RIGATONI IN A WOODSMAN'S SAUCE

6 Servings

3 tablespoons olive oil
½ cup chopped onions
¼ pound sweet Italian sausage, removed from the casing
2 cups sliced mixed mushrooms
2 tablespoons unsalted butter
1 cup canned Italian peeled tomatoes, crushed
½ cup fresh ricotta cheese
1 cup cooked fresh peas, or thawed frozen
1 cup half-and-half or light cream
Salt and freshly ground pepper
1 pound rigatoni
1 cup freshly grated Parmigiano-Reggiano cheese (4 ounces)

1. In a large nonreactive saucepan, heat the oil. Add the onions and cook over moderate heat until wilted. Add the sausage and cook, stirring, for 10 minutes. Drain all the fat from the pan. Add the mushrooms and butter and cook for 3 minutes. Add the tomatoes and simmer gently until thick, about 10 minutes. Add ¼ cup of the ricotta to the sauce and mix well, then add the peas and half-and-half and boil lightly for 4 minutes. Season with salt and pepper.

2. Cook the rigatoni in a large pot of boiling salted water until al dente. Drain well. Add the pasta to the sauce and mix well over low heat. Fold in the Parmigiano and the remaining ¼ cup ricotta and serve.

—Lidia Bastianich

• • •

PENNE WITH BROCCOLI RABE AND SAUSAGE

6 Servings

1 pound penne
¼ cup olive oil
3 large garlic cloves, crushed
1½ pounds broccoli rabe, florets and tender leaves and stems only
¼ teaspoon crushed red pepper
¼ teaspoon salt
1 cup chicken stock or canned broth
½ pound cooked sweet Italian sausage, crumbled or chopped
2 teaspoons unsalted butter
½ cup freshly grated Parmigiano-Reggiano cheese

1. Cook the penne in a large pot of boiling salted water until al dente. Drain well.

2. Meanwhile, in a large deep skillet, heat the oil. Add the garlic and cook over moderately high heat until golden. Add the broccoli rabe, crushed red pepper and salt; cover and steam for 5 minutes, stirring occasionally. Stir in the chicken stock, sausage and butter and cook over high heat until the sauce reduces slightly, about 3 minutes.

3. Add the penne to the skillet and toss gently. Sprinkle half of the Parmigiano on top and toss again. Serve immediately, sprinkled with the remaining cheese.

—Lidia Bastianich

• • •

POTATO GNOCCHI WITH VENISON STEW

6 Servings

½ cup dried porcini mushrooms (1½ ounces)
¼ cup olive oil
1 medium onion, minced
¼ cup minced pancetta or bacon (1 ounce)
Salt and freshly ground pepper
2½ pounds boneless venison from the leg or shoulder, cut into 1-inch cubes
½ cup dry red wine
2 bay leaves
2 whole cloves
1 sprig of fresh rosemary or 1 teaspoon dried
2 tablespoons tomato paste
3½ cups chicken stock or canned broth
Potato Gnocchi (recipe follows)

1. Soak the porcini in 2 cups of hot water until softened, about 30 minutes. Drain the mushrooms, reserving the liquid. Rinse and chop the mushrooms,

discarding any tough bits. Strain the liquid through a sieve lined with cheesecloth and reserve.

2. Meanwhile, in a large nonreactive casserole, heat the oil over moderately high heat. Add the onion and pancetta and sauté until golden, about 6 minutes. Season lightly with salt and pepper. Increase the heat to high, add the venison and cook until all the meat juices have evaporated, about 15 minutes.

3. Add the chopped porcini to the casserole, along with the wine, bay leaves, cloves and rosemary. Cook, stirring, for 5 minutes, until the wine is nearly evaporated.

4. Stir in the tomato paste and season lightly with salt and pepper. Add the stock and the reserved mushroom liquid and bring to a boil. Reduce the heat to moderately low and simmer, partially covered, until the meat is tender, about 1½ hours. Remove the meat and boil the sauce until reduced to 2 cups, about 5 minutes. Remove the bay leaves and rosemary sprig. *(The venison stew can be made up to 2 days ahead and refrigerated, covered.)*

5. In a large pot of boiling salted water, cook the Potato Gnocchi in 3 or 4 batches until they rise to the surface, 2 to 3 minutes. Using a slotted spoon, transfer the gnocchi to a warm platter and cover with foil. Toss the gnocchi with the hot venison sauce and serve immediately.

—Lidia Bastianich

• • •

POTATO GNOCCHI

6 Servings

3 large Idaho or russet potatoes, unpeeled (1½ pounds)
1 teaspoon salt
Dash of freshly ground white pepper
1 egg, beaten
1½ cups unbleached flour, sifted

1. In a large saucepan, boil the potatoes in lightly salted water until easily pierced with a fork, 30 to 40 minutes. Drain and cool.

2. Peel the potatoes and pass them through a ricer or push them through a coarse sieve. Spread the potatoes out on a large plate or platter and let them cool completely.

3. On a cool work surface, gather the cold riced potatoes into a mound and form a well in the center. Stir the salt and pepper into the egg and pour the mixture into the well. Using both hands, work the egg into the potatoes, gradually adding the flour and scraping the dough up from the work surface as necessary. Work the dough just until all of the ingredients are blended, 4 to 5 minutes.

4. Lightly dust the dough, your hands and the work surface with flour and cut the dough into 3 parts. Using both hands, roll each piece of dough into a ½-inch-thick rope, then cut the rope at ½-inch intervals. Indent the gnocchi with your thumb, or roll them with the back of a fork to produce a ribbed effect.

—Lidia Bastianich

• • •

RAVIOLACCI STUFFED WITH SPRING HERBS AND CHEESE

4 Servings

1½ teaspoons olive oil
1 small scallion, minced
2 tablespoons minced leek
¼ cup cooked and minced Swiss chard or spinach
½ pound fresh ricotta cheese
¼ cup mascarpone cheese
2 ounces ricotta salata cheese,* coarsely grated
½ cup freshly grated Parmigiano-Reggiano cheese
2 tablespoons chopped flat-leaf parsley
Salt and freshly ground pepper
1 egg, beaten
Egg Pasta (p. 127)
1 stick (4 ounces) unsalted butter
¼ cup milk
¼ cup heavy cream
8 fresh sage leaves
****Available at Italian markets and specialty cheese shops***

1. In a small skillet, heat the oil. Add the scallion and leek and cook over moderately low heat until softened. Stir in the Swiss chard. Set aside to cool.

2. In a bowl, combine the fresh ricotta, mascarpone, ricotta salata, ¼ cup of the Parmigiano and the parsley. Add the reserved greens and mix well. Season with salt and pepper. Stir in half of the beaten egg.

3. Divide the Egg Pasta dough in half and roll each piece to the next to the last setting on a manual pasta machine. Lay the pasta sheets on a work surface. Mound 1 tablespoon of the filling at 2½-inch intervals along the lengths of the sheets, ½ inch up from the bottoms. Lightly brush around the filling with the remaining beaten egg. Loosely fold the top of the pasta sheets over to cover the mounds of filling; press around the filling to release any air. Cut into 2½-by-3-inch squares with a jagged pastry cutter or a large ravioli stamp.

4. In a large pot of boiling salted water, cook the *raviolacci* until they rise to the surface and are tender. Drain well in a colander, reserving ¼ cup of the pasta water.

5. Meanwhile, in a large deep skillet, melt the butter over moderately high heat. Stir in the milk, cream, sage leaves and the reserved pasta water and bring to a gentle boil. Cook for 3 minutes. Add the cooked *raviolacci*, stir gently with a wooden spoon to coat and add the remaining ¼ cup Parmigiano. Shake the pan until the sauce is lightly syrupy and coats the *raviolacci*. Season with salt and pepper. Transfer to warm plates and serve.

—Lidia Bastianich

• • •

CHEESE AND POTATO KREPLACH

Kreplach, like ravioli, can be filled with cheese, potato, kasha, chicken or meat. They are boiled and served in soup or fried and then eaten as an appetizer or side dish, with or without sour cream.

Makes About 40 Kreplach

4 medium waxy potatoes
2 tablespoons unsalted butter
1 small onion, minced
1 egg, lightly beaten
¾ cup cottage cheese
1 teaspoon salt
1½ cups all-purpose flour
3 eggs, lightly beaten, plus 1 beaten egg for sealing
1 tablespoon corn oil

1. In a medium saucepan of boiling water, cook the potatoes until tender, about 20 minutes. Set aside in a colander to drain and cool.

2. Meanwhile, in a small skillet, melt the butter over moderately low heat. Add the onion and cook, stirring occasionally, until soft and beginning to brown, about 15 minutes.

3. Peel the potatoes and transfer to a medium bowl. Mash the potatoes; add the egg, cottage cheese and ½ teaspoon of the salt. If the mixture is quite lumpy, strain it through a coarse sieve. Stir in the onion. *(The filling can be made up to 1 day ahead and refrigerated, covered.)*

4. Mound the flour on a work surface and make a well in the center. Add the 3 beaten eggs, oil and the remaining ½ teaspoon salt to the well. Mix with a fork, drawing in the flour, until all the liquid is incorporated. Using your hands, gather the dough into a ball and knead it until smooth and elastic, about 10 minutes. Cut in half.

5. Set a pasta machine on the thickest setting and roll one piece of the dough through the machine. Continue to roll the dough through the machine, decreasing the setting each time, until you reach the next to the last setting and the dough is about ¹⁄₁₆ inch thick. Trim the dough to form a strip, 6 inches wide by 30 inches long. Cut the strip in half lengthwise, cover with a towel and set aside. Repeat with the remaining dough.

6. Cut each strip crosswise into ten 3-inch squares. Place a rounded tablespoon of the filling in the center of each square and brush the edges with the remaining beaten egg. Let sit until tacky, about 2 minutes, then fold over a corner of each square to form triangles; pinch the edges together to seal. Transfer to a baking sheet and cover with a dish towel. Repeat with the remaining dough.

7. Bring a large pot of salted water to a boil over high heat. Add the *kreplach* and cook until the dough is tender and the filling is cooked, about 9 minutes. Drain in a colander.

—Susan R. Friedland

• • •

LAYERED FRESH PASTA WITH CHICKEN, MUSHROOMS AND CHEESE

8 Servings

Egg Pasta (p. 127)
¼ cup olive oil
1 large onion, diced
2 slices of bacon, diced
1 chicken, cut into 8 pieces
1 teaspoon fresh rosemary, chopped
4 whole cloves
Salt and freshly ground pepper
2 teaspoons tomato paste
1 cup dry white wine
2½ cups chicken stock or canned broth
3 bay leaves
2 cups sliced mixed mushrooms
2 tablespoons unsalted butter
Salsa Besciamelle (recipe follows)
1½ cups freshly grated Parmigiano-Reggiano cheese (6 ounces)
1½ cups shredded Italian Fontina cheese (8 ounces)

1. Cut the Egg Pasta dough in half and roll out each piece to the next to the last setting on a pasta machine. Cut the dough crosswise into 3½-inch-wide strips. Let rest for at least 30 minutes.

2. In a large nonreactive casserole, heat 3 tablespoons of the oil. Add the onion and bacon and sauté over high heat until golden. Add the chicken, rosemary and cloves, sprinkle with salt and pepper and cook until the chicken is lightly browned all over, about 5 minutes. Add the tomato paste and stir to coat the chicken. Stir in the wine, scraping the bottom of the pan, then add the stock and bay leaves and simmer over low heat for 25 minutes.

3. Remove the chicken and set aside to cool. Strain the sauce and skim off the fat. Return the sauce to the casserole and cook over high heat until it has reduced to 1½ cups, about 12 minutes. Shred the chicken; discard the skin and bones. Return the meat to the sauce.

4. In a medium skillet, sauté the mushrooms in the butter over moderately high heat for 4 minutes. Season with salt and pepper and add to the chicken sauce. Cook the sauce gently for 5 minutes, then set aside to cool to room temperature.

5. Bring a large pot of salted water to a boil. Fill a large bowl with cold water and add the remaining 1 tablespoon olive oil. Drop 4 strips of the pasta into the boiling water, stir and let return to a boil; boil for 6 seconds. Transfer the cooked pasta to the bowl of cold water and separate the strips with your hands. Spread the strips out on a damp towel. Repeat with remaining pasta strips.

6. Preheat the oven to 450°. Line a well-buttered 9-by-13-inch ceramic or glass baking dish with 7 strips of pasta, allowing the ends to hang 2 inches over the edge. Set aside 1 cup of the Salsa Besciamelle, 3 tablespoons of the chicken sauce and 2 tablespoons each of the Parmigiano and Fontina cheeses.

7. Spread one-fourth of the remaining Salsa Besciamelle evenly over the pasta and sprinkle with one-third of the Fontina. Cover with 4 pasta strips. Sprinkle one-third of the Parmigiano on top and cover with one-third of the chicken sauce. Top with 5 pasta strips. Repeat this layering 2 more times and top with a final layer of Salsa Besciamelle. Cover with any remaining pasta strips and fold in the ends to seal. Top with the reserved Salsa Besciamelle, chicken sauce and cheeses and bake for 30 minutes. Let cool for 15 minutes, then cut into squares and serve.

—Lidia Bastianich

• • •

SALSA BESCIAMELLE

Makes 4 Cups

3½ cups milk, at room temperature
2 bay leaves
Pinch of freshly grated nutmeg
6 tablespoons unsalted butter
½ cup all-purpose flour
Salt and freshly ground white pepper

1. In a small saucepan, combine the milk, bay leaves and nutmeg and bring to a simmer over moderate heat.

2. Meanwhile, in a heavy medium saucepan, melt the butter. Stir in the flour and cook over moderate heat, mixing frequently, until smooth, about 1 minute. Gradually whisk in the milk until smooth. Cook over low heat, whisking frequently, until the sauce thickens and no floury taste remains, about 10 minutes. Strain the sauce through a fine sieve and season with salt and pepper to taste. Let cool.

—Lidia Bastianich

• • •

ROASTED ASPARAGUS LASAGNA

This dish could take center stage at lunch as well as at dinner, accompanied with a simple salad and crusty bread.

🍷 The onions and asparagus add sweetness to the flavors here, which are buttressed by the richness of the cheese and cream. For balance, a cuttingly acidic white with contrasting flavor, such as Sauvignon Blanc, would be required. Italian examples include 1988 Eno Friulia or 1988 Avignonesi Il Vignola; alternately, a crisp California bottling, such as 1989 Grgich Hills Fumé Blanc, would work as well.

6 Servings

5 tablespoons unsalted butter
3 tablespoons unbleached flour
1½ cups hot milk
1½ teaspoons coarse (kosher) salt
2 tablespoons plus 1 teaspoon pure olive oil
2 large onions (1 pound), halved vertically and thinly sliced
2 pounds fresh asparagus, trimmed
4 wide lasagna noodles (see Note)
½ cup plus 1 tablespoon heavy cream
1¼ cups freshly grated Parmigiano-Reggiano cheese (about 3½ ounces)
Twelve ⅛-inch-thick slices fresh mozzarella cheese (about 4 ounces)

1. In a heavy medium saucepan, melt 3 tablespoons of the butter over low heat. Add the flour and stir with a wooden spoon until thoroughly incorporated. Cook, stirring, until the mixture has bubbled for 1 minute; do not allow the flour to brown.

2. Remove from the heat and very slowly whisk in the hot milk. Return the saucepan to low heat and cook, whisking, until the sauce thickens and loses its floury taste, about 10 minutes. Stir in ½ teaspoon of the salt and transfer to a bowl. Press a piece of plastic wrap or wax paper directly on the surface of the sauce and set aside. *(The béchamel can be made several hours ahead; let cool to room temperature and refrigerate. It will thicken as it cools; rewarm it very slowly until it reaches spreading consistency before using.)*

3. Preheat the oven to 500°. In a large skillet, melt the remaining 2 tablespoons butter in 1 tablespoon of the olive oil. Add the onions and sprinkle with ½ teaspoon of the salt. Cook over low heat, stirring occasionally, until very soft and light gold, 15 to 20 minutes.

4. On a baking sheet, toss the asparagus with the remaining 1 tablespoon plus 1 teaspoon olive oil until evenly coated. Spread them in a single layer and bake until tender, about 10 minutes. Remove from the oven and let cool slightly. Thinly slice the asparagus on the diagonal and add to the onions. Reduce the oven temperature to 375°.

5. In a large saucepan, bring 5 quarts of water to a boil and add the remaining ½ teaspoon salt. Drop the lasagna noodles into the boiling water and cook until soft and pliable, about 3 minutes for instant and 30 seconds for fresh. Drain and lay the lasagna noodles on a damp tea towel. (If using fresh pasta, refresh the noodles under cold running water to stop the cooking process and to prevent the noodles from sticking to one another.)

6. Set aside 2 tablespoons of the béchamel sauce, 1 tablespoon of the heavy cream and ½ cup of the Parmigiano. To assemble, spread 2 tablespoons of the béchamel on the bottom of an 8-inch square baking pan and drizzle 2 tablespoons of the heavy cream on top. Cover with one lasagna noodle and 2 more tablespoons of béchamel. Spread 1 cup of the asparagus and onions on the sauce, cover with 4 slices of the mozzarella and sprinkle ¼ cup of the Parmigiano on top. Drizzle with 2 tablespoons of the heavy cream. Top with another noodle and repeat the layering twice, using 2 tablespoons of béchamel, 1 cup of the asparagus and onions, 4 slices of mozzarella, ¼ cup of the Parmigiano, 2 tablespoons cream and 1 noodle each time, ending with the noodle. Spread the reserved béchamel, cream and Parmigiano on top.

7. Cover the lasagna loosely with foil and bake for 10 minutes. Uncover and bake for an additional 20 to 30 minutes, or until golden and bubbling. Let cool for 10 minutes before cutting.

NOTE: *We suggest using Delverde Instant Lasagne Ondine for this dish; the noodles are wide, light and delicate. If unavailable, use half a pound of fresh wide lasagna noodles instead. Do not substitute curly-edged dried lasagna noodles; they are too thick for this dish.*

—*Johanne Killeen & George Germon*

• • •

SPICY SUMMER NOODLES WITH FRESH VEGETABLES

These noodles can be cooked, dressed and then refrigerated overnight. Simply add the vegetables at the last minute and toss well.

6 Main-Course or 10 First-Course or Side-Dish Servings

1 pound very thin Chinese or Italian egg noodles (1/16 inch)
Ice water
¾ pound fresh mung bean sprouts

DRESSING:
¼ cup black soy sauce*
¼ cup unseasoned Japanese rice vinegar*
¼ cup plus 1 tablespoon Chili-Lemon Oil (p. 263)
2 tablespoons sugar
1½ teaspoons coarse (kosher) salt

2 teaspoons finely grated lemon zest
3 tablespoons black sesame seeds* (optional)
1 European seedless cucumber, cut into thin julienne strips
2 red bell peppers, cut into thin julienne strips
½ pound carrots, cut into thin julienne strips
1 large bunch of scallions, thinly sliced crosswise
****Available at Asian markets***

1. Fluff the noodles to separate the strands. In a large pot of boiling water, cook the noodles until al dente, swishing with chopsticks, about 2 minutes. Drain and plunge the noodles into ice water to chill, then drain well.

2. In a medium saucepan of boiling water, blanch the bean sprouts for 5 seconds. (This seals their color and dulls any grassy taste.) Drain and then plunge into ice water to chill. Drain the bean sprouts well and set aside until just before using.

3. In a small bowl, combine the dressing ingredients and whisk to blend. In a large bowl, toss the noodles with the dressing, using your fingers to coat and separate the strands. Sprinkle half of the lemon zest on the noodles and toss to mix. Taste and add the remaining lemon zest if desired. Let the noodles sit for 10 minutes.

4. In a small dry skillet, toast the black sesame seeds over moderate heat, tossing until fragrant, about 2 minutes. Remove from the pan and let cool.

5. Toss the noodles again. Sprinkle the toasted sesame seeds on top. Add the reserved bean sprouts and the cucumber, bell peppers, carrots and most of the scallions. Toss well to mix and arrange on a platter or in bowls. Garnish with the reserved scallions.

—Barbara Tropp

• • •

CHILLED SOBA WITH ORANGE WALNUT DIPPING SAUCE

Both the *soba* and the dipping sauce should be prepared several hours ahead so they will be well chilled when it's time to serve.

6 First-Course or 4 Main-Course Servings

2½ cups Dashi (p. 46)
7 tablespoons plus 2 teaspoons soy sauce
½ cup rice vinegar
⅓ cup sugar
¼ cup sake
¼ cup (loosely packed) bonito flakes
2 tablespoons minced orange zest
2 tablespoons plus ½ cup minced walnuts
1 pound dry soba noodles, preferably yamaimo soba
5 scallions, thinly sliced

1. In a medium nonreactive saucepan, combine the Dashi, soy sauce, vinegar, sugar, sake and bonito flakes. Bring to a boil over high heat. Reduce the heat to moderate and simmer for 2 minutes. Stir in the orange zest and remove from the heat. Let cool slightly, then refrigerate until chilled, 1 to 2 hours. Just before serving, stir in the walnuts.

2. Bring a large pot of water to a boil over high heat. Add the *soba* noodles and when the water returns to a boil, boil until tender, about 5 minutes. Drain the noodles in a colander and toss gently but thoroughly under cold running water. Spread the noodles out on paper towels and pat dry. Cover and refrigerate until chilled, about 1 hour. If the noodles stick together when chilled, rinse under cold water and pat dry again. Transfer to dinner bowls.

3. Sprinkle each serving with the walnuts and garnish with the scallions. Serve the orange walnut dipping sauce in small bowls on the side. Swish portions of noodles in the sauce before each bite.

—Linda Burum

• • •

SEAFOOD LO MEIN WITH PEPPERED EGG GARNISH

Timing is everything when stir-frying noodles, so it's best to prepare and measure out all the ingredients before starting to cook.

🍷 The squid and shrimp in this dish call for white wine, and the spicy accents point to a California Sauvignon Blanc, such as 1990 White Oak, or an Italian Pinot Grigio, such as 1989 Bollini Valdadige for a refreshing foil.

4 Servings

1 egg white
1 tablespoon plus 2 teaspoons Chinese rice wine* or dry sherry
1¼ teaspoons salt
1 tablespoon plus 1 teaspoon cornstarch
½ cup plus 1½ tablespoons peanut or vegetable oil
¾ pound small shrimp, shelled and deveined
¾ pound fresh thin Chinese egg noodles* or 9 ounces dried
1 tablespoon Oriental sesame oil
⅓ cup chicken stock or canned broth
2 tablespoons light Chinese soy sauce*
1½ tablespoons oyster sauce*
¾ teaspoon sugar
2 whole eggs, at room temperature
2 jalapeño peppers, partially seeded and minced (see Note)
½ pound cleaned squid, cut into thin rings
1½ tablespoons minced fresh ginger
1 tablespoon minced garlic
1 small red onion, halved and sliced lengthwise into thin strips

1 medium red bell pepper, cut into thin strips
½ of a small head of bok choy, white and green separately cut crosswise into very thin strips
2 scallions, thinly sliced
Fresh coriander (cilantro) sprigs, for garnish
****Available at Asian markets***

1. In a medium bowl, combine the egg white, 2 teaspoons of the rice wine, 1 teaspoon of the salt and 1 tablespoon of the cornstarch and whisk to blend. Blend in 2 teaspoons of the peanut oil. Add the shrimp and toss to coat completely. Let marinate for 1 hour at room temperature or cover and refrigerate for up to 24 hours. The longer marinating time is preferable.

2. Cook the noodles in a large pot of boiling water until al dente, about 2 minutes for fresh or 4 to 5 minutes for dried. Drain and rinse under cold running water. Drain well and pat dry with paper towels. Toss the noodles with 1 teaspoon of the sesame oil and set aside. *(The noodles can be prepared to this point up to 2 days ahead. Store in a plastic bag in the refrigerator.)*

3. In a small bowl, combine the stock, soy sauce, oyster sauce, sugar and the remaining ¼ teaspoon salt, 1 teaspoon cornstarch and 2 teaspoons sesame oil; set aside.

4. In a small bowl, lightly beat the whole eggs with 2 teaspoons of the peanut oil. In a small nonstick skillet, heat 2 more teaspoons of the peanut oil over moderately high heat. Add the jalapeños and cook, stirring, until softened, about 45 seconds. Stir in the eggs and scramble them until dry, about 1 minute. Transfer the eggs to a small plate.

5. About 30 minutes before you are ready to assemble the *lo mein*, bring a large pot of water to a simmer over high heat. Add the shrimp and remove from the heat. Stir briskly. Let stand until the shrimp are almost opaque but not quite fully cooked, about 1 minute. Drain in a colander and set aside.

6. In a wok, heat 1½ tablespoons of the peanut oil over high heat and swirl to coat the pan. Add the squid and stir-fry until almost opaque, about 30 seconds; it should not be thoroughly cooked. Transfer to the colander. Wipe out the wok.

7. Heat 2 tablespoons of the peanut oil in the wok over high heat. Add the ginger and garlic and stir-fry for 20 seconds. Add the onion, bell pepper and white portion of the bok choy and stir-fry until almost crisp-tender, 45 seconds to 1 minute. Stir in the bok choy greens and stir-fry for 5 seconds. Add the seafood and toss it with the vegetables until well combined. Add the remaining 1 tablespoon rice wine and stir-fry for another 30 seconds. Slide the mixture onto a large plate.

8. Wipe out the wok with a damp paper towel. Return it to high heat and add the remaining 3 tablespoons peanut oil. When it is almost smoking, sprinkle in the noodles and stir them briskly in a circular motion; then stir in the opposite direction. With two large spoons, lift and toss the noodles as you would a salad for about 30 seconds.

9. Add the vegetables and seafood and toss well. Stir the reserved stock mixture well and sprinkle it over the noodles. Toss until the liquid is distributed and clings to the noodles. Toss in half of the reserved scrambled eggs, breaking them into small chunks. Transfer the noodles to a large platter. Garnish with the scallions and heap the remaining scrambled eggs in the center of the noodles. Garnish with the coriander sprigs.

NOTE: *For a mild dish, remove all the seeds; a medium dish, half the seeds; a very hot dish, leave in all the seeds.*

—*Linda Burum*

• • •

CHOW MEIN

In Canton, *yuk see chau mein* is a classic dish in which noodles are panfried into a pancake and topped with stir-fried pork and vegetables. Here is the dish that became chow mein when it came to America.

6 Servings

½ pound fresh Chinese egg noodles* or fresh or dried capellini
⅓ cup dried Chinese black mushrooms*
1 cup boiling water

MARINADE:
1½ teaspoons finely grated fresh ginger
1½ teaspoons oyster sauce*
1 teaspoon Oriental sesame oil
½ teaspoon dry white wine
½ teaspoon light soy sauce
½ teaspoon sugar
½ teaspoon cornstarch
⅛ teaspoon salt
Pinch of freshly ground white pepper

¼ pound boneless pork loin, trimmed and cut into 2-by-¼-inch strips

SAUCE:
1 cup Chicken Stock (p. 48) or canned low-sodium chicken broth
1 tablespoon plus 1½ teaspoons cornstarch
*1 tablespoon oyster sauce**
1 teaspoon Oriental sesame oil
1 teaspoon sugar
*½ teaspoon dark soy sauce**
⅛ teaspoon salt
Pinch of freshly ground white pepper

5 tablespoons peanut oil
1½ tablespoons finely grated fresh ginger
1½ teaspoons minced garlic
1½ cups yellow Chinese chives or green chives, cut into 1½-inch lengths*
1 cup fresh bean sprouts, both ends picked off
**Available at Asian markets*

1. Bring a large saucepan of salted water to a boil over high heat. Add the noodles and cook, stirring with chopsticks or a large fork to prevent sticking, until just tender, about 20 seconds for fresh, 2 to 3 minutes for dried. Drain in a colander and rinse thoroughly under cold running water to remove the starch; set aside to cool. Spread the noodles in a single layer on a large kitchen towel and let them dry for 2 hours, tossing occasionally.

2. Place the dried mushrooms in a small bowl and pour in the boiling water; set aside until softened, about 30 minutes. Drain the mushrooms and rinse under cold running water. Discard the stems; cut the caps into thin strips and set aside.

3. *Make the marinade:* Place the grated ginger in a small strainer set over a medium bowl. Press hard with the back of a spoon to extract ½ teaspoon of juice; discard the ginger pulp. Stir in the remaining marinade ingredients. Add the pork strips, stir to coat well. Cover and marinate for 30 minutes.

4. *Make the sauce:* Combine all the sauce ingredients in a small bowl; set aside.

5. Heat a large cast-iron skillet over high heat for 5 minutes, then add 2 tablespoons of the peanut oil. When a wisp of white smoke appears, after about 2 minutes, place the reserved noodles in the skillet, spreading them in an even layer. Cook until nicely browned on the bottom, 4 to 5 minutes. Remove the pan from the heat and, using a spatula, slide the noodle cake onto a large, flat plate. Place another plate on top and invert. Add 1 tablespoon of the oil to the skillet and slide in the noodle cake. Cook until well browned and crisp on the second side, about 4 minutes. Remove from the heat and cover to keep warm.

6. Heat a wok over high heat for 40 seconds. Add the remaining 2 tablespoons oil and stir with a metal spatula to coat the wok. When a wisp of white smoke appears, about 2 minutes, add the ginger and stir-fry for 20 seconds. Stir in the garlic and add the pork and its marinade, spreading the meat in an even layer. Cook for 30 seconds; then stir in the reserved mushrooms. Stir the sauce to blend, then add it to the wok and bring to a boil. Stir in the chives and bean sprouts and stir-fry until heated through, about 3 minutes.

7. Transfer the noodle cake to a large warm plate and spoon the pork on top. Serve immediately.

—*Eileen Yin-Fei Lo*

• • •

TIBETAN CRISP-FRIED NOODLES WITH LAMB AND VEGETABLES

This dish, a version of *chow-chow*, is eaten on festive occasions in Tibet. Although this recipe for a noodle cake topped with a stir-fried lamb mixture is more elaborate than typical Tibetan food, it is easy for a Westerner to prepare, quick to cook and the ingredients are not exotic.

🍷 Lamb has a natural affinity with California Cabernets, Bordeaux and Tuscan reds. For this hearty dish, a straightforward Médoc, such as 1986 Château Greysac, or a Chianti, such as 1985 Ruffino Riserva Ducale, would be an appropriate match.

4 Servings

1 pound dried egg vermicelli
4 tablespoons unsalted butter
2 tablespoons vegetable oil
1 large onion, thinly sliced
3 garlic cloves, minced
½ teaspoon turmeric
1 pound lean lamb (from the leg), cut into ¾-inch cubes
One ½-inch piece of fresh ginger, peeled and minced
2 tablespoons soy sauce
2 large tomatoes—peeled, halved and cut into chunks
1 green bell pepper, sliced into ¼-inch-wide strips
2 scallions, thinly sliced crosswise
¼ cup chopped fresh coriander (cilantro)

1. Preheat the oven to 250° and place a large ovenproof platter inside to warm. Bring a large saucepan of water to a rolling boil over high heat. Add the vermicelli and cook according to the

package directions until al dente, about 8 minutes. Drain the noodles in a colander and return them to the saucepan off the heat. Stir in 2 tablespoons of the butter and set aside.

2. Heat a large skillet or wok over moderately high heat for 4 minutes. Add the vegetable oil and heat until shimmering. Add the onion and stir-fry for 1 minute. Add the garlic and stir-fry until the onion is translucent and the garlic begins to brown, 5 to 6 minutes. Add the turmeric, lamb cubes and ginger and stir-fry until the meat begins to darken, 3 to 4 minutes.

3. Stir in the soy sauce, tomatoes and green bell pepper. Reduce the heat to moderately low and cook, stirring occasionally and scraping the bottom of the pan to prevent sticking, until the lamb is cooked through and the tomatoes are soft, 10 to 15 minutes. Remove from the heat and cover to keep warm.

4. In another large heavy skillet, melt the remaining 2 tablespoons butter over low heat. Add the reserved noodles and spread and press them with a spatula into an even layer in the pan. Fry without stirring, until the underside is crisp and brown and the noodles hold together and are warmed through, about 15 minutes.

5. Remove the platter from the oven and invert the noodle cake on top. Spoon the lamb and vegetable mixture over the noodles, sprinkle the scallions and coriander on top and serve hot.

—Jennifer Brennan

• • •

FRESH RICE NOODLES WITH CHILE SAUCE, SHRIMP AND PEANUTS

The Thai, or bird, chile peppers used to flavor the oil are quite hot.

5 Servings

2 pounds fresh flat rice noodles* (see Note)
¾ cup chicken stock or canned broth
About 2½ tablespoons Chinese soy sauce*
2½ tablespoons oyster sauce*
2 teaspoons Oriental sesame oil
1 teaspoon cornstarch
⅔ cup unsalted dry roasted peanuts (3½ ounces)
½ cup plus 1½ tablespoons peanut or vegetable oil
⅓ cup fresh red Thai, or bird, chiles* (optional)
1 large onion, halved and thinly sliced lengthwise
1 medium green bell pepper, cut into thin strips
1 medium red bell pepper, cut into thin strips
1 tablespoon minced fresh ginger
4 large garlic cloves, minced
About 2½ teaspoons Chinese chile paste with garlic*
1 teaspoon sugar
1¼ pounds medium shrimp, shelled and deveined
3 scallions, thinly sliced, for garnish
****Available at Asian markets***

1. Put the noodles in a colander and rinse them under hot running water. Unfold the noodles, gently breaking them apart into skeins. Pour on more hot water and separate as many of the noodles as you can without breaking them. Drain very well. Gently pat dry and set aside.

2. In a small bowl, combine the chicken stock, 2½ tablespoons of the soy sauce, the oyster sauce, sesame oil and cornstarch. Set aside.

3. Place a wok over moderately high heat. After about 45 seconds, add the peanuts and stir to sear lightly, about 30 seconds. Transfer the peanuts to a small bowl and set aside. Increase the heat to high and add 1 tablespoon of the peanut oil to the wok. Add the Thai chiles, if using, and stir-fry until blistered, about 45 seconds. Remove them with a slotted spoon and set aside.

4. Add 2 tablespoons of the oil to the wok, and when it is hot, add the onion and bell peppers. Stir-fry until the onion is soft and almost translucent, about 2 minutes. Transfer the onion and peppers to a large bowl and set aside.

5. Wipe out the wok. Heat 2 more tablespoons of the oil over moderate heat and add the ginger. Stir-fry until aromatic, about 30 seconds. Add the garlic and stir-fry for 20 seconds. Add 2½ teaspoons of the chile paste and stir-fry until the garlic is completely soft, about 2 minutes. Stir in the sugar. Scrape the mixture into a small bowl.

6. Heat about 1½ tablespoons of the oil in the wok over high heat and add the shrimp. Stir-fry for 1 minute, then add the reserved chile paste-garlic mixture and continue to stir-fry until the shrimp are pink and barely cooked through, about 1 minute. Transfer the shrimp to the bowl with the vegetables.

7. Wipe out the wok, add 2 more tablespoons of the oil and heat over high heat. Gently slide half of the rice noodles into the wok, taking care not to splatter the oil. Using a wooden spoon, stir-fry them briskly, folding them under and over to separate them, until softened slightly, about 30 seconds. Don't worry if they do not separate completely. Transfer to a plate.

8. Stir-fry the remaining noodles and then return the first batch of noodles to the pan. Quickly stir in the reserved stock mixture. When the sauce begins to thicken and coat the noodles, after about 30 seconds, add the reserved shrimp and vegetables. Using two large wooden spoons, toss everything together in the wok as you would a salad. Work quickly so that the noodles do not overcook. Taste and add additional soy sauce and chile paste if desired. Stir in about half of the toasted peanuts.

9. Transfer the noodles to a large platter. Sprinkle the scallions on top and pile the remaining peanuts in the center of the noodles. Arrange the fried Thai chiles around the noodles and serve immediately.

NOTE: *You can substitute 12 ounces of dried flat rice noodles. Soak them for 15 to 20 minutes, until softened, then boil for 2½ to 3 minutes, drain and rinse with cold water. Drain well and mix with 1 teaspoon of oil.*

—Linda Burum

• • •

KOREAN NOODLE STIR-FRY WITH BLACK MUSHROOMS AND BEEF

Though *chap chae* resembles chow mein, Koreans don't consider it a noodle dish but rather a vegetable or side dish.

4 to 5 Main-Course or 8 Side-Dish Servings

⅓ cup dried tree ear or wood ear mushrooms* (about ½ ounce)
8 dried Chinese black mushrooms* or medium shiitakes (about ½ ounce)
8 ounces Korean vermicelli (dang myun) or coarse bean thread noodles*
1 tablespoon sesame seeds
¼ cup plus 2 tablespoons soy sauce
5 scallions—3 minced, 2 thinly sliced
3 medium garlic cloves, minced
1 tablespoon Oriental sesame oil
2¼ teaspoons sugar
¼ teaspoon freshly ground pepper
1 pound beef top round or sirloin, sliced ⅛ inch thick and cut into 2-inch strips
¼ teaspoon salt
¼ cup plus 1 teaspoon vegetable oil
1 large carrot, cut into 1½-by-¼-inch matchsticks
1 medium onion, halved and thinly sliced lengthwise
1 medium zucchini, cut into 1½-by-¼-inch matchsticks
½ pound nappa cabbage, thinly sliced crosswise
Sesame Omelet Strips (recipe follows)
Kimchi*
****Available at Asian markets***

1. Place the tree ear and Chinese black mushrooms in separate small bowls. Add warm water to cover and weigh down to keep them submerged until soft, about 20 minutes. Set aside. Rinse the vermicelli thoroughly, drain and set aside for 30 minutes to soften.

2. Heat a small heavy skillet over moderate heat until hot. Add the sesame seeds and stir constantly until golden, about 3 minutes. Let cool slightly. Pound the sesame seeds in a mortar or place in a plastic bag and crush with a rolling pin until a coarse powder forms.

3. In a medium bowl, combine the crushed sesame seeds with 2 tablespoons of the soy sauce, the minced scallions, garlic, 1 teaspoon of the sesame oil, 1¼ teaspoons of the sugar and the pepper. Add the beef to the bowl and toss to coat with the marinade. Set aside for 20 minutes to 2 hours.

4. In a small bowl, combine the remaining 1 teaspoon sugar, ¼ cup soy sauce, 2 teaspoons sesame oil and the salt; mix well and set aside.

5. Bring a large pot of water to a boil. Meanwhile, drain the tree ear and Chinese black mushrooms. Trim off the tough stems and cut the mushrooms into ¼-inch strips.

6. Add the vermicelli to the boiling water and simmer until soft, about 50 seconds. Pour immediately into a colander and refresh with cold water. Drain well. Add the 1 teaspoon vegetable oil and mix to coat each noodle; set aside.

7. In a wok or large skillet, heat 2 tablespoons of the vegetable oil over high heat. Add the carrot and stir-fry until beginning to soften, about 25 seconds. Add the onion and stir-fry until beginning to soften, about 30 seconds. Add the zucchini and cabbage and stir-fry until wilted, about 30 seconds. Transfer to a plate.

8. Heat the remaining 2 tablespoons vegetable oil in the wok. Add the beef and mushrooms and stir-fry until the meat is browned, about 3 minutes. Stir in the reserved noodles and stir-fry until warmed through, about 30 seconds. Add the reserved soy sauce mixture and stir-fry for 1 minute. Stir in the cooked vegetables and toss until warmed through, about 30 seconds. Season with additional soy sauce. Transfer to a platter and sprinkle the sliced scallions on top. Garnish with the Sesame Omelet Strips and serve with a bowl of *kimchi*.

—Linda Burum

• • •

SESAME OMELET STRIPS

4 to 8 Servings

2 teaspoons sesame seeds
2 eggs
2 tablespoons chicken stock or canned broth
2 teaspoons peanut or vegetable oil
Scant 1/4 teaspoon sugar
Pinch of salt

1. In a small heavy skillet, toast the sesame seeds over moderate heat, stirring constantly, until golden, about 2 minutes. Let cool slightly. Then lightly crush in a mortar.

2. In a medium bowl, lightly beat the eggs with the stock, oil, sugar, salt and crushed sesame seeds.

3. Heat a lightly oiled, medium nonstick skillet over moderate heat. Pour in one-third of the egg mixture and swirl to coat the bottom of the pan with a paper-thin layer. Cook the omelet until firm but not brown, adjusting the heat as necessary, about 3 minutes. Loosen the omelet with a spatula and turn out onto a plate. Repeat with the remaining egg mixture in 2 batches. When the omelets are cool, stack and roll them into a cylinder, then slice crosswise into 1/8-inch strips.

—Linda Burum

• • •

SALADS

CHERRY TOMATO SALAD WITH FRESH HERBS

6 Generous Servings

2 pints cherry tomatoes, halved
10 scallions, very thinly sliced
¼ cup minced fresh mint
¼ cup minced fresh basil
¼ cup minced flat-leaf parsley
½ cup rice vinegar
¼ cup sunflower oil
2 tablespoons fresh orange juice
Pinch of sugar (optional)
Freshly ground pepper
12 large Bibb lettuce leaves

1. In a large bowl, toss the tomatoes, scallions, mint, basil and parsley. In a small bowl, whisk the vinegar, oil, orange juice, sugar and pepper to taste. Pour the dressing over the tomatoes and toss to coat. Set the tomatoes aside for 20 to 30 minutes.

2. Place 2 lettuce leaves on each plate and top with the tomatoes.

—*Mary Anne Dolan*

• • •

ARUGULA SALAD

8 Servings

¼ cup plus 2 tablespoons extra-virgin olive oil
2½ ounces thinly sliced double-smoked bacon or pancetta, cut crosswise in thin strips
1 medium shallot, minced
2 tablespoons balsamic vinegar
12 cups (loosely packed) arugula, torn into bite-size pieces (about 3 bunches)
Freshly ground pepper
Coarse (kosher) salt

1. In a small nonreactive skillet, heat 2 tablespoons of the oil over moderate heat. Add the bacon and cook, stirring constantly, until cooked through but not browned, 2 to 3 minutes. Remove from the heat and whisk in the shallot, vinegar and the remaining ¼ cup oil until well blended.

2. Place the arugula in a large bowl and toss with enough of the dressing to coat thoroughly and wilt the greens slightly. Season to taste with pepper and coarse salt.

—*Perla Meyers*

• • •

SALAD WITH HARD-BOILED EGG DRESSING

Old-fashioned salad dressings were made with quantities of vinegar and sugar that are unacceptable to today's tastes. This recipe is not so much an adaptation as it is a tribute to the old style.

6 to 8 Servings

2 hard-cooked eggs
1 tablespoon white wine vinegar
1 teaspoon Dijon mustard
2 tablespoons minced chives, or a mix of chives and parsley
3 tablespoons extra-virgin olive oil
3 tablespoons heavy cream
1 teaspoon sugar (optional)
Salt and freshly ground pepper
10 cups of bite-size pieces of lettuce

1. Chop the eggs very fine or sieve them into a small bowl.

2. In another bowl, whisk together the vinegar, mustard, chives, oil and cream. Add the sugar and season with salt and pepper to taste. Stir in the eggs.

3. Toss the dressing with the greens and serve.

—*Nancy Harmon Jenkins*

• • •

BITTER GREENS WITH TOASTED WALNUTS AND ROQUEFORT CHEESE

4 Servings

⅓ cup walnuts, coarsely chopped (1½ ounces)
1 tablespoon sherry wine vinegar
Pinch of salt and freshly ground pepper
1½ tablespoons olive oil
1½ tablespoons walnut oil
8 cups mixed bitter greens, cut or torn in pieces
⅓ cup crumbled Roquefort cheese (2 ounces)

1. Preheat the oven to 425°. Spread the nuts on a baking sheet and toast in the oven until fragrant, 7 to 10 minutes.

2. In a small bowl, whisk the vinegar with the salt and pepper. Then whisk in the olive oil and walnut oil. Toss the greens with the vinaigrette, walnuts and Roquefort; serve.

—*Stephanie Lyness*

• • •

ITALIAN SALAD

6 Servings

½ cup distilled white vinegar
3 small scallions, white and tender green, minced
1 large garlic clove, lightly crushed
2 tablespoons minced parsley
1 teaspoon salt
1 teaspoon sugar
¼ teaspoon freshly ground pepper
1 cup olive oil
2 medium carrots, sliced crosswise ¼ inch thick
2 cups small cauliflower florets
2 cups small broccoli florets
1 head of iceberg lettuce, shredded
18 pitted green olives
6 anchovy fillets, coarsely chopped
2 tablespoons freshly grated Parmesan cheese

1. In a medium bowl, whisk together the vinegar, scallions, garlic, parsley, salt, sugar and pepper. Gradually pour in the olive oil in a fine stream, whisking until incorporated. Set aside.

2. Bring a stockpot of salted water to a boil. Add the carrots. After 1 minute, add the cauliflower. After 3 more minutes, add the broccoli. When the broccoli has cooked for 5 minutes, drain all the vegetables and plunge them into a basin of cold water until cool. Drain very well.

3. Place all the vegetables in a medium bowl and add ½ cup of the dressing. Toss very gently. Set aside to marinate for 1 to 6 hours, stirring occasionally.

4. Toss the lettuce with the remaining dressing and place on 6 plates. Spoon the marinated vegetables, olives and anchovies on top. Sprinkle 1 teaspoon of Parmesan over each portion and serve at once.

—Diane Darrow & Tom Maresca

• • •

SPINACH AND CABBAGE SALAD WITH PECANS

4 Servings

⅓ cup pecan halves (about 1½ ounces), coarsely chopped
10 ounces spinach, torn into bite-size pieces
¼ of a small head of red cabbage, thinly sliced (3 lightly packed cups)
½ of a small red onion, thinly sliced
1½ tablespoons red wine vinegar
½ teaspoon grainy mustard
3 tablespoons extra-virgin olive oil
3 tablespoons buttermilk
Salt and freshly ground pepper

1. Preheat the oven to 400°. Spread the pecans in a baking pan and toast, stirring once, for about 8 minutes. Set aside to cool.

2. In a large bowl, toss together the spinach, red cabbage and red onion. Refrigerate until serving time.

3. In a small bowl, whisk the vinegar with the mustard. Whisk in the oil, then the buttermilk. Season to taste with salt and pepper.

4. Just before serving, toss the salad with the pecans and dressing.

—Susan Shapiro Jaslove

• • •

RUTABAGA REMOULADE

4 Servings

1½ pounds rutabaga, peeled
6 tablespoons mayonnaise
3 to 4 tablespoons Dijon mustard
2 tablespoons olive oil
2 tablespoons white wine vinegar
Salt and freshly ground pepper

1. With a large heavy knife, slice the rutabaga into ¼-inch julienne strips. In a large pot of boiling salted water, cook the rutabaga strips until crisp-tender, about 5 minutes. Drain well and let cool to room temperature. Pat dry.

2. In a bowl, whisk the mayonnaise, mustard, oil and vinegar until creamy. Season with salt and pepper to taste. Add the rutabaga and toss to coat well. Cover and chill for at least 2 hours before serving.

—Barbara Lee Hanson

• • •

HOT AND SWEET CUCUMBER SALAD

In this Southeast Asian-style salad, crisp vegetables are tossed in a light dressing with mint and coriander.

4 Servings

2 cucumbers—peeled, halved lengthwise, seeded and thinly sliced crosswise
½ of a small red onion, thinly sliced in rings
1 large red bell pepper, cut into thin julienne strips
1 carrot, cut into thin julienne strips
¼ cup rice vinegar
2 tablespoons sugar

1 tablespoon chopped fresh coriander (cilantro)
½ teaspoon crushed red pepper
Salt and freshly ground white pepper

Combine all the ingredients in a large bowl and toss well.

—Chris Schlesinger & John Willoughby

• • •

TROPICAL FRUIT COCKTAIL WITH CHILE PEPPERS

4 Servings

1 large pear—peeled, cored and cut into ½-inch chunks
1 large ripe banana, cut into ½-inch chunks
1 large ripe papaya—peeled, seeded, and cut into ½-inch chunks
2 jalapeño chiles (seeded and deribbed if desired), finely minced
¼ cup grated fresh coconut or unsweetened flaked coconut
½ cup fresh orange juice
6 tablespoons fresh lime juice
1 tablespoon sugar

Combine all the ingredients in a bowl and toss well.

—Chris Schlesinger & John Willoughby

• • •

PEAR PISTOU SALAD

In this salad, the *pistou* (the French version of *pesto*) is in effect created in each mouthful rather than mixed and blended in a bowl in advance. Each forkful should contain some of the cool, sweet pear, the nutty, salty Parmesan and the intense basil for a balanced contrast. Use the best oil and vinegar you can find for this salad.

1 Serving

5 to 6 leaves of interesting lettuce, such as curly red leaf
½ of a ripe Bartlett pear, cored and cut into 8 thin lengthwise slices
8 thin slices of a dry, pungent, well-aged, salty Parmesan cheese (½ ounce)
4 large fresh basil leaves, roughly cut
1 tablespoon extra-virgin olive oil
2 teaspoons balsamic vinegar
Freshly ground pepper
Salt (optional)
1 teaspoon toasted pine nuts, for garnish (see Note)

Arrange the lettuce leaves on a flat plate or in a soup plate and place the pear slices decoratively on top. Set a slice of cheese on each slice of pear and sprinkle the basil on top. Drizzle the olive oil over the salad, followed by the vinegar, pepper and salt, if using. Garnish with the toasted pine nuts.

NOTE: *To toast pine nuts, stir them in a dry hot skillet over moderate heat for 1 to 2 minutes.*

—Ann Haskell

• • •

BEET AND PEAR SALAD WITH ARUGULA

6 Servings

6 medium beets, roots intact
1 medium firm pear, peeled and coarsely chopped
1 teaspoon fresh lemon juice
1 tablespoon minced red onion
3 tablespoons safflower oil
3 tablespoons mild olive oil
2 tablespoons sherry vinegar
1 teaspoon dry sherry (optional)
½ teaspoon Dijon mustard
½ teaspoon salt
½ teaspoon freshly ground black pepper
¼ teaspoon hot pepper sauce
1 bunch of arugula, large stems removed

1. Preheat the oven to 400°. Line a small pan with aluminum foil. Place the beets in the pan and cover tightly with another piece of foil. Bake for about 1¼ hours or until the beets feel tender when pierced with a knife. Uncover and let cool. Peel and trim the beets. Cut into medium wedges and transfer to a large bowl.

2. In a small bowl, sprinkle the pear with the lemon juice. Add the pear and the onion to the beets.

3. In a small bowl, whisk together the safflower oil, olive oil, vinegar, sherry, mustard, salt, black pepper and hot pepper sauce. Add half of the vinaigrette to the beets and toss.

4. In a bowl, toss the arugula with the remaining vinaigrette. Arrange alongside the beet salad and serve.

—Lee Bailey

• • •

SICILIAN ORANGE SALAD

This traditional Sicilian winter salad adds brilliant color to the buffet table. If you are fortunate enough to have a fireplace, throw in some of the orange peels to perfume the house. The oranges can be peeled up to one day ahead but must be sliced shortly before serving.

20 Servings

18 navel oranges
2 large red onions, very thinly sliced crosswise
1 cup Moroccan oil-cured olives
1 tablespoon crushed red pepper
½ cup extra-virgin olive oil
Salt

1. Using a sharp knife, peel the oranges; make sure to remove all the bitter white pith. Slice the oranges crosswise about ¼ inch thick.

2. Arrange half of the orange slices on a large platter. Scatter half the onion slices, olives, red pepper and oil over the oranges and season lightly with salt. Top with the remaining ingredients and serve at room temperature.

—*Evan Kleiman*

• • •

ARUGULA AND FRIED OKRA SALAD WITH ROASTED-CORN VINAIGRETTE

This salad combines my southern passion for fried okra and corn with sophisticated arugula.
🍷 1989 Fetzer Gewürztraminer

12 Servings

4 large ears of fresh corn
1 large shallot, minced
2 garlic cloves, minced
2 tablespoons white wine vinegar
⅔ cup chicken stock or canned low-sodium broth
½ cup olive oil
½ cup corn oil, plus more for frying
Salt
2 eggs
2 tablespoons milk
24 large okra spears (about 12 ounces), cut into ⅓-inch rounds
1 cup cornmeal
2 pounds arugula, large stems removed
2 medium tomatoes—peeled, seeded and diced

1. Preheat the oven to 400°. Using a sharp knife, cut the corn kernels off the cobs. On a large heavy baking sheet, spread the kernels in an even layer. Roast in the preheated oven, stirring occasionally for about 20 minutes, until lightly browned but still moist. Set aside to cool. Reduce the oven temperature to 300°.

2. In a blender or food processor, combine the cooled corn kernels with the shallot, garlic, vinegar and chicken stock; process until the corn is pureed. With the machine on, slowly drizzle in the olive oil and ½ cup corn oil. Pour the vinaigrette into a bowl and season to taste with salt; cover and set aside.

3. In a medium cast-iron skillet, heat ¼ inch of corn oil over moderately high heat until lightly smoking. Meanwhile, in a medium bowl, beat the eggs with the milk.

4. Working in three batches, dip the okra rounds in the egg wash and then dredge in the cornmeal to coat thoroughly. Fry in the hot oil, stirring occasionally, until golden brown and crisp, about 2 minutes. Using a slotted spoon, transfer the okra to a baking sheet lined with paper towels to drain. Keep the fried okra warm in the oven while you fry the rest.

5. Place the arugula on a large serving platter. Drizzle with the corn vinaigrette and toss thoroughly. Garnish the salad with the fried okra and diced tomato and serve at once.

—*Stephan Pyles*

• • •

WARM POTATO SALAD WITH THYME

4 Servings

1½ pounds small red potatoes
Salt
2 tablespoons dry white wine
1 generous teaspoon chopped fresh thyme or ½ teaspoon dried
1 tablespoon plus 1 teaspoon red wine vinegar
2 teaspoons Dijon mustard
⅛ teaspoon freshly ground pepper
¼ cup mild olive oil
1 tablespoon chopped scallion

1. Place the potatoes in a medium saucepan and add enough water to cover by 1 inch. Salt the water and bring to a boil over moderately high heat. Reduce the heat to moderate and simmer the potatoes until tender, about 15 minutes. Drain well. While the potatoes are still hot, quarter or halve them, depending on their size. Transfer the potatoes to a serving bowl and toss gently with the wine and thyme.

2. In a small bowl, whisk the vinegar with the mustard, pepper and ¼ teaspoon salt. Gradually whisk in the oil. Pour the dressing over the potatoes and toss gently to coat. Sprinkle the scallion on top and serve warm.

—*Stephanie Lyness*

• • •

YUKON GOLD POTATO SALAD

Yukon Gold potatoes have a pleasant sweetness and a firm waxy texture. Don't substitute the Yellow Finn, which turns mushy when boiled.

8 Servings

3½ pounds small Yukon Gold potatoes or new red potatoes
Salt
½ pound lean slab bacon, cut into ¼-inch dice
1 large bunch of scallions, white and tender green, finely chopped
3 tablespoons white wine vinegar
½ teaspoon freshly ground pepper
¼ cup mild olive oil

1. In a small stockpot, combine the potatoes, a large pinch of salt and enough water to cover by 1 inch. Bring to a boil over moderately high heat, then reduce the heat to moderate and boil until the potatoes are just tender, 10 to 12 minutes. Drain and set aside to cool.

2. Meanwhile, heat a large heavy skillet over moderately high heat until very hot, about 4 minutes. Reduce the heat to moderate, add the bacon and cook, stirring often, until the fat is rendered and the bacon is crisp, about 10 minutes. Using a slotted spoon, transfer the bacon to paper towels. Set aside 2 tablespoons of the bacon fat in a small bowl.

3. Peel and quarter the potatoes. Place in a bowl, add the scallions and half of the bacon and toss.

4. Whisk the vinegar, pepper and ¾ teaspoon salt into the reserved bacon fat. Gradually whisk in the oil. Pour the dressing over the potatoes and toss. Garnish with the remaining bacon and serve.

—*Janie Hibler*

• • •

HOME-STYLE POTATO SALAD

Make this dish in advance so that the flavors can come together.

6 Servings

2½ pounds white boiling potatoes
2 large celery ribs, minced
1 medium red or green bell pepper, finely diced
1 small onion, minced
3 hard-cooked eggs, coarsely chopped
About 1 cup mayonnaise
1 teaspoon salt
½ teaspoon freshly ground pepper

1. Place the potatoes in a large saucepan with enough water to cover and bring to a boil over high heat. Reduce the heat to moderately high and cook until tender but not mushy, about 20 minutes. Drain, peel and set aside to cool.

2. In a large bowl, combine the celery, bell pepper and onion.

3. When the potatoes have cooled, cut them into ½-inch cubes and add to the vegetables. Add the eggs. Gradually stir in 1 cup of the mayonnaise. Add more if desired. The potato salad should not be too wet or too dry.

4. Add the salt and pepper and mix gently but thoroughly to incorporate. Cover and refrigerate for at least 3 hours or overnight. Serve cold.

—*Jessica B. Harris*

• • •

MALAY SALAD

5 Servings

1 teaspoon vegetable oil
Two 2-ounce cakes of pressed bean curd (tau kua) (see Note)
2 tablespoons sesame seeds
1½ teaspoons shrimp paste (belacan)*
5 tablespoons hoisin sauce*
1 tablespoon soy sauce
1 fresh cayenne or serrano chile, finely chopped
2 medium garlic cloves, finely chopped
1 teaspoon palm sugar or dark brown sugar
1 tablespoon fresh lime juice
½ of a medium pineapple—peeled, cored and cut into bite-size chunks
1 ripe guava (about 6 ounces)—peeled, seeded and cut into bite-size chunks
1 medium green mango or 1 large tart green apple—peeled, pitted or cored, cut into bite-size chunks
½ of a European seedless cucumber, cut into bite-size chunks
½ pound jicama, peeled and cut into bite-size chunks

⅓ cup raw shelled and skinned peanuts (about 2 ounces), roasted and coarsely chopped
1 medium star fruit (carambola), thinly sliced crosswise
****Available at Asian markets***

1. In a small skillet, heat the oil over moderately high heat. Add the pressed bean curd and fry until browned, about 4 minutes per side. Drain on paper towels. Cut the bean curd into bite-size cubes and set aside.

2. In a small cast-iron skillet, toast the sesame seeds over moderately high heat, stirring constantly, until they begin to brown, about 1 minute. Transfer the seeds to a small bowl and set aside.

3. Toast the shrimp paste in a dry skillet over moderately high heat for 5 minutes, flattening it against the pan to ensure that it cooks well. (It will be lighter and more powdery when cooked.) Set aside.

4. In a small saucepan, combine the hoisin sauce with 5 tablespoons of water. Bring to a boil over high heat, stirring to prevent sticking. Simmer until thickened slightly, about 5 minutes. Crumble the toasted shrimp paste into the sauce and stir well. Mix in the soy sauce, chile, garlic and sugar. Reduce the heat to low and stir for 1 minute. Remove from the heat and stir in the lime juice.

5. In a large serving bowl, combine the reserved bean curd, pineapple, guava, mango, cucumber and jicama. Pour the sauce over the fruit and vegetables and toss well. Sprinkle half of the chopped peanuts and half of the sesame seeds over the salad and garnish with the sliced star fruit. Serve immediately, with the remaining peanuts and sesame seeds passed separately.

NOTE: *To make pressed bean curd, place two 2-ounce cakes of tofu between two towels and weigh down with a cast-iron skillet for two to three hours.*

—Jeffrey Alford & Naomi Duguid

• • •

PEANUT PASTA SALAD

A little cayenne pepper can be substituted for the chili oil.

4 Servings

2 heaping cups bow-tie pasta
½ of a small head of Chinese cabbage, coarsely chopped (4 cups)
½ of a medium red bell pepper, cut into ¼-inch dice
4 large scallions, white and tender green, thinly sliced
½ cup natural peanut butter
¼ cup rice vinegar
3 tablespoons soy sauce
2 tablespoons honey
1 tablespoon Oriental sesame oil
About ¾ teaspoon chili oil*
¾ cup unsalted dry-roasted peanuts
****Available at Asian markets***

1. Cook the pasta in a medium saucepan of boiling water until al dente, about 12 minutes. Drain, then rinse with cold water and drain again. Transfer the pasta to a large bowl. Add the cabbage, red bell pepper and scallions and toss well.

2. In a medium bowl, whisk the peanut butter, vinegar, soy sauce, honey and sesame oil until smooth. Whisk in ¼ cup of water. Add the chili oil, ¼ teaspoon at a time, to taste. Set aside ¼ cup of the peanut dressing in a small bowl. Pour the rest over the salad, sprinkle the peanuts on top and toss until well coated. Transfer to a bowl and pass the reserved dressing alongside.

—Susan Shapiro Jaslove

• • •

THAI GLASS-NOODLE SALAD WITH SHRIMP

6 Servings

6 ounces bean thread noodles*
1 small head of Bibb or butter lettuce
4 Chinese sausages,* sliced ¼ inch thick
¾ cup chicken stock or canned broth
½ pound cooked and peeled tiny shrimp
Chile-Lime Basil Dressing (p. 257)
½ of a medium red onion, cut lengthwise into thin strips
1 cup bean sprouts
1 small cucumber—peeled, halved lengthwise, seeded and sliced ½ inch thick
1 tomato, cut into wedges
2 limes, cut into wedges
Fresh coriander (cilantro) sprigs
Fresh basil sprigs, preferably Asian*
****Available at Asian markets***

1. Soak the bean threads in warm water to cover until pliable, about 15 minutes. Drain and rinse. Snip into 10-inch lengths. Line a large platter with the lettuce leaves.

2. In a large skillet, fry the sausage slices over moderate heat until cooked through and slightly crisp, about 4 minutes. Drain on paper towels. Discard the grease.

3. In the same skillet, heat the chicken stock. Add the bean threads and stir just until they begin to turn translucent, about 2 minutes. Add a little water if the pan is dry. Remove the skillet from the heat and stir in the sausage, shrimp and ½ cup of the Chile-Lime Basil Dressing. Toss very well.

4. Turn the noodles out onto the prepared platter. Sprinkle the onion and bean sprouts on top. Encircle with the cucumber, tomato and limes and garnish with the coriander and basil. Pass any remaining dressing separately.

—Linda Burum

• • •

THAI CELLOPHANE NOODLE SALAD

This spicy noodle salad often comes wrapped in a banana leaf, accompanied with a little bag of fresh salad vegetables and herbs. It can be eaten either hot or at room temperature.

6 First-Course Servings

3½ ounces cellophane noodles*
1 teaspoon peanut or vegetable oil
2 garlic cloves, finely chopped
2 ounces lean pork, thinly sliced
1 teaspoon minced fresh lemon grass*
2 Thai, or bird, chiles,* or 1 to 2 serrano chiles, finely chopped
½ cup chicken stock or canned broth
8 medium shrimp, shelled and deveined
2 large shallots, thinly sliced crosswise
12 lettuce leaves
1 large tomato, thinly sliced
2 tablespoons fresh lime juice
1 tablespoon fish sauce (nam pla)*
1 teaspoon sugar
2 tablespoons fresh coriander (cilantro) leaves
****Available at Asian markets***

1. Soak the cellophane noodles in a bowl of cold water for 30 minutes. Drain well and cut into 2- to 3-inch lengths.

2. Meanwhile, in a medium saucepan, heat the oil over moderately high heat. Add the garlic and stir-fry until lightly browned, about 30 seconds.

3. Add the pork, lemon grass and chiles and stir-fry until no trace of pink remains in the pork, about 1 minute.

4. Add the stock and bring to a boil. Add the shrimp and cook until they turn pink, 2 to 3 minutes. Stir in the shallots. Add the noodles and cook until heated through and somewhat soft to the bite, 1 to 2 minutes.

5. Layer the lettuce leaves on a large plate and surround with the tomato slices. Turn the noodle mixture out on the plate.

6. In a small bowl, combine the lime juice, fish sauce and sugar. Pour evenly over the noodles. Garnish with the coriander leaves and serve.

—Jeffrey Alford & Naomi Duguid

• • •

WILD ASIAN SALAD

6 to 8 Servings

½ cup slivered, blanched almonds
1 cup wild rice
2 cups plus 2 tablespoons vegetable oil
10 wonton skins, cut into ¼-inch-wide strips
2 ounces rice vermicelli,* cut with scissors into 3-inch lengths
3½ tablespoons fresh lime juice
2 tablespoons light brown sugar
2 tablespoons fish sauce*
½ teaspoon chili sauce
1 tablespoon minced fresh ginger
¼ cup minced fresh basil
2 tablespoons minced fresh mint
1 pound spinach, stems removed, cut into ⅛-inch strips
1 cup mung bean sprouts
1 large red bell pepper—cored, seeded and cut into ⅛-inch strips
1 package (3½ ounces) enoki mushrooms (optional), trimmed and separated
****Available at Asian markets***

1. Preheat the oven to 350°. On a baking sheet, bake the almonds until lightly golden, about 5 minutes. Set aside.

2. In a medium saucepan, cover the wild rice with 4 cups of water. Bring to a boil over high heat, reduce the heat to low, cover and cook until the rice is tender, 30 to 40 minutes. Drain well, cover and refrigerate until chilled.

3. In a medium saucepan, heat 2 cups of the oil over moderately high heat until shimmering. Scatter the wonton strips over the surface of the oil and cook, stirring frequently, until light golden and crisp, about 4 minutes. Using a slotted spoon, transfer to paper towels to drain. Add a handful of the rice vermicelli and cook until the noodles puff up, about 5 seconds. Turn and cook for about 2 more seconds. Using a slotted spoon, transfer to paper towels to drain. Repeat with the remaining vermicelli, one handful at a time.

4. In a medium bowl, combine the remaining 2 tablespoons oil, the lime juice, brown sugar, fish sauce, chili sauce, ginger, basil and mint.

5. To serve, combine the almonds, wild rice, spinach, bean sprouts, red bell pepper and mushrooms in a large bowl. Toss with the dressing and gently fold in the wontons and rice sticks; serve immediately.

—Hugh Carpenter

• • •

Pear Pistou Salad (p. 144).

MAR

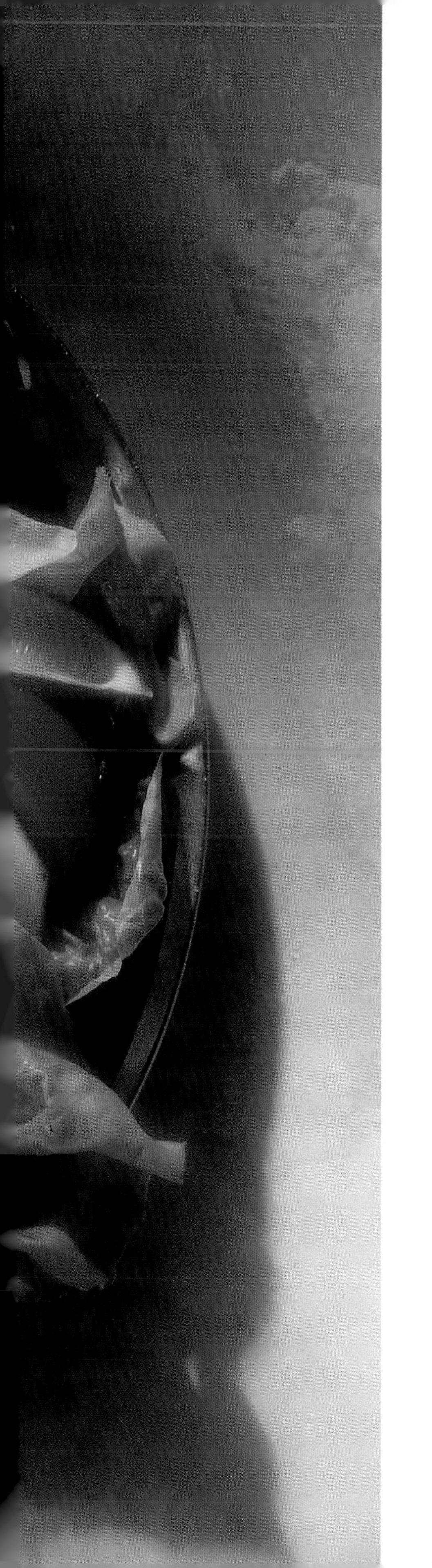

Left, Thai Glass-Noodle Salad with Shrimp (p. 147) and Chile-Lime Basil Dressing (p. 257). Above, Sicilian Orange Salad (p. 145).

SOUTHWESTERN PASTA SALAD WITH SMOKED CHICKEN AND OVEN-DRIED CHERRY TOMATOES

If you do not own a home smoker, and smoked chicken is unavailable, substitute diced grilled or roasted chicken.
🍷 1988 Beringer Vineyards Private Reserve Chardonnay

6 to 8 Servings

2 tablespoons chopped fresh coriander (cilantro)
1 tablespoon chopped fresh thyme
2 tablespoons chopped fresh basil
2 garlic cloves, minced
2 shallots, minced
1 tablespoon dry white wine
2 tablespoons white wine vinegar
1 tablespoon balsamic vinegar
½ cup plus 3 tablespoons olive oil
¼ cup corn oil
Salt and freshly ground black pepper
9 ounces pasta, such as fusilli or penne
½ cup cooked black beans
½ of a medium red bell pepper, cut into ¼-inch strips
½ of a medium yellow bell pepper, cut into ¼-inch strips
1 small carrot, coarsely chopped
5 fresh tomatillos—husked, rinsed, cored and cut into ¼-inch dice
4 ounces fresh mozzarella, cut into ⅓-inch dice
One 8-ounce boneless smoked chicken breast, cut into ⅓-inch dice
1 cup Oven-Dried Cherry Tomatoes (p. 266)

1. In a small bowl, combine the coriander, thyme and 1 tablespoon of the basil, half of the minced garlic and the shallots. Whisk in the wine, wine vinegar and balsamic vinegar. Slowly drizzle in ½ cup of the olive oil and the corn oil, whisking constantly. Season to taste with salt and black pepper; set aside.

2. Cook the pasta in a large pot of boiling salted water until al dente. Drain and place in a large serving bowl. Add the remaining 3 tablespoons olive oil and toss well; set aside to cool.

3. When the pasta is thoroughly cool, add the black beans, red and yellow bell peppers, carrot, tomatillos, mozzarella, smoked chicken, Oven-Dried Cherry Tomatoes and the remaining basil and garlic. Toss with the reserved vinaigrette and season to taste with salt and black pepper. Cover the salad and refrigerate to chill slightly, about 20 minutes. *(The salad can be made up to 3 hours ahead.)*

—*Stephan Pyles*

Cold Chicken Salad with Sweet Mustard Dressing (p. 155).

• • •

SEARED AHI SALAD WITH CILANTRO-SOY DRESSING

Ahi is the Hawaiian name for yellowfin, or bigeye, tuna. Any fresh tuna will work well in this recipe.

4 Servings

1 pound small red bliss potatoes
1 medium zucchini or summer squash
2 medium carrots, cut into thin 1½-inch-long matchsticks
One 1½-pound tuna steak, cut about 1¼ inches thick
Salt and freshly ground pepper
2 teaspoons corn or other vegetable oil
1 pound bok choy, bottom part of white stems trimmed, coarsely chopped
Cilantro-Soy Dressing (p. 256)
12 leaves of butter lettuce
12 leaves of red oak leaf lettuce
Sunflower sprouts or alfalfa sprouts and fresh coriander (cilantro) leaves, for garnish

1. In a large saucepan, combine the potatoes and enough salted water to cover. Bring to a boil over moderately high heat and cook until the potatoes are just tender, 10 to 12 minutes. Drain and set the potatoes aside to cool.

2. Slice off the skin of the zucchini in ¼-inch-thick lengthwise strips. Cut the strips into 1½-by-¼-inch batons. Discard the skinless core (or save for another use).

3. Have a bowl of ice water handy. Bring a medium saucepan of water to boil over high heat. Add the carrots and cook for 1 minute; then, using a slotted spoon, transfer to the ice water. Repeat the process with the zucchini. Remove the carrots and zucchini from the ice water, pat dry, place in a medium bowl and set aside. *(The recipe can be made to this point up to 1 day ahead. Cover and refrigerate the potatoes and the carrot and zucchini mixture separately. Return to room temperature before continuing.)*

4. Heat a large heavy skillet over high heat until very hot, about 5 minutes. Slice the tuna on the diagonal ⅓ inch thick. Season lightly with salt and pepper. Add the oil to the skillet and tilt the pan to coat. Divide the tuna slices into 3 batches. Add 1 batch and cook until the underside of the tuna is browned, about 1 minute. Turn the fish over and cook until the underside is browned and the fish is cooked to medium, 30 to 45 seconds longer. Using a spatula, transfer the fish to a plate.

Repeat with the remaining 2 batches. Set aside.

5. Quarter the cooled potatoes and add to the carrots and zucchini. Add the bok choy. Toss with 6 tablespoons of the Cilantro-Soy Dressing. Season to taste with salt and pepper. Arrange 3 leaves of butter lettuce and 3 leaves of red oak leaf lettuce on each plate. Mound the dressed vegetables on top of the lettuce in the center of each plate. Arrange 3 to 4 slices of the seared tuna around the vegetables. Garnish with the sunflower sprouts and coriander leaves. Pass the extra dressing.

—The Lodge at Koele,
Lanai City, Hawaii

• • •

SEAFOOD SALAD

4 Servings

¾ pound cleaned squid, bodies cut into ¼-inch rings, tentacles halved if large
¾ pound shelled, cooked medium shrimp
½ pound lump crabmeat, picked over
1 large red bell pepper, quartered lengthwise and cut crosswise into ¼-inch-thick strips
2 medium scallions, finely chopped
1 medium celery rib, finely chopped
2 tablespoons minced fresh basil
¼ cup fresh lemon juice
Salt and freshly ground black pepper
½ cup extra-virgin olive oil
8 leaves of radicchio

1. In a medium saucepan, bring 2 inches of water to a boil over moderately high heat. Stir in the squid, cover and cook until just tender, 2 to 3 minutes. Drain and rinse under cold running water; drain thoroughly. Transfer to a large bowl and add the shrimp, crabmeat, bell pepper, scallions, celery and basil. Toss well.

2. Whisk the lemon juice with ¼ teaspoon salt and black pepper to taste. Whisk in the oil. Pour over the salad and toss gently.

3. Place 2 radicchio leaves on each plate or line a platter with the leaves; mound the salad on top.

—Stephanie Lyness

• • •

SALAD OF GINGER-POACHED SHRIMP WITH SESAME RICE AND NORI

🍷 The flavors of sushi bar items, both raw and cooked, are great with a variety of Champagnes. A fairly substantial Champagne stands up well to the many flavors of this sushi-like dish. Serve a full-bodied Brut, like Taittinger Brut La Française, or a vintage Champagne, such as 1983 Veuve Clicquot Brut or a 1983 Bollinger Grande Année.

2 Servings

¼ cup plus ½ teaspoon Japanese rice vinegar*
3 tablespoons vegetable oil
3¼ teaspoons Japanese soy sauce
¼ teaspoon Oriental sesame oil
Salt
1 teaspoon sesame seeds
3-inch piece of fresh ginger, peeled and sliced ½ inch thick
8 large shrimp (about 8 ounces), shelled, with tails left on
3 tablespoons short-grain rice
⅛ teaspoon sugar
1 small head of Boston or Bibb lettuce
½ cup (loosely packed) watercress leaves
⅓ cup alfalfa sprouts
8 thin slices of Hass avocado
1 sheet nori (dried seaweed)*
****Available at Asian markets***

1. In a small bowl, combine 3 tablespoons of the rice vinegar with the vegetable oil, soy sauce and sesame oil; whisk vigorously until smooth and season to taste with salt.

2. In a small, heavy, dry skillet, toast the sesame seeds over moderate heat, stirring frequently, until golden brown, about 2 minutes.

3. Place 2 cups of water in a medium saucepan. Add the ginger, 1 tablespoon of the rice vinegar and ¼ teaspoon salt and bring to a boil over high heat. Reduce the heat to moderately low and simmer for 20 minutes. Remove from the heat.

4. Meanwhile, make a long deep slit down the back of the shrimp and devein them. Spread the shrimp open in butterfly fashion, keeping them attached at the tail.

5. Add the shrimp to the warm ginger broth, cover and set aside until the shrimp are just cooked, about 1 minute. Using a slotted spoon, transfer the shrimp to a small bowl and toss with 1 tablespoon of the rice vinegar dressing.

6. Remove and discard the ginger slices from the broth. Add the rice to the broth and bring to a boil over high heat. Reduce the heat to moderately high and boil, uncovered, until the rice is just cooked, about 15 minutes. Toss the rice with the sugar and the remaining ½ teaspoon rice vinegar. Add the toasted sesame seeds.

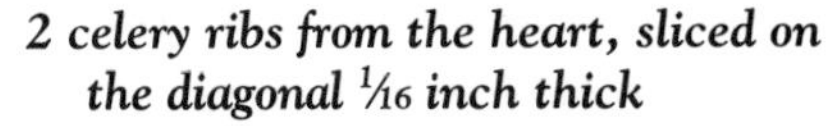

7. In a large bowl, toss the lettuce, watercress and alfalfa sprouts. Add about two-thirds of the rice vinegar dressing and toss well. Arrange the salad on 2 large plates. Place 4 slices of avocado on top of each salad in pinwheel fashion. Nestle 4 of the shrimp on each plate between avocado slices. Pat the rice lengthwise down the top of each shrimp. Drizzle the remaining dressing over the avocado slices and the shrimp.

8. Hold the sheet of nori about 3 inches from an open flame. Toast on both sides until crisp, about 30 seconds. Alternatively, broil the nori on both sides, rotating to toast evenly, until crisp, about 10 seconds per side. Cut into thin shreds and crisscross a pair of shreds on top of each shrimp.

—David Rosengarten

• • •

DUNGENESS CRAB SALAD

In this salad, the sweet substantial meat of the West Coast Dungeness crab is combined with peppery watercress and bitter endive.

8 First-Course Servings

1 pound Dungeness or lump crabmeat, picked over
1 bunch of watercress (about 4 ounces), large stems discarded
2 Belgian endives (4 ounces each), sliced crosswise ¼ inch thick
2 tablespoons minced fresh chives
2 tablespoons drained capers
2 tablespoons mild olive oil
1½ teaspoons fresh lemon juice
¼ teaspoon salt
8 large Boston lettuce leaves
8 cherry tomatoes, halved

1. In a large bowl, toss the crab, watercress, endives, chives and capers. In a small bowl, whisk the olive oil, lemon juice and salt. Pour the dressing over the salad and toss.

2. Line 8 salad plates with a lettuce leaf and top with the crab salad. Garnish each salad with 2 tomato halves and serve at once.

—Janie Hibler

• • •

COLD CHICKEN SALAD WITH SWEET MUSTARD DRESSING

All the elements can be prepared up to one day ahead and then tossed together just before serving.

4 Main-Course or
6 First-Course Servings

1 whole chicken breast, bone-in, with skin (1½ pounds), at room temperature
4 quarter-size slices of fresh ginger, lightly smashed
4 scallions, 2 cut into finger lengths and smashed, 2 thinly sliced crosswise
⅛ teaspoon Szechuan peppercorns*
½ cup sliced almonds (1½ ounces)

MUSTARD DRESSING:
½ cup rice bran oil* or corn oil
¼ cup juice from Homemade Pickled Ginger (p. 264)
3 tablespoons Dijon mustard
2 teaspoons Japanese sesame oil*
1 tablespoon sugar
¼ teaspoon fine sea salt

1 small red bell pepper, cut into thin julienne strips
1 small yellow or orange bell pepper, cut into thin julienne strips
2 celery ribs from the heart, sliced on the diagonal 1/16 inch thick
8 cups assorted small lettuces, including tender spinach leaves and radicchio, cut into ribbons
About 3 tablespoons thinly slivered Homemade Pickled Ginger (p. 264)
****Available at Asian markets***

1. In a heavy medium saucepan, combine the chicken, fresh ginger slices, smashed scallions and Szechuan peppercorns. Add enough cold water to cover and bring to a simmer over moderately high heat. Reduce the heat to moderately low and simmer gently until the chicken is cooked, about 35 minutes. Transfer the chicken to a plate and let cool.

2. Meanwhile, preheat the oven to 350°. Place the almonds in a pie tin and toast in the oven, shaking occasionally, for about 8 minutes, until fragrant and lightly browned. Set aside to cool.

3. Remove the skin, bones, cartilage and any membranes from the chicken breast and discard. Thinly slice the chicken against the grain.

4. In a small bowl, combine the dressing ingredients and whisk until emulsified.

5. In a medium bowl, toss the chicken with the bell peppers, celery and about one-third of the dressing. In a large bowl, toss the lettuces, sliced scallions, Pickled Ginger and half the toasted almonds with one-third of the dressing. Then toss the chicken and the lettuce mixture together, adding more dressing if desired. To serve, mound the salad on individual plates and garnish with the remaining toasted almonds.

—Barbara Tropp

• • •

ROASTED RABBIT AND WINTER VEGETABLE SALAD WITH MUSTARD

Ask your butcher to prepare the rabbit for you.

🍷 The mild flavor of rabbit and root vegetables, here pointed up by a mustard seed dressing, is an excellent foil for a fine red Bordeaux.

2 Servings

¼ cup plus 3 tablespoons olive oil
2½ tablespoons grainy mustard
2 tablespoons chopped fresh thyme or 1 tablespoon dried
¼ cup all-purpose flour
Salt and freshly ground pepper
One 2½-pound rabbit, sectioned into hind legs and boneless loins
4 small red potatoes
2 medium beets, peeled and quartered
2 shallots
1 small fennel bulb, trimmed and cut into 4 wedges
1 large carrot, cut into 3-inch-long matchsticks
4 large shiitake mushrooms, stems discarded
1 teaspoon yellow mustard seeds
1½ teaspoons fresh lemon juice
2 cups mixed greens, such as escarole, frisée and the inner tender leaves of green cabbage

1. Preheat the oven to 375°. In a small bowl, whisk 2 tablespoons each of the oil and grainy mustard with the thyme and set aside. Place the flour on a plate and season with salt and pepper. Dredge the rabbit legs lightly in the seasoned flour.

2. In a large ovenproof skillet, heat 1 tablespoon of the olive oil over moderately high heat. Add the rabbit legs and cook until lightly browned on both sides, about 1½ minutes per side. Remove from the skillet. Coat the rabbit legs and the loins liberally with the reserved mustard-thyme oil.

3. In a medium bowl, toss the potatoes, beets, shallots, fennel and carrot with 2 tablespoons of the olive oil. Season lightly with salt and pepper.

4. Arrange the rabbit legs and oiled vegetables in an even layer in the skillet and cook over moderate heat just until they begin to sizzle, about 30 seconds. Cover and roast in the oven for 20 minutes, until the vegetables are tender. Remove from the oven and preheat the broiler.

5. Add the rabbit loins and shiitakes to the skillet and broil on the middle shelf for 5 to 7 minutes, or until the loins are no longer pink but still juicy. Set aside to cool.

6. Meanwhile, in a small dry skillet, toast the mustard seeds over high heat, shaking the pan, until they pop and are fragrant, about 1 minute. In a small bowl, combine the toasted mustard seeds with the remaining 2 tablespoons oil and ½ tablespoon grainy mustard and the lemon juice. Whisk in 3 tablespoons of the pan juices.

7. When the rabbit is cool enough to handle, remove the meat from the legs and cut into thick strips. Slice the loins evenly into rounds.

8. Arrange the greens on large plates. Top with the roasted vegetables and the rabbit. Drizzle the mustard dressing over the salads and serve.

—John Ash & Sid Goldstein

• • •

VEGETABLES

ASPARAGUS WITH OYSTER MUSHROOMS

4 Servings

2 pounds medium asparagus, trimmed
3½ tablespoons unsalted butter
1 cup minced shallots
1¼ cups chicken stock or low-sodium broth
1 tablespoon Pernod
2½ teaspoons hazelnut oil
Salt and freshly ground pepper
8 ounces oyster mushrooms (pleurotes), halved if large
8 chives, snipped
Chervil leaves, for garnish

1. Cut the asparagus tips 3 inches long. Coarsely chop the remaining stalks.

2. In a heavy medium saucepan, melt 2 tablespoons of the butter over moderate heat. Add the shallots and cook, stirring occasionally, until softened, about 5 minutes. Reduce the heat to low and add the chicken stock and Pernod. Add the asparagus stalks and simmer until tender, about 20 minutes.

3. Puree the mixture in a food processor and strain into the saucepan. Stir in 2 teaspoons of hazelnut oil and season with salt and pepper to taste.

4. Bring a saucepan of salted water to a boil. Drop in the asparagus tips and cook until just tender, about 5 minutes. Drain and return to the pan. Add ½ tablespoon of the butter and season with pepper. Shake the pan to mix. Set aside, covered.

5. Melt the remaining 1 tablespoon butter in a large skillet over moderately high heat. Add the oyster mushrooms and sauté, tossing, until golden brown, about 2 minutes. Stir in the remaining ½ teaspoon hazelnut oil and season with salt and pepper.

6. Arrange the asparagus tips in 4 shallow bowls. Bring the asparagus puree to a boil, whisking constantly, and add a few drops of Pernod. Pour the puree over the asparagus and top with the mushrooms. Garnish with the chives and chervil.

—*David Rosengarten*

• • •

ASPARAGUS WITH LEMON VINAIGRETTE

4 Servings

1¼ to 1½ pounds asparagus, trimmed
¼ teaspoon finely grated lemon zest
1 tablespoon fresh lemon juice
3 tablespoons extra-virgin olive oil
Salt and freshly ground pepper
1 tablespoon finely chopped scallion

1. In a large pot of boiling salted water, blanch the asparagus stalks until just tender, about 4 minutes. Drain thoroughly and transfer to a serving plate.

2. In a small bowl, whisk the lemon zest and lemon juice. Gradually whisk in the oil. Season to taste with salt and pepper.

3. Spoon the vinaigrette over the asparagus and sprinkle the scallion on top. Serve warm or at room temperature.

—*Stephanie Lyness*

• • •

ASIAN LONG BEANS WITH HAZELNUTS

Long beans, or yard-long beans, are so called because their green, string bean-like pods can grow as long as three feet, though they are generally picked at half that size. You will find them at Asian markets and some produce markets. Firmer and less sweet than a common green bean, they are delicious with hazelnuts (also called filberts).

6 to 8 Servings

¼ cup hazelnuts
2 cups canned low-sodium chicken broth
1 pound Asian long beans or string beans, trimmed
2 tablespoons mild olive oil
1 tablespoon rice vinegar
¼ teaspoon salt
¼ teaspoon freshly ground pepper

1. Preheat the oven to 350°. Spread the hazelnuts on a baking sheet and toast in the oven for about 8 minutes, until fragrant. Transfer the hot nuts to a kitchen towel and rub them together vigorously to remove most of the skins. Finely chop the hazelnuts and set aside.

2. In a large saucepan, bring the chicken broth to a boil over moderate heat. Add the beans and cook until tender, about 6 minutes. Drain.

3. In a small bowl, whisk the oil and vinegar. Pour over the beans and toss. Season with the salt and pepper. *(The recipe can be made up to 1 day ahead; cover and refrigerate.)* Transfer to a serving platter, sprinkle with the reserved hazelnuts and toss.

—*Janie Hibler*

• • •

YELLOW WAX BEANS WITH SUMMER SAVORY

Summer savory is a pungent counterpoint to the slightly nutty flavor of wax beans. These beans can be served hot or lukewarm; and they are delicious cold the next day.

4 to 6 Servings

1 pound yellow wax beans, cut into 1½-inch lengths
2 tablespoons olive oil
1 large garlic clove, minced
1 tablespoon chopped fresh summer savory
½ teaspoon freshly ground pepper
¼ teaspoon salt

1. In a large pot of boiling salted water, blanch the beans for 3 minutes. Drain and refresh under cold running water; drain and set aside.

2. In a large skillet, heat the oil over moderate heat. Stir in the garlic, then add the beans. Cook, stirring frequently, until the beans are quite tender and the garlic is translucent, 12 to 15 minutes. Stir in the savory, pepper and salt.

—*MaryLee Johnson, Johnny's Selected Seeds, Albion, Maine*

• • •

FRIJOLES CHARROS

These tasty whole pinto beans, flavored with bacon, onion and chiles, are a nice change from the ubiquitous refried beans served at every Mexican restaurant.

Makes 10 Cups

1 pound dried pinto beans—rinsed, soaked overnight in water to cover and drained
2 garlic cloves, crushed
½ of a medium onion, peeled, plus 1 medium onion, chopped
1½ teaspoons salt
3 strips of bacon, diced
2 to 4 serrano chiles—halved, seeded and finely diced
1 medium tomato, diced
½ cup chopped fresh coriander (cilantro) leaves

1. Place the beans in a large pot and add fresh cold water to cover by 2 inches. Add the garlic and ½ onion and bring to a rolling boil over high heat. Reduce the heat to moderately low, cover and simmer until the beans are tender, 1 to 1½ hours. Add the salt and continue cooking until the beans are very tender, about 20 minutes longer, The beans should be covered by about ½ inch of water during cooking; replenish as necessary. Discard the onion and garlic.

2. Meanwhile, in a medium skillet, fry the bacon until crisp. Drain the bacon. Let cool and then crumble it.

3. Add the chopped onion and the chiles to the bacon grease in the skillet and cook over moderate heat until softened, about 5 minutes.

4. Add the tomato and cilantro and cook for 10 minutes. Stir the mixture into the beans and add the crumbled bacon. Serve hot.

—*Chata DuBose*

• • •

FRICASSEE OF WHITE BEANS WITH PRESERVED LEMONS

At Mondrian in New York, Tom Colicchio serves these lemon-perfumed beans with pan-seared or grilled tuna or swordfish.

4 to 6 Servings

2 cups (about 11 ounces) dried white beans, preferably Great Northern, rinsed and picked over
6 whole black peppercorns, tied in cheesecloth
1 small onion, unpeeled
½ pound double-smoked slab bacon, cut into large pieces
1 large sprig of thyme
1 large sprig of parsley, plus ¼ cup minced parsley
½ teaspoon salt
6 slices of Preserved Lemons* (p. 264)
Freshly ground pepper
Extra-virgin olive oil, for serving
****Available at Middle Eastern markets***

1. In a large bowl, cover the beans with several inches of water. Set aside to soak overnight at room temperature.

2. Preheat the oven to 325°. Drain and rinse the beans. Transfer them to a heavy, medium, flameproof casserole and add enough water to cover the beans by 2 inches. Add the peppercorns, onion, bacon, thyme sprig and parsley sprig. Bring to a boil over moderately high heat and boil for 1 minute. Cover tightly and bake for about 1¼ hours, until the beans are just tender. Do not overcook. Remove the casserole from the oven and discard the onion, herbs, bacon and peppercorns. Stir in the salt and set aside, uncovered. *(The beans can be prepared to this point up to 5 days ahead. Let cool, then refrigerate, covered, in their cooking liquid.)*

3. Carefully rinse the Preserved Lemon slices under running water to remove the salt. Drain well and set aside.

4. Drain the beans in a colander and reserve the cooking liquid. In a medium skillet, combine the beans and ½ cup of their cooking liquid. Add the preserved lemon slices and cook over moderately low heat, stirring occasionally, until the beans are warmed through. Add more of the bean liquid if necessary; the mixture should be quite moist but not soupy.

5. Season generously with salt and pepper to taste and stir in the minced parsley. Serve with the lemon slices on top and extra-virgin olive oil drizzled over the beans.

—*Perla Meyers*

• • •

BROCCOLI WITH GARLIC CHIPS

4 Servings

1 bunch of broccoli (about 1⅓ pounds)
¼ cup extra-virgin olive oil
6 medium garlic cloves, thinly sliced lengthwise
Salt and freshly ground pepper

1. Using a small sharp knife, peel off the outer woody layer of the broccoli stalks and trim 1 to 2 inches from the bottom. Cut each broccoli stalk lengthwise to make long skinny "trees," about ½ inch thick each.

2. In a large skillet, bring 1 cup of water to a boil over high heat. Add the broccoli and cook uncovered, turning the stalks once, until tender and the water evaporates, 5 to 6 minutes. Transfer the broccoli to a bowl and set aside.

3. Wipe out the skillet. Heat the oil over moderate heat until hot. Add the garlic and cook, stirring often, until just golden brown, about 3 minutes; do not burn the garlic. Using a slotted spoon, transfer the garlic to a paper towel to drain.

4. Add the broccoli to the oil in the skillet and cook over moderately high heat until heated through, browned in spots and crisp-tender, about 3 minutes. Season to taste with salt and pepper. Arrange on a serving platter with the garlic chips scattered over the top.

—*Susan Shapiro Jaslove*

• • •

FRIED CABBAGE

Many African-American dishes call for bacon fat. Substituting another fat will not yield the same flavor.

4 Servings

2 tablespoons rendered bacon fat
One 2-pound green cabbage, quartered, cored and finely shredded
1 tablespoon sugar
Salt

1. Heat a large cast-iron skillet over moderately high heat for 5 minutes. Add the bacon fat and heat until melted. Add the cabbage and sugar and season with salt. Reduce the heat to moderate and cook, stirring occasionally, until the cabbage browns lightly, about 10 minutes.

2. Stir in ¼ cup of water. Cover, reduce the heat to moderately low and cook until the cabbage is tender and the water has evaporated, about 8 minutes. Serve hot.

—*Jessica B. Harris*

• • •

RED CABBAGE WITH WINE AND APPLES

This side dish upgrades plain pork chops and buttered egg noodles to first-class, turns grilled sausages and mashed potatoes into party fare and makes a supermarket duck seem as festive as the Cratchits' Christmas goose.

8 Servings

2 medium heads of red cabbage (4 pounds)
4 tablespoons unsalted butter
1½ tablespoons dark brown sugar
2 medium onions, finely chopped
2 small Granny Smith apples—peeled, cored and coarsely chopped
¼ cup plus 2 tablespoons red wine vinegar
1 teaspoon coarse (kosher) salt
¼ cup plus 2 tablespoons dry red wine
1 to 1⅓ cups meat stock, canned beef broth or water
3 tablespoons red currant jelly

1. Quarter and core the cabbages. Wash, drain and cut into ¼-inch shreds. In a large, heavy, nonreactive flameproof casserole, melt the butter over moderately low heat. Stir in the brown sugar and cook, stirring, until melted. Add the onions and apples. Cover

tightly and cook over low heat for 5 minutes, stirring twice.

2. Add the shredded cabbage and toss to coat lightly. Pour the vinegar over the cabbage and stir to mix. Cover and cook for 10 minutes.

3. Sprinkle the salt over the cabbage and add the wine and 1 cup of the stock. Cover and simmer over moderately low heat until the cabbage is very tender, 1½ to 2 hours, adding more stock as necessary to keep the cabbage fairly moist but never soupy. Add the currant jelly and stir until melted. Remove from the heat and serve hot. *(The cabbage can be made up to 2 days ahead. Let cool completely, then cover and refrigerate. Let return to room temperature before reheating.)*

—Leslie Newman

• • •

FRESH CORN SOUFFLE

6 Generous Servings

3 large ears of corn
1½ cups milk
1 stick (4 ounces) unsalted butter
½ cup all-purpose flour
4 eggs, separated
¾ cup grated extra-sharp white Cheddar cheese (3 ounces)
½ teaspoon salt
¼ teaspoon cayenne pepper
Pinch of freshly ground white pepper
3 egg whites, at room temperature

1. Preheat the oven to 375°. Butter a 1½-quart soufflé dish and set aside.

2. Cut the kernels from the corn cobs with a sharp knife and reserve in a bowl. Working over a nonreactive saucepan, scrape down the cobs with the knife to extract any liquid. Cut the cobs crosswise in 2-inch pieces and add to the saucepan along with the milk and ½ cup of the corn kernels. Bring to a simmer. Reduce the heat to low and cook gently for 8 minutes. Remove from the heat and discard the cobs. Transfer the contents of the saucepan to a blender and blend on low speed until smooth.

3. Bring a small saucepan of salted water to a boil. Add the remaining corn kernels and cook for 3 minutes. Drain and reserve.

4. In a medium saucepan, melt the butter over moderately low heat. Whisk in the flour. Reduce the heat to low and cook, stirring frequently, for 10 minutes; do not let the roux brown.

5. Whisk in the pureed corn and milk mixture and cook over low heat until the mixture resembles mashed potatoes. Remove from the heat. With a wooden spoon, beat in the 4 egg yolks, one at a time.

6. Stir in the grated cheese, salt, cayenne, white pepper and the whole corn kernels.

7. In a large bowl, beat the 7 egg whites with an electric mixer until firm but not dry. Fold one-fourth of the whites into the corn mixture with a rubber spatula, then fold in the remaining whites just until combined.

8. Scrape the mixture into the prepared soufflé dish and bake for about 40 minutes, until puffed and golden. Serve immediately.

—Mary Anne Dolan

• • •

CREAMY CORN CUSTARDS

Chef Terrance Brennan serves these delicate custards with a black bean and corn salsa as an accompaniment to grilled or roasted pork at the New York restaurant Prix Fixe. As an appetizer, they can be served on a bed of mixed greens dressed with a lemon vinaigrette or served in a pool of homemade tomato sauce.

8 Servings

2 cups heavy cream
1 package (10 ounces) frozen corn kernels, thawed
¾ teaspoon salt
¾ teaspoon freshly ground pepper
Pinch of freshly grated nutmeg
4 eggs, lightly beaten
Boiling water

1. Preheat the oven to 325°. Butter eight ½-cup porcelain ramekins and set aside.

2. In a large saucepan, combine the cream, corn, salt, pepper and nutmeg and bring to a boil over moderate heat. Reduce the heat to moderately low and simmer until the liquid reduces by one-fourth, about 8 minutes.

3. In a blender, puree the contents of the saucepan on low speed for several seconds, then increase the speed gradually to high, blending until very smooth. Strain the puree through a very fine sieve set over a large bowl, pressing to extract as much liquid as possible; discard the corn in the sieve and reserve the strained corn cream. Thoroughly whisk the eggs into the corn cream.

4. Set the prepared ramekins in a heavy baking dish and pour in the corn custard. Carefully pour enough boiling water into the baking dish to reach halfway up the sides of the ramekins. Bake in the center of the oven for about 25 minutes, until the custards are set but still wobbly in the center. A toothpick inserted into the custard should come out slightly moist. Let cool for 5 minutes in the water bath, then remove the ramekins and let cool for 5 more minutes. Run a thin sharp knife around the edge of a ramekin and invert a serving plate over it. Holding the plate, turn the ramekin over and tap gently to release the custard. Repeat with the remaining ramekins and serve warm.

—Perla Meyers

• • •

CORN MACQUE CHOUX

This version of the traditional Cajun dish is from Billy and Tracy Fava.

8 to 10 Servings

4 tablespoons unsalted butter
1 medium onion, chopped
1 garlic clove, minced
1 medium green bell pepper, chopped
2 boxes (10 ounces each) frozen corn kernels, thawed
1 can (16 ounces) creamed corn
1 can (14 ounces) Italian peeled tomatoes, drained and chopped
½ teaspoon salt
¼ teaspoon freshly ground black pepper
Pinch of cayenne pepper
½ pound crawfish tails or shelled and deveined small shrimp (optional)

In a large nonreactive skillet, melt the butter over moderate heat. Add the onion and cook until translucent, about 3 minutes. Add the garlic and bell pepper and cook until all the vegetables are tender, 2 to 3 minutes longer. Add the corn kernels, creamed corn, tomatoes, salt, black pepper and cayenne. Bring to a simmer, cover partially and cook over low heat for 10 minutes to blend the flavors. Add the seafood, if using, and cook for 5 minutes longer.

—Billy & Tracy Fava, Mayers Famous Plate Lunches, Lafayette, Louisiana

• • •

GRILLED CORN WITH FLAVORED BUTTERS

If you don't have an outdoor grill, you can always broil the husked corn several inches from the heat; keep turning them and basting them with water.

The possibilities for other compound butter flavorings are endless. You can serve the butters on grilled vegetables and meats or on hot crusty bread.

8 Servings

8 large ears of fresh corn, unhusked
Sun-Dried Tomato Butter (p. 258) or Fresh Herb Butter (p. 258) or both, at room temperature

1. Light the grill. Soak the ears of corn in their husks in water for at least 30 minutes; drain.

2. Pull back the corn husks but do not remove them; discard all the corn silk. Spread each ear of corn with 1 tablespoon of the flavored butter of your choice; save the remaining butter for another use. Re-cover the ears with their husks and secure with string or a strip of one of the outside leaves.

3. Lay the corn on the hot grill, 3 to 6 inches above the coals and grill, turning often, until the corn kernels feel tender when pierced through the husks with a long kitchen fork, 20 to 25 minutes. Working over plates to catch the dripping butter, peel back the corn husks; the corn kernels should be hot and opaque. If not, rewrap and grill the corn for a little longer.

—Susan Costner

• • •

AN ESPECIALLY GOOD CORN PUDDING

Tender corn soufflé puddings are made without flour. The eggs and the starch from the corn are sufficient thickeners. The best dish for a corn pudding is a shallow one. Since it takes longer to bake in a deep dish, by the time the heat penetrates to the center of the pudding, it will have curdled.

6 Servings

6 to 8 large ears of fresh corn
1 cup heavy cream, at room temperature
3 large eggs, separated, at room temperature
2 tablespoons unsalted butter, melted
1 tablespoon sugar
¾ teaspoon salt
¼ teaspoon freshly ground white pepper or a pinch of cayenne

1. Preheat the oven to 350°. Butter an 8-inch-square glass baking dish.

2. Using a thin sharp knife, slice the corn kernels from each cob into a large bowl, scraping the cobs with the knife to extract any juices. Whisk the cream, egg yolks, butter, sugar, salt and pepper into the corn.

3. In a separate bowl, beat the egg whites until stiff but not dry. Fold the egg whites into the corn mixture.

4. Gently pour the batter into the prepared baking dish. Place in a larger pan of hot water and bake for about 30 minutes, or until firm and a knife inserted into the center comes out fairly clean. Serve at once.

—Camille H. Glenn

• • •

CREAMED FRESH CORN

If your corn isn't just-picked, bring out its sweetness by adding a teaspoon or so of sugar to the cream. Creamed corn is delicious with roast chicken.

4 to 6 Servings

4 to 6 large ears of fresh corn
1½ cups heavy cream
3 tablespoons unsalted butter
2 tablespoons finely chopped flat-leaf parsley
1 tablespoon finely chopped fresh sage
Salt and freshly ground pepper

1. Using a thin sharp knife, slice the corn kernels from each cob into a large measuring cup, scraping the cobs with the knife to extract any juices, until you have 3 cups.

2. In a large heavy saucepan, bring the cream to a boil over moderately high heat (it tends to foam up and boil over, so be ready to stir it down). Add the corn kernels and return to a boil, then reduce the heat to moderately low and boil gently, stirring, until the cream is thick and coats the corn, about 15 minutes.

3. Stir in the butter, parsley and sage. Season with salt and pepper to taste. *(The recipe can be made up to 3 hours ahead. Set aside at room temperature, partially covered. Rewarm over moderate heat until hot.)*

—John Phillip Carroll

• • •

BRAISED LENTILS WITH ARUGULA SALAD

Lentils are delicious hot, warm or at room temperature tossed in various vinaigrettes. They make an excellent accompaniment to pan-seared fish steaks, such as swordfish or salmon, and are just as satisfying as a side dish to a hearty stew or roast chicken. Served on top of a light salad of peppery greens, as Bradley Ogden does at The Lark Creek Inn in Larkspur, California, they become a modern and unusual side dish. This recipe can also be served on its own as an appetizer or main course (it will serve about four as a main dish).

8 Servings

10 ounces double-smoked slab bacon in one piece
2 medium carrots
2 medium celery ribs
2 medium onions
½ pound (1¼ cups) French green lentils (lentilles du Puy),* picked over
2 tablespoons extra-virgin olive oil
1 large garlic clove, minced
½ teaspoon freshly ground pepper
¼ teaspoon coarse (kosher) salt
1 tablespoon balsamic vinegar or more to taste
⅓ to ½ cup crème fraîche
Arugula Salad (p. 142)
****Available at specialty and health food stores***

1. Cut half of the bacon into ½-inch pieces and place in a large saucepan. Cut one of the carrots and one celery rib into ½-inch lengths and add to the bacon. Peel and quarter one of the onions and add to the bacon and vegetables along with the lentils. Add enough water to cover and bring to a boil over moderately high heat. Reduce the heat to moderately low and simmer, skimming occasionally, until the lentils are tender, 30 to 35 minutes. Strain the mixture through a sieve set over a medium bowl. Reserve the lentils and their cooking liquid; pick out and discard the bacon and vegetables.

2. Cut the remaining bacon into ⅓-inch dice. In a large heavy skillet, heat the olive oil over moderately high heat. Add the diced bacon and cook, stirring occasionally, until almost crisp, about 5 minutes. Transfer to paper towels with a slotted spoon; set aside.

3. Finely chop the remaining onion and add it to the skillet along with the garlic. Reduce the heat to moderately low and cook, stirring occasionally, until the onion is soft but not browned, about 4 minutes. Cut the remaining carrot and celery into ¼-inch dice and add to the pan along with the reserved crisp bacon. Stir in 2 to 3 tablespoons of the reserved lentil broth. Cover and simmer until the onion, carrot and celery are very tender, 8 to 10 minutes. Stir in the cooked lentils, the pepper and coarse salt and cook, stirring occasionally, until heated through, 8 to 10 minutes. *(The lentils can be prepared to this point up to 1 day ahead. Let cool, cover and refrigerate. Let the lentils return to room temperature before proceeding.)*

4. Add the vinegar and ⅓ cup of the crème fraîche to the lentils and cook, stirring, until heated through, 2 to 3 minutes. Add more crème fraîche if desired; season with salt and pepper to taste and serve hot, either alongside or on top of the Arugula Salad.

—*Perla Meyers*

• • •

WILD MUSHROOM AND GOAT CHEESE GRATIN

4 Servings

2 tablespoons unsalted butter, plus 1 tablespoon, melted
½ cup minced shallots (about 4 large)
2 teaspoons minced garlic (about 2 large cloves)
1 pound small, delicate chanterelles or oyster mushrooms
¼ cup minced chervil or a combination of parsley and tarragon
Salt and freshly ground pepper
½ cup fresh bread crumbs
Freshly grated nutmeg
3 tablespoons crumbled dry, aged goat cheese

1. Preheat the broiler. In a large heavy skillet, melt the 2 tablespoons butter over low heat. Add the shallots and garlic and cook, stirring, until the shallots brown slightly, 6 to 7 minutes. Stir in the mushrooms, cover and cook until tender, 5 to 7 minutes. Remove from the heat, stir in the chervil and season with salt and pepper. Set aside.

2. In a small bowl, toss the bread crumbs with the 1 tablespoon melted butter and season with ⅛ teaspoon each of salt and pepper; grate in a pinch of nutmeg and toss to combine.

3. Spoon the mushrooms into 4 individual shallow gratin dishes and place on a baking sheet. Sprinkle the crumbled goat cheese evenly over the mushrooms and top with the buttered crumbs.

4. Broil for 1 to 2 minutes, rotating the pan, until the gratins bubble and the tops are golden brown. Serve hot.

—*David Rosengarten*

• • •

STIR-FRIED WILD MUSHROOMS WITH BACON, GARLIC AND CILANTRO

This can be served as an appetizer or as a side dish.

4 Servings

2 teaspoons peanut oil
5 slices of bacon (5 ounces), cut into 1-inch squares
2 teaspoons coarsely chopped garlic
4 ounces medium shiitake mushrooms, stemmed and quartered
4 ounces Chinese black mushrooms, stemmed and cut into ½-inch dice
4 ounces golden chanterelle mushrooms, stemmed and quartered
4 ounces enoki mushrooms
2 tablespoons minced fresh coriander (cilantro)
½ teaspoon salt
¼ teaspoon freshly ground pepper

1. In a wok, heat the peanut oil over moderately high heat until it starts to smoke. Add the bacon and cook, stirring occasionally, until light brown, 6 to 7 minutes. Using a slotted spoon, transfer the bacon to paper towels to drain.

2. Pour off all but 3 tablespoons of the fat. Add the garlic and stir-fry for 20 seconds; do not let the garlic burn. Add the shiitakes and black mushrooms and stir-fry for 2 minutes. Stir in the chanterelles and then the enokis and stir-fry until all the mushrooms are tender and softened, about 2 minutes longer.

3. Just before serving, stir in the coriander, salt, pepper and bacon.

—*Jean-Marie Josselin, A Pacific Cafe, Kapaa, Kauai, Hawaii*

• • •

GRILLED GREEN ONIONS

In Mexico, green onions are frequently prepared on outdoor grills. The slightly smoky, slightly charred result is a prime example of a good ingredient simply prepared.

4 Servings

2 pounds golf-ball-size green onions, split lengthwise
¼ cup olive oil
Salt and freshly ground pepper

Light a medium fire or preheat the broiler. Rub the onions with the oil and season with salt and pepper. Grill or broil the onions as far from the heat as possible, turning occasionally, until the bulbs are tender and golden and the greens are slightly crisp, about 15 minutes. Serve hot.

—*Chris Schlesinger & John Willoughby*

• • •

A MESS OF PEAS

Salmon and fresh peas are traditional Independence Day fare north of Boston. The peas are simply cooked to bring out their natural flavor.

6 to 8 Servings

1 tablespoon unsalted butter
1 tablespoon vegetable oil
1 cup finely chopped onions
4 cups freshly shelled peas (about 4 pounds in the pod)
3 tablespoons light cream
Salt and freshly ground pepper

1. In a large saucepan, melt the butter in the oil over moderately low heat. Add the onions and cook, stirring occasionally, until soft and golden, about 15 minutes.

2. Add the peas and pour in just enough water to reach the top of the peas. Bring to a gentle simmer, cover and cook for about 15 minutes; the peas should be very tender and most of the water should have been absorbed or boiled away.

3. Add the cream and cook until the liquid in the pan thickens into an unctuous sauce, about 5 minutes longer. Season with salt and pepper to taste and serve hot.

—Nancy Harmon Jenkins

• • •

POTATO AND CORN PANCAKES

These delicious potato pancakes were created 50 years ago by La Mère Blanc, grandmother of the famous three-star French chef Georges Blanc, and have since been adapted by many chefs on both sides of the Atlantic. Georges Paineau, of the two-star restaurant Bretagne in Brittany, serves them in a light crème fraîche sauce enhanced with a pinch of allspice, but they are delicious by themselves as a topping to a mixed salad or as a side dish for both seafood and meat dishes.

8 Servings

1¼ pounds baking potatoes, peeled and cut into ½-inch pieces
Salt
3 tablespoons flour
⅓ cup crème fraîche
3 whole eggs
4 egg whites, lightly beaten
1 cup frozen corn kernels, thawed
½ teaspoon freshly ground pepper
Corn oil, for frying

1. Place the potatoes in a medium saucepan and add enough water to cover the potatoes by 1 inch; salt the water generously. Bring to a boil over moderately high heat and boil until the potatoes are very tender, 15 to 20 minutes. Drain thoroughly. Puree the potatoes in a food mill fitted with a medium disk and set over a large bowl.

2. Add the flour, crème fraîche, whole eggs, egg whites and corn kernels to the potatoes, stirring until thoroughly incorporated. Season with ½ teaspoon salt and the pepper; set aside at room temperature for 30 minutes.

3. In a 10-inch nonstick skillet, heat 2 teaspoons of corn oil over moderate heat. For each pancake, ladle 2 tablespoons of the batter into the skillet, spacing the pancakes 1½ inches apart. Cook the pancakes until golden brown on both sides, about 2 minutes per side.

4. Using a spatula, transfer the pancakes to a rack set over a baking sheet and place in a low oven to keep warm. Repeat with the remaining batter, adding more oil as necessary. Serve warm.

—Perla Meyers

• • •

MARJORIE MOSSER'S POTATO PANCAKES

Marjorie Mosser was the niece and secretary of the great Maine novelist Kenneth Roberts. Her cookbook, called with becoming modesty, *Good Maine Food,* was compiled from family recipes and those Roberts had collected in his travels. This is an adaptation of their recipe for potato pancakes.

6 Servings

4 medium baking potatoes
1 medium onion
2 eggs, well beaten
1 teaspoon salt
½ teaspoon freshly ground pepper
Dash of freshly grated nutmeg
3 tablespoons bacon fat, lard or vegetable oil, or more if necessary

1. Peel the potatoes, rinse well and pat dry. Grate the potatoes on the large holes of a box grater. Roll the potatoes up in a towel and squeeze to extract as much liquid as possible. Transfer the potatoes to a bowl. Grate the onion onto paper towels and pat dry. Add to the potatoes.

2. Add the eggs, salt, pepper and nutmeg to the bowl and blend thoroughly so that all the potato bits are well covered with egg.

3. In a large heavy skillet, heat 1 tablespoon of the fat over moderately high heat. Just before it starts to smoke, drop in mounded tablespoons of the potatoes, spreading them to about 2½ inches. Fry, turning once, until browned and crisp, about 3 minutes per side. Keep warm on a rack-lined baking sheet in a low oven while you fry the rest in the remaining fat. Serve hot.

—Nancy Harmon Jenkins

• • •

BOILED POTATOES WITH SHALLOT-GARLIC BUTTER

6 Servings

2 pounds waxy potatoes, cut into 1-inch cubes
1½ teaspoons salt
3 tablespoons unsalted butter
2 medium shallots, finely chopped
1 medium garlic clove, minced
⅓ cup minced fresh chives
¼ teaspoon freshly ground pepper

1. In a medium saucepan, combine the potatoes and 1 teaspoon of the salt. Add enough water to cover by about 2 inches. Bring to a boil over moderately high heat and cook until just tender, about 12 minutes. Drain in a colander.

2. Add the butter to the saucepan and melt over moderately low heat. Add the shallots and garlic and cook, stirring occasionally, until well softened but not browned, 4 to 5 minutes.

3. Increase the heat to moderate, add the potatoes and toss to coat with the butter. Add the chives, pepper and the remaining ½ teaspoon salt and cook, stirring, until heated through, about 5 minutes. Serve at once.

—Lee Bailey

• • •

POTATO GRATIN

4 Servings

4 baking potatoes, peeled
1 garlic clove, minced
1 teaspoon salt
½ teaspoon freshly ground pepper
1½ cups chicken stock or canned low-sodium broth
½ cup heavy cream
1 tablespoon unsalted butter, softened

1. Preheat the oven to 375°. Grease a nonreactive 9-by-13-by-2-inch baking dish. In a food processor fitted with a medium slicing disk or using a large knife, slice the potatoes crosswise about ⅛ inch thick.

2. Arrange half of the potato slices, overlapping, in the bottom of the prepared dish. Sprinkle the garlic, ½ teaspoon of the salt and ¼ teaspoon of the pepper on top. Cover with the remaining potatoes, salt and pepper. Pour in the stock and cream and dot with the butter.

3. Bake the gratin for 45 to 50 minutes, until the potatoes are tender and the top is brown. Let cool for 10 to 15 minutes before serving.

—Stephanie Lyness

• • •

FRIED GREEN PLANTAINS

4 Servings

2 cups vegetable oil
2 green plantains (1 pound), peeled and sliced into 1-inch rounds
Salt and freshly ground pepper

1. In a medium saucepan, heat the oil until hot but not smoking, about 375°. Fry the plantain rounds in the hot oil, 4 at a time, until well browned, 2 to 3 minutes. Drain on paper towels. Keep the oil hot.

2. Using a rolling pin, squash the fried plantains flat. They should have a more or less round shape.

3. Refry the flattened plantains, 4 at a time, until golden brown all over, about 2 minutes. Drain well on paper towels. Season with salt and pepper and serve hot or at room temperature.

—Chris Schlesinger & John Willoughby

• • •

SCOTS-IRISH COLCANNON

4 Servings

1¼ pounds rutabaga, peeled and cubed
1½ pounds all-purpose potatoes, peeled and cubed
1 stick (4 ounces) unsalted butter
2 medium onions, coarsely chopped
6 ounces Canadian bacon, cut into ¼-inch strips
3 tablespoons heavy cream
Salt and freshly ground pepper

1. Bring a large pot of salted water to a boil. Add the rutabaga and potatoes and cook until quite tender, about 25 minutes. Drain well.

2. Meanwhile, melt 2 tablespoons of the butter in a medium skillet. Add the onions and cook over moderate heat, stirring, until golden.

3. In a large cast-iron skillet, fry the Canadian bacon strips, stirring, until beginning to brown.

4. Preheat the broiler. In a large bowl, mash the hot rutabaga and potatoes with 4 tablespoons of the butter and the cream until smooth. Stir in the onions and season with salt and pepper.

5. Spread the vegetable mixture over the bacon in the skillet. Dot with the remaining 2 tablespoons butter, broil until browned and serve hot.

—Barbara Lee Hanson

• • •

RUTABAGA PUREE WITH CRISPY SHALLOTS

This assertive, versatile puree of rutabaga is a favorite at the Union Square Cafe in New York, where the chef Michael Romano sometimes makes the puree with white turnips. Either way it goes well with hearty main courses, such as braised Cornish hens, roast turkey, a ragout of veal or roast pork tenderloin.

6 Servings

5 tablespoons unsalted butter
2 tablespoons peanut oil
6 large shallots, thinly sliced
2 medium or 1 large rutabaga (about 3 pounds), peeled and cut into 1-inch pieces
Salt
1 medium all-purpose or baking potato, peeled and cut into 1-inch pieces
3 tablespoons sour cream
Freshly ground white pepper

1. In a heavy 8-inch skillet, melt 2 tablespoons of the butter in the oil over moderately high heat. Add the shallots and fry, stirring, until nicely browned and crisp-tender, about 6 minutes. Transfer the shallots to paper towels with a slotted spoon and set aside.

2. Place the rutabaga in a large saucepan and add enough water to cover by 1½ inches. Add a pinch of salt and bring to a boil over high heat. Reduce the heat to moderate and boil gently until tender, 35 to 40 minutes. Drain and return to the saucepan. Cook over very low heat, stirring occasionally, for 8 to 10 minutes to dry out the rutabaga.

3. Meanwhile, preheat the oven to 350°. Place the potato in a small saucepan and add water to cover and a pinch of salt. Bring to a boil over high heat, reduce the heat to moderate and boil gently until tender, about 15 minutes. Drain well.

4. Puree the cooked rutabaga and potato in a food mill fitted with a medium disk set over a bowl. Beat the remaining 3 tablespoons butter and the sour cream into the puree. Fold in half of the crisp shallots and season generously with salt and white pepper. Transfer to an ovenproof serving platter or bowl and sprinkle the remaining crisp shallots on top. *(The puree can be prepared to this point several hours in advance. Cover and set aside at room temperature.)* Bake uncovered for about 20 minutes, or until heated through.

—Perla Meyers

• • •

NUTMEG-GLAZED RUTABAGA

4 to 6 Servings

3 tablespoons unsalted butter
2 pounds rutabaga, peeled and cut into ½-inch cubes
2 cups chicken stock or canned broth
3 tablespoons sugar
Freshly grated nutmeg

1. In a large skillet, melt the butter. Add the rutabaga, stock, sugar and three gratings of nutmeg and bring to a boil over high heat. Reduce the heat, cover and simmer until the rutabaga is tender, about 25 minutes.

2. Uncover and boil until the liquid reduces to a syrup and coats the rutabaga, about 15 minutes. Dust with nutmeg before serving.

—Barbara Lee Hanson

• • •

GRATIN OF ROOT VEGETABLES

Jimmy Schmidt serves this gratin at The Rattlesnake Club in Detroit with fowl, pheasant, roast duck and turkey—even with rack of venison. For a variation, sprinkle with a mixture of mild blue cheese and coarsely grated Parmesan and run it under the broiler until nicely browned and bubbly.

You can also make the gratin in individual five-inch gratin dishes to serve as an appetizer or even as a simple supper dish.

8 Servings

1½ cups heavy cream
1¾ teaspoons salt

1¼ teaspoons freshly ground white pepper
¼ teaspoon freshly ground nutmeg
1 large baking potato (½ pound), peeled and sliced crosswise ⅛ inch thick
1 large parsnip, peeled and sliced crosswise ⅛ inch thick
1 large sweet potato (½ pound), peeled and sliced crosswise ⅛ inch thick
½ cup snipped fresh chives
½ cup freshly grated Parmesan cheese
1 medium celery root, peeled and sliced crosswise ⅛ inch thick

1. Preheat the oven to 350°. Butter an 8-by-8-by-2-inch baking dish and set aside.

2. In a small bowl, whisk together the cream, salt, pepper and nutmeg. Layer half of the baking potato slices in the prepared baking dish, overlapping them slightly. Drizzle enough of the cream over the potato to just cover. Layer the parsnip slices over the potato, then top with the sweet potato. Sprinkle the chives and half of the grated Parmesan over the sweet potato. Top with the celery root and then the remaining baking potato. Pour the remaining cream evenly over the potato and top with the remaining Parmesan; cover the pan with aluminum foil.

3. Bake on the lowest rack of the oven for 30 minutes. Remove the foil and continue baking for about 30 minutes more, until bubbly and browned on top. Transfer the baking dish to a rack to cool for about 10 minutes. Serve warm. *(The gratin can be prepared several hours ahead. Reheat in a 300° oven.)*

—Perla Meyers

• • •

SAUTEED SPINACH WITH SHIITAKE MUSHROOMS AND TOASTED SESAME SEEDS

4 Servings

½ teaspoon sesame seeds
½ tablespoon unsalted butter
1 tablespoon olive oil
4 ounces shiitake mushrooms, stems discarded and caps thinly sliced
¼ teaspoon salt
2 large bunches of spinach (1½ to 2 pounds), stems trimmed, leaves washed but not dried
Freshly ground pepper

1. In a skillet, toast the sesame seeds over moderate heat, stirring, until fragrant, about 5 minutes.

2. In a large skillet, melt the butter in the oil over moderately high heat. Add the mushrooms, season with the salt and cook until softened, about 5 minutes. Transfer to a plate.

3. Wipe out the skillet. Add the spinach with the water clinging to it, season with salt and pepper and cook, stirring, until all the water has evaporated, about 7 minutes. Stir in the mushrooms. Transfer the spinach to a dish and sprinkle the toasted sesame seeds on top.

—Stephanie Lyness

• • •

ANNE OGLETREE NOBLE'S FRIED GREEN TOMATOES

The greatest gift a friend can bring to your weekend table is a piece of his own family history. This tomato recipe came to us from the Noble family of Tallassee, Alabama.

Salting the sliced tomatoes draws out moisture and helps the cornmeal adhere.

6 Generous Servings

3 large green tomatoes (2¼ pounds), sliced crosswise ⅓ inch thick
1 teaspoon salt
1 cup yellow cornmeal
¼ teaspoon cayenne pepper
¼ cup vegetable shortening or vegetable oil

1. Arrange the tomato slices on paper towels and sprinkle with the salt. Set aside for about 30 minutes to draw out the moisture.

2. Dredge the tomato slices in the cornmeal and sprinkle with the cayenne. Set aside in a single layer.

3. In a large heavy skillet, melt 2 tablespoons of the shortening over moderately high heat. When the fat is hot, add a single layer of tomatoes and fry, turning once, until golden, about 3 minutes per side. Transfer the tomatoes to paper towels to drain. Wipe out the skillet if necessary and repeat with the remaining shortening and tomatoes. Serve immediately.

—Mary Anne Dolan

• • •

Ragout of Fall Vegetables (p. 183).

Fricassee of White Beans with Preserved Lemons (p. 159).

Gratin of Root Vegetables (p. 167).

CHERRY TOMATOES WITH CRUNCHY GREMOLADA

These tomatoes are an ideal accompaniment for grilled fish or roast chicken and are also splendid with old-fashioned macaroni and cheese.

4 to 6 Servings

1 tablespoon olive oil
2 teaspoons finely grated lemon zest
½ cup medium-fine dry bread crumbs made from a baguette
2 pounds cherry tomatoes, preferably Sweet Chelsea, rinsed and thoroughly dried
1 large garlic clove, minced
3 tablespoons minced flat-leaf parsley
½ teaspoon salt

1. Preheat the oven to 475°. In a small heavy skillet, heat 1 teaspoon of the oil over moderate heat. When it shimmers, add the lemon zest and cook, stirring, until the zest begins to color. Add the bread crumbs and sauté until golden brown. Remove from the heat and set aside to cool.

2. Put the remaining 2 teaspoons oil in a shallow pan or gratin dish just large enough to hold the tomatoes in one layer. Add the tomatoes to the pan and roll them around in the oil until evenly coated. Bake the tomatoes, shaking the pan once or twice, for about 10 minutes, or just until the tomatoes are heated through and their skins have begun to split.

3. Meanwhile, toss the bread crumb mixture with the garlic, parsley and salt. Sprinkle the topping over the hot tomatoes and serve at once.

—*Leslie Land*

• • •

SUMMER RATATOUILLE

Ratatouille, or *bohémienne* as it's referred to in Provence, comes in as many varieties as there are cooks. This one requires less heat than the long-baked versions. Use leftover ratatouille as an omelet filling or serve over pasta.

🍷 Dishes as rich and intense as this call for an assertive red with enough tannic texture to cut across the flavors. Think Côtes du Rhône, such as 1988 Guigal; Australian Shiraz, such as 1986 Taltarni; California Syrah, such as 1989 Joseph Phelps Vin du Mistral, and similar beefy bottlings.

4 Servings

About 6 tablespoons olive oil
1 medium onion, chopped
2 garlic cloves, minced
1 green bell pepper, sliced lengthwise ¼ inch thick
1 yellow bell pepper, sliced lengthwise ¼ inch thick
½ red bell pepper, sliced lengthwise ¼ inch thick
1 medium eggplant, sliced ¼ inch thick
1 cup thinly sliced mushrooms
Salt and freshly ground black pepper
⅓ cup (lightly packed) fresh basil leaves, chopped
3 large tomatoes, halved lengthwise and sliced crosswise ⅓ inch thick
⅔ cup coarsely grated hard Italian cheese, such as Romano, Pecorino or Parmesan

1. Preheat the oven to 400°. In a large, heavy, nonreactive skillet, heat 3 tablespoons of the oil over moderately high heat. Add the onion, garlic, bell peppers, eggplant and mushrooms and sauté, tossing and adding more oil as necessary, until the vegetables soften, about 15 minutes. Season with salt and black pepper and add the basil. Stir in the tomatoes and cook for 1 minute longer.

2. Transfer the vegetables to a 14-inch oval gratin dish and sprinkle the cheese on top. Cover with foil and bake for about 30 minutes, until the vegetables are very tender. Serve hot, warm or cold. *(The ratatouille can be made up to 3 days ahead and refrigerated, covered.)*

—*Ann Haskell*

• • •

SIMPLE STUFFED TOMATOES

Fresh thyme, oregano or basil can be substituted for the chives, and the recipe can easily be doubled or tripled.

4 Servings

4 firm-ripe tomatoes (5 to 6 ounces each)
Salt
2 slices firm-textured white bread, crusts removed, bread cut into ⅓-inch cubes
1 tablespoon cold unsalted butter, cut into bits
¼ teaspoon freshly ground pepper
2 teaspoons minced fresh chives
2 teaspoons freshly grated Parmesan cheese

1. Preheat the oven to 400°. Remove the top fourth of each tomato and discard. Using a small sharp paring knife, cut around the core of each tomato at a

Home-Style Potato Salad (p. 146).

45-degree angle, leaving a large cone-shaped hole in the top. Place the tomatoes on a small baking sheet, cored side up, and sprinkle lightly with salt.

2. In a medium bowl, toss the bread cubes with the butter bits, pepper and chives. Lightly pack the bread mixture into the tomatoes, mounding it as high as possible.

3. Sprinkle each tomato with ½ teaspoon of the Parmesan cheese and bake for 16 to 18 minutes, until the stuffing is browned and the tomatoes are heated through and beginning to wrinkle. Serve hot.

—Tracey Seaman

• • •

HOT AND SOUR HUNAN VEGETABLES

Ladled over a big bowl of rice or noodles laced with Chili-Lemon Oil or Chili-Orange Oil, this becomes an exceptional one-dish vegetarian meal. The vegetable variations are endless; simply use what's freshest and most colorful. This dish is also good cold.

2 to 3 Main-Course Servings

1 pound baby or young slender zucchini and/or yellow summer squash, halved lengthwise if tiny or sliced crosswise ¼ inch thick
Ice water
¾ pound cauliflower florets, cut into walnut-size nuggets (2 cups)
½ pound carrots, cut into diagonal rounds ⅛ inch thick (2 cups)

AROMATICS:
2½ tablespoons Chinese fermented black beans* (do not rinse them), coarsely chopped
1½ tablespoons finely minced fresh ginger
1½ tablespoons finely minced garlic
1 teaspoon dried red chili flakes* or seasonings drained from Chili-Lemon Oil or Chili-Orange Oil ***(p. 263)***

SAUCE:
¾ cup vegetable or light chicken stock
2½ tablespoons distilled white vinegar
2 tablespoons mushroom soy sauce*
Scant ½ teaspoon sugar

2 to 3 tablespoons corn or peanut oil
6 ounces wild and/or domestic mushrooms, halved or quartered if large
1 tablespoon cornstarch dissolved in 1½ tablespoons cold stock or water
Cooked rice or noodles, for serving
****Available at Asian markets***

1. In a large pot of boiling water, blanch the zucchini until crisp-tender, then promptly plunge into ice water to chill. Drain well. Repeat with the cauliflower and then the carrots. Set aside.

2. In a small bowl, combine the aromatics. In another bowl, combine the sauce ingredients.

3. About 10 minutes before serving, heat a wok or a large heavy skillet over high heat until hot enough to sizzle a bead of water on contact. Add 2 tablespoons of the corn oil and swirl to coat the wok. Reduce the heat to moderately high, add the aromatics and stir-fry until fully fragrant, about 1 minute. Adjust the heat if necessary to prevent scorching. Add the mushrooms and stir-fry until they start to sing, about 1½ minutes; if needed, drizzle a bit more corn oil down the side of the pan to prevent sticking. Add the blanched zucchini, cauliflower and carrots and stir-fry until heated through, about 3 minutes longer.

4. Give the sauce a stir, add it to the pan and increase the heat to high. Bring to a simmer, stirring. Stir the cornstarch mixture, then add it to the wok and stir until the sauce turns glossy, 30 seconds to 1 minute. Serve over rice or noodles.

—Barbara Tropp

• • •

LOW-CALORIE DISHES

SMOKED SALMON DIP WITH CRUDITES

This appetizing dip will keep for a couple of days in the refrigerator.

8 Servings
74 Calories per Serving

5 ounces smoked salmon
⅔ cup low-fat cottage cheese
¼ cup plain nonfat yogurt
2 tablespoons fresh lemon juice
1 teaspoon Dijon mustard
Freshly ground pepper
½ pound snow peas or sugar snap peas
One ½-pound fennel bulb—trimmed, cored and sliced lengthwise in sticks
½ bunch of celery, cut into sticks

1. In a food processor, pulse the smoked salmon until coarsely chopped. Add the cottage cheese, yogurt, lemon juice and mustard and puree until smooth, scraping down the sides occasionally. Season to taste with pepper. Transfer the dip to a serving bowl, cover and refrigerate for at least 1 hour or up to 2 days.

2. In a medium saucepan of boiling water, blanch the snow peas for 1 minute; drain and refresh with cold water. Arrange the snow peas, fennel sticks and celery sticks on a platter. Stir the dip and serve with the vegetables.

—*Martha Rose Shulman*

• • •

TOFU HUMMUS DIP

The dip and vegetables can also be used as a pita sandwich filling.

12 Servings (4½ Cups)
338 Calories per Serving

1 can (19 ounces) chickpeas, rinsed and drained
¼ cup plus 2 tablespoons tahini*
4 garlic cloves, coarsely chopped
1 pound regular tofu, drained
½ cup fresh lemon juice
1¼ teaspoons salt
½ teaspoon freshly ground pepper
¼ cup plus 2 tablespoons unhulled sesame seeds**
1 tablespoon cumin
2 large scallions, minced, plus 2 tablespoons sliced scallion greens, for garnish
Twelve 6-inch pita pockets (24 ounces), cut into eighths
1½ pounds broccoli, cut into 1½-by-½-inch spears
1 pound carrots, cut into 2-by-⅓-inch sticks
****Available at supermarkets***
*****Available at health food stores or Asian markets***

1. Preheat the oven to 375°. In a food processor, combine the chickpeas, tahini and garlic and puree, scraping occasionally, until smooth and thick. Add the tofu, lemon juice, salt and pepper and process until creamy.

2. In a heavy medium skillet, cook the sesame seeds over moderate heat until they begin to pop, about 3 minutes; cook, stirring, until lightly toasted and fragrant, about 3 minutes longer. Add three-fourths of the hot seeds to the food processor and pulse briefly to incorporate. Set the remaining seeds aside.

3. Add the cumin to the skillet and cook over moderate heat, stirring, until fragrant, about 1 minute. Add to the food processor along with the minced scallions and pulse briefly to combine. Season to taste with salt and pepper.

4. Transfer the dip to a large platter, stirring to evenly combine the ingredients. Sprinkle the reserved toasted sesame seeds and the sliced scallion greens on top.

5. Spread the pita triangles on 2 large baking sheets and bake, turning once, for about 10 minutes until lightly toasted. Serve the pita, broccoli spears and carrot sticks alongside the hummus.

—*Diana Sturgis*

• • •

TRENDY TRAIL MIX

Every ingredient here is a source of calcium. Munch the trail mix for a lunch snack or serve it as breakfast cereal moistened with apple juice, low-fat or skim milk or soy milk. Store this wheat-free mix in an airtight container in the refrigerator. It will keep for three to four weeks.

8 Servings (8 Cups)
462 Calories per Serving

4 cups old-fashioned rolled oats (¾ pound)
⅓ cup raw sunflower seeds (1½ ounces)
⅓ cup coarsely chopped natural almonds (2 ounces)
¼ cup unhulled sesame seeds** (about 1⅓ ounces)
¼ cup finely diced orange peel (including the white pith)
¼ cup plus 2 tablespoons pure maple syrup
¼ cup fresh orange juice

*2 tablespoons tahini**
2 teaspoons cinnamon
6 ounces dried figs, cut into ¼-inch dice (1 packed cup)
4 ounces dried California (sour) apricots, cut into ¼-inch dice (1 cup)
1 cup raisins (4 ounces)
**Available at supermarkets*
***Available at health food stores or Asian markets*

1. Preheat the oven to 375°. On a large baking sheet with sides, toss the oats, sunflower seeds, almonds, sesame seeds and orange peel to combine. Drizzle the maple syrup and orange juice on top and add the tahini; toss well and spread the mixture evenly in the pan. Bake for 30 minutes, stirring every 10 minutes.

2. Sprinkle the cinnamon on top, toss again and bake for 5 to 10 minutes longer, until nicely toasted.

3. Transfer the mixture to a large bowl and stir in the figs, apricots and raisins. Set aside to cool.

—*Diana Sturgis*

• • •

CALYPSO BEAN SOUP

Dried legumes are a highly concentrated source of protein and many other nutrients; they contain only a trace of vegetable fat and are deliciously filling. The Calypso Bean Soup uses a newly available black-and-white bean. Although I'm not sure why these pretty beans are called calypso, their name suggested a Caribbean treatment for this soup—hence the spices, sweet potato and coriander. Black-eyed peas, cranberry beans or navy beans would work just as well.

4 Servings (10 Cups)
409 Calories per Serving

1 cup dried calypso beans (8 ounces), picked over
8 cups Vegetable Stock (p.178)
1 medium sweet potato, peeled and cut into ½-inch dice
¼ pound green beans, cut into ½-inch lengths
2 tablespoons olive oil
2 medium onions, finely chopped
5 garlic cloves, minced
1 tablespoon minced fresh ginger
1 bay leaf
¼ teaspoon cayenne pepper
½ teaspoon ground coriander
½ teaspoon ground cumin
½ teaspoon tomato paste
¼ teaspoon finely grated orange zest
Salt and freshly ground black pepper
3 tablespoons fresh coriander (cilantro) leaves

1. In a large bowl, combine the calypso beans and enough cold water to cover by 2 inches and let soak overnight. Drain.

2. In a medium saucepan, bring the Vegetable Stock to a boil over moderately high heat. Add the sweet potato and cook until tender, about 5 minutes. Using a slotted spoon, transfer the sweet potato to a colander to drain; then transfer to a plate and set aside. Add the green beans to the saucepan and cook until tender, about 4 minutes. Using a slotted spoon, transfer the green beans to the colander to drain. Set the stock aside.

3. In a large saucepan, heat the oil over moderately high heat. Add the onions, garlic and ginger and cook, stirring occasionally, until wilted, about 5 minutes. Add the calypso beans, bay leaf and the reserved stock. Bring to a boil, reduce the heat to low, and simmer, skimming occasionally, until the calypso beans are very tender, about 1 hour. If the beans are not yet tender, add 1 cup of water and cook them a little longer.

4. Stir in the reserved sweet potato and green beans. Keep the soup at a gentle simmer over very low heat while you proceed.

5. In a small skillet, combine the cayenne, coriander and cumin and toast over high heat, stirring often with a metal spatula, until fragrant, about 1 minute. Stir in the tomato paste until well blended and cook for 1 minute longer. Scrape the spice mixture and the orange zest into the soup and whisk well. Season the soup with salt and black pepper to taste. Serve at once, garnished with the coriander leaves.

—*Marcia Kiesel*

• • •

COOL LEEK SOUP

This emerald soup is an adaptation of a recipe from José Gutierrez, a chef I worked with in Memphis, Tennessee. It can be served warm if you like, but cool is better. Make the Cool Leek Soup for lunch on a sunny day that hints of warm weather to come. This recipe uses the whole leek, since the green stalk, which is often discarded, contains essential nutrients such as Vitamin A, calcium, potassium, phosphorous and some Vitamin C and iron.

6 Servings (8 Cups)
112 Calories per Serving

1 tablespoon olive oil
6 medium leeks, white and all of the green—split lengthwise, and sliced crosswise ¼ inch thick
6 shallots, thinly sliced

3 garlic cloves, minced
6 cups Vegetable Stock (at right)
1 cup flat-leaf parsley leaves
1½ tablespoons fresh lemon juice
Salt and freshly ground pepper
Sweet Hungarian paprika, for garnish

1. In a large flameproof casserole, heat the oil over high heat. Stir in the leeks, shallots and garlic and reduce the heat to low. Cover and cook, stirring occasionally, until the leeks have wilted, about 10 minutes. Add the Vegetable Stock, increase the heat to high and bring to a boil. Stir in the parsley and remove from the heat.

2. Working in batches, spoon the leeks with some of the broth into a blender. Blend the soup, covering the top of the blender with a kitchen towel to prevent the soup from splattering, until smooth. Pour the soup through a coarse sieve into a large bowl, pressing to extract as much fine pulp as possible; discard the solids. Continue blending and straining the remaining soup. Set the bowl of soup in a larger bowl of ice water and stir constantly to cool it as quickly as possible. This keeps the soup bright green. *(The soup can be made up to 2 days ahead; cover and refrigerate.)*

3. Just before serving, season the soup with the lemon juice and salt and pepper to taste. Pour into bowls and dust lightly with paprika.

—Marcia Kiesel

• • •

CELERY-RICE SOUP WITH PEAS, SORREL AND MINTED GREMOLATA

Because cooked rice doesn't hold up well in broth, this soup is best eaten shortly after it is made. The Celery-Rice Soup with Peas, Sorrel and Minted Gremolata is an Italian-style, rib-sticking, stewlike preparation thick with rice. The strong flavors of celery, tart sorrel leaves and a minty gremolata stirred in at the last moment add a tasty punch with few calories. Sweet peas are high in Vitamin A and fiber and, if cooked soon after picking, retain a respectable amount of Vitamin C.

5 Servings (10 Cups)
227 Calories per Serving

1 tablespoon olive oil
2 medium onions, cut into ¼-inch dice
5 large celery ribs, peeled and cut crosswise ¼ inch thick
4 garlic cloves, minced
2 fresh thyme sprigs or ¼ teaspoon dried
½ cup rice, rinsed
8½ cups Vegetable Stock (recipe follows)
1 cup fresh or frozen peas
¼ pound sorrel or Swiss chard, stems trimmed and leaves coarsely chopped
Minted Gremolata (p. 179)
Salt and freshly ground pepper

1. In a large flameproof casserole, heat the oil over moderate heat. Add the onions, celery, garlic and thyme and cook, stirring occasionally, until wilted, about 5 minutes. Stir in the rice until evenly coated and increase the heat to moderately high. Add the Vegetable Stock and bring to a boil. Reduce the heat to low and simmer, skimming occasionally, until the rice is tender, about 20 minutes.

2. Add the peas to the soup and cook until tender, about 5 minutes for fresh, 2 minutes for frozen. Stir in the sorrel and cook until wilted, about 1 minute. Just before serving, stir in the Minted Gremolata and season to taste with salt and pepper.

—Marcia Kiesel

• • •

VEGETABLE STOCK

This flavorful meatless broth can be prepared up to five days in advance and kept in the refrigerator.

Makes 10 Cups
48 Calories per Cup

1 pound green or Chinese cabbage, cored and cut into large pieces
2 large carrots, coarsely chopped
2 large celery ribs, coarsely chopped
1 large onion, cut into 8 wedges
10 garlic cloves
1 bunch of flat-leaf parsley
4 fresh thyme sprigs or 1 teaspoon dried

1. In a large stockpot, combine all the ingredients and cover with 16 cups of cold water. Bring to a boil over high heat, then reduce the heat to low and simmer, uncovered, for 1½ hours.

2. Strain the stock through a fine-mesh sieve, pressing lightly on the vegetables with the back of a spoon to extract any excess liquid. Discard the solids and set the stock aside to cool to room temperature.

—Marcia Kiesel

• • •

MINTED GREMOLATA

This condiment can be used in numerous ways. Stir it into fish soup or risotto. Use it to marinate fish or chicken, to spread on fish fillets before broiling and to top plain pasta or potatoes.

Makes ¼ Cup

1 large garlic clove, minced
1 teaspoon finely grated lemon zest
1 teaspoon fresh lemon juice
1 tablespoon minced flat-leaf parsley
2 tablespoons minced fresh spearmint

In a small bowl, combine all the ingredients. Stir well and set aside until ready to serve.

—Marcia Kiesel

• • •

SWEET CORN AND CLAM SOUP

Fresh fish from nearby Atlantic and Gulf waters are delivered daily to the Doral Saturnia spa. Chef Ron Hook also relies on the spa's own herb garden and a small but expanding organic vegetable garden. Pureed fresh corn adds a subtle sweetness and a creamy consistency to this soup.

Makes 4 Cups
222 Calories per Cup

6 to 7 medium ears of fresh corn
4 cups chicken stock or canned low-sodium broth
½ cup bottled clam juice
12 freshly shucked littleneck clams, liquid reserved, clams chopped
½ cup canned evaporated skimmed milk
Freshly ground pepper
Minced chives, for garnish

1. Using a thin sharp knife and working over a large bowl, cut the kernels from 6 ears of corn, scraping the cobs with the knife to extract any juices. You should have 4 cups of corn. Repeat with the remaining ear if you need more. Reserve the cobs.

2. In a medium flameproof casserole, combine the corn and the cobs with the chicken stock, clam juice, reserved fresh clam liquid and evaporated milk. Cook over moderate heat for 45 minutes.

3. Remove and discard the cobs. In a blender, puree the soup in 2 batches until fairly smooth. Strain into a medium saucepan. *(The recipe can be made to this point up to 2 hours ahead; cover and refrigerate. Bring to room temperature before proceeding.)*

4. Bring the soup to a boil over moderately high heat. Stir in the chopped clams and cook for 30 seconds, then remove from the heat. Season to taste with pepper. Pour the soup into shallow bowls and garnish with the chives.

—Ron Hook, Doral Saturnia International Spa Resort, Miami

• • •

ZUCCHINI AND MIXED GREENS WITH LEMON-YOGURT DRESSING

Be sure to slice the zucchini paper thin; use a mandoline if possible. To save on last-minute preparations, cut the zucchini and also wash the greens up to one day ahead; seal them in separate plastic bags and refrigerate. This salad was inspired by one at the Paris bistro Le Caméléon.

8 Servings
51 Calories per Serving

1 pound small zucchini, very thinly sliced crosswise
1 tablespoon chopped fresh tarragon
1 tablespoon chopped flat-leaf parsley
1 medium head of frisée or young chicory, tough outer leaves removed, inner leaves torn into bite-size pieces
1 small head of radicchio or 1 small bunch of arugula, torn into bite-size pieces
Leaves of 1 small bunch of fresh chervil (optional)
¼ cup plus 2 tablespoons plain low-fat yogurt
2½ tablespoons fresh lemon juice
2 teaspoons red wine vinegar or sherry vinegar
1 teaspoon Dijon mustard
1 small garlic clove, minced (optional)
1 tablespoon plus 1 teaspoon extra-virgin olive oil
Salt and freshly ground pepper

1. In a medium bowl, toss the zucchini with 1 teaspoon each of the tarragon and parsley. In a large salad bowl, combine the frisée and radicchio, the remaining tarragon and parsley and half the chervil.

2. In a medium bowl, whisk the yogurt, lemon juice, vinegar, mustard and garlic. Whisk in the oil and 1½ tablespoons of water. Season with salt and pepper to taste and set aside. *(The dressing can be made up to 3 hours ahead; cover and refrigerate. Stir well before using.)*

3. Shortly before serving, toss the zucchini with half the dressing and the greens with the other half. Arrange the zucchini in the middle of each salad plate and surround with the greens. Garnish with the remaining chervil and serve.

—Martha Rose Shulman

• • •

FRESH MOZZARELLA, OLIVE AND ARUGULA SALAD WITH TOMATO VINAIGRETTE

Guests at New York City's Peninsula Spa can sample spa food at Adrienne, The Peninsula hotel's restaurant. Chef Adam Odegard's emphasis is on deliciously dressed salads instead of vegetables tossed in butter, which often accompany a main dish. In his low-calorie dressings he replaces most of the oil with low-fat yogurt or emulsions of pureed vegetables, as demonstrated in the tomato vinaigrette here.

4 Servings
305 Calories per Serving

2 large plum tomatoes (½ pound), peeled and seeded
1 tablespoon fresh lemon juice
1 small garlic clove, minced
3 tablespoons olive oil
¼ teaspoon salt
¼ teaspoon freshly ground white pepper
6 cups arugula leaves
8 ounces fresh part-skim mozzarella cheese,* cut into 12 slices
12 oil-cured black olives, pitted
****Available at cheese shops and some Italian markets***

1. In a blender, combine the tomatoes, lemon juice and garlic. Blend well. Add the olive oil in a steady stream and blend until emulsified. Stir in the salt and pepper.

2. Pour ¼ cup of the tomato vinaigrette onto each of 4 plates and tilt to coat. Pile 1½ cups of the arugula in the center of each plate. Arrange 3 slices of cheese and 3 olives around the arugula.

—Adam Odegard, Adrienne, New York City

• • •

CRISP SALAD WITH ORANGE-MISO DRESSING

6 Servings
81 Calories per Serving

1 head of romaine lettuce, torn in bite-size pieces
1 bunch of watercress, large stems removed
2 medium carrots, coarsely shredded or grated
9 medium red radishes, very thinly sliced
Orange-Miso Dressing (recipe follows)

Place the lettuce in 6 individual salad bowls and add the watercress. Top with the carrots and radishes. Refrigerate until well chilled. Stir the Orange-Miso Dressing and spoon over each salad. Serve at once.

—Diana Sturgis

• • •

ORANGE-MISO DRESSING

Scrub the orange under cold water before removing the zest.

6 Servings (1¼ Cups)
54 Calories per Serving

¾ cup fresh orange juice (from 2 or 3 large juicy oranges)
3 tablespoons medium- or light-colored miso (soybean paste)*
1 tablespoon Japanese dark sesame oil*
1 tablespoon finely grated orange zest
2 teaspoons light tamari sauce*
****Available at Japanese markets***

In a small bowl, whisk all the ingredients until combined. Refrigerate and serve chilled if desired. *(The dressing can be made up to 5 hours ahead.)*

—Diana Sturgis

• • •

POTATO PANCAKES STUFFED WITH SHIITAKE MUSHROOMS

In frying the pancakes, lightly brush the pan with oil at the start and then use only as much of the remaining oil as needed to prevent them from sticking.

6 Servings
153 Calories per Serving

3 large baking potatoes (1½ pounds), scrubbed but not peeled
2 red bell peppers
3 tablespoons olive oil

2 small onions, finely chopped
4 garlic cloves, minced
½ pound shiitake mushrooms, stems discarded, caps coarsely chopped
Salt
1 tablespoon dry white wine
2 tablespoons thinly sliced scallion greens
Freshly ground black pepper
2 tablespoons minced flat-leaf parsley

1. In a large saucepan of lightly salted water, boil the potatoes until tender, 50 minutes to 1 hour. Drain and let cool.

2. Meanwhile, roast the bell peppers directly over a gas flame or under the broiler, turning, until charred black all over. Transfer the peppers to a bowl, cover and set aside to steam for 10 minutes. Peel the peppers and remove the cores, seeds and ribs. Cut the peppers in thin lengthwise strips and set aside.

3. In a large nonstick skillet, heat 1 tablespoon of the oil over moderately high heat. Add the onions and cook, stirring, until softened and browned on the edges, about 5 minutes. Stir in the garlic, reduce the heat to moderately low and cook for 1 minute. Stir in the mushrooms and season with salt. Cover and cook, stirring occasionally, until tender, about 6 minutes. Uncover, stir in the wine and cook until evaporated. Remove from the heat. Stir in the scallion greens and season to taste with salt and pepper.

4. Peel the potatoes. Cut them in 1½-inch chunks and pass them through a food mill set over a large bowl. Using a wooden spoon, beat in the parsley. Season to taste with salt and pepper.

5. Line a baking sheet with wax paper. Using your hands, pat 2 tablespoons of the mashed potatoes into a 2½-inch pancake and place on the prepared baking sheet. Repeat with the remaining potatoes to form 24 pancakes.

6. Spoon 1 tablespoon of the mushroom mixture in the center of 12 of the potato pancakes. Top with the remaining pancakes and press gently around the edges to seal.

7. Lightly brush a large nonstick skillet with some of the remaining olive oil and heat over moderately high heat. Add half of the potato pancakes and cook, turning once, until browned, crisp and heated through, about 3 minutes per side. Transfer to a warm platter. Re-oil the skillet and fry the remaining pancakes. Arrange 2 potato pancakes on each plate and garnish with the roasted red pepper strips.

—Jacques Pépin

• • •

PUREE OF ROASTED CARROTS AND LEEKS WITH GINGER

6 Servings
107 Calories per Serving

2 medium leeks, white and tender green, cut into 2-inch lengths
1 teaspoon minced fresh ginger
2½ pounds carrots, cut into 2-inch pieces
1 tablespoon olive oil
¼ teaspoon salt
½ teaspoon freshly ground pepper
¼ cup low-fat buttermilk

1. Preheat the oven to 375°. Wrap the leeks and ginger in aluminum foil.

2. Cut any thick pieces of carrot in half lengthwise to ensure even cooking. Place the carrots in a medium roasting pan in a single layer. Toss with the oil and salt and pour in ⅓ cup of water. Cover the pan tightly with foil. Bake the carrots and the packet of leeks for 50 minutes, uncovering the carrots after 30 minutes. The vegetables are done when the carrots are tender and lightly browned on the undersides and the leeks are soft.

3. Transfer the carrots and gingered leeks to a food processor. Process until a coarse puree forms. Add the pepper and buttermilk and process until smooth. Season with salt to taste. Transfer the puree to a warmed dish and serve.

—Jacques Pépin

• • •

BAKED TOMATOES WITH GOAT CHEESE EN PAPILLOTE

4 Servings
361 Calories per Serving

2½ pounds zucchini, halved lengthwise
2½ pounds yellow summer squash, halved lengthwise
1 teaspoon salt
12 plum tomatoes—cored, halved lengthwise and seeded
8 ounces Montrachet goat cheese, at room temperature
¾ teaspoon freshly ground pepper
¾ cup chopped fresh basil
1 teaspoon olive oil

1. Using a spoon, scoop out the seeds and the surrounding pulp from the zucchini and summer squash and discard. In a food processor, shred the zucchini and summer squash. Place in a colander and toss with ½ teaspoon of the salt. Set aside for 1 hour to drain.

2. Meanwhile, sprinkle the cut sides

of the tomatoes with ¼ teaspoon of the salt. Place the halves on paper towels in pairs, cut sides down, and let drain for 30 minutes.

3. In a small bowl, combine the goat cheese with ½ teaspoon of the pepper and ½ cup of the basil. Mix thoroughly. Form the cheese mixture into a log 1 inch in diameter, then cut into 12 equal portions.

4. Place a slice of the goat cheese on the cut side of half of the tomatoes and cover with the remaining tomato halves.

5. Press lightly on the squash to remove any excess liquid. Toss the squash with the olive oil and the remaining ¼ teaspoon each of salt and pepper and ¼ cup basil.

6. To assemble the papillotes, fold a 12-by-16-inch piece of parchment paper in half (to form a 12-by-8-inch rectangle) and draw a large half heart. Holding on to the crease, cut out the heart. Repeat to form 4 parchment wrappers.

7. Spoon the squash onto one side of the wrappers. Arrange 3 stuffed tomatoes on top of the squash on each one. Fold and seal the papillote packages with overlapping crimps. Place them on a large baking sheet and refrigerate for up to 5 hours.

8. Preheat the oven to 350°. Bake the papillotes on the bottom rack of the oven for 20 minutes. Transfer the papillotes to plates, cut them open and serve immediately.

—Bob Chambers

• • •

SESAME COLLARDS ON BUCKWHEAT NOODLES

This tasty lunch or light supper can be made in less than half an hour. Buckwheat (or wheat and buckwheat) noodles cook very quickly and make a nice change from the usual all-wheat pasta.

2 Servings
444 Calories per Serving

8 ounces trimmed collard greens (from a 12-ounce bunch), cut crosswise ½ inch thick
2 tablespoons unhulled sesame seeds*
1 tablespoon Oriental sesame oil
1 tablespoon minced garlic
1 tablespoon plus 1 teaspoon light tamari sauce,* plus more for serving
6 ounces soba (buckwheat noodles)*
****Available at health food stores or Asian markets***

1. In a medium saucepan, bring 4 inches of water to a boil. Add the collards and boil over moderate heat until tender but still green, about 15 minutes. Drain in a colander set over a bowl. Set the collards aside and return the cooking liquid to the saucepan. Add 4 cups of water and set the pan over low heat.

2. Meanwhile, in a heavy medium skillet, cook the sesame seeds in ½ teaspoon of the sesame oil over moderate heat, stirring occasionally, until lightly toasted, about 5 minutes. Transfer to a small bowl and set aside.

3. Let the skillet cool for 5 minutes, then add 1 more teaspoon of the sesame oil. Add the garlic and cook over moderately low heat, stirring, until softened but not browned, about 2 minutes. Remove from the heat and stir in the drained collards, toasted sesame seeds and 2 teaspoons of the tamari sauce.

4. Bring the saucepan of simmering water to a boil over high heat, add the soba and cook until al dente, about 3 minutes if they are all buckwheat (a few minutes longer if they are part wheat). Drain the noodles, transfer to a warm bowl and toss with the remaining 2 teaspoons tamari sauce and 1½ teaspoons sesame oil.

5. Quickly rewarm the collards and place them on top of the noodles. Pass extra tamari sauce.

—Diana Sturgis

• • •

ROOT VEGETABLE CAKES

At Patina in Los Angeles, Joachim Splichal serves these "cakes" of finely diced root vegetables with an unusual thyme-scented sauce made from reduced potato cooking liquid, potato puree and olive oil.

4 Servings
275 Calories per Serving

¼ of a small celery root, peeled and cut into ¼-inch dice (1 cup)
1 medium parsnip, peeled and cut into ¼-inch dice (1 cup)
¼ of a small rutabaga, peeled and cut into ¼-inch dice (1 cup)
1 medium kohlrabi, peeled and cut into ¼-inch dice (1 cup)
2 large red cabbage leaves
2 large savoy cabbage leaves
2 tablespoons unsalted butter
1 large beet, peeled and cut into ¼-inch dice (1 cup)
Salt and freshly ground pepper
1 pound Idaho potatoes

2 tablespoons olive oil
1 teaspoon chopped fresh thyme

1. Bring a large saucepan of salted water to a boil over high heat. Add the celery root, parsnip, rutabaga and kohlrabi; blanch until almost tender, 2 to 3 minutes. Using a slotted spoon, transfer the vegetables to a colander and refresh under cold running water. Drain well.

2. Bring the water back to a boil and add the red and savoy cabbage leaves. Cook until tender, about 4 minutes. Refresh under cold water and drain thoroughly. Transfer to a clean kitchen towel and pat dry. Using a 2-inch round cookie cutter, cut out 4 neat circles from the red cabbage leaves; repeat with the savoy cabbage leaves. Cut the remaining cabbage into thin julienne strips.

3. In a large skillet, melt the butter over moderately high heat. Add the reserved blanched root vegetables, the beet and julienned cabbage and cook, stirring, until just tender, about 5 minutes. Season with salt and pepper to taste.

4. Line the bottom of 4 straight-sided ½-cup ramekins with a savoy cabbage circle. Fill the ramekins with the diced root vegetables, packing them tightly. Top each ramekin with a red cabbage circle.

5. Peel and quarter the potatoes. In a medium saucepan, cover the potatoes with 4 cups of water; bring to a boil over moderately high heat. Cook until the potatoes are tender, about 20 minutes. Using a slotted spoon, transfer the potatoes to a plate. Reserve the cooking water; you should have about 1½ cups.

6. Mash one-fourth of the cooked potatoes in a medium bowl; discard the remaining potatoes. Boil the potato cooking liquid over moderately high heat until reduced to 1 cup, about 5 minutes. Whisk in the mashed potatoes and the olive oil. The sauce should be the consistency of pancake batter. Set aside.

7. Preheat the oven to 350°. Place the ramekins in a small roasting pan. Pour enough hot water into the pan to reach halfway up the sides of the ramekins. Cover with foil and bake until the vegetables are heated through and the beets are tender, 25 to 30 minutes.

8. To serve, reheat the potato sauce over moderate heat. Season with salt and pepper to taste and add the thyme. Invert the vegetable cakes onto serving plates and ladle the warm potato sauce around them.

—Baba S. Khalsa

• • •

RAGOUT OF FALL VEGETABLES

At Mondrian in Manhattan, chef Tom Colicchio varies the vegetables he adds to a base of braised artichokes according to what's fresh and in season at the market.

6 Servings
295 Calories per Serving

6 large artichokes
1 lemon, halved
⅓ cup plus 2 tablespoons olive oil
1 medium carrot, coarsely chopped
1 medium onion, coarsely chopped
1 leek, white and tender green portions, thinly sliced crosswise
3 garlic cloves, lightly crushed
1 sprig of fresh thyme
1 sprig of fresh rosemary
1 bay leaf
1 cup dry white wine
¼ pound chanterelle mushrooms, cut into 1-inch pieces
¼ pound shiitake mushrooms, stemmed, caps cut into 1-inch pieces
Salt and freshly ground pepper
3 small parsnips, peeled and cut into ½-inch dice
1 large tomato—peeled, seeded and cut into ¼-inch dice

1. Break off the stems of the artichokes. Trim the artichokes by snapping off the tough outer leaves near the base. Using a sharp stainless steel knife, cut off all the leaves. Trim the base of any remaining dark green parts. Rub the base well with the cut lemon to prevent discoloration. Trim the base to an even round shape and scoop out the hairy chokes with a spoon. Rub the surfaces again with the cut lemon and set aside.

2. In a large nonreactive skillet, heat 1½ tablespoons of the oil over moderately low heat. Add the carrot, onion and leek and cook, stirring, until softened, about 3 minutes. Add the artichoke bottoms, garlic, thyme and rosemary sprigs, bay leaf, wine, ⅓ cup of the olive oil and 3 cups of water. Cook, covered, over low heat, turning the artichokes once, until they are easily pierced, about 20 minutes.

3. Meanwhile, in a large skillet, heat the remaining 1½ teaspoons olive oil over moderately high heat. Add the chanterelle and shiitake mushrooms and season with salt and pepper. Cover and cook, stirring once, until softened, about 3 minutes.

4. Bring a small saucepan of water to a boil over high heat. Add the parsnips and cook until tender, about 4 minutes. Drain and set aside.

5. Cut each artichoke bottom in half and then slice crosswise ¼ inch thick. Return to the pan and add the chanterelles, shiitakes, parsnips and tomato. Warm over moderately high heat until heated through, about 3 minutes. Spoon the ragout onto 6 serving plates and serve hot.

—*Baba S. Khalsa*

• • •

SPINACH-STUFFED EGGPLANT ROLLATINI WITH FRESH TOMATO SAUCE

This vegetable main dish provides protein in the form of a cheese filling made mostly of part-skim ricotta mixed with a little feta and Parmesan. At Cal-a-Vie, it's served with steamed broccoli, a green salad and a slice of the spa's whole-grain baguette.

🍷 A grapy, flavorful red, such as 1989 William Wheeler R.S. Reserve or 1988 Kendall-Jackson Syrah from California or 1989 Prosper Maufoux Côtes du Rhône from France, would provide a nice counterpoint to the earthy and rich tastes of this dish.

10 Servings
273 Calories per Serving

3 pounds fresh spinach, stems discarded, or 1 pound frozen leaf spinach, thawed
10 walnut halves
¾ cup fresh whole wheat bread crumbs
3 tablespoons plus 1 teaspoon olive oil
1 large onion, finely chopped
1 large garlic clove, minced
1½ cups part-skim ricotta cheese
½ cup crumbled feta cheese
3 tablespoons freshly grated Parmesan cheese
¼ cup minced flat-leaf parsley
2 tablespoons minced fresh basil
1 teaspoon freshly ground pepper
¼ teaspoon salt
¼ teaspoon cumin
1 egg plus 1 egg white, lightly beaten
Vegetable oil cooking spray
Two 1- to 1½-pound eggplants, peeled and cut lengthwise into twenty ¼-inch-thick slices
Fresh Tomato Sauce (recipe follows)
12 brine-cured black olives, pitted and sliced, for garnish

1. Preheat the oven to 350°. Place half of the spinach leaves in a large pot or medium flameproof casserole with 1 cup of water. Cover and cook over high heat until wilted, about 10 minutes. Transfer the spinach to a colander, rinse briefly under cool water and set aside to drain. Repeat with the remaining spinach. When cool enough to handle, squeeze the spinach in small bunches to extract as much liquid as possible. (Alternatively, squeeze the thawed frozen spinach.) Chop well and set aside in a large bowl.

2. Meanwhile, place the walnuts on a small baking sheet. Bake for 7 to 8 minutes, until fragrant and toasted. Transfer to a plate and set aside to cool. Place the bread crumbs on the baking sheet and bake, stirring once or twice, for 5 minutes, or until dry and lightly browned. Let cool briefly. Finely chop the walnuts and stir into the spinach. Stir in the bread crumbs.

3. In a medium skillet, heat 1 teaspoon of the olive oil over low heat. Add the onion and garlic and cook, stirring occasionally, until very soft, about 15 minutes.

4. Stir into the spinach mixture. Stir in the ricotta, feta, 2 tablespoons of the Parmesan, 2 tablespoons of the parsley, the basil, pepper, salt and cumin. *(The spinach filling can be prepared up to 2 days ahead; cover and refrigerate. Return to room temperature before proceeding.)*

5. Increase the oven temperature to 450°. Stir the egg and egg white into the spinach mixture and set aside. Lightly oil 2 large baking sheets with vegetable oil cooking spray. Spread the eggplant slices on both sheets. Brush lightly with 2 tablespoons of the olive oil and bake for 10 minutes. Brush again lightly with the remaining 1 tablespoon oil, rotate the baking sheets and bake the eggplant for 8 to 10 minutes longer, until browned and soft. Set aside to cool, about 10 minutes.

6. Lower the oven temperature to 375°. Spread ½ cup of the Fresh Tomato Sauce in a 9-by-13-inch nonreactive baking pan. Lay a few eggplant slices on a work surface. Place 2 heaping tablespoons of the spinach mixture at the short end of each piece of eggplant. Roll up from the short end and place the rollatini, seam side down, in rows in the prepared pan. Repeat with the remaining eggplant slices and spinach stuffing.

7. Pour 1 cup of the tomato sauce over the rollatini. Cover loosely with foil and bake for 30 minutes, until heated through. Let rest for 5 minutes. *(The rollatini can be prepared to this point up to 1 day ahead; cover and refrigerate. Reheat in a 350° oven.)*

8. Meanwhile, in a medium nonreactive saucepan, reheat the remaining 1½ cups tomato sauce over moderately low heat. Sprinkle the remaining 1 tablespoon Parmesan cheese, 2 tablespoons parsley and the olives over the rollatini. Serve 2 rollatini per person. Pass the warm tomato sauce alongside.

—*Rose Daley, Cal-a-Vie, Vista, California*

• • •

FRESH TOMATO SAUCE

Makes 3 Cups
36 Calories per ¼ Cup

½ pound white mushrooms, coarsely chopped
2 teaspoons olive oil
1 medium onion, chopped
1 small green bell pepper, cut into ¼-inch dice
1 large garlic clove, crushed
¼ cup dry white wine
9 plum tomatoes (1⅓ pounds)—peeled, seeded and pureed—or 1 can (35 ounces) Italian peeled tomatoes, drained and pureed
1½ teaspoons tomato paste
3 tablespoons minced fresh basil
1 tablespoon minced fresh oregano
½ teaspoon freshly ground pepper
¼ teaspoon salt (optional)

1. Heat a medium cast-iron or other heavy skillet over moderately high heat for 5 minutes. Add the mushrooms and cook, stirring occasionally, until well browned, about 8 minutes. Reduce the heat to low and stir in the olive oil, onion, green bell pepper and garlic. Cook, stirring frequently, until the onion is translucent, about 10 minutes.

2. Transfer the contents from the skillet to a medium nonreactive saucepan. Stir in the wine and cook over moderate heat until the mixture is almost dry, 1 to 2 minutes. Add the pureed tomatoes, tomato paste, basil, oregano, black pepper and salt. Bring to a gentle boil and cook, stirring occasionally, until thick, about 45 minutes. *(The sauce can be made up to 3 days ahead. Refrigerate but do not freeze.)*

—Rose Daley, Cal-a-Vie, Vista, California

• • •

SWORDFISH WITH SWEET PEPPERS AND ONIONS

You can use any other substantial but lean fish for this dish, such as halibut or tuna.

8 Servings
332 Calories per Serving

2 tablespoons olive oil
3 medium onions, halved and thinly sliced
1 cup dry white wine
4 large red bell peppers, or a combination of red and yellow peppers, cut into 1½-by-¼-inch strips
4 garlic cloves, minced
¼ teaspoon coarse sea salt or coarse (kosher) salt
2 tablespoons balsamic vinegar
1 teaspoon fresh thyme
Freshly ground black pepper
Eight 6-ounce swordfish steaks (about 1 inch thick)
Table salt
Cayenne pepper
Fresh thyme sprigs and lemon wedges, for garnish

1. Oil a 9-by-13-inch baking dish. In a large, nonstick skillet, heat 1 tablespoon of the oil over moderate heat. Add the onions and cook, stirring, until translucent and limp, about 7 minutes. Stir in 3 tablespoons of the wine and cook until the onions begin to turn golden, about 5 minutes longer.

2. Add the remaining 1 tablespoon oil to the skillet along with the bell peppers, garlic and coarse salt and cook, stirring, until the peppers are very tender, about 15 minutes.

3. Add 3 more tablespoons of the wine and cook, stirring, for 5 minutes. Stir in the vinegar and cook until the liquid has evaporated, about 2 minutes. Season with the thyme and black pepper to taste. Transfer the mixture to the baking dish and set aside. *(The recipe can be prepared to this point up to 5 hours ahead; cover and set aside at room temperature.)*

4. Preheat the oven to 450°. Heat the skillet used for the vegetables over moderately high heat. Add half of the fish steaks and cook until the undersides are lightly browned, about 1 minute. Turn the steaks and season lightly with table salt, black pepper and a tiny pinch of cayenne. Cook until lightly browned on the second side, about 1 minute longer. Repeat with the remaining fish steaks.

5. Transfer the fish to the baking dish, arranging the vegetables around and on top of the steaks. Pour in the remaining ½ cup plus 2 tablespoons wine and season lightly with table salt and black pepper. Cover the dish tightly with aluminum foil and bake for 10 to 12 minutes, until the fish is firm to the touch and opaque.

6. Transfer the fish to plates and spoon the vegetables and any accumulated juices on top. Garnish with the thyme and lemon.

—Martha Rose Shulman

• • •

SHRIMP AND SCALLOPS WITH PEPPERS AND FENNEL EN PAPILLOTE

🍷 The mild but briny flavor of shellfish requires a contrasting, crisp white, and the fennel, basil and peppers suggest a Sauvignon Blanc to harmonize with those tastes. A 1989 Montpellier or 1989 St. Supéry from California would be excellent.

4 Servings
268 Calories per Serving

2 tablespoons olive oil
4 shallots, thinly sliced
1 red bell pepper, cut into thin 2-inch-long matchsticks
1 yellow bell pepper, cut into thin 2-inch-long matchsticks
1 green bell pepper, cut into thin 2-inch-long matchsticks
2 pounds fennel bulbs, cored and thinly sliced
½ teaspoon salt
½ teaspoon freshly ground black pepper
2 teaspoons fennel seeds
16 large shrimp (¾ pound), shelled and deveined
¾ pound medium sea scallops of even size, membranes removed
½ cup shredded fresh basil

1. In a large nonstick skillet, heat the oil over moderately high heat. Add the shallots and cook, stirring constantly, until beginning to brown, about 3 minutes. Add the bell peppers, fennel, salt, black pepper and fennel seeds. Cook, stirring occasionally, until softened, 5 to 6 minutes. Remove from the heat and set aside to cool completely.

2. To assemble the papillotes, fold a 12-by-16-inch piece of parchment paper in half (to form a 12-by-8-inch rectangle) and draw a large half heart. Holding on to the crease, cut out the heart. Repeat to form 4 parchment wrappers.

3. Spoon the fennel and pepper mixture onto one side of the wrappers. Arrange 4 shrimp, one-fourth of the scallops and the basil on top of the vegetables. Season with salt and black pepper. Fold and seal the papillote packages with overlapping crimps. Place them on a large baking sheet and refrigerate for up to 5 hours.

4. Preheat the oven to 350°. Bake the papillotes on the bottom rack of the oven for 18 minutes. Transfer the papillotes to plates, cut them open and serve immediately.

—Bob Chambers

• • •

SALMON FILLET WITH LEEKS AND CARROTS EN PAPILLOTE

4 Servingss
425 Calories per Serving

¼ cup plus 4 teaspoons fresh lemon juice
2 tablespoons chopped fresh dill
¾ teaspoon salt
½ teaspoon freshly ground black pepper
Pinch of cayenne pepper
3 tablespoons olive oil
Four 6-ounce pieces of center-cut salmon fillet
1½ pounds leeks, white parts only, halved lengthwise and thinly sliced crosswise
1 garlic clove, minced
1 pound carrots, coarsely shredded

1. In a small nonreactive bowl, combine ¼ cup of the lemon juice with 1 tablespoon of the dill, ½ teaspoon of the salt, ¼ teaspoon of the black pepper and the cayenne. Slowly whisk in 2 tablespoons of the olive oil. Place the salmon in a glass or ceramic dish and pour the marinade on top. Turn to coat. Cover and refrigerate for up to 3 hours, turning occasionally.

2. Meanwhile, in a large nonstick skillet, heat the remaining 1 tablespoon olive oil over moderately high heat. Add the leeks and toss to coat with the oil. Cook, stirring frequently, until translucent, 3 to 4 minutes. Add the garlic and cook for 1 minute longer. Add the carrots and the remaining ¼ teaspoon each of salt and black pepper. Cook, stirring, until the carrots soften, about 2 minutes. Remove from the heat and set aside to cool completely.

3. To assemble the papillotes, fold a 12-by-16-inch piece of parchment paper in half (to form a 12-by-8-inch rectangle) and draw a large half heart. Holding on to the crease, cut out the heart. Repeat to form 4 parchment wrappers.

4. Spoon the leek and carrot mixture onto one side of the wrappers and top with the salmon fillets. Sprinkle each fillet with 1 teaspoon of the remaining lemon juice and ¾ teaspoon of the remaining dill. Fold and seal the papillote packages with overlapping crimps. Place them on a large baking sheet and refrigerate for up to 5 hours.

5. Preheat the oven to 350°. Bake the papillotes on the bottom rack of the oven for 15 minutes. Transfer to plates, cut them open and serve immediately.

—Bob Chambers

• • •

BAKED SALMON WITH CHEVRE SAUCE

Chef Graham Griswold turns to such regional ingredients as jicama, cilantro, chile peppers and black beans for his inventive meals. He also uses an array of sauces to "paint" a plate. Made without cream or butter, these low-calorie sauces include everything from this goat cheese version to fresh vegetable salsas.

🍷 A rich Chardonnay would match the flavors of the salmon and cheese sauce. Consider 1988 Cuvaison Carneros Reserve from California or 1989 Chablis Les Clos Domaine de la Maladière William Fèvre from Burgundy.

4 Servings
218 Calories per Serving

One 8.45-ounce container soy milk
2 ounces soft, mild goat cheese
3 garlic cloves, lightly crushed
Four 3-ounce pieces of salmon fillet, cut about 1 inch thick
¼ cup Yellow Pepper Sauce (recipe follows)
12 steamed broccoli florets, for garnish
4 steamed cauliflower florets, for garnish
¼ cup diced red bell pepper, for garnish

1. In a small nonreactive saucepan, whisk together the soy milk, goat cheese and garlic over low heat. Cook, whisking occasionally, until the mixture thickens to the consistency of a light cream sauce, about 5 minutes. Strain through a fine sieve. Keep warm.

2. In a large saucepan fitted with a flat steamer over 1 inch of water, steam the salmon over moderately high heat until firm, 3 to 5 minutes.

3. To serve, ladle about ¼ cup of the warm goat cheese sauce into the center of each of 4 large warmed plates; tilt the plates slightly to coat evenly with the sauce. Spoon 1 tablespoon of the Yellow Pepper Sauce in small amounts on each plate, using the tip of a knife to swirl the sauce decoratively. Place a salmon fillet on each plate and garnish with the broccoli and cauliflower florets and the diced red pepper.

—Graham Griswold, Vista Clara Spa and Health Resort, Galisteo, New Mexico

• • •

YELLOW PEPPER SAUCE

Makes ¾ Cup
29 Calories per ¼ Cup

½ cup chicken stock or canned low-sodium broth
½ cup diced yellow bell pepper
4 ounces all-purpose potatoes, peeled and diced (½ cup)
Pinch of saffron threads

1. Combine all the ingredients in a small saucepan. Cover and simmer over moderately low heat until the pepper is soft, 20 to 25 minutes.

2. Transfer the mixture to a blender and puree until smooth. Strain through a fine sieve into a small heatproof bowl. *(The sauce can be made up to 1 day ahead. Cover tightly and refrigerate. Rewarm over moderate heat.)*

—Graham Griswold, Vista Clara Spa and Health Resort, Galisteo, New Mexico

• • •

GRILLED SEA BASS WITH SAFFRON-TOMATO SAUCE, BULGUR RISOTTO AND JULIENNED VEGETABLES

Michael Flynn, chef at the Sonoma Mission Inn and Spa in the heart of northern California, calls upon local organic farmers, ranchers specializing in farm-raised veal and free-range chicken, and Pacific ocean fishermen. One of the backbones of Flynn's cooking is a flavorful vegetable stock, which replaces higher-fat meat and poultry stocks whenever possible.

4 Servings
513 Calories per Serving

Four 5-ounce skinless sea bass fillets
½ cup dry white wine
3 medium garlic cloves, smashed
1 medium shallot, finely chopped
1 teaspoon finely grated lemon zest
½ teaspoon freshly ground pepper
Pinch of thyme
1 celery rib, cut into medium dice
1 medium carrot, cut into medium dice
1 medium yellow onion, cut into medium dice
4 to 5 tomatoes (2 pounds), chopped and liquid reserved
1¾ cups chicken stock or canned low-sodium broth
Pinch of saffron threads
Fresh lemon juice
Olive oil, for grilling (optional)
Bulgur Risotto (p. 197)
Julienned Vegetables (recipe follows)

1. Place the bass fillets in a medium bowl and add the wine, 1 of the garlic cloves, the shallot, lemon zest, pepper and thyme. Set aside at room temperature for at least 45 minutes and up to 2 hours.

2. Meanwhile, in a medium nonreactive saucepan, combine the celery, carrot, onion and the remaining 2 garlic cloves. Cover and cook over moderately low heat, stirring occasionally, until the vegetables are tender, about 25 minutes.

3. Add the tomatoes and their liquid, the chicken stock and the saffron and simmer until reduced by half, about 30 minutes. Transfer the sauce to a food mill fitted with a medium disk and puree into a bowl. Season to taste with additional pepper and lemon juice.

4. Light a grill or preheat the broiler. Rub olive oil on the grill, if using. Grill or broil the sea bass fillets, turning once, for 6 to 7 minutes, until firm and white throughout.

5. To serve, spoon ½ cup of the tomato sauce onto each of 4 warm dinner plates. Place 1 sea bass fillet on the sauce. Spoon the Bulgur Risotto and Julienned Vegetables alongside the bass. Serve at once.

—Michael Flynn, Sonoma Mission Inn and Spa, Sonoma, California

• • •

JULIENNED VEGETABLES

4 Servings
69 Calories per Serving

1 medium red bell pepper
1 yellow bell pepper
1 green bell pepper
1 medium (1 pound) daikon radish
1 medium carrot
1 medium yellow squash
1 medium zucchini
½ cup Vegetable Stock (p. 197)

1. Using a sharp knife, core the red, yellow and green bell peppers, then slice into thin 1-inch-long strips. Slice the daikon and carrot into thin 1-inch-long strips.

2. Halve the yellow squash and zucchini. Using a spoon, scoop out the pulp to about ¼-inch from the skin and discard. Slice the skins into thin 1-inch-long strips.

3. Heat a large skillet over moderately high heat until hot. Add all of the vegetables and the Vegetable Stock, cover and cook until crisp-tender, 1 to 2 minutes.

—Michael Flynn, Sonoma Mission Inn and Spa, Sonoma, California

• • •

CHICKEN BREASTS WITH MUSHROOMS AND THYME EN PAPILLOTE

4 Servings
320 Calories per Serving

2 tablespoons olive oil
6 large shallots, thinly sliced
1 pound shiitake mushrooms, stems discarded, caps sliced ¼ inch thick
1 pound white mushrooms, stems discarded, caps sliced ¼ inch thick
1 teaspoon salt
½ teaspoon freshly ground pepper
2 tablespoons fresh thyme
Juice of ½ a lemon
Four 6-ounce skinless, boneless chicken breast halves, trimmed of visible fat

1. In a large nonstick skillet, heat 1½ tablespoons of the olive oil over moderately high heat. Add the shallots and cook, stirring frequently, until translucent, 4 to 5 minutes. Add the shiitake and white mushrooms. Cover, reduce the heat to moderate and cook until wilted, about 5 minutes. Uncover and increase the heat to moderately high. Add ½ teaspoon of the salt, ¼ teaspoon of the pepper, 1 tablespoon of the thyme and the lemon juice. Cook, stirring occasionally, until the liquid in the pan has evaporated and the mushrooms are thoroughly browned, about 5 minutes. Set aside and let cool completely.

2. To assemble the papillotes, fold a 12-by-16-inch piece of parchment paper in half (to form a 12-by-8-inch rectangle) and draw a large half heart. Holding on to the crease, cut out the heart. Repeat to form 4 parchment wrappers.

3. Spoon the mushroom mixture onto one side of the wrappers. Place the chicken on top of the mushrooms and brush with the remaining ½ tablespoon olive oil. Sprinkle with the remaining ½ teaspoon salt, ¼ teaspoon pepper and 1 tablespoon thyme. Fold and seal the papillote packages with overlapping crimps. Place them on a large baking sheet and refrigerate for up to 5 hours.

4. Preheat the oven to 350°. Bake the papillotes on the bottom rack of the oven for 18 minutes. Transfer the papillotes to plates, cut them open and serve immediately.

—Bob Chambers

• • •

Mixed Grain Trio (p. 196) with Herb Coulis (p. 196).

Left, Italian Salad (p. 143). Above, Sfinciuni Pizza (p. 37).

BROILED MARINATED QUAIL

If you are seriously trying to limit your calorie and fat intake, simply remove the skin from the birds before eating them.

This marinade for quail is also delicious with lean pork tenderloins; for six, you'll need two 14-ounce tenderloins, trimmed of excess fat. Once marinated, broil them, basting and turning frequently, until evenly browned and just cooked through.

🍷 Quail is a relatively mild bird, easily overwhelmed by a powerful red. Look for one with soft, enveloping flavors—such as a California Merlot—that will underscore the subdued spiciness here. Excellent choices are 1989 Geyser Peak or 1988 Cuvaison.

6 Servings
465 Calories per Serving

3 medium shallots, minced
3 large garlic cloves, minced
3 tablespoons Vietnamese fish sauce (nuoc mam)*
1½ teaspoons sugar
1 teaspoon minced fresh jalapeño pepper
12 partially boned quail (4 ounces each)
****Available at Asian markets***

1. In a small bowl, combine the shallots, garlic, fish sauce, sugar, jalapeño and 1 tablespoon of water. Place the quail in a glass dish, pour the marinade on top and turn to coat completely. Cover and refrigerate for 3 to 4 hours.

2. Preheat the broiler. Place the quail on a broiler pan and broil on the top rack for 4 minutes on each side, until the skin is bubbly, browned and crisp. Serve immediately.

—*Jacques Pépin*

• • •

Salmon Fillet with Leeks and Carrots en Papillote (p. 186).

ROASTED BREAST OF PHEASANT WITH KASHI PILAF AND WARM AUTUMN FRUIT SAUCE

Seasonings play a large part in the spa cuisine at Connecticut's Norwich Inn & Spa. The founder, Edward Safdie, and chef Priscilla Martell emphasize the importance of contrasting flavors. They use a minimum of salt and rely instead on a combination of fresh herbs and spices, onions and garlic, lemon and lime, and homemade low-sodium stocks. This main course is accented with fresh rosemary and stewed fruit.

🍷 Balance the pheasant's relatively mild game flavor with a fruity, medium-bodied red, such as 1989 Rosemount Pinot Noir from Australia, or a red Burgundy, such as 1988 Jaffelin Volnay.

3 Servings
450 Calories per Serving

Vegetable oil cooking spray
One 3½-pound pheasant
Kashi Pilaf (recipe follows)
¼ cup plus 2 tablespoons Warm Autumn Fruit Sauce (p. 194)
Sprigs of fresh rosemary, for garnish

1. Preheat the oven to 350°. Spray a heavy 9-by-13-inch roasting pan with vegetable oil cooking spray and place over moderately high heat. Add the pheasant and cook, turning with tongs as necessary, until browned on all sides, 6 to 8 minutes. Place the pan in the oven and roast the pheasant for about 30 minutes, until the juices run clear when a thigh is pierced with a fork. Set aside to cool for 10 minutes.

2. Using a thin sharp knife and using the breast bone as your guide, remove the breasts from the bird. (Reserve the remaining parts for another use.) If the underside of the meat is still cold or pink, return the breasts to the oven, skin side up, and cook for an additional 10 to 15 minutes, but do not overcook the meat. Set aside for 5 minutes, then remove and discard the skin.

3. To serve, spoon an equal amount of the warm Kashi Pilaf onto each of 3 warmed plates. Slice the pheasant breasts and fan out the meat on top of the pilaf. Spoon 2 tablespoons of the Warm Autumn Fruit Sauce over each serving of pheasant and garnish with rosemary sprigs. Serve at once.

—*Patricia Martell, Norwich Inn & Spa, Norwich, Connecticut*

• • •

KASHI PILAF

3 Servings
273 Calories per Serving

Vegetable oil cooking spray
1 small onion, finely chopped
1 medium shallot, finely chopped
1 cup seven-grain Kashi Pilaf
2 cups poultry stock or canned low-sodium chicken broth
2 teaspoons minced fresh chives
2 teaspoons chopped parsley
1 teaspoon chopped fresh thyme
Salt and freshly ground white pepper

1. Spray a heavy saucepan with vegetable oil cooking spray. Add the onion and shallot and cook over low heat, stirring frequently, until translucent, about 10 minutes.

2. Stir in the Kashi Pilaf until well mixed, then add the stock. Increase the heat to high and bring to a boil. Reduce the heat to moderate and boil, uncovered, checking occasionally, until the liquid is absorbed and the Kashi Pilaf is tender but slightly chewy, about 25 minutes. (If the liquid is evaporating too quickly, reduce the heat slightly, add ¼ cup hot water, cover and cook to desired tenderness.) *(The recipe can be prepared to this point up to 1 day ahead; cover and refrigerate. Reheat, covered, over low heat.)*

3. Stir in the chives, parsley and thyme. Season with salt and white pepper to taste. Serve at once.

—Patricia Martell, Norwich Inn & Spa, Norwich, Connecticut

• • •

WARM AUTUMN FRUIT SAUCE

This savory fruit compote goes well with all manner of poultry and game.

Makes 2 Cups
13 Calories per Tablespoon

½ teaspoon whole black peppercorns
Two 1-inch sprigs of fresh rosemary
4 juniper berries
1 medium Golden Delicious or Granny Smith apple—peeled, cored and coarsely chopped
1 medium Anjou pear—peeled, cored and coarsely chopped
¼ cup dried apricots, coarsely chopped
2 cups rich chicken stock or canned low-sodium broth
2 tablespoons pear brandy, such as Poire Williams

1. Cut out a 5-inch single-layer square of cheesecloth. Place the peppercorns, rosemary sprigs and juniper berries in the center. Gather up the corners and tie with cotton string.

2. In a medium nonreactive saucepan, combine the spice bundle, apple, pear and dried apricots. Stir in the stock, pear brandy and ½ cup of water and bring to a boil over moderately high heat. Reduce the heat to moderately low and simmer until the fruit is tender and the liquid is syrupy, about 35 minutes.

—Patricia Martell, Norwich Inn & Spa, Norwich, Connecticut

• • •

PORK TENDERLOIN WITH CAPELLINI AND SPICY CABBAGE EN PAPILLOTE

4 Servings
461 Calories per Serving

2 tablespoons fresh lemon juice
2 tablespoons plus 1½ teaspoons olive oil
¾ teaspoon salt
¼ teaspoon freshly ground black pepper
¼ teaspoon cayenne pepper
½ teaspoon marjoram, crumbled
1½ pounds pork tenderloin, trimmed of all membranes and visible fat and sliced ½ inch thick
6 ounces capellini
1 medium onion, thinly sliced
1 garlic clove, minced
1 pound green cabbage, finely shredded
½ teaspoon curry powder
½ teaspoon chili powder

1. In a medium nonreactive bowl, combine the lemon juice, 2 tablespoons of the olive oil, ½ teaspoon of the salt, the black and cayenne peppers and the marjoram. Add the sliced pork and toss to coat well. Cover and refrigerate for 4 hours, stirring from time to time.

2. Meanwhile, in a large pot of boiling salted water, cook the pasta until slightly firm to the bite, about 3 minutes. (The pasta will finish cooking in the papillotes.) Drain the pasta and rinse under cold running water. Drain thoroughly and toss with the remaining 1½ teaspoons olive oil. Set aside.

3. Reserving the marinade, drain the pork slices. In a large nonstick skillet, heat the marinade over moderately high heat until it begins to bubble. Add the onion and garlic and cook until translucent, about 3 minutes. Add the cabbage, curry powder, chili powder and the remaining ¼ teaspoon salt and toss well. Cover and cook, stirring frequently, until the cabbage is wilted, 4 to 5 minutes. Remove from the heat and let cool completely.

4. To assemble the papillotes, fold a 12-by-16-inch piece of parchment paper in half (to form a 12-by-8-inch rectangle) and draw a large half heart. Holding on to the crease, cut out the heart. Repeat to form 4 parchment wrappers.

5. Spoon the spicy cabbage onto one side of the wrappers. Surround the cabbage with the pasta. Arrange the pork slices on top of the cabbage, overlapping them slightly. Fold and seal the papillote packages with overlapping crimps. Place them on a large baking sheet and refrigerate for up to 5 hours.

6. Preheat the oven to 350°. Bake the papillotes on the bottom rack of the

oven for 20 minutes. Transfer the papillotes to plates, cut them open and serve immediately.

—Bob Chambers

VEAL ROLLS WITH PROSCIUTTO, GORGONZOLA AND SPINACH EN PAPILLOTE

4 Servingss
415 Calories per Serving

3 pounds fresh spinach, stemmed
1 tablespoon olive oil
1 medium onion, finely chopped
½ teaspoon salt
½ teaspoon freshly ground pepper
Pinch of freshly grated nutmeg
Four 6-ounce veal scallops, pounded thin
4 ounces thinly sliced prosciutto, all visible fat removed
4 ounces Gorgonzola cheese, cut into 4 pieces
2 teaspoons minced parsley

1. Place the spinach in a large saucepan and add ¼ cup of water. Cover and cook over moderately high heat, stirring occasionally, until the spinach is wilted, 5 to 6 minutes. Drain the spinach and press it against the side of the strainer to squeeze out excess water. Coarsely chop the spinach.

2. In a large nonstick skillet, heat the oil over moderately high heat. Add the onion and cook until translucent, about 3 minutes. Add the chopped spinach, salt, ¼ teaspoon of the pepper and the nutmeg. Cook, tossing, to dry out the spinach, 3 to 4 minutes. Set aside and let cool completely.

3. Sprinkle the veal scallops with the remaining ¼ teaspoon pepper. Cover the scallops with the prosciutto. Place 1 piece of Gorgonzola on top of the prosciutto at one end of each scallop. Tightly roll up the scallops to enclose the cheese. Press slightly to flatten.

4. To assemble the papillotes, fold a 12-by-16-inch piece of parchment paper in half (to form a 12-by-8-inch rectangle) and draw a large half heart. Holding on to the crease, cut out the heart. Repeat to form 4 parchment wrappers.

5. Spoon the spinach onto one side of the wrappers. Set the veal rolls on the spinach and sprinkle the parsley on top. Fold and seal the papillote packages with overlapping crimps. Place them on a large baking sheet and refrigerate for up to 5 hours.

6. Preheat the oven to 350°. Bake the papillotes on the bottom rack of the oven for 15 minutes. Transfer the papillotes to plates, cut them open and serve immediately.

—Bob Chambers

• • •

ORZO WITH LEMON AND HERBS

Rice-shaped orzo pasta is popular in Greece as well as in Italy. This is a lightened version of a Greek dish.

8 Servings
243 Calories per Serving

7 cups chicken stock or canned low-sodium broth
2 heaping cups orzo (1 pound)
1 tablespoon olive oil
¼ cup fresh lemon juice
¾ cup chopped fresh parsley, chervil or basil, or a combination
Salt and freshly ground pepper

1. In a large nonreactive saucepan, bring the chicken stock to a rolling boil over moderate heat. Add the orzo and cook, stirring often to prevent sticking, until most of the broth is absorbed and the orzo is tender and creamy, about 10 minutes.

2. Remove the pan from the heat and stir in the oil, then the lemon juice and herbs. Season with salt and pepper. Serve, or transfer to a baking dish and keep warm in a 350° oven for up to 20 minutes.

—Martha Rose Shulman

• • •

BULGUR WITH CURRANTS AND SCALLIONS

6 Servings
167 Calories per Serving

1½ teaspoons extra-virgin olive oil
1 bunch of scallions, white and tender green, coarsely chopped (1 cup)
1½ cups bulgur wheat
¼ cup dried currants
3 cups chicken stock or canned low-sodium broth
1 teaspoon salt
½ teaspoon freshly ground pepper

In a medium skillet, heat the oil over moderately high heat. Add the scallions and cook, stirring, until softened, about 2 minutes. Stir in the bulgur, currants, stock, salt and pepper and bring to a boil. Cover, reduce the heat to moderately low and simmer gently until the bulgur is tender, about 20 minutes. Season with salt and pepper to taste. Fluff with a fork and serve.

—Jacques Pépin

• • •

MIXED GRAIN TRIO

At his restaurant in Chicago, Charlie Trotter accents three harmonious, grain-based mixtures with a pungent pesto-like sauce of tarragon, parsley, spinach and basil.

4 Servings
264 Calories per Serving

¼ cup barley
¼ cup quinoa
½ cup instant couscous
2 tablespoons pine nuts
1 tablespoon plus 1 teaspoon olive oil
6 ounces chanterelle mushrooms, stemmed and coarsely chopped
4 ounces shiitake mushrooms, stemmed and finely chopped
1 shallot, minced
Salt and freshly ground black pepper
1 tablespoon finely chopped scallions
1 tablespoon finely chopped parsley
¼ cup fresh corn kernels
½ of a small red bell pepper, cut into ¼-inch dice
3-inch piece of cucumber—peeled, seeded and cut into ¼-inch dice
1 tablespoon chopped fresh mint
1 tablespoon chopped basil
Herb Coulis (recipe follows)

1. In a medium saucepan, combine the barley and 1¼ cups water. Cover and cook over low heat until tender, about 45 minutes. Drain and set aside.

2. In a small saucepan, combine the quinoa and ½ cup water. Cover and cook over low heat until all the water has been absorbed and the quinoa is cooked, about 15 minutes. Set aside.

3. In a small saucepan, bring ⅓ cup water to a boil over high heat. Stir in the couscous, cover and remove from the heat. Let stand for 5 minutes, then uncover and fluff lightly with a fork. Set aside.

4. Preheat the oven to 400°. Place the pine nuts in a pie plate and bake until browned, about 4 minutes. Set aside. Leave the oven on.

5. In a small skillet, heat 1 tablespoon of the olive oil over moderately high heat. Add the chanterelles and cook, stirring occasionally, until tender, about 4 minutes. Using a slotted spoon, transfer the chanterelles to a small bowl. Increase the heat to high and add the remaining 1 teaspoon of the olive oil to the skillet. When hot, add the shiitakes and the shallot and cook, stirring constantly, until wilted, 2 to 3 minutes. Season with a pinch of salt and pepper.

6. In a medium bowl, combine the shiitakes with the reserved quinoa and the chanterelles. Season with salt and pepper.

7. In another bowl, combine the barley with the scallions, parsley, corn kernels and red pepper. Season with salt and pepper.

8. In a third bowl, combine the couscous, cucumber, mint, basil and toasted pine nuts. Pack each of the three grain mixtures into four ½-cup ramekins, making a total of 12.

9. Arrange the ramekins in a large roasting pan. Pour enough hot water into the pan to reach halfway up the sides of the ramekins. Cover with foil and bake for about 20 minutes, until the grains are heated through.

10. To serve, spread one-fourth of the Herb Coulis on each serving plate and invert one of each molded grain mixture onto each plate. Serve warm.

—*Baba S. Khalsa*

• • •

HERB COULIS

Makes ⅘ Cup

½ cup (packed) fresh tarragon leaves
1 cup (packed) spinach leaves, coarsely chopped
½ cup (packed) parsley leaves
¼ cup (packed) basil leaves, coarsely chopped
2 tablespoons chopped fennel fronds
1 tablespoon extra-virgin olive oil
½ teaspoon fresh lemon juice
Salt and freshly ground pepper

In a food processor, combine the tarragon, spinach, parsley, basil and fennel. Puree until a coarse paste forms. With the machine running, slowly pour in the olive oil and ⅓ cup water. Add the lemon juice and season with salt and pepper to taste.

—*Baba S. Khalsa*

• • •

NOODLE GALETTES WITH BASIL WATER AND TOMATOES

Charlie Trotter's rectangles of sautéed capellini are served floating in a basil-infused vegetable broth. The pasta is cooked the day before and refrigerated overnight before being cut into compact noodle *galettes*.

6 Servings
237 Calories per Serving

¼ pound capellini
2 tablespoons plus 1½ teaspoons pure olive oil
Salt and freshly ground pepper
½ pound celery root, peeled and coarsely chopped

½ pound leeks, white and tender green portions, coarsely chopped
1 large onion, chopped
4 celery ribs, chopped
2 parsnips, chopped
2 large bunches of basil (about ½ pound) plus 1 tablespoon finely shredded basil leaves
1 medium red tomato—peeled, seeded and diced
1 medium yellow tomato—peeled, seeded and diced
2 tablespoons extra-virgin olive oil

1. Bring a large pot of salted water to a boil. Add the pasta, bring back to a boil and cook, stirring, until al dente, about 4 minutes. Drain in a colander and toss with 2 tablespoons of the pure olive oil. Season with salt and pepper. In a baking pan, shape the capellini into a 10-by-9-inch rectangle about ⅓-inch thick. Cover and refrigerate overnight.

2. In a large saucepan, combine the celery root, leeks, onion, celery and parsnips and 3 quarts of water. Simmer over low heat for 2 hours. Strain the broth into a clean saucepan and discard the solids. Boil the broth over high heat, skimming occasionally, until reduced to 2 cups, about 20 minutes. Add the basil bunches and remove from the heat. Cover and let steep for 2 minutes. Strain and set aside.

3. In a medium bowl, combine the red and yellow tomato with the extra-virgin olive oil and shredded basil. Set aside.

4. Cut the chilled capellini into six 5-by-3-inch rectangles. In a large nonstick skillet, heat the remaining 1½ teaspoons pure olive oil over moderately high heat. Add the noodle galettes and fry until lightly browned and crisp, about 5 minutes per side. Transfer to paper towels to drain. Meanwhile, reheat the basil water, if necessary.

5. To serve, place a noodle galette in each of 6 large, shallow soup bowls. Place a spoonful of the tomato mixture on top of each galette and pour the hot basil water into each bowl. Serve hot.

—Baba S. Khalsa

• • •

BULGUR RISOTTO

4 Servings
246 Calories per Serving

2 medium shallots, minced
1½ cups cracked wheat bulgur (about ½ pound)
3 cups hot Vegetable Stock (recipe follows)
2 tablespoons chopped mixed herbs, such as chervil and thyme
1½ teaspoons canola or other vegetable oil
2 teaspoons freshly grated Parmesan cheese (optional)
Freshly ground pepper

1. Place the shallots in a medium saucepan, cover and cook over moderately low heat, stirring, until translucent, about 5 minutes.

2. Stir in the bulgur and 2 cups of the hot Vegetable Stock. Cook, stirring, for 5 minutes; if the bulgur is not tender, add another ½ cup of the hot stock and cook for several minutes longer. Check and repeat the process if necessary. Stir in the herbs, oil and Parmesan. Season to taste with pepper.

—Michael Flynn, Sonoma Mission Inn and Spa, Sonoma, California

• • •

VEGETABLE STOCK

You can freeze any remaining stock for up to three months.

Makes 6 Cups
22 Calories per ½ Cup

6 medium celery ribs, cut into 1-inch lengths
4 medium carrots, cut into 1-inch lengths
4 medium tomatoes, quartered
2 onions, coarsely chopped
1 leek, white and tender green portions, coarsely chopped
6 sprigs of parsley
2 bay leaves
10 whole black or white peppercorns
1 bottle (750 ml) dry white wine

1. In a food processor, coarsely chop the celery. Transfer to a large nonreactive flameproof casserole. Repeat with the carrots, then the tomatoes. Add the onions, leek, parsley, bay leaves, peppercorns and ½ cup of water. Cover tightly and cook over moderately low heat until the vegetables are soft but not brown, 30 to 40 minutes.

2. Stir in the wine and increase the heat to moderate. Simmer until reduced by half, about 45 minutes. Add 3½ cups more water, return to a simmer and reduce by half again, about 45 minutes longer. Strain through a sieve.

—Michael Flynn, Sonoma Mission Inn and Spa, Sonoma, California

• • •

GINGERBREAD PANCAKES WITH APPLE BUTTER

The spa serves these pancakes with the apple butter that follows and with "fitness cheese," a 21-calorie-per-tablespoon topping: Whisk 1 cup part-skim ricotta cheese with 2 tablespoons plain nonfat yogurt and refrigerate for at least two hours.

8 Servings
171 Calories per Serving

1 cup whole wheat flour
1 teaspoon baking powder
½ teaspoon ground ginger
½ teaspoon cinnamon
¼ teaspoon salt
¼ teaspoon ground cloves
2 teaspoons instant decaffeinated coffee powder
¼ cup boiling water
1 egg, beaten
1 can (6 ounces) frozen unsweetened apple juice concentrate, thawed
2 tablespoons corn oil or melted and cooled corn oil margarine
Vegetable oil cooking spray
1 cup Apple Butter (recipe follows)

1. In a medium bowl, toss together the flour, baking powder, ginger, cinnamon, salt and cloves; set aside.

2. In a small bowl, stir the instant coffee into the boiling water; let cool for 1 minute. Using a fork, beat in the egg, apple juice concentrate and corn oil until well blended. Stir into the dry ingredients until barely combined (the batter will be lumpy).

3. Heat a griddle or large skillet over moderate heat until hot, about 5 minutes. Spray lightly with vegetable oil cooking spray. Using a measuring scoop or ladle, spoon about ¼ cup of the batter onto the griddle for each pancake, allowing room for them to spread to 3 inches. Cook until the surfaces are covered with tiny bubbles and the undersides are brown, about 1½ minutes, then flip and cook until the other side is brown. If the pancakes are cooking too quickly, reduce the heat slightly. Repeat with the remaining batter. Place 1 pancake on each plate. Top each one with 2 tablespoons of the Apple Butter.

—Bernd Schmitt, Canyon Ranch Vacation Fitness Resort, Tucson

• • •

APPLE BUTTER

Makes 2 Cups
16 Calories per Tablespoon

2 cups unsweetened apple juice
¼ pound unsulphured dried sliced apples (2 cups)*
1 teaspoon cinnamon
Pinch of allspice
Pinch of ground cloves
****Available at health food stores***

1. Combine all of the ingredients in a large saucepan and bring to a boil over high heat. Reduce the heat to moderately low, cover and simmer, stirring occasionally, until the apples are very soft and the liquid is syrupy, about 20 minutes. Set aside to cool for 5 minutes.

2. Scrape the mixture into a blender and puree, about 1 minute. Set aside to cool to room temperature.

—Bernd Schmitt, Canyon Ranch Vacation Fitness Resort, Tucson

• • •

BLUEBERRY-BRAN MUFFINS

Makes 12 Muffins
98 Calories per Muffin

1 cup wheat bran*
1 cup whole wheat flour
¼ cup unprocessed oat bran*
1¼ teaspoons ground cinnamon
1 teaspoon baking soda
¼ cup mashed very ripe banana
¼ cup wild-sage or other herb honey
1 egg
1 teaspoon vanilla extract
1 cup low-fat buttermilk
1 cup (5 ounces) fresh or frozen blueberries or raspberries, coarsely chopped
****Available at health food stores***

1. Preheat the oven to 375°. Line 12 standard muffin cups (2½ inches in diameter) with foil liners.

2. In a medium bowl, toss together the wheat bran, flour, oat bran, cinnamon and baking soda.

3. In a large bowl, whisk the banana, honey, egg and vanilla. Whisk in the buttermilk. Stir the liquid mixture into the dry ingredients until just barely combined.

4. Fold in the berries. Spoon the batter into the muffin cups and bake for 25 to 30 minutes, or until the centers spring back when pressed. Turn out on a rack to cool for 30 minutes.

—Ramon Flores Guerrero, Rancho La Puerta, Baja California, Mexico

• • •

PEAR AND APPLE PHYLLO NESTS

The Golden Door spa in Escondido, California has its own organic orchards and garden. This fruit-and-phyllo pastry creation is an example of chef Tracy Pikhart Ritter's penchant for baking.

8 Servings
130 Calories per Serving

¼ cup light brown sugar
2 tablespoons fresh lemon juice
2 Granny Smith apples (1 pound)—peeled, cored and cut into ½-inch dice
1 pear (8 ounces)—peeled, cored and cut into ⅓-inch dice
Pinch of ground nutmeg
4 sheets of phyllo dough
Butter-flavored vegetable oil cooking spray
20 almonds
4 amaretti cookies, crushed
1 tablespoon confectioners' sugar

1. Preheat the oven to 400°. In a nonreactive saucepan, melt 2 tablespoons of the brown sugar in 1 tablespoon of the lemon juice over moderate heat. Stir in the apples and bring to a boil. Cover and cook, stirring occasionally, until tender, about 10 minutes. Using a slotted spoon, transfer the apples to a bowl.

2. Add the remaining 2 tablespoons brown sugar and 1 tablespoon lemon juice to the cooking juices in the saucepan and melt over moderate heat. Stir in the pear. Cover and simmer, stirring occasionally, until tender, about 5 minutes. Using a slotted spoon, add the pear to the apples.

3. Increase the heat under the cooking juices to moderately high. Bring to a boil and reduce until syrupy, about 3 minutes. Remove from the heat and stir in the nutmeg. Toss with the fruit and set aside.

4. On a work surface, spread out 1 sheet of the phyllo dough and spray lightly with vegetable oil cooking spray. Top with a second sheet of phyllo. Using a large sharp knife, cut the phyllo into four 5-inch squares. Gently mold the pastry squares into 4 standard (2½-inch) muffin cups, with 1 inch of overhang. Repeat with the remaining 2 sheets of phyllo to make 8 pastry nests.

5. Bake the pastry nests for 5 to 7 minutes, until crisp and brown. Transfer the muffin pan to a rack to cool for 10 minutes.

6. Place the almonds on a small baking sheet and roast for about 5 minutes, until lightly browned and fragrant. Let cool, then chop coarsely.

7. Place the phyllo nests on individual dessert plates. Fill each nest with ¼ cup of the apple-pear mixture. Sprinkle the chopped almonds and crumbled amaretti on top. Sift the confectioners' sugar over the nests and serve at once.

—*Tracy Pikhart Ritter*

• • •

GINGERED BAKED APPLES WITH DRIED FRUIT EN PAPILLOTE

4 Servings
380 Calories per Serving

1 pound plums, sliced ¼ inch thick
1 pound Bosc pears—peeled, cored and cut into ½-inch cubes
¼ cup golden raisins
¼ cup dried currants
1 tablespoon minced candied ginger
½ teaspoon vanilla extract
⅓ cup confectioners' sugar
1 tablespoon potato starch
1 teaspoon finely grated lemon zest
1 tablespoon plus 1 teaspoon fresh lemon juice
2 Granny Smith apples—peeled, halved and cored
2 teaspoons granulated sugar
1 pint vanilla low-fat yogurt

1. In a medium nonreactive bowl, toss the plums, pears, raisins, currants, ginger and vanilla.

2. In a small bowl, stir together the confectioners' sugar and potato starch. Sprinkle evenly over the fruit. Add the lemon zest and 2 teaspoons of the lemon juice and toss well.

3. In another bowl, toss the apple halves with the remaining 2 teaspoons lemon juice and the granulated sugar.

4. Preheat the oven to 400°. To assemble the papillotes, fold a 12-by-16-inch piece of parchment paper in half (to form a 12-by-8-inch rectangle) and draw a large half heart. Holding on to the crease, cut out the heart. Repeat to form 4 parchment wrappers.

5. Spoon the fresh and dried fruit mixture onto one side of the wrappers. Set an apple half, cut side up, on top of the fruit. Fold and seal the papillote packages with overlapping crimps. Place them on a large baking sheet and bake on the bottom rack of the oven for 18 minutes.

6. Transfer the papillotes to plates and cut them open. Serve with the vanilla yogurt.

—*Bob Chambers*

• • •

PINEAPPLE-ORANGE SORBET

You can substitute other berries for the strawberries in this dessert.

8 Servings (2 Quarts)
82 Calories per Serving

½ cup sugar
Six ½-inch-wide strips of orange zest
1½ ripe medium pineapples (about 4½ pounds)—peeled, cored and cut into ½-inch chunks
2 cups strained fresh orange juice
3 tablespoons fresh lime juice
1 pint strawberries, thinly sliced lengthwise
1½ tablespoons orange liqueur

1. In a medium saucepan, combine the sugar, orange zest and 1 cup of water and bring to a boil over moderately high heat. Reduce the heat to moderate and simmer until the liquid is reduced by half, 5 to 7 minutes. Set the syrup aside to cool.

2. In a food processor, process two-thirds of the pineapple chunks until relatively smooth, scraping down once or twice. Transfer to a large nonreactive bowl and stir in the orange and lime juices. Pour the reserved sugar syrup through a strainer into the puree. Stir thoroughly.

3. Working in batches if necessary, transfer the mixture to an ice cream maker and freeze according to the manufacturer's instructions. Pack in an airtight container and freeze for up to 1 day.

4. In a medium bowl, toss together the remaining pineapple chunks, the strawberries and the orange liqueur and set aside to macerate for at least 30 minutes and up to 3 hours.

5. To serve, let the sorbet soften slightly in the refrigerator. Spoon into dessert dishes and surround with the macerated fruit.

—*Martha Rose Shulman*

• • •

HAZELNUT CAKE

Serve this cake with any seasonal fresh fruit.

10 Servings
231 Calories per Serving

½ teaspoon plus 1 tablespoon canola or safflower oil
2 cups hazelnuts (6 ounces)
¼ cup potato starch
¾ cup granulated sugar
3 egg yolks
2 tablespoons milk
1 tablespoon unsalted butter, at room temperature
1 teaspoon vanilla extract
5 egg whites
Confectioners' sugar, for dusting

1. Preheat the oven to 325°. Grease an 8-by-1-inch round cake pan with ½ teaspoon of the oil. Line the pan with a circle of parchment or wax paper and set aside.

2. Place the hazelnuts in a pie tin or a baking pan and roast in the oven for 10 to 12 minutes, until very fragrant and golden brown. Immediately wrap the hot hazelnuts in a kitchen towel and firmly rub them together to loosen the skins. Discard the skins. Set the hazelnuts aside to cool completely.

3. In a food processor, combine the cooled hazelnuts, potato starch and ½ cup plus 2 tablespoons of the granulated sugar. Process in long pulses, scraping down the sides of the bowl as necessary, until the nuts are finely ground. Add the egg yolks, milk, butter, vanilla and the remaining 1 tablespoon oil. Process just until smooth. Scrape the batter into a medium bowl.

4. In a large bowl, beat the egg whites with an electric mixer at medium speed until soft peaks form. Increase the speed to high, gradually sprinkle in the remaining 2 tablespoons granulated sugar and beat the whites until firm.

5. Fold one-fourth of the beaten whites into the hazelnut batter to lighten it, then fold in the remaining whites. Do not overfold. Scrape the batter into the prepared pan and bake for about 35 minutes, until a cake tester inserted in the center comes out clean. Transfer the cake to a rack and let it cool in the pan for 10 minutes; it will sink at least ½ inch.

6. Run a sharp knife around the edge of the cake and invert it onto the rack. Remove the pan, peel off the parchment paper and let the cake cool completely, about 45 minutes. Transfer the cake to a platter. Sift a light dusting of confectioners' sugar over the top just before serving.

—*Jacques Pépin*

• • •

BREADS

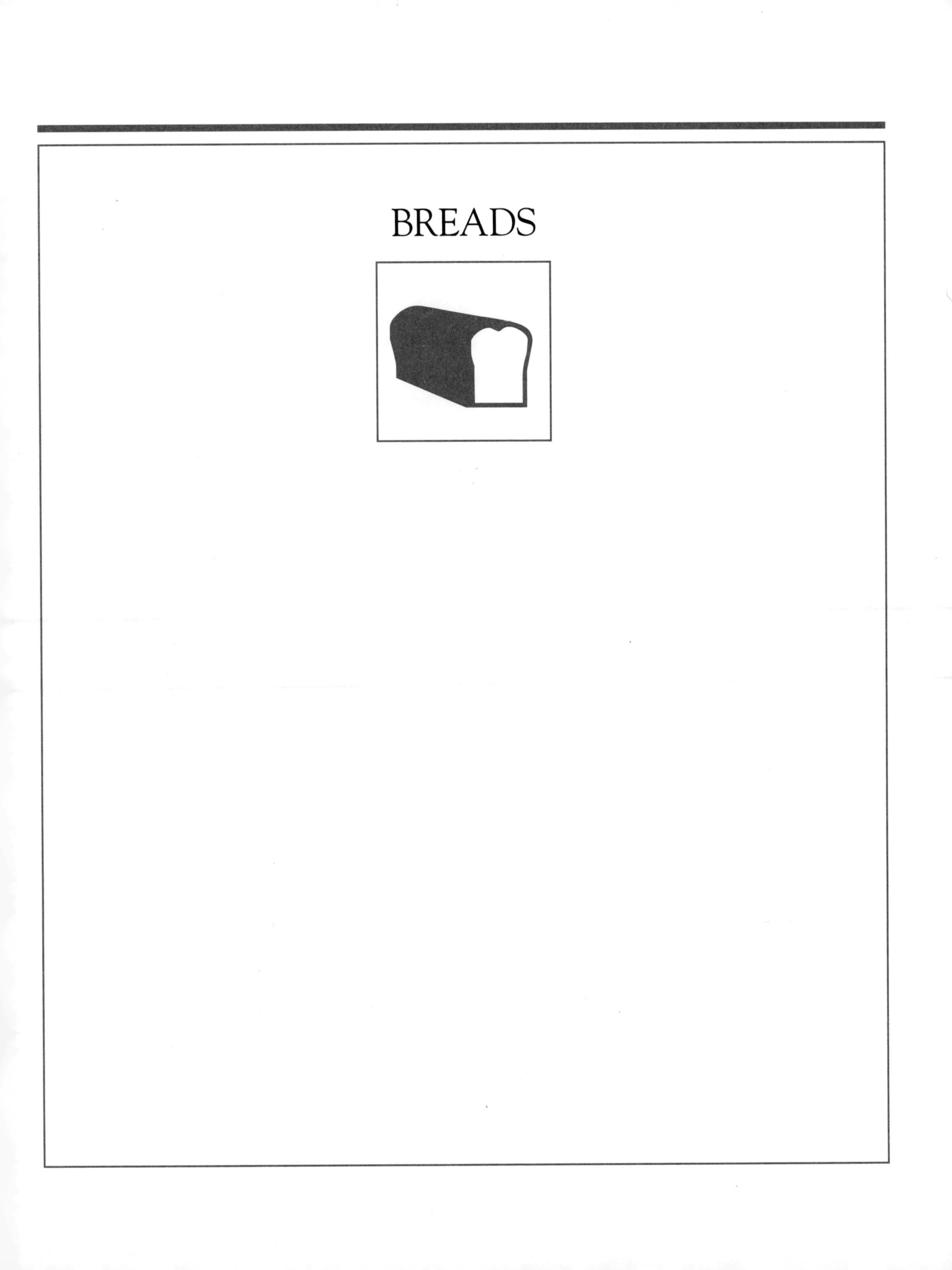

PANETTONE

Panettone is the traditional Italian Christmas bread. Although Milan claims panettone as its own, this light, rich sweet bread studded with orange peel and raisins is available throughout Italy. Today, however, panettone is mostly the province of industrial bakeries, which bake it in rigid waxed paper molds to form loaves that are taller by half than they are wide.

This recipe is for *panettone alla casalinga*, a less lofty home-style version that is simple to prepare. Just observe the following precautions. Make sure all ingredients are at room temperature; cold butter or eggs can cause the dough to separate, making a coarse-textured loaf. Do not let the dough overferment during the final rising or the panettone will fall during baking.

Makes 1 Loaf

½ cup milk
1 envelope (¼ ounce) active dry yeast
3⅔ cups unbleached all-purpose flour
1 stick (4 ounces) unsalted butter, softened, plus 2 tablespoons melted
½ teaspoon salt
⅓ cup sugar
1 teaspoon finely grated lemon zest
2 teaspoons vanilla extract
1 tablespoon white rum
3 whole eggs, at room temperature
3 egg yolks, at room temperature
½ cup diced candied orange peel
½ cup dark raisins
½ cup golden raisins

1. In a small saucepan, heat the milk until lukewarm (110°). Remove from the heat and whisk in the yeast. Place ⅔ cup of the flour in a bowl and stir in the milk-yeast mixture until smooth. Cover tightly with plastic and let rise at room temperature until almost tripled, about 1 hour. (The sponge may fall abruptly toward the end; this is normal.)

2. Fifteen minutes before the sponge is ready, place the stick of butter in a heavy-duty mixer fitted with a paddle. Beat at medium-high speed until light. Add the salt, sugar, lemon zest, vanilla and rum and beat until fluffy, about 5 minutes.

3. In a small bowl, combine the eggs and egg yolks. Beat one-third of the eggs into the butter mixture until smooth. On lowest speed, beat in 1 cup of the flour until fully incorporated. Scrape the bowl and paddle. Repeat with the remaining eggs and flour in two batches, beating well after each addition. Add the sponge and beat on the lowest speed until the dough is smooth and slightly elastic, about 5 minutes. Finally, beat in the candied orange peel and the raisins.

4. Scrape the dough into a buttered 2½-quart bowl, cover tightly with plastic wrap and let rise at room temperature until doubled, about 2 hours.

5. Butter and flour a 9-by-3-inch springform pan. Stir the dough with a rubber spatula to deflate, then scrape it into the prepared pan. Cover loosely with a buttered piece of plastic wrap. Set aside until the dough reaches the top of the pan, about 1 hour. Meanwhile, preheat the oven to 375°.

6. Discard the plastic wrap. Bake the panettone in the middle of the oven for about 20 minutes, until well risen and deeply colored. Cover loosely with foil and bake for 20 to 30 minutes longer, or until a thin knife inserted in the center emerges clean. Transfer to a rack to cool in the pan for 5 minutes, then remove the sides of the pan and slide the panettone off the base onto the rack. Brush all over with the melted butter and let cool completely. *(The panettone can be refrigerated wrapped in plastic for up to 5 days or frozen for up to 1 month. Unwrap, cover loosely with a towel and bring to room temperature before serving.)*

—Nick Malgieri

• • •

HERB BREAD

Indigo serves this bread steaming hot and partially sliced, with a ramekin of soft butter. The next day it makes wonderful toast or diced herbed croutons for salad.

Makes Two 8-Inch Loaves

1 cup lukewarm water (105° to 115°)
2 envelopes (¼ ounce each) active dry yeast
1 small onion, coarsely chopped
6 garlic cloves, minced
¼ cup fresh rosemary leaves
¼ cup fresh thyme leaves
2½ tablespoons extra-virgin olive oil
1 tablespoon plus 1 teaspoon salt
About 5¾ cups unbleached flour or bread flour

1. Place the lukewarm water in a large bowl of a standing electric mixer fitted with a dough hook. Sprinkle the yeast on top and let sit until dissolved, about 5 minutes. In a food processor, combine the onion, garlic, rosemary, thyme and ¾ cup of warm tap water. Process until just combined.

2. Add the herb mixture, olive oil, salt and 1 cup of the flour to the yeast mixture and whisk to combine. Add 4 more cups of flour and beat on low speed until incorporated. Increase the speed to medium and beat until the dough cleans the bowl and springs back

when poked, about 10 minutes. If possible, beat in up to ½ cup more flour, a little at a time.

3. Transfer the dough to a lightly floured surface and knead until quite stiff, 1 to 2 minutes. Knead in as much of the remaining ¼ cup flour as the dough can absorb. Form the dough into a ball and place in a lightly oiled bowl, turning the dough to coat it. Cover the bowl with a warm damp cloth and set aside in a warm place to rise until doubled in bulk and a finger pressed lightly into the dough leaves an indentation, 1½ to 2 hours.

4. Grease two 8-by-4-inch loaf pans. Turn the dough out on a lightly floured surface and knead a little more flour into it if possible. Using a dough scraper or large knife, halve the dough. Flatten 1 piece and roll it up tightly to form a log the length of the loaf pan. Place seam-side down in 1 of the prepared pans and flatten the dough evenly so that it fills the corners of the pan. Cover with a warm damp cloth. Repeat with the remaining dough. Set aside in a warm place until the dough has risen to the top of the pans, 1 to 1½ hours.

5. Preheat the oven to 450°. Sift 1½ teaspoons of flour over the tops of the loaves. Using a sharp serrated knife, slash down the length of each loaf. Place the pans on the bottom rack of the oven and, using a plant sprayer filled with water, spray the oven walls and roof 3 to 5 times. Bake for about 30 minutes, until the tops are quite brown. Reduce the heat to 350° and bake for 10 to 15 minutes longer, until the bottom of the bread sounds hollow when tapped. Transfer the loaves, out of their pans, to a rack to cool.

—*Tony DiLembo, Indigo, Los Angeles*

• • •

GOLDEN RAISIN BRIOCHE

This recipe shortens Nancy Silverton's traditional sourdough-making process into an overnight sensation that contains only a minimal amount of yeast. At the Los Angeles restaurant this bread is used for French toast at breakfast and in a bread pudding with apples for dessert.

Makes Two 8-Inch Loaves

4¼ cups unbleached flour or bread flour
1 cup plus 2 tablespoons lukewarm water (105° to 115°)
½ cup milk, at room temperature
1 teaspoon active dry yeast
2 whole eggs, lightly beaten, at room temperature
3 tablespoons sugar
1¼ teaspoons salt
6 tablespoons unsalted butter, softened
2 cups golden raisins
1 egg yolk

1. Make the sponge: In a medium bowl, combine 1¾ cups of the flour with the water, milk and yeast until blended. Cover with a warm damp cloth and set aside in a warm place until bubbly, about 1 hour.

2. Transfer the sponge to a large bowl of a standing electric mixer fitted with a dough hook. Add the beaten eggs, sugar, salt and the remaining 2½ cups flour. Using a rubber spatula, mix to incorporate. Beat on medium-high speed for 8 minutes, occasionally scraping down the sides of the bowl. The dough will look like a sticky batter and will not pull away from the sides of the bowl. Reduce the speed to low and add the butter. Increase the speed to medium-high and beat, scraping down the bowl once, until incorporated, about 4 minutes. Add the raisins and beat for 2 minutes longer, scraping down the bowl to evenly distribute the raisins.

3. Lightly butter a medium bowl. Scrape the dough into the bowl, cover tightly and refrigerate for at least 8 but no more than 12 hours, until the dough has a web-like surface and has risen slightly.

4. Butter two 8-by-4-inch loaf pans. Turn the dough out onto a floured surface and knead briefly with floured hands. Using a dough scraper or large knife, halve the dough. Using floured hands, flatten 1 piece and roll it up to form a log the length of the loaf pan. Pinch the seam to seal. Place seam-side down in 1 of the prepared pans and flatten the dough evenly with floured hands so that it fills the corners of the pan. Cover the pan with a piece of buttered plastic wrap. Repeat with the remaining dough. Set aside in a warm place until the dough rises to the top of the pan and feels very airy and delicate to the touch, 1 to 1½ hours. Preheat the oven to 425°.

5. In a small bowl, beat the egg yolk with 1 tablespoon of water. Gently brush the top of the loaves with the egg wash. Place the pans on the bottom rack of the oven and, using a plant sprayer filled with water, spray the oven walls and roof 3 to 5 times. Bake for 40 to 50 minutes, until the tops of the loaves are quite dark and the bottoms of the bread are nicely browned and sound hollow when lightly tapped. (It may be necessary to run a knife around the bread to loosen it from the pan.) Set the loaves on a rack to cool.

—*Nancy Silverton, Campanile, Los Angeles*

• • •

WHOLE WHEAT WALNUT-RAISIN BREAD

You can vary the amount of raisins in this bread (the restaurant's recipe called for one cup). Allow time to refrigerate this dough overnight.

Makes 2 Round Loaves

2 cups raisins
3 cups broken walnut halves (about 9 ounces)
2⅓ cups lukewarm water (105° to 115°)
1 envelope (¼ ounce) active dry yeast
2 tablespoons walnut oil
2 tablespoons honey
3 cups whole wheat flour
About 2¾ cups unbleached flour or bread flour
1 tablespoon plus 1 teaspoon salt

1. Preheat the oven to 350°. Soak the raisins in warm tap water to cover until plump, about 1 hour.

2. Meanwhile, place the walnuts on a small baking sheet and toast in the oven for about 10 minutes, until fragrant. Set aside to cool. Drain the raisins and set aside.

3. Pour the lukewarm water into a large bowl of a standing electric mixer fitted with a dough hook. Sprinkle the yeast on top. Set aside until dissolved, about 2 minutes. Using a rubber spatula, stir in the oil, honey and whole wheat flour until combined. Add 2½ cups of the white flour and the salt and beat on low speed until combined. Increase the speed to medium and beat for 6 minutes. Add the nuts and raisins and beat for 3 minutes, scraping the sides of the bowl occasionally.

4. Transfer the dough to a lightly floured surface and knead to distribute the nuts and raisins, 2 to 3 minutes. If the dough is sticky, knead in up to ¼ cup more flour.

5. Form the dough into a ball and place in a lightly oiled medium bowl, turning the dough to coat it. Cover the bowl tightly with plastic wrap and refrigerate overnight.

6. Place the dough on a lightly floured surface and shape it into a ball. Transfer to a well-floured baking sheet, cover with a warm damp cloth and set aside in a draft-free place until the dough has lost its chill and begins to rise, 30 to 45 minutes.

7. Using a dough scraper or large knife, cut the dough into 2 even pieces (about 2 pounds each). Flatten each piece, fold the rim in toward the center and shape each piece into a firm round ball, pinching the underside to seal. Dust lightly with flour. Line 2 medium bowls with kitchen towels and dust with flour. Place the dough, seam-side up, in the bowls. Bring the corners of the towels up to cover the dough and set aside to rise in a draft-free place until doubled in bulk, 1 to 3 hours.

8. Preheat the oven with a hearthstone on the bottom to 425°. Heavily dust a baking sheet without sides with flour. Gently turn out the balls of dough seam-side down onto the baking sheet. If your oven is too small to bake both breads simultaneously, place 1 ball of dough on a floured tray, cover with a warm damp cloth and refrigerate until the oven is free. Sift 1½ teaspoons of flour over each ball of dough. Using a sharp serrated knife, slash a deep "X" on the tops. Slide the dough off the baking sheet onto the hearthstone with a quick jerk. Using a plant sprayer filled with water, spray the oven walls and roof 3 to 5 times. Immediately close the oven door. Spray the oven again 3 minutes later. Bake for 20 minutes, reduce the temperature to 350° and bake for 15 to 20 minutes longer, until the bottoms of the loaves sound hollow when tapped. If you are baking the breads separately, be sure to heat the oven to 425° before baking the second loaf. Transfer the breads to a rack to cool.

—*Amy Scherber, Mondrian, New York City*

• • •

SICILIAN FLATBREAD

This bread is great cut into squares and used for open-faced sandwiches.

Makes 2 Rectangular Flatbreads

1 cup semolina flour*
1 envelope (¼ ounce) active dry yeast
1¼ cups lukewarm water (105° to 115°)
¾ cup ale, at room temperature but not flat
½ cup plus 1 tablespoon extra-virgin olive oil
1 tablespoon sugar
About 3¾ cups unbleached flour or bread flour
1 tablespoon table salt
Cornmeal, for dusting
6 garlic cloves, finely minced
¼ cup plus 1 tablespoon freshly grated Romano cheese
40 fresh sage leaves
1½ teaspoons coarse (kosher) salt
****Available at specialty food stores or Italian markets***

1. In a large bowl of a standing electric mixer fitted with a dough hook, whisk the semolina with the yeast. Whisk in the lukewarm water, ale, 1 tablespoon of the oil and the sugar. Cover the bowl with a warm damp cloth and set aside in a warm place until the mixture is bubbly, 20 to 30 minutes.

2. Using a rubber spatula, stir in 2 cups of the white flour and the table salt. Turn the mixer to low and gradually beat in 1½ cups more flour. Increase the speed to medium and beat until the dough pulls away from the bowl, about 5 minutes. If the dough doesn't pull away, add up to ¼ cup more flour.

3. Transfer the dough to a lightly floured surface and knead by hand until smooth and elastic, a minute or so. Form the dough into a ball and place in a lightly oiled medium bowl, turning the dough to coat it. Cover the bowl with a warm damp cloth and set in a warm place until the dough has doubled in bulk and a finger pressed lightly into it leaves an indentation, 1 to 1¾ hours.

4. Generously dust two 11-by-13-inch baking sheets without sides with cornmeal. Punch down the dough to deflate it and turn it out on a lightly floured surface. Using a dough scraper or large knife, halve the dough and shape 1 piece into an 11-by-13-inch rectangle by stretching gently from the center out. Transfer the dough to 1 of the baking sheets by carefully lifting it with both arms. (Alternatively, dust the top of the dough with flour, roll it up on a rolling pin and unroll it on the baking sheet.) Reshape the dough rectangle on the baking sheet and prick it all over with a fork. Repeat with the remaining dough.

5. Brush the dough with some of the remaining ½ cup oil and evenly distribute the garlic on top. Sprinkle 1½ tablespoons Romano on each rectangle. Finely chop half of the sage leaves and set aside. Dip the remaining whole sage leaves in the remaining oil and arrange 10 of them on each rectangle. Sprinkle each rectangle with ¾ teaspoon coarse salt. (If your hearthstone is too small to bake both pieces at once, cover 1 baking sheet with a warm damp cloth and refrigerate until 30 minutes before the oven is free.) Set aside in a warm place until the dough is puffy, 20 to 30 minutes. Preheat the oven with a hearthstone on the bottom to 425°.

6. Shake the baking sheet gently to be sure the dough is not adhering. If it is, slide a knife underneath to loosen it. Slide the dough off the baking sheet onto the hearthstone with a quick jerk. Using a plant sprayer filled with water, spray the oven walls and roof 3 to 5 times. Bake for 12 to 15 minutes, until the bread is nicely browned. Remove from the oven and immediately sprinkle the reserved chopped sage and remaining 2 tablespoons Romano over the dough. Drizzle a little of the remaining oil on top and serve.

—*Greg Higgins, The Heathman Bakery and Pub, Portland, Oregon*

• • •

FOCACCIA WITH FENNEL AND ANCHOVIES

In addition to the ingredients used here, any other focaccia or pizza topping would taste great on this crisp and chewy flatbread.

Makes Two 10-Inch Focaccias

½ cup lukewarm water (105° to 115°)
1 envelope (¼ ounce) active dry yeast
¼ cup plus 2⅔ cups unbleached flour or bread flour
½ cup whole wheat flour
2 teaspoons fennel seeds
2 teaspoons salt
¼ cup plus 2 tablespoons extra-virgin olive oil, plus more for brushing
½ cup finely chopped flat-leaf parsley
1 tin (2 ounces) anchovies in oil, drained
2 fennel bulbs, tops trimmed
Cornmeal, for dusting
½ cup small shards of Parmesan cheese
Freshly cracked pepper

1. In a medium bowl, combine the lukewarm water and yeast. Stir in the ¼ cup white flour and the whole wheat flour until combined. Pour the remaining 2⅔ cups white flour over this sponge but do not stir it in. Set aside in a warm place until the sponge bubbles up through the flour, 15 to 30 minutes.

2. Using a mortar and pestle, grind the fennel seeds and salt.

3. Scrape the sponge into a large bowl of a standing electric mixer fitted with a dough hook. Add the fennel mixture, 2 tablespoons of the olive oil and 1 cup of water and beat on low speed until combined, scraping the bottom of the bowl occasionally. Increase the speed to medium and continue beating until the dough is elastic and comes away from the bowl cleanly, 8 to 10 minutes. If it seems too stiff, beat in up to ¼ cup more water.

4. Transfer the dough to a lightly floured surface and knead by hand for another minute or so. The dough should be soft and elastic. Form the dough into a ball and place in a lightly oiled medium bowl, turning the dough to coat it. Cover the bowl with a warm damp cloth and set in a warm place until the dough has doubled in bulk and a finger pressed lightly into it leaves an indentation, 1 to 1½ hours. Punch down the dough, re-cover with plastic wrap and refrigerate overnight.

5. Using a dough scraper or knife, halve the dough and form into 2 balls. Place the balls on a large, generously floured baking sheet. Slip a large plastic bag over each end, overlapping them, and set in a warm place until the dough is doubled in bulk, 1 to 1¾ hours.

6. Preheat the oven with a hearthstone on the bottom to 450°. Meanwhile, make the topping. Set aside 2 teaspoons of the chopped parsley. Finely chop the anchovies with the remaining parsley, place in a small bowl and mix in the remaining ¼ cup olive oil; set aside.

7. Using a large sharp knife, halve each fennel bulb. In a medium saucepan, cover the fennel with water and bring to a boil. Boil for 10 minutes. Transfer the fennel, cut-sides down, to paper towels to drain. Slice the fennel crosswise ¼ inch thick.

8. When the dough has risen, use floured hands to stretch and flatten each ball into a 10-inch disk. Dust 2 baking sheets without sides with cornmeal and place 1 disk of dough on each. Prick the dough all over with a fork. Spread the parsley mixture on the dough. Arrange the sliced fennel in a circular pattern on top. Brush the fennel with some olive oil. Scatter the Parmesan shards on top and dust with a little pepper. If your hearthstone is too small to bake both pieces at once, refrigerate 1 baking sheet until the oven is free.

9. Slide the dough off the baking sheet onto the hearthstone with a quick jerk. Using a plant sprayer filled with water, spray the walls and roof of the oven 3 to 5 times. Bake for about 20 minutes, until golden. Transfer the focaccias to a rack to cool slightly, sprinkle the reserved parsley on top and serve warm.

—The Sign of the Dove, New York City

• • •

GRAPE FOCACCIA

This is a sweet version of the traditional flat Italian bread. In Tuscany, where it is eaten as a mid-afternoon snack, it is typically made with flavorful red wine grapes during the harvest season; the seedless table grapes used here are easier to find and to eat.

8 Servings

⅓ cup extra-virgin olive oil
2 tablespoons fresh rosemary leaves
1 envelope (¼ ounce) rapid-rise dry yeast
1 cup lukewarm water (105° to 115°)
3 to 3¼ cups unbleached flour
¼ cup sugar
1 teaspoon salt
2½ cups seedless red or green grapes (about 14 ounces), rinsed and thoroughly dried
1 cup walnut pieces (4 ounces)

1. In a small saucepan, heat the oil over moderate heat until hot, about 5 minutes. Add the rosemary and set aside to cool.

2. In a large bowl, sprinkle the yeast over the warm water. Let stand until the yeast is dissolved, about 5 minutes. Stir in the rosemary oil, 3 cups of the flour, 2 tablespoons of the sugar and the salt until a soft dough forms.

3. Turn the dough out on a very lightly floured surface and knead until smooth and elastic and the rosemary starts to fall out, adding more flour by tablespoons if the dough feels sticky, 8 to 10 minutes.

4. Transfer the dough to a lightly oiled large bowl, turn to coat with the oil. Cover with a towel and let rise in a warm place until doubled in bulk, about 45 minutes.

5. Preheat the oven to 375°. Dust a 15-by-10-by-1-inch jelly-roll pan with flour. Punch down the dough and transfer it to the prepared pan. Using your hands, firmly press and stretch the dough to the edges of the pan. Scatter the grapes and walnuts evenly over the dough, pressing them lightly to adhere. Sprinkle the remaining 2 tablespoons sugar on top.

6. Bake the focaccia for 30 to 35 minutes, or until lightly browned and crisp. Using a knife or spatula, lift and slide the focaccia onto a rack to cool briefly. Serve warm or at room temperature, cut in squares.

—Michele Scicolone

• • •

SAUSAGE BREAD

The ample filling for these savory loaves has a tendency to seep out the sides of the loaves as they bake, which is fine.

Makes 4 Loaves

FILLING:
2 tablespoons vegetable oil
1 pound spicy smoked pork sausage, such as andouille
1½ pounds mozzarella cheese, grated
1 cup chopped green olives
½ cup freshly grated Parmesan cheese
4 scallions, finely chopped
3 tablespoons chopped parsley
2 fresh jalapeño peppers, seeded and finely chopped

BREAD DOUGH:
1 envelope (¼ ounce) active dry yeast
2 teaspoons sugar
½ cup lukewarm water (105° to 115°)
4 cups unbleached flour
1 tablespoon salt
1 egg, beaten

1. *Make the filling:* In a large skillet, heat the oil over moderately high heat. Add the sausage and reduce the heat to moderate. Cook, turning, until browned all over, about 5 minutes. Drain off the oil and set the sausage aside to cool, then chop in small pieces.

2. In a bowl, combine the mozzarella, olives, Parmesan, scallions, parsley and jalapeños. Add the sausage and toss well to mix thoroughly. Cover and refrigerate the filling for at least 3 hours but preferably 24.

3. *Make the dough:* In a large bowl, dissolve the yeast and sugar in the lukewarm water. Set aside in a warm place until starting to foam, about 5 minutes.

4. Add the flour, salt and ¾ cup of warm water. Mix until a dough forms, then transfer the dough to a lightly floured surface and knead well until smooth and elastic, 7 to 10 minutes. If the dough seems dry, add up to ¼ cup more warm water. Transfer the dough to an oiled bowl, cover with a towel and let rise in a warm place until doubled in bulk, about 1 hour.

5. Preheat the oven to 350°. Punch down the dough and knead briefly. Cut the dough in 4 pieces. Working with 1 piece at a time, roll it out into a 10-by-12-inch rectangle. Brush the edges with the beaten egg. Spread one-fourth of the filling to within ½ inch of the edges. Beginning with a longer side, roll up the dough jelly-roll style. Seal the seam and the ends with beaten egg and pinch to close. Transfer the loaf to a greased baking sheet, seam-side down. Repeat with the remaining 3 pieces of dough and filling. Bake the loaves for about 25 minutes, until very lightly browned all over. Let cool slightly before slicing and serving warm.

—John Ed Laborde

• • •

BASIL AND SUN-DRIED TOMATO ROLLS

At The Herbfarm, this dough is turned into a bread and served in warm, fat slices with nasturtium butter on the side. Redolent of basil and sun-dried tomatoes and with a hint of fresh garlic, it is wonderful with everything from soup to salads.

Sun-dried tomatoes are available either dry or packed in olive oil. Soak dry tomatoes in boiling water to reconstitute them. Drain the oil-packed tomatoes thoroughly before using, and since they have probably been salted, decrease the amount of salt accordingly.

Makes 16 Rolls

2 cups (firmly packed) fresh basil leaves
1 large garlic clove, coarsely chopped
¼ cup olive oil
2¾ cups lukewarm water (105° to 115°)
2 tablespoons active dry yeast
⅓ cup sun-dried tomatoes, finely chopped (2 ounces)
6 to 6½ cups all-purpose flour
1¾ teaspoons salt
Fine cornmeal, for dusting
Egg wash: 1 egg yolk mixed with 3 tablespoons water

1. In a food processor, combine the basil leaves and garlic. With the machine on, pour in the olive oil in a stream and process until a rough-textured pesto forms.

2. In a large bowl, combine the lukewarm water and yeast and set aside until dissolved, stirring once or twice. Stir in the pesto and tomatoes, then add 1 cup of the flour and the salt and mix well. Work in 5 more cups of flour, 1 cup at a time, until the dough is soft but not sticky. Turn the dough out onto a lightly floured surface and knead, adding up to ½ cup flour if necessary, until it is elastic and satiny, about 10 minutes. (Alternatively, using an electric mixer fitted with a dough hook, mix the dough ingredients and add the flour as described above, then knead the dough for about 5 minutes at medium-high speed.) Form the dough into a ball. Place the dough in a large, lightly oiled bowl, cover loosely, set aside in a warm place and let rise until doubled in bulk, about 1 hour.

3. Dust 2 baking sheets heavily with cornmeal. Punch down the dough. Cut it into 16 equal pieces and shape each piece into a ball. Place the balls about 2 inches apart on the baking sheets and cover loosely. Set aside in a warm place and let rise until nearly doubled in bulk, about 45 minutes.

4. Preheat the oven to 400°. Brush the rolls with the egg wash and bake for 15 minutes. Switch the pans and bake for another 15 minutes, until the rolls are golden. (If you like crustier rolls, use a plant sprayer filled with water to spray the oven walls and roof several times.)

5. Serve the rolls immediately, or transfer to a rack to cool.

—Jerry Traunfeld, The Herbfarm, Fall City, Washington

• • •

OLIVE ROLLS

Instead of rolls, this dough can also be formed into one large or two small loaves, or it can be formed into a ring. The only salt comes from the olives and olive paste, so feel free to sprinkle a good amount of coarse salt over the top to bring out the flavor.

Makes 16 Rolls

1½ cups lukewarm water (105° to 115°)
2 envelopes (¼ ounce each) active dry yeast
⅔ cup olive paste* (about 2½ ounces)
¼ cup extra-virgin olive oil plus more for brushing
5 cups unbleached flour or bread flour
1 cup oil-cured black olives, pitted
Cornmeal, for dusting
2 teaspoons coarse (kosher) salt
****Available at specialty food stores***

1. Place the lukewarm water in a large bowl of a standing electric mixer fitted with a dough hook. Sprinkle the yeast on top and let sit until dissolved, about 5 minutes.

2. Stir in the olive paste, olive oil and 1 cup of the flour. Add 3 more cups of flour and beat on low speed until incorporated. Add the remaining 1 cup flour and beat until incorporated. Increase the speed to medium and beat for 6 minutes. Add the olives and beat for 2 minutes. Transfer the dough to a lightly floured surface and knead by hand for another minute to evenly distribute all the olives. The dough should be springy, smooth and soft but not sticky.

3. Form the dough into a ball and place in a lightly oiled bowl, turning the dough to coat it. Cover the bowl with a warm damp cloth and set in a warm place to rise until the dough has doubled in bulk and a finger lightly pressed into it leaves an indentation, 1 to 1¼ hours.

4. Transfer the dough to a lightly floured surface and roll it evenly into a rope about 16 inches long. Using a dough scraper or large knife, halve the rope and cut each half into 8 even pieces (about 3 ounces each). Cover the dough with plastic wrap or a damp cloth while you work. Flatten 1 piece of dough, fold the rim in toward the center and roll with your palms to form a tight ball; pinch the bottom seam. Repeat with the remaining pieces of dough.

5. Dust cornmeal evenly over a large baking sheet without sides. Place the rolls on the baking sheet a few inches apart and cover with a warm damp cloth. Set aside in a warm place until the dough is almost doubled in bulk, the surface is taut and there is very little spring left when poked, 1¼ to 1¾ hours.

6. Preheat the oven with a hearthstone on the bottom to 425°.

7. If your oven is too small to bake all the rolls at once (allowing about 3 inches between each roll), transfer half of them to another baking sheet, cover with a warm damp cloth and refrigerate until the oven is free. Using a pastry brush, gently brush a little olive oil over each roll. Sprinkle the coarse salt on top. Using a sharp serrated knife, deeply slash each roll.

8. Slide the rolls off the baking sheet onto the hearthstone with a quick jerk. Alternatively, pick up each roll gently and place it on the stone, but work quickly so that the oven doesn't lose heat. Using a plant sprayer filled with water, spray the oven walls and roof 3 to 5 times. Bake the rolls for 15 to 20 minutes, until lightly browned and the bottoms sound hollow when tapped. Transfer to a rack to cool.

—*Roberto Donna, Galileo, Washington, D.C.*

• • •

BUTTERMILK BISCUITS

Makes 8 Biscuits

1 cup unbleached flour
½ cup whole wheat pastry flour*
1½ teaspoons baking powder
¾ teaspoon salt
½ teaspoon baking soda
½ teaspoon sugar
6 tablespoons cold unsalted butter, cut into teaspoon-size pieces
½ cup buttermilk
****Available at health food stores***

1. Preheat the oven to 400°. In a large bowl, mix together the unbleached flour, pastry flour, baking powder, salt, baking soda and sugar. Using your fingers or a pastry blender, cut in the butter until the mixture resembles coarse crumbs. Stir in the buttermilk with a fork.

2. Turn the dough out onto a lightly floured surface and knead about 8 times until it just becomes a smooth mass. Pat the dough into an 8-by-4-inch rectangle. Cut the dough into eight 2-inch square biscuits.

3. Place the biscuits about 1 inch apart on an ungreased baking sheet. Bake for about 15 minutes, until golden brown. Serve warm.

—*Susan Shapiro Jaslove*

• • •

Corn Muffins with Bell Peppers and Scallions (p. 213).

Left, Blueberry Crostata with a Cornmeal Crust (p. 217). Above, Red Beet Devil's Food Cake (p. 225).

REAL-GOOD SOUTHERN BISCUITS

Real southern biscuits should really be made with southern flour, but Real-Good Southern Biscuits can be made with Yankee flour too. To preserve their tender and flaky texture, southern biscuits are never cut with a knife but are gently pulled or split apart by hand.

Measure the flour by spooning it into a 2-cup dry measure and then leveling it off with the edge of a knife.

Makes 10 to 12 Biscuits

2 cups all-purpose flour, preferably southern soft wheat flour
1 tablespoon baking powder
1 teaspoon coarse (kosher) salt
1 teaspoon sugar
3 tablespoons chilled vegetable shortening
2 tablespoons chilled unsalted butter, cut into bits
⅔ cup cold milk

1. In a bowl, combine the flour, baking powder, salt and sugar and mix well. Sift the dry ingredients into a large wide bowl. Using cool fingertips, a pastry blender or 2 knives, cut the shortening and butter into the dry ingredients just until the mixture resembles coarse meal with some lumps that are the size of baby peas.

2. Make a well in the center of the flour and fat mixture; pour in ½ cup of the milk. Begin stirring with a large fork. Gradually stir in the remaining milk until the dough comes together in a loose mass and leaves the sides of the bowl.

3. Turn the dough out onto a very lightly floured work surface. Knead gently about 8 times, going through the motions without applying any real pressure, just until the dough begins to look smooth and no longer feels sticky. (Any further kneading will overdevelop the gluten in the flour and make the biscuits tough.)

4. Using lightly floured hands and a very light touch, pat the dough from the center outward into a square or rectangle about ½ inch thick. Dip a 2-inch biscuit cutter in flour, tap off the excess and cut straight down through the dough; do not twist or the biscuits will be lopsided. Repeat the process, reflouring the cutter and tapping off the excess each time, until you have cut as many rounds as possible. Trim away the excess dough. (Although you can use the remaining dough, reworking the scraps would produce only 2 or 3 more biscuits, and they would be tougher than the others.)

5. Preheat the oven to 450°. Using a spatula, transfer the cut biscuits to an ungreased baking sheet arranging them about ½ inch apart. Cover with plastic wrap and refrigerate for 15 minutes to let the dough relax.

6. Bake the biscuits in the middle of the oven for 12 to 14 minutes, rotating the baking sheet once, until delicately golden brown. Serve hot.

—Leslie Newman

• • •

Benne Seed Wafers (p. 231).

CORN MUFFINS WITH BELL PEPPERS AND SCALLIONS

These corn muffins are best eaten on the day they are made.

Makes 20 Muffins

3 large ears of fresh corn
2 cups unbleached flour
1 cup yellow cornmeal
¼ cup sugar
2 teaspoons baking powder
1 teaspoon salt
¼ cup finely diced green bell pepper
¼ cup finely diced red bell pepper
¼ cup thinly sliced scallion greens
2 cups heavy cream
2 eggs, lightly beaten
4 tablespoons unsalted butter, melted

1. Preheat the oven to 350°. Grease two ½-cup muffin tins thoroughly. Using a thin sharp knife, slice the corn kernels from each cob into a large measuring cup until you have 1½ cups.

2. In a large bowl, sift together the flour, cornmeal, sugar, baking powder and salt. Stir in the corn kernels, green and red bell peppers and scallions. Make a well in the center and add the cream and eggs. Using a fork, stir in the dry ingredients until lightly mixed. Fold in the butter until incorporated.

3. Pour about ⅓ cup batter per muffin into the prepared muffin tins. Bake the muffins for 20 to 25 minutes, or until a cake tester inserted in their centers comes out clean. Transfer the muffin tins to a rack to cool slightly, then invert and let the muffins cool completely.

—Hay Day, The Country Farm Market, Greenwich, Connecticut

• • •

SERRANO CHILE-BLUE CORNSTICKS

Makes 1½ Dozen Cornsticks

6 tablespoons vegetable shortening
1 stick (4 ounces) butter
1 tablespoon vegetable oil, plus more for brushing
2 to 3 serrano chiles—seeded and minced
1 red bell pepper, cut into ¼-inch dice
1 green bell pepper, cut into ¼-inch dice
¼ cup minced red onion
3 garlic cloves, minced
1½ cups blue cornmeal
1 cup all-purpose flour
2 tablespoons sugar
1 teaspoon baking powder
2 eggs
1 cup buttermilk, at room temperature, mixed with a pinch of baking soda
½ cup heavy cream, at room temperature
3 tablespoons chopped cilantro (fresh coriander)

1. Preheat the oven to 400°. In a small saucepan, melt the shortening with the butter over low heat. Let cool to room temperature.

2. In a small skillet, heat the vegetable oil over low heat. Add the chiles, red and green bell peppers, onion and garlic, and cook until softened, about 5 minutes. Set aside.

3. Heat 1 or 2 cast-iron cornstick molds in the oven for 5 minutes. Meanwhile, in a large bowl, sift together the cornmeal, flour, sugar and baking powder. In a medium bowl, lightly beat the eggs. Add the melted shortening and butter, then stir in the buttermilk, cream, cilantro and the bell pepper mixture. Add to the flour mixture and stir just until smooth; do not overmix.

4. Brush the hot molds generously with oil. Return the molds to the oven for about 2 minutes. Spoon about ¼ cup of the batter into each mold and bake for 20 to 25 minutes, until brown and crisp on the bottom and springy to the touch. Turn the cornsticks out of the pan and let cool slightly on a rack. Repeat with the remaining batter, brushing the molds generously with oil before refilling. Serve warm.

—Stephan Pyles

• • •

GREEN-CHILE SPOON BREAD

This quintessentially southern recipe is one of the most elegant dishes made from cornmeal. Chiles add a distinctive southwestern flavor.

8 Servings

2 large garlic cloves, unpeeled
1 large ear of corn, unshucked
1 large green poblano chile
¾ cup milk
¾ cup chicken stock or canned low-sodium broth
½ cup yellow cornmeal
2 tablespoons unsalted butter
¼ teaspoon white pepper
1½ teaspoons salt
3 tablespoons finely diced green bell pepper
3 tablespoons finely diced red bell pepper
1 serrano chile, seeded and minced
½ cup heavy cream
3 eggs, separated

1. Preheat the oven to 400°. Loosely wrap the garlic cloves in foil and roast until soft, about 25 minutes. At the same time, roast the corn until the husk is browned and the kernels are tender, about 45 minutes. Squeeze the garlic pulp from the skins into a small bowl and mash to a paste; set aside. When the corn is cool enough to handle, shuck the ear. Using a sharp knife, slice the kernels off the cob. Set aside.

2. Roast the poblano directly over a gas flame or under the broiler as close to the heat as possible, turning occasionally until charred all over. Immediately transfer to a brown paper bag, seal and set aside to steam for a few minutes. Peel the poblano and remove the core, seeds and ribs. Cut the chile into ¼-inch dice and set aside. *(The recipe can be prepared to this point up to 1 day ahead. Cover and refrigerate the garlic, corn and diced poblano chile separately.)*

3. In a large saucepan, combine the milk and chicken stock and bring to a boil over high heat. Boil for 30 seconds, then reduce the heat to moderate and whisk in the cornmeal until smooth. Remove from the heat and add the butter, pepper and the salt. Stir in the green and red bell peppers, serrano chile, garlic, roasted corn, poblanos and cream. Let cool slightly, then whisk in the egg yolks.

4. Preheat the oven to 325°. Beat the egg whites to soft peaks and gently fold them into the batter. Pour into a lightly oiled 1½-quart ceramic baking dish or soufflé mold and place inside a larger pan. Add enough very hot water to reach about 1 inch up the sides of the baking dish. Place the pan in the middle of the oven and bake for 45 minutes, or until a knife inserted in the center comes out clean. Check after 30 minutes. If the top is browning too quickly, cover with foil. Serve immediately.

—Stephan Pyles

• • •

PIES, CAKES & COOKIES

CHERRY-FRANGIPANE TART

The pastry for this tart was inspired by a recipe of Jacques Pépin's. If desired, serve with vanilla ice cream.

Makes One 11-Inch Tart

PASTRY:
1 cup all-purpose flour
¼ teaspoon salt
¼ teaspoon sugar
6 tablespoons cold unsalted butter, cut into small pieces
4 to 5 tablespoons ice water

FILLING:
¼ cup almond paste (2 ounces), at room temperature
2 tablespoons unsalted butter, at room temperature
3 tablespoons plus 1½ teaspoons granulated sugar
1 tablespoon plus ¾ teaspoon all-purpose flour
½ of a lightly beaten egg white
2 pounds ripe Bing cherries, pitted (4 to 4½ cups)
1 teaspoon kirsch
Confectioners' sugar, for dusting

1. *Make the pastry:* In a large bowl, toss the flour with the salt and sugar to mix well. Using a pastry blender or 2 knives, cut in 3 tablespoons of the cold butter until the mixture resembles coarse meal. Then cut in the remaining 3 tablespoons butter until only pea-size pieces remain. Using a fork, stir in ¼ cup ice water. The dough should hold together when pinched; if not, add a few more drops of ice water. Pat the dough into a disk, wrap in wax paper and refrigerate until firm, at least 30 minutes.

2. *Prepare the filling:* In a medium bowl, using a hand-held electric mixer, beat the almond paste and butter at high speed until fluffy. In a small bowl, combine the 1½ teaspoons granulated sugar and ¾ teaspoon flour and beat into the almond mixture until incorporated. Beat in the egg white. Set the frangipane filling aside.

3. Preheat the oven to 400°. On a lightly floured surface, roll out the pastry into a 14-inch round. Gently place the dough in an 11-inch tart pan with a removable bottom, fitting it evenly into the pan without stretching. Trim the overhanging dough to 1 inch, then fold this in against the inside of the pan to make a double-thick rim. (Smooth out the dough to seal any cracks.)

4. Using a rubber spatula, gently spread the frangipane evenly over the bottom of the tart shell. Sprinkle the remaining 1 tablespoon flour and 1 tablespoon of the granulated sugar evenly over the frangipane.

5. In a large bowl, toss the cherries with the kirsch. Spread the cherries evenly in a single layer over the frangipane. Sprinkle the remaining 2 tablespoons granulated sugar on top.

6. Bake the tart for 55 to 60 minutes, or until the edge of the pastry is brown. Transfer to a rack to cool for 15 minutes, then remove the tart pan. Serve slightly warm or at room temperature, dusted with confectioners' sugar.

—*Lindsey Shere*

• • •

STRAWBERRY-RHUBARB CROSTATA

Assemble this rustic tart before guests arrive and refrigerate it. Bake the *crostata* just before serving the main course so that it will still be warm at dessert time.

🍷 A fruity, just-sweet wine that will underscore this dish, not compete with it, would be ideal. Italian Moscatos, such as 1991 Rivetti Moscato d'Asti "La Spinetta" or California versions, such as 1989 Robert Mondavi Moscato d'Oro, are just the ticket for this tart, fruity dessert. Alternatively, serve a small glass of chilled grappa, such as Nonino Fragola.

6 Servings

1 cup unbleached flour
¼ cup plus 1 teaspoon superfine sugar
¼ teaspoon coarse (kosher) salt
1 stick (4 ounces) very cold unsalted butter, cut into ½-inch cubes
2 to 3 tablespoons ice water
2 medium ribs of fresh rhubarb, cut on the diagonal ¼ inch thick
½ pint strawberries, sliced lengthwise ¼ inch thick
Confectioners' sugar, for dusting
Mint Crème Anglaise (recipe follows)

1. In a food processor, combine the flour, 2 tablespoons of the superfine sugar and the salt and pulse to blend. Add the butter and pulse about 15 times, until the butter is the size of small peas.

2. With the machine on, add 2 tablespoons of the ice water through the feed tube and process for about 10 seconds, until the dough barely begins to form a ball. If the dough is dry and

crumbly, add up to 1 tablespoon more water and process briefly until incorporated.

3. Transfer the dough to a sheet of aluminum foil and pat to form a 5-inch disk. Wrap the dough completely in the foil and refrigerate until thoroughly chilled, at least 1 hour or up to 2 days.

4. Preheat the oven to 425°. On a lightly floured surface, roll out the dough to a 12-inch round. Carefully transfer it to a heavy flat baking sheet and sprinkle with 1 tablespoon of the superfine sugar.

5. Cover the dough with an even layer of rhubarb, leaving a 1½-inch border all around. Sprinkle with 1 tablespoon of the superfine sugar. Arrange the strawberry slices over the rhubarb in concentric circles, with the berries pointing toward the center. Sprinkle with the remaining 1 teaspoon superfine sugar.

6. Fold the edge of the dough inward to form a 2-inch rim, letting the dough drape gently over the fruit. Lightly press the rim of the dough to the baking sheet, taking care not to mash the fruit. Gently pinch together any pleats that formed when the dough was folded over.

7. Bake the tart for 20 to 25 minutes, or until the pastry is thoroughly cooked and golden brown and the fruit has given off some of its juice. Let the *crostata* cool for about 10 minutes, then dust with confectioners' sugar. Cut into wedges and serve warm with the Mint Crème Anglaise.

—Johanne Killeen & George Germon

• • •

MINT CREME ANGLAISE

Makes 1¼ Cups

1 cup heavy cream
½ cup fresh mint leaves
2 egg yolks
2 tablespoons sugar
¼ teaspoon pure vanilla extract

1. In a heavy medium saucepan, combine the cream and mint and bring just to a boil over high heat. Remove from the heat and set aside to steep for 45 minutes. Strain the cream and return it to the saucepan; reheat until warmed through.

2. In a medium bowl, whisk the egg yolks with the sugar until blended. Gradually whisk in the hot cream. Pour the mixture into a clean saucepan and cook over moderate heat, stirring constantly with a wooden spoon, until it reaches 160°, is slightly thickened and just coats the back of a spoon, 6 to 8 minutes. Do not let the custard boil, or it will curdle.

3. Immediately strain the custard into a metal bowl and set it in a larger bowl of ice water to cool, stirring occasionally. Stir in the vanilla. Cover and refrigerate until chilled or for up to 1 day.

—Johanne Killeen & George Germon

• • •

BLUEBERRY CROSTATA WITH A CORNMEAL CRUST

The fruit filling for this Italian tart is like a blueberry jam. When blueberries are plentiful, make extra batches of the filling (it freezes well). It is a good spread for toast and other breakfast breads.

8 Servings

3 cups blueberries
1 cup granulated sugar
⅛ teaspoon cinnamon
2 cups all-purpose flour
⅓ cup yellow cornmeal
1 teaspoon baking powder
½ teaspoon salt
1½ sticks (6 ounces) cold unsalted butter, cut into bits
2 teaspoons finely grated lemon zest
1 egg plus 1 egg yolk, lightly beaten
Confectioners' sugar, for dusting

1. In a medium nonreactive saucepan, combine the blueberries, ½ cup of the granulated sugar and the cinnamon. Cover and bring to a simmer over moderate heat. Uncover and cook, stirring occasionally, until the mixture has thickened, about 20 minutes. Set aside to cool. The mixture will thicken further as it cools. *(The recipe can be made to this point up to 1 day ahead. Transfer to a small container, cover and refrigerate.)*

2. In a large bowl, toss the flour with the cornmeal, baking powder, salt and the remaining ½ cup granulated sugar. Using a pastry blender or 2 knives, cut in the butter until the mixture resembles coarse crumbs. Stir in the lemon zest. Using a fork, lightly stir the beaten eggs into the flour mixture until the dough is moist and crumbly.

3. Scatter about two-thirds of the crumb mixture in a 9-inch round tart pan with a removable bottom. Pat the crumbs evenly over the bottom and up the sides of the pan to form a shell. Spoon the chilled blueberry mixture into the shell and smooth the surface.

4. Preheat the oven to 350°. On a very lightly floured surface, pat the remaining crumb mixture into a square; cut in 9 even pieces. Roll each piece into a ½-inch-thick rope. Crisscross the ropes 1 inch apart over the surface of the tart to form a lattice. Press the rope ends against the inside rim of the shell.

5. Bake the tart for 45 to 50 minutes, or until golden brown. Let cool on a wire rack for 10 minutes. Remove the tart from the pan and let cool completely. Just before serving, sift confectioners' sugar over the top of the *crostata.*

—Michele Scicolone

• • •

A-MACE-ING BANANA CREAM PIE WITH COCONUT

8 Servings

CRUST:

1¼ cups all-purpose flour
½ teaspoon sugar
Pinch of salt
5 tablespoons cold vegetable shortening
3½ tablespoons ice water

CUSTARD FILLING:

½ cup sugar
⅓ cup cornstarch
2½ cups milk
3 egg yolks
½ teaspoon vanilla extract
¼ teaspoon freshly grated nutmeg
3 bananas, sliced ¼ inch thick

TOPPING:

½ cup unsweetened shredded coconut
½ cup heavy cream
2 tablespoons confectioners' sugar
1 can (14 ounces) unsweetened coconut milk,* well chilled
½ teaspoon ground mace
****Available at Asian markets***

1. *Make the crust:* In a large bowl, combine the flour, sugar and salt. Cut in the shortening until the mixture has particles the size of small peas. Drizzle the ice water on top and, using a fork, stir to combine. Using your hands, shape the dough into a disk, wrap well and refrigerate for at least 30 minutes.

2. *Make the filling:* In a small bowl, combine the sugar and cornstarch. In a heavy medium saucepan, whisk together the milk and egg yolks. Place over moderate heat and whisk in the cornstarch mixture. Cook, whisking constantly, until the mixture boils once or twice and begins to thicken, about 5 minutes. Remove from the heat while still whisking. Pour the custard into a clean bowl and whisk until slightly cooled, about 1 minute. Place a piece of plastic wrap directly on the surface of the custard and let stand at room temperature until just barely warm, about 30 minutes.

3. Preheat the oven to 350°. On a lightly floured surface, roll out the dough to a circle about ⅛ inch thick. Fold the dough in quarters and place it in a 9-inch pie pan. Unfold the dough and press it gently into the pan without stretching. Trim off any long overhang and crimp the rim. Freeze the dough until very firm, about 10 minutes.

4. Line the dough with aluminum foil and fill with pastry weights. Bake in the middle of the oven for about 30 minutes, until the rim starts to brown. Remove the foil and weights and bake for another 10 minutes, until the crust is golden brown all over and cooked through. Transfer to a rack to cool.

5. Stir the vanilla and nutmeg into the cooled custard, then fold in the sliced bananas. Pour the filling into the cooled pie crust. Press plastic wrap directly on the surface of the custard and refrigerate for at least 2 hours or overnight.

6. *Make the topping:* Preheat the oven to 350°. Spread the shredded coconut on a baking sheet and bake, stirring a few times, for about 5 minutes, or until golden brown. Transfer to a plate and set aside.

7. In a large bowl, whip the cream until soft peaks form. Add the confectioners' sugar and whip just until firm. Cover and refrigerate.

8. Open the can of chilled coconut milk and measure out ½ cup of the thickened milk from the surface. Reserve the remaining coconut milk for another use. Whip the coconut "cream" gently into the whipped cream. The mixture should be firm but spreadable.

9. Spread the topping over the banana custard. Sprinkle the toasted coconut around the edge of the pie near the crust. Using a small sieve, dust the top of the pie evenly with the mace. Serve at once.

—Marcia Kiesel

• • •

CHOCOLATE MACADAMIA NUT TART

If you can find only salted macadamia nuts, rinse them, pat them thoroughly dry and roast as indicated.

Makes One 11-Inch Tart

1½ cups macadamia nuts (about 7 ounces)
6 ounces bittersweet chocolate, coarsely chopped
2 tablespoons unsalted butter
2 whole eggs
1 egg white
⅔ cup sugar
⅔ cup dark corn syrup
1 teaspoon dark rum
Chocolate Pastry Shell (recipe follows)
Unsweetened whipped cream, for serving

1. Preheat the oven to 300°. Spread the macadamia nuts on a small baking sheet and roast, shaking and turning once or twice, for about 8 minutes, until fragrant and golden. Let cool, then chop coarsely. Place in a medium skillet and toast over low heat, stirring often, until golden brown all over, about 8 minutes; be careful not to let them burn. Set aside to cool completely. Increase the oven temperature to 350°.

2. In a double boiler, combine the chocolate and butter and melt, stirring, over moderate heat. Set aside to cool slightly.

3. In a large bowl, whisk the whole eggs, egg white, sugar and corn syrup until combined. Stir in the rum and the cooled chocolate mixture and nuts until blended. Pour the filling into the partially baked Chocolate Pastry Shell and bake for about 45 minutes, until the center is set and does not wiggle when shaken. Set aside on a rack to cool. Serve at room temperature or chilled, garnished with whipped cream.

—*Teresa Gannon, Haliimaile General Store, Haliimaile, Maui, Hawaii*

• • •

CHOCOLATE PASTRY SHELL

This is a chocolate cookie-like crust. The dough softens quickly once out of the refrigerator and is a bit difficult to transfer to the tart pan, but scraps can be used to repair any cracks.

Makes One 11-Inch Tart Shell

2 cups all-purpose flour
¼ cup unsweetened cocoa powder
1½ sticks (6 ounces) unsalted butter, cut into pieces and softened to room temperature
½ cup sugar
2 egg yolks
1 tablespoon heavy cream
1 teaspoon vanilla extract
½ teaspoon salt

1. On a work surface, mix the flour and cocoa until well blended; form into a mound. Make a well in the center and add the remaining ingredients. Using your hands, slowly blend the ingredients in the well until partially mixed, then incorporate the flour and cocoa until completely combined and a soft dough forms. Pat the dough into a disk, wrap well and refrigerate for at least 2 hours or overnight.

2. Between sheets of wax paper, roll out the dough into a 13-inch round. Refrigerate for 10 minutes. Remove the wax paper and transfer the dough to an 11-inch fluted tart pan with a removable bottom. Fit the dough evenly into the pan and trim any overhanging pastry. Refrigerate for at least 10 minutes more. Preheat the oven to 425°.

3. Line the chilled shell with aluminum foil and weigh down with pie weights or dried beans. Bake for 10 minutes, then remove the foil and weights and bake for 5 minutes longer, until just set but slightly soft.

—*Teresa Gannon, Haliimaile General Store, Haliimaile, Maui, Hawaii*

• • •

ORANGE-RHUBARB BREAKFAST CAKE

Makes One 13-by-9-Inch Cake

⅓ cup granulated sugar
1 tablespoon unsalted butter, softened
½ cup finely chopped walnuts
1½ teaspoons finely grated orange zest
1 teaspoon cinnamon
1⅓ cups (packed) light brown sugar
⅔ cup vegetable oil
1 cup buttermilk
1 egg
1 teaspoon vanilla extract
2¼ cups all-purpose flour
¼ cup oat bran
1 teaspoon baking soda
Pinch of salt
2 cups fresh or partially thawed frozen rhubarb, cut into ½-inch pieces
1 tablespoon confectioners' sugar

1. Preheat the oven to 350°. Lightly butter a 13-by-9-by-2-inch baking pan.

2. In a small bowl, using your fingers, rub the granulated sugar and butter together until blended. Mix in the walnuts and ½ teaspoon each of the orange zest and cinnamon. Set the streusel topping aside.

3. In a large bowl, blend the brown sugar and oil. Add the buttermilk, egg and vanilla and stir to combine. In a medium bowl, toss the flour, oat bran, baking soda, salt and remaining 1 teaspoon orange zest and ½ teaspoon cinnamon. Stir the dry ingredients into the buttermilk mixture until combined. Fold in the rhubarb.

4. Spoon the batter into the prepared pan. Sprinkle the reserved streusel topping over the top. Bake for about 50 minutes, or until a cake tester inserted in the center comes out clean. Let cool on a rack for at least 10 minutes. Sift the confectioners' sugar on top and serve.

—*Marcy Goldman*

• • •

PUMPKIN BOURBON POUND CAKE

10 to 12 Servings

2 sticks (8 ounces) unsalted butter, softened
1 cup granulated sugar
1 cup light brown sugar
4 eggs, at room temperature, beaten
¼ cup milk
2 tablespoons bourbon
1 teaspoon vanilla extract
2 cups fresh or canned unsweetened pumpkin puree
3 cups all-purpose flour
2 teaspoons baking soda
2 teaspoons baking powder
1¾ teaspoons cinnamon
½ teaspoon ground ginger
¼ teaspoon ground allspice
¼ teaspoon freshly grated nutmeg
Small pinch of salt
1 cup plus 2 tablespoons pecan halves, coarsely chopped
Bourbon Caramel Glaze (recipe follows)

1. Preheat the oven to 350°. Generously grease and flour a 12-cup angel food cake pan or bundt pan.

2. In a large bowl, using an electric mixer, cream the butter, granulated sugar and brown sugar until fluffy. Gradually beat in the eggs on low speed. Beat in the milk, bourbon, vanilla and pumpkin puree.

3. In a bowl, sift the flour with the baking soda, baking powder, cinnamon, ginger, allspice, nutmeg and salt. Add the dry ingredients to the pumpkin mixture and mix just until blended. Stir in 1 cup of the pecans.

4. Spoon the batter into the prepared pan and bake for about 1 hour, or until a cake tester inserted in the center comes out clean. Let the cake cool in the pan for 10 minutes before inverting onto a rack to cool completely. Transfer to a plate.

5. Drizzle the warm Bourbon Caramel Glaze over the top of the cake. Garnish with the remaining 2 tablespoons pecans.

—*Marcy Goldman*

• • •

BOURBON CARAMEL GLAZE

Makes 1¼ Cups

1 stick (4 ounces) unsalted butter
½ cup (packed) light brown sugar
About 3 tablespoons heavy cream
1½ cups confectioners' sugar, sifted
3 tablespoons bourbon
¼ teaspoon vanilla extract

In a small heavy saucepan, melt the butter over moderately low heat. Stir in the brown sugar until incorporated. Stir in the 3 tablespoons cream and simmer, stirring, for 3 minutes. Using an electric mixer, beat in the confectioners' sugar, bourbon and vanilla. If necessary, add more cream to achieve a heavy glaze consistency. Use warm.

—*Marcy Goldman*

• • •

BUTTERNUT SQUASH, APPLESAUCE AND DATE CAKE

Makes Two 9-Inch Loaves

2 cups (loosely packed) pitted dates
1 small butternut squash
2 cups sugar
1½ cups vegetable oil
4 eggs
1 cup unsweetened applesauce
1 teaspoon vanilla extract
1 teaspoon finely minced lemon zest
3⅔ cups all-purpose flour
2 teaspoons baking powder
2 teaspoons baking soda
2 teaspoons cinnamon
¼ teaspoon ground ginger
½ cup finely chopped walnuts

1. Preheat the oven to 350°. Generously grease two 9-inch loaf pans. Soak the dates in a bowl of very hot water for 5 minutes. Drain, halve lengthwise and set aside.

2. Halve the squash lengthwise and scoop out and discard the seeds. Place on a baking sheet cut side down and bake for about 30 minutes, until soft. Let cool, then scoop the pulp into a food processor; puree until smooth. Measure 1 cup of the puree for the cake and save the remainder for another use.

3. In a large bowl, beat the sugar, oil, eggs, squash puree, applesauce, vanilla and lemon zest with an electric mixer until well combined.

4. In a medium bowl, sift the flour with the baking powder, baking soda, cinnamon and ginger. On low speed, gradually beat the dry ingredients into the wet ingredients just until blended. Stir in the dates and walnuts.

5. Spoon the batter into the prepared pans. Bake the cakes for 1 hour, or until golden brown and a cake tester inserted in their centers comes out clean. Transfer to a rack to cool slightly, then invert the cakes onto the rack to cool completely.

—Marcy Goldman

• • •

GA'S SUNDAY NIGHT CAKE

This was the first recipe my mother ever gave me. It is as simple as it seems and works flawlessly.

Makes One 8-Inch Loaf

⅔ cup unsalted butter, softened
⅔ cup granulated sugar
2 eggs, at room temperature
3 drops of vanilla or almond extract
⅔ cup all-purpose flour
½ teaspoon baking powder
1 tablespoon fresh orange juice
1 tablespoon confectioners' sugar

1. Preheat the oven to 350°. Grease an 8-inch loaf pan.

2. In a medium bowl, using a hand-held electric mixer, beat the butter with the sugar on high speed, until light and fluffy. Add the eggs, one at a time, and beat until incorporated. Beat in the vanilla. Sift in the flour and baking powder and beat on low speed until blended.

3. Scrape the batter into the prepared pan and bake for 30 to 40 minutes, until a cake tester inserted in the center comes out clean.

4. Leave the cake in the pan for 5 minutes, then turn it out onto a rack. In a small bowl, combine the orange juice and confectioners' sugar and spread it over the top of the cake while still hot. Let cool slightly before slicing.

—Mary Anne Dolan

• • •

BASIC NUT CAKE

This simple cake can be made with just about any nut. Depending on the variety you choose, you'll need four to five ounces of nuts to yield the one cup of ground nuts called for. The batter can be baked in a 9-inch round cake pan or a jelly-roll pan—only the baking times will vary. For a chocolate nut cake, see the variation below.

Makes One 9-by-2-Inch Round or One 10½-by-15½-by-¾-Inch Rectangle

4 eggs
⅓ cup light brown sugar
1 teaspoon vanilla extract
Pinch of salt
⅓ cup granulated sugar
1 cup ground nuts
½ cup all-purpose flour
4 tablespoons unsalted butter, melted and cooled

1. Preheat the oven to 350°. Butter the cake pan. Line the bottom of the pan with parchment or wax paper and butter the paper.

2. Separate 3 of the eggs, placing the yolks and whites in separate bowls. Add the remaining whole egg to the yolks and beat at medium speed until blended. Slowly beat in the brown sugar and then the vanilla. Continue beating at high speed until the mixture is very light, about 3 minutes. Clean and dry the beaters.

3. Add the salt to the egg whites and beat at medium speed until the whites are opaque and just begin to hold their shape. Increase the speed to high and gradually beat in the granulated sugar. Continue beating until the whites are glossy and hold firm peaks.

4. Using a large rubber spatula, gently fold the whites into the yolk mixture. Stir the ground nuts to aerate them and then pour them on one side of the egg mixture. Fold in the ground nuts until half incorporated. Sift the flour over the batter and continue folding just until the batter is smooth; be careful not to deflate the batter by overmixing.

5. In a small bowl, gently stir ½ cup of the batter into the melted butter, then fold it back into the remaining batter until incorporated. Scrape the batter into the prepared pan and smooth the surface with a metal spatula. Bake for 15 to 17 minutes for a rectangular layer and about 25 minutes for a round one, or until the cake is light golden and a toothpick inserted in the center comes out clean.

6. Loosen the cake from the pan with the point of a small sharp knife. Invert the cake on a rack, remove the pan and peel off the paper. Cover the cake with another rack and turn it right side up. Let cool to room temperature.

BASIC CHOCOLATE NUT CAKE

Follow the Basic Nut Cake recipe, but replace 3 tablespoons of the flour with 3 tablespoons of unsweetened cocoa powder.

—Nick Malgieri

• • •

HAZELNUT MARSALA ROLL

10 Servings

Basic Nut Cake (p. 221), made with ground skinned hazelnuts (see Note)
1½ cups heavy cream
¼ cup sweet Marsala, such as Florio or Pellegrino
3 tablespoons sugar
1 tablespoon dark rum
¼ cup skinned hazelnuts (see Note), coarsely chopped

1. Make the Basic Nut Cake batter using ground hazelnuts. Bake it in a 10½-by-15½-by-¾-inch jelly-roll pan and cool as directed. Slide the cake onto a piece of parchment or wax paper, right side up.

2. In a bowl, combine the cream, Marsala, sugar and rum. Beat at medium speed until firm. Spread half of the Marsala whipped cream over the cake using a metal spatula. Fold in 1 inch of the long edge of the cake closest to you and tightly roll up the cake. Center the roll on the paper, tightly wrap the paper around it and twist the ends to seal. Refrigerate the roll and the remaining Marsala whipped cream for 1 hour.

3. Unwrap the roll and transfer it to a large platter, seam side down. Spread the remaining Marsala whipped cream over the roll. Trim the ends on the diagonal for a neat appearance. Garnish the roll with the chopped hazelnuts and refrigerate until just before serving.

NOTE: *To skin hazelnuts, bake them at 350° for 10 minutes, until the skins are cracked and loose and the nuts are lightly toasted. Rub the hot hazelnuts in a towel to loosen the skins, then peel with your fingers. Return recalcitrant nuts to the oven for a few more minutes if necessary. Let the nuts cool before grinding.*

—*Nick Malgieri*

• • •

CHOCOLATE MOCHA WALNUT ROLL

The slight bitterness of the walnuts combines with the chocolate and coffee to make a rich but not excessively sweet cake.

10 Servings

Basic Nut Cake (p. 221), made with ground walnuts
1 cup heavy cream
⅓ cup strong brewed coffee
12 ounces semisweet chocolate, finely chopped
4 tablespoons unsalted butter, softened
2 tablespoons dark rum
10 walnut halves, for garnish

1. Make the Basic Nut Cake batter using ground walnuts. Bake it in a 10½-by-15½-by-¾-inch jelly-roll pan and cool as directed.

2. In a medium saucepan, combine the cream and coffee and bring to a boil over moderate heat. Remove from the heat and add the chocolate. Stir once to mix and set aside for 5 minutes. Add the butter and rum and whisk until smooth. Pour the ganache into a bowl, cover and set aside until thickened and beginning to set.

3. Slide the cooled cake onto a piece of parchment or wax paper, right side up. Spread half of the ganache over the cake using a metal spatula. Fold in 1 inch of the long edge of the cake closest to you and tightly roll up the cake. Center the roll on the paper, tightly wrap the paper around it and twist the ends to seal. Refrigerate the roll for about 30 minutes; leave the remaining ganache at room temperature.

4. Unwrap the roll and transfer it to a large platter, seam side down. Spread the remaining ganache over the roll in a smooth layer. Using the tines of a fork, streak the ganache to give it a decorative grooved appearance. Trim the ends of the roll on the diagonal for a neat appearance. Arrange the walnut halves on top of the roll to mark each portion. Refrigerate the cake until 30 minutes before serving.

—*Nick Malgieri*

• • •

PINEAPPLE AND MACADAMIA CAKE

Cooking the pineapple for the filling makes it sweet and tender, even if the pineapple is underripe.

10 Servings

Basic Nut Cake (p. 221), made with ground macadamia nuts
1 medium pineapple (about 2 pounds)—peeled, quartered, cored and sliced crosswise ¼ inch thick
⅓ cup plus 2 tablespoons granulated sugar
2 tablespoons kirsch or white rum
¾ cup heavy cream
Confectioners' sugar, for dusting

1. Make the Basic Nut Cake batter using ground macadamias. Bake it in a 9-by-2-inch round cake pan and cool as directed.

2. Meanwhile, in a medium nonreactive saucepan, combine the pineapple, ⅓ cup of the granulated sugar, ¼ cup of water and the kirsch. Bring to a simmer over moderately low heat and cook the pineapple until softened, about 5 minutes. Remove from the heat and let the pineapple cool in the syrup. Drain the pineapple in a colander set over a bowl; chill the pineapple and syrup separately.

3. In a medium bowl, combine the cream and the remaining 2 tablespoons granulated sugar. Beat at medium speed until firm peaks form.

4. Using a long serrated knife, split the cake in half horizontally. Place the bottom of the cake on a platter, cut side up, and brush 2 tablespoons of the pineapple syrup on top. Spread half of the whipped cream on the cake. Arrange the drained pineapple slices on the whipped cream, overlapping them slightly. Top with the remaining cream.

5. Moisten the cut side of the top layer with 2 tablespoons of the pineapple syrup, then invert it onto the cake. Lightly sift confectioners' sugar over the top of the cake and serve soon after assembling.

—*Nick Malgieri*

• • •

LEMON PISTACHIO CAKE

To dress this cake up, spread a thin layer of raspberry preserves under the lemon frosting and decorate the top of the cake with fresh raspberries when they are in season.

10 Servings

Basic Nut Cake (p. 221), made with ground blanched pistachios (see Note)
¾ cup milk
¾ cup granulated sugar
1 teaspoon finely grated lemon zest
3 egg yolks
3 tablespoons flour
¼ cup strained fresh lemon juice
2 tablespoons kirsch
2 sticks (8 ounces) unsalted butter
Chopped blanched pistachios, for garnish
Confectioners' sugar, for dusting

1. Make the Basic Nut Cake batter using ground blanched pistachios. Bake it in a 9-by-2-inch round cake pan and cool as directed.

2. In a medium nonreactive saucepan, combine the milk, ¼ cup of the granulated sugar and the lemon zest. Whisk once and bring to a boil over low heat.

3. Meanwhile, in a medium bowl, whisk the egg yolks, then whisk in ¼ cup of the granulated sugar. Sift in the flour and whisk to blend, then add the lemon juice.

4. Whisk in one-third of the hot milk. Return the remaining milk in the pan to a boil and whisk in the egg yolk mixture. Whisk constantly until the custard thickens and comes to a boil. Boil, whisking constantly, for 30 seconds. Scrape the custard into a nonreactive container, press plastic wrap directly against the surface and refrigerate until cold.

5. In a small saucepan, combine the remaining ¼ cup granulated sugar with ¼ cup of water and bring to a boil over high heat. Remove from the heat and let cool, then add the kirsch. Set the syrup aside.

6. In a medium bowl, beat the butter until very soft and light. Add the cold lemon custard all at once, then continue beating until the frosting is smooth and light, about 5 minutes. (If it appears curdled, continue beating—it is only because the cold custard caused the butter to firm up. The butter will soften again, and the frosting will easily smooth out.)

7. Using a long serrated knife, cut the cake in half horizontally. Place the bottom on a platter, cut side up, and brush with half the syrup. Spread a little less than half the lemon frosting on top. Top with the second layer and brush with the remaining syrup. Frost the outside of the cake. Press the chopped pistachios all over the top and sides and refrigerate until the frosting is set. Remove the cake from the refrigerator about 30 minutes before serving. Lightly sift confectioners' sugar over the cake.

NOTE: *To blanch pistachios, place in a saucepan, cover with water and bring to a boil. Drain immediately and rub the nuts in a towel to loosen the skins, then peel the nuts. Place the nuts in a baking pan and crisp them in a 300° oven for about 7 minutes, without allowing them to take on any color. Let cool completely before grinding.*

—*Nick Malgieri*

• • •

PECAN RUM TEA CAKE

10 Servings

Basic Nut Cake (p. 221), made with ground pecans
1 tablespoon granulated sugar
3 tablespoons dark rum
⅔ cup confectioners' sugar
24 pecan halves, for garnish

1. Make the Basic Nut Cake batter using ground pecans. Bake it in a 9-by-2-inch round cake pan and unmold as directed.

2. Meanwhile, in a small saucepan, combine the granulated sugar and 2 tablespoons of water and bring to a boil, stirring to dissolve the sugar. Remove from the heat and let cool, then stir in 1 tablespoon of the rum.

3. While the cake is still warm, brush the rum syrup evenly over the top. Let the cake cool completely.

4. In a small saucepan, combine the confectioners' sugar and the remaining 2 tablespoons rum. Stir until smooth. Place over low heat and stir until very warm. Drizzle the glaze over the cooled cake from a fork. Arrange the pecan halves in a ring around the top rim of the cake.

—*Nick Malgieri*

• • •

CHOCOLATE ALMOND LOAF CAKE

To vary the flavoring of the cake, spread one tablespoon of orange marmalade on each layer before spreading it with the ganache.

10 Servings

Basic Chocolate Nut Cake (p. 221), made with ground almonds
1 cup heavy cream
12 ounces semisweet chocolate, finely chopped
4 tablespoons unsalted butter, softened
3 tablespoons orange liqueur
2½ tablespoons sugar
¼ cup toasted sliced almonds (1½ ounces), for garnish

1. Make the Basic Chocolate Nut Cake batter using ground almonds. Bake it in a 10½-by-15½-by-¾-inch jelly-roll pan and cool as directed.

2. In a medium saucepan, bring the cream to a boil over moderately high heat. Remove from the heat and add the chocolate. Stir once to mix and set aside for 5 minutes. Whisk in the butter and 2 tablespoons of the orange liqueur until smooth. Pour the ganache into a bowl, cover and let cool until thickened and beginning to set.

3. In a small saucepan, combine the sugar with 2½ tablespoons of water and bring to a boil over high heat. Remove from the heat and let cool, then add the remaining 1 tablespoon orange liqueur. Set the syrup aside.

4. Cut the cooled cake in thirds crosswise; each piece will measure 5 by 10 inches. Position one piece on a platter. Brush with one-third of the syrup and spread with a thin layer of the ganache. Repeat with the 2 remaining cake layers, syrup and some of the ganache. Spread the remaining ganache over the cake and decorate with the sliced almonds. If desired, use a pastry bag fitted with a small star tube to pipe a series of ganache rosettes around the top border of the cake. Refrigerate the cake until 30 minutes before serving.

—*Nick Malgieri*

• • •

CHOCOLATE-PECAN CAKE WITH CHERIMOYA CUSTARD SAUCE

10 to 12 Servings

¾ cup coarsely chopped pecans (about 3½ ounces)
1 cup heavy cream
4 tablespoons unsalted butter
10½ ounces semisweet chocolate, coarsely chopped
2 ounces unsweetened baking chocolate, coarsely chopped
5 eggs
⅓ cup sugar
1 teaspoon vanilla extract
Boiling water
Cherimoya Custard Sauce (recipe follows)

1. Preheat the oven to 350°. Line the bottom of a 9-by-2-inch round cake pan with parchment or wax paper. Butter and flour the pan and paper, tapping out the excess flour. In a small pie pan, toast the pecans until fragrant, stirring once, about 10 minutes. Let cool.

2. In a medium saucepan, combine the cream and butter and bring to a boil over moderately high heat. Remove from the heat and stir in the semisweet and unsweetened chocolate. Cover the pan and set aside until the chocolate is melted, about 5 minutes. Stir to blend completely and let cool.

3. In a large bowl, combine the eggs, sugar and vanilla. Set the bowl over a saucepan of simmering water and whisk over low heat until the mixture is warm to the touch, about 1 minute. Remove the bowl from the water and beat the eggs with an electric mixer at high speed, until tripled in volume, about 8 minutes.

4. Beat one fourth of the egg mixture into the melted chocolate until incorporated. Stir in the toasted pecans. Then, using a rubber spatula, gently fold the chocolate mixture into the remaining egg mixture just until blended.

5. Pour the batter into the prepared cake pan and place in a larger pan. Pour enough boiling water into the larger pan to reach halfway up the sides of the cake pan. Bake in the middle of the oven until a skewer inserted in the center of the cake comes out clean, 45 to 50 minutes. Remove from the oven and leave the cake in the water bath for 30 minutes.

6. When cool, remove the cake pan from the water bath and dry the bottom and sides. Invert the cake, right side up, onto a serving platter and carefully peel off the parchment paper. *(The cake can* *be prepared to this point up to 3 days ahead. Cover and refrigerate. Let return to room temperature before serving.)* Serve at room temperature with the chilled Cherimoya Custard Sauce.

—*Stephan Pyles*

• • •

CHERIMOYA CUSTARD SAUCE

The cherimoya, or custard apple, is an amazingly rich, complex fruit with subtle flavors of papaya, mango, coconut, pineapple and sometimes even vanilla. It can be found at specialty or Latin markets and should be used when completely ripe and soft to the touch. Ripe mango or pineapple, or a combination of the two, can be substituted here.

Makes 2 Cups

2 very ripe cherimoyas (about 1¼ pounds)
1 cup milk
½ vanilla bean, halved lengthwise
⅓ cup sugar
3 egg yolks
⅓ cup heavy cream or crème fraîche

1. Peel the cherimoyas and place in a coarse sieve set over a medium bowl. Using a rubber spatula, strain the pulp; discard the seeds. In a food processor, puree the pulp until smooth. Transfer to a small bowl and set aside.

2. In a medium saucepan, bring the milk and vanilla bean to a boil over high heat. Remove, cover and set aside for 5 minutes to infuse.

3. In a medium bowl, whisk the sugar with the egg yolks until thick and light, about 2 minutes.

4. Remove the vanilla bean from the milk. (Rinse the bean and store for another use.) Strain the warm milk into the egg yolk-sugar mixture, then transfer to a clean medium saucepan. Cook over moderate heat, stirring constantly with a wooden spoon, until the mixture reaches 175° on a candy thermometer, is slightly thickened and coats the back of the spoon, 5 to 8 minutes. Remove from the heat and immediately whisk in the cream. Let cool slightly, then refrigerate until completely chilled.

5. When cold, whisk in the cherimoya puree; serve cold. *(The sauce can be made up to 1 day ahead and kept, covered, in the refrigerator.)*

—*Stephan Pyles*

• • •

RED BEET DEVIL'S FOOD CAKE

Serve this cake with whipped cream or à la mode with coffee ice cream.

Makes One 13-by-9-Inch Cake

6 medium beets
3 ounces unsweetened chocolate
1½ cups granulated sugar
3 eggs
1 cup vegetable oil
1¾ cups all-purpose flour
1½ teaspoons baking soda
Confectioners' sugar, for dusting

1. In a medium saucepan, combine the beets and enough water to cover. Bring to a boil over high heat, reduce the heat to moderately low and simmer until tender, about 1 hour. Drain, rinse with cold water and peel the beets. In a food processor, puree until completely smooth.

2. Preheat the oven to 350°. Lightly grease a 13-by-9-by-2-inch baking pan. In a small double boiler, melt the chocolate. Set aside to cool.

3. In a medium bowl, whisk the granulated sugar with the eggs and oil until blended. Stir in the pureed beets and the cooled chocolate.

4. Sift the flour with the baking soda. Stir the dry ingredients into the chocolate-beet mixture. Spoon the batter into the prepared pan and bake for 25 to 30 minutes, or until the cake springs back slightly when touched. Transfer to a rack to cool completely. Dust the top of the cake with confectioners' sugar.

—*Marcy Goldman*

• • •

RICH GINGERBREAD

This moist cake will sink slightly.

6 Servings

2 cups all-purpose flour
1½ teaspoons ground ginger
1 teaspoon cinnamon
1 teaspoon baking soda
¾ teaspoon salt
½ teaspoon ground allspice
1½ sticks (6 ounces) unsalted butter, softened
½ cup (packed) light brown sugar
1 egg
¾ cup molasses
¾ cup milk
Unsweetened lightly whipped cream

1. Preheat the oven to 350°. Butter a 9-inch round cake pan.

2. In a bowl, sift the flour with the ginger, cinnamon, baking soda, salt and allspice. In a large bowl, cream the butter and brown sugar. Beat in the egg and then the molasses. Add the dry ingredients and the milk in 5 parts, beginning and ending with the dry ingredients and beating after each addition just to mix.

3. Using a rubber spatula, scrape the batter into the prepared pan and smooth the top. Bake for about 50 minutes, until a tester inserted in the center of the cake comes out clean and the sides pull away slightly from the pan. Transfer to a rack to cool for 15 minutes before serving with the whipped cream. *(The gingerbread will keep for up to 1 week; wrap well and refrigerate.)*

—Stephanie Lyness

• • •

MINT AND BLACK PEPPER CAKE WITH PISTACHIO CRUST

🍷 Desserts always call for some sweetness in sparkling wine. With this not-too-sweet loaf, serve a Mumm's Extra Dry Champagne (which is actually a little sweet) or a 1990 Cascinetta Moscato d'Asti from Italy (which will echo the cake's minty flavor).

Makes One 8-Inch Loaf

1 stick (4 ounces) unsalted butter, at room temperature
⅔ cup plus 2½ tablespoons sugar
2½ tablespoons white crème de menthe
1 teaspoon whole black peppercorns, crushed
6 egg whites, at room temperature
Pinch of salt
Pinch of cream of tartar
1 cup all-purpose flour, sifted
½ cup unsalted shelled pistachio nuts
Whipped cream, for serving

1. Preheat the oven to 350°. Butter and flour an 8-by-2-inch loaf pan.

2. Using an electric mixer on medium speed, cream the butter with ⅓ cup of the sugar, until light and fluffy. Beat in the crème de menthe and crushed peppercorns.

3. With clean beaters, in a clean bowl, beat 5 of the egg whites on high speed with the salt and cream of tartar until soft peaks form. While still beating, sprinkle in ⅓ cup of the sugar, a tablespoon at a time, until the whites are stiff and glossy.

4. Alternately fold the beaten egg whites and the flour into the butter in 3 batches. Fold carefully but thoroughly; the less the batter is manipulated, the lighter the cake will be. Scrape the batter into the prepared pan and bake for 30 minutes.

5. Meanwhile, in a food processor, combine the pistachio nuts and the remaining egg white and 2½ tablespoons of sugar. Pulse until the nuts are coarsely chopped.

6. Remove the loaf from the oven after 30 minutes. If it hasn't cracked, make a few shallow slits on top. Spread the pistachio mixture over the top, letting it seep into the cracks. Bake the loaf for 25 minutes longer or until a cake tester inserted in the center comes out clean. Transfer to a rack, let cool slightly and unmold the loaf; let cool for 1 hour. *(The cake can be made 1 day ahead and kept at room temperature, tightly wrapped.)* Serve in slices with a dollop of whipped cream if desired.

—David Rosengarten

• • •

INDIVIDUAL WARM CHOCOLATE TORTES

At Chez Panisse this dessert has been served with vanilla, coffee, raspberry, caramel, anise, Cognac, eggnog, mint, noyau, Chartreuse, maraschino and macaroon ice creams.

Bake these tortes in 4-by-1-inch flan rings or in 6-ounce pineapple cans (which have a 3¼-inch diameter) with their tops, bottoms and labels removed.

10 Servings

10 ounces bittersweet chocolate, such as Callebaut or Valrhona, coarsely chopped
2½ sticks (10 ounces) unsalted butter, at room temperature
9 egg yolks, at room temperature
½ cup granulated sugar
5 egg whites, at room temperature
¼ teaspoon cream of tartar
Confectioners' sugar, for dusting
1 quart Vanilla Ice Cream (p. 249) or another ice cream
Bittersweet Chocolate Sauce (recipe follows)

1. Preheat the oven to 300°. Butter a large baking sheet that won't flex in the oven and liberally butter the inside of ten 3¼- or 4-inch rings (see headnote). Set the rings about 1 inch apart on the baking sheet. (You may need 2 sheets, depending on their size.)

2. In a double boiler, melt the chocolate over moderately low heat, stirring until smooth. Remove the top of the double boiler from the heat and set aside to cool slightly.

3. In a medium bowl, using an electric mixer, cream the butter at high speed until fluffy. Beat in the cooled chocolate.

4. In a large bowl, beat the egg yolks with 6 tablespoons of the sugar at high speed until the mixture holds a ribbon for 3 seconds, 4 to 5 minutes. Beat in the chocolate mixture on low speed, scraping down as necessary, until thoroughly incorporated.

5. In a large bowl, using clean beaters, beat the egg whites until foamy. Add the cream of tartar and beat at medium speed until soft peaks form. Beat in the remaining 2 tablespoons sugar at high speed just until the egg whites hold soft peaks again. Then, using a rubber spatula, fold one-third of the whites into the chocolate mixture. Fold in the remaining whites just until mixed.

6. Fill each of the prepared rings about half full; smooth the tops. *(The recipe can be made to this point up to 3 hours ahead. Set the tortes aside at room temperature.)* Bake the tortes until puffed and just set in the middle, about 15 minutes for 3¼-inch rings and 20 minutes for 4-inch rings.

7. Set the baking sheet on a rack to cool. As the tortes cool, they will sink; push in their edges so that they fall evenly into the rings. After 10 minutes, twist the rings and remove from the tortes. Using a metal spatula, transfer the tortes to individual dessert plates and dust their tops lightly with confectioners' sugar. Serve warm with a couple of scoops of ice cream. Drizzle the Bittersweet Chocolate Sauce over the ice cream and around the tortes.

—Lindsey Shere

• • •

BITTERSWEET CHOCOLATE SAUCE

For the best texture, this sauce should be made the day before serving.

Makes 1⅔ Cups

5 ounces bittersweet chocolate, such as Callebaut or Valrhona, coarsely chopped
2 tablespoons butter

In a small heavy saucepan, combine the chocolate and 1¼ cups of warm water and stir over low heat, until the chocolate is just melted. Remove from the heat and whisk in the butter. Set aside to cool to room temperature, about 30 minutes; then cover and refrigerate overnight. Set aside at room temperature for 1 hour before serving.

—Lindsey Shere

• • •

PINA COLADA CHEESECAKE

This very large, tall cake should be made a day ahead so that it can be refrigerated overnight.

Makes One 10-Inch Cake

3 cups finely ground graham cracker crumbs (12 ounces)
1 cup unsweetened shredded coconut (2 ounces)
2½ cups granulated sugar
6 tablespoons unsalted butter, melted
2½ cups coarsely chopped fresh pineapple, from a 2½-pound pineapple (see Note)
¼ cup light brown sugar
3 pounds cream cheese, at room temperature
6 eggs
½ cup unsweetened coconut milk*
2 cups heavy cream
¼ cup cream of coconut, such as Coco Lopez brand
2 teaspoons vanilla extract
****Available at Asian markets***

1. In a large bowl, toss together the graham cracker crumbs, ¾ cup of the coconut and ¼ cup of the granulated sugar. Using a fork, stir in the melted butter. Transfer the crumb mixture to a 10-by-3-inch springform pan and press evenly all over the bottom and up the sides of the pan. Refrigerate for 15 minutes. Preheat the oven to 350°.

2. In a medium nonreactive saucepan, stir together the pineapple and brown sugar. Bring to a simmer over moderate heat and cook until soft and syrupy, about 10 minutes. Drain and set aside to cool. Reserve the syrup for another use.

3. Using an electric mixer, beat the cream cheese and the remaining 2¼ cups granulated sugar at medium speed, scraping the bowl. Beat in the eggs one at a time, blending well after each addition. Beat in the unsweetened coconut milk.

4. Pour one-fourth of the cream cheese mixture into the chilled crust. Spoon the cooled pineapple on top in an even layer. Pour the remaining cream cheese mixture over the pineapple. Bake for 1½ hours, then prop open the oven door and let the cake cool completely in the oven. Refrigerate the cake overnight.

5. Preheat the oven to 350°. Spread the remaining ¼ cup coconut on a baking sheet and toast until golden, about 5 minutes. Let cool.

6. In a medium mixer bowl, whip the heavy cream, cream of coconut and vanilla until stiff. Unmold the cheesecake on a platter. Spread or pipe the coconut cream over the top. Sprinkle the toasted coconut over the cream.

NOTE: *If fresh pineapple is unavailable, substitute a 16-ounce can of crushed pineapple packed in its own juice, drained; then delete Step 2.*

—Teresa Gannon, Haliimaile General Store, Haliimaile, Maui, Hawaii

• • •

STRAWBERRY AND PASSION FRUIT SHORTCAKES

12 Servings

½ cup unbleached all-purpose flour
⅓ cup cake flour
½ teaspoon non-aluminum baking powder (see Note)
Pinch of salt
5 large eggs, at room temperature
¾ cup plus ⅓ cup sugar
2 teaspoons vanilla extract
¼ teaspoon finely grated lemon zest
2 tablespoons milk, warmed
Confectioners' sugar, for dusting
4 pints strawberries
6 passion fruits (about ½ pound)
2 cups heavy cream

1. Preheat the oven to 325°. Butter and flour a 10-by-15-inch jelly-roll pan.

2. In a medium bowl, toss the all-purpose flour, cake flour, baking powder and salt. Sift 3 times to blend and lighten the mixture and set aside.

3. In a medium heatproof bowl set over simmering water, whisk the eggs and the ¾ cup sugar over moderate heat until warm to the touch, about 3 minutes. Remove the bowl from the heat, and using an electric mixer, beat at high speed until almost quadrupled in volume and thick enough to hold a ribbon for 3 seconds.

4. Sprinkle 1 teaspoon of the vanilla and the lemon zest over the egg yolk mixture. Then, in 3 additions, sift the dry ingredients on top and fold in gently with a large whisk until thoroughly incorporated. Using a rubber spatula, quickly fold in the warm milk. Scrape the mixture evenly into the prepared pan, tilting if necessary.

5. Bake for about 25 minutes, or until the top of the cake is lightly browned and springs back when lightly pressed in the center. Set aside on a rack to cool for 10 minutes. Run a small knife around the sides of the pan. Place a clean kitchen towel over a cooling rack and lightly sift confectioners' sugar over it. Invert the cake on the towel, remove the pan and let the cake cool completely, about 1 hour. *(The cake can be baked 1 day ahead; wrap well and store in a cool place.)*

6. In a large bowl, using a potato masher, crush one-fourth of the strawberries with ¼ cup of the remaining sugar. Slice the remaining berries ¼ inch thick and stir into the crushed fruit. Let macerate for 1 to 2 hours at room temperature.

7. Halve the passion fruits over a strainer set over a bowl and scoop out the seeds. Press on the seeds with a fork to extract as much juice as possible; set the juice aside.

8. In a medium bowl, whip the cream with the remaining 1 tablespoon plus 1 teaspoon sugar and 1 teaspoon vanilla just until it holds a soft shape.

9. To assemble the shortcakes, turn the sponge cake right side up on a work surface. Using a large serrated knife, slice the sponge cake evenly into 12 squares or any other shape. Place on individual serving plates and spoon about ½ cup of the strawberries and ½ tablespoon of the passion fruit juice over and around each portion of cake. Garnish with the whipped cream.

NOTE: *Many commercial baking powders contain sodium aluminum sulfate, which can leave a slightly bitter flavor in baked goods. Rumford baking powder is a nationally available brand that does not contain any aluminum compounds. You can also make your own. For ½ teaspoon baking powder, mix ¼ teaspoon cream of tartar, ⅛ teaspoon baking soda and ⅛ teaspoon cornstarch and use at once.*

—Lindsey Shere

• • •

CORNMEAL CAKE WITH SUMMER BERRIES

The glorious berries of summer—raspberries, blackberries, blueberries and strawberries—are cooked just enough that they give off their juices and are then spooned warm over a tender cornmeal cake.

6 to 8 Servings

1½ sticks (6 ounces) unsalted butter, softened
1¼ cups superfine sugar
¼ teaspoon salt
1 teaspoon vanilla extract
3 eggs, at room temperature
3 egg yolks, at room temperature
½ cup all-purpose flour
½ cup yellow cornmeal
1½ teaspoons baking powder
8 cups mixed berries: blueberries, halved strawberries, raspberries and blackberries
Sweetened whipped cream, for serving
Sprigs of mint, for garnish (optional)

1. Preheat the oven to 350°. Butter a 9-by-5-inch glass loaf pan and coat with cornmeal, shaking out the excess. In a medium bowl, using an electric mixer at medium speed, cream the butter with ¾ cup of the sugar and salt until light and fluffy, about 2 minutes. Add the vanilla. Add the eggs and egg yolks, one at a time, beating well after each addition. Sift in the flour, cornmeal and baking powder; mix to incorporate.

2. Scrape the batter into the prepared pan and bake for 40 to 45 minutes, until the center springs back when lightly pressed and the cake begins to pull away from the sides of the pan. Run a sharp paring knife around the inside of the pan and invert onto a cooling rack for about 15 minutes; then lift off the pan, turn the cake right side up and let cool completely. *(The cake can be made several hours ahead. Once cooled, return the cake to the loaf pan, cover tightly and set aside.)*

3. In a large nonreactive saucepan, combine the blueberries and strawberries with the remaining ½ cup sugar and cook over moderate heat, stirring occasionally, until the sugar is dissolved, 2 to 3 minutes. Adjust the amount of sugar to the sweetness of the berries. Gently stir in the raspberries and blackberries and cook until the berries are softened but still intact, about 1 minute longer. Drain the berries in a coarse strainer set over a medium bowl; reserve the juices. Transfer the berries to a serving bowl.

4. Cut the cornmeal cake into ¾-inch slices. Spoon some of the berry juice onto individual dessert plates and place a slice of the cake on top. Spoon some of the berries over half the cake and garnish with the whipped cream and mint sprigs. Pass the remaining berries separately.

—Peggy Cullen

• • •

OATMEAL-CHOCOLATE CHIP BARS

Makes 12 Bars

1 stick (4 ounces) cold unsalted butter, cut into pieces
½ cup (packed) light brown sugar
1 egg
½ teaspoon vanilla extract
½ cup unbleached flour
½ teaspoon baking soda
¼ teaspoon salt
1¼ cups old-fashioned rolled oats
1 package (6 ounces) chocolate chips

1. Preheat the oven to 375°. Butter an 8-inch square baking pan and set aside.

2. In a food processor, process the butter and brown sugar until light and fluffy, scraping down the bowl occasionally. Add the egg and vanilla and process until just combined.

3. In a medium bowl, toss together the flour, baking soda and salt. Add the dry mixture to the processor and process, scraping down the bowl once, until blended. Using a rubber spatula, scrape the batter into the medium bowl. Stir in the oats and chocolate chips.

4. Scrape the batter into the prepared pan and spread evenly. Bake until set and golden brown, 20 to 25 minutes. Cut into 12 bars while still slightly warm. Remove from the pan and serve at once or set aside on a rack to cool.

—Susan Shapiro Jaslove

• • •

PINEAPPLE-FILLED OATMEAL SQUARES

Makes 16 Squares

2½ cups 1-inch cubes of fresh pineapple (from a 4-pound pineapple)
⅓ cup plus 2 tablespoons sugar
1 cup all-purpose flour
1 cup quick-cooking rolled oats
½ cup (packed) light brown sugar, pushed through a coarse sieve
½ teaspoon salt
½ teaspoon freshly grated nutmeg
1 egg, beaten
¼ cup plus 1 tablespoon canola oil

1. Lightly oil a 9-inch square baking pan and set aside. In a medium nonreactive saucepan, combine the pineapple, sugar and ⅓ cup of water and bring to a boil over moderately high heat. Reduce the heat to low, cover and simmer until the pineapple is tender, about 15 minutes.

2. Transfer the pineapple and cooking liquid to a food processor and puree until smooth, about 1 minute. Return the puree to the saucepan and simmer over moderate heat, stirring, until it is quite dry, about 12 minutes. Transfer the puree to a bowl and set aside to cool to room temperature. *(The recipe can be prepared to this point up to 1 day ahead; cover and refrigerate.)*

3. Preheat the oven to 350°. In a large bowl, combine the flour, oats, brown sugar, salt and nutmeg. Stir in the egg and then the oil, blending until the mixture is uniformly moist and crumbly.

4. Pack half the oat mixture into the bottom of the prepared pan. Evenly spread the pineapple filling over the base. Sprinkle the remaining oat mixture over the top to cover, but don't press or pack it. Bake on the top rack of the oven for about 10 minutes, or until golden brown on top. Let cool to room temperature, then cut into 16 squares.

—Marcia Kiesel

• • •

PEANUT BUTTER, WHITE CHOCOLATE AND MACADAMIA NUT COOKIES

These are terrific served with ice cream or sorbet.

Makes 2½ Dozen

6 ounces macadamia nuts, coarsely chopped (1 generous cup)
1 cup all-purpose flour
½ teaspoon baking soda
Pinch of salt
½ cup chunky peanut butter
1 stick (4 ounces) unsalted butter, at room temperature
½ cup (firmly packed) light brown sugar
2 tablespoons granulated sugar
1 egg
1 teaspoon vanilla extract
6 ounces white chocolate, coarsely chopped

1. In a medium skillet, toast the nuts over moderately low heat, stirring occasionally, until fragrant and golden, about 5 minutes. Set aside to cool.

2. Preheat the oven to 375°. In a medium bowl, toss together the flour, baking soda and salt. Set aside.

3. In a large bowl, using an electric mixer, cream the peanut butter, butter, brown sugar and granulated sugar until smooth and light, about 3 minutes. Add the egg and beat until fluffy, about 3 minutes. Add the vanilla and beat until incorporated. Using a wooden spoon, stir in the flour mixture until well blended. Stir in the toasted nuts and the white chocolate.

4. Spoon heaping tablespoons of the dough about 1 inch apart on 2 large ungreased cookie sheets. Flatten the dough mounds slightly with your fingers. Bake for 12 to 15 minutes, or until golden brown. Do not overbake or the cookies will be dry. Let cool on the baking sheets for 5 minutes, then transfer with a spatula to a rack and let cool completely. *(The cookies can be made up to 3 days ahead; store in an airtight container.)*

—Lee Bailey

• • •

PINE NUT CRESCENTS

Provençal cooks make frequent use of pine nuts, and they like to keep their desserts simple. This cookie combines both tendencies.

🍷 A fragrant, fruity dessert wine, such as 1989 J. Vidal-Fleury Muscat de Beaumes de Venise or 1989 Markham Muscat Blanc, would add a grace note to this refreshing light dessert.

Makes 3 Dozen

1 stick (4 ounces) unsalted butter, softened
½ cup sugar, plus more for sprinkling
1 teaspoon vanilla extract
¼ cup hot water
2 cups all-purpose flour, sifted
½ teaspoon salt
1 egg white, lightly beaten
⅔ cup pine nuts (3 ounces)

1. Preheat the oven to 375°. Grease a large cookie sheet.

2. In a bowl, cream the butter with the ½ cup sugar. Gradually beat in the vanilla and hot water. Sift the flour and salt over the butter mixture and stir until blended. Scrape the dough onto a piece of wax paper, pat into a disk and refrigerate for 30 minutes.

3. Roll out the dough ¼ inch thick and cut with a 2-inch crescent-shaped cookie cutter. Transfer the cookies to the prepared baking sheet and brush with the egg white. Sprinkle the pine nuts over the cookies, pressing lightly to help them adhere. Sprinkle the cookies with sugar and bake for about 15 minutes, until lightly browned. Let cool on a rack.

—Ann Haskell

• • •

PECAN GINGERSNAPS

Makes 5 Dozen

¾ cup vegetable shortening
1 cup plus 3 tablespoons sugar
¼ cup pure maple syrup
1 egg, lightly beaten
1½ cups all-purpose flour
2 teaspoons baking soda
1½ teaspoons ground ginger
1 teaspoon cinnamon
1 cup finely chopped pecans

1. Preheat the oven to 375°. Generously spray 2 large cookie sheets with nonstick cooking spray.

2. In a large mixing bowl, cream the shortening with 1 cup of the sugar until fluffy. Beat in the maple syrup and egg until well blended.

3. In a medium bowl, sift together the flour, baking soda, ginger and cinnamon. Toss in the pecans. Add the dry ingredients to the shortening mixture in 4 batches, mixing well between each addition.

4. Form the dough into 1-inch balls.

Roll the cookies in the remaining 3 tablespoons sugar and place at least 2 inches apart on the cookie sheets. Bake for 12 to 14 minutes, until golden brown. Let cool for about 1 minute, then transfer to a rack to cool. Store in an airtight container for up to 1 week.

—*Lee Bailey*

• • •

BENNE SEED WAFERS

Benne, a West African word for sesame, is still commonly used in South Carolina. Legend has it that eating sesame seeds brings good luck.

Makes 4 Dozen

1 cup sesame seeds (4 ounces)
1 cup (lightly packed) light brown sugar
4 tablespoons unsalted butter, slightly softened
1 egg, lightly beaten
½ cup all-purpose flour
¼ teaspoon salt
⅛ teaspoon baking powder
1 teaspoon fresh lemon juice
½ teaspoon vanilla extract

1. In a heavy medium skillet, toast the sesame seeds over moderate heat, stirring, until golden brown, about 10 minutes. Immediately transfer the seeds to a plate and let cool.

2. Preheat the oven to 325°. Using an electric mixer, cream the brown sugar and butter. Add the egg, flour, salt and baking powder and blend to form a soft dough.

3. Using a spoon, stir in the toasted sesame seeds, lemon juice and vanilla until combined.

4. Drop teaspoons of the dough about 1 inch apart onto well-greased cookie sheets. Bake for about 15 minutes, or until brown at the edges.

5. Let the wafers cool briefly on the cookie sheets, then transfer to a rack and let cool completely.

—*Jessica B. Harris*

• • •

ALMOND COOKIES

This version of *ricciarelli* comes from my pastry chef, Sandy Soto Teich. It is the apotheosis of a macaroon: soft and chewy, not too sweet, with just a lingering hint of orange. Finely ground almond flour is also sold as blanched almond meal.

Makes 3½ Dozen

2 egg whites, at room temperature
Pinch of salt
1¼ cups granulated sugar
Finely grated zest of 1 medium orange
1 teaspoon vanilla extract
½ teaspoon almond extract
3 scant cups almond flour (13 ounces)*
¼ cup all-purpose flour
Confectioners' sugar, for dusting
****Available at specialty food shops***

1. Preheat the oven to 250°. Spray 2 nonstick cookie sheets with nonstick spray.

2. In a medium bowl, beat the egg whites with the salt until soft peaks form. Gradually beat in 1 cup of the granulated sugar and continue beating until the whites are stiff and shiny. Stir in the orange zest, vanilla and almond extracts and finally the almond flour until incorporated and the dough is thick and stiff.

3. In a small bowl, toss the remaining ¼ cup granulated sugar with the all-purpose flour. Lightly dust the prepared cookie sheets with this mixture and scatter the rest on a work surface.

4. With greased hands, divide the dough in 3 pieces. Roll 1 piece into a rope at least ¾ inch in diameter and flatten slightly. Using a wet knife, cut the strip of dough on the diagonal to form 1-inch diamonds. Arrange the diamonds on 1 of the prepared cookie sheets. Repeat with the remaining dough.

5. Bake the cookies for about 15 minutes, or until puffed and set. They should not color. Remove from the oven and immediately sift confectioners' sugar generously over the tops. Transfer to wire racks to cool completely, then store in airtight containers for up to 3 days.

—*Evan Kleiman*

• • •

GRANOLA BISCOTTI

For this recipe, use your favorite granola, homemade or storebought.

Makes 4 Dozen

1 cup all-purpose flour
⅔ cup sugar
1 teaspoon finely grated lemon zest
1 teaspoon coarsely chopped anise seeds
¾ teaspoon baking powder
Pinch of salt
5 tablespoons cold unsalted butter, cut into small pieces
2 cold eggs, lightly beaten
1 teaspoon vanilla extract
2 cups granola, big pieces broken up

1. In a food processor, combine the flour, sugar, lemon zest, anise seeds, baking powder and salt and process a few times to blend. Add the butter and pulse about 5 times to incorporate the butter without softening it. Pour in the eggs and vanilla all at once and process until just combined, about 5 seconds. Scrape the dough into a bowl and stir in the granola until incorporated. Cover and refrigerate the dough until firm, about 20 minutes.

2. Preheat the oven to 350°. Lightly grease a baking sheet. Quarter the chilled dough and form each quarter into a 6-by-1-inch log; flatten the logs slightly to make a rectangular shape. Transfer the logs to the prepared baking sheet and bake for 20 minutes, until golden brown and almost firm. Remove the baking sheet from the oven and set aside to let the logs rest for 5 minutes.

3. Using a spatula, transfer the logs to a cutting board and slice crosswise ½ inch thick with a serrated knife, using a gentle sawing motion. Return the biscotti to the baking sheet, cut sides down, and bake for about 12 minutes longer, until very firm and beginning to brown. Transfer to a rack to cool. *(The biscotti can be made up to 2 weeks ahead; wrap well and freeze.)*

—*Marcia Kiesel*

• • •

ROSEMARY SHORTBREAD

The rosemary in these cookies may seem unconventional, but it provides a welcome surprise. Its flavor is mellowed by the butter and flour. Once you've tried rosemary, you'll understand that there are nearly endless herb possibilities: thyme, lavender or mint to name a few.

Serve these cookies in the afternoon with herbal tea or with ice cream or fruit for dessert.

Makes 4 Dozen Cookies

3 sticks (12 ounces) unsalted butter, at room temperature
⅔ cup sugar, plus 2 teaspoons sugar for sprinkling
2 tablespoons minced fresh rosemary or 2 teaspoons dried
2⅓ cups all-purpose flour
½ cup brown rice flour*
¼ teaspoon salt
****Available at health food stores and specialty food markets***

1. Preheat the oven to 375°. Line 2 large baking sheets with parchment.

2. In a large bowl, using an electric mixer, cream the butter at medium-high speed until pale yellow, about 2 minutes. Add the ⅔ cup sugar and beat until fluffy, about 1 minute.

3. If using dried rosemary, crush it with a mortar and pestle or with a rolling pin until finely ground but not pulverized.

4. Add the all-purpose flour, rice flour, salt and rosemary to the butter mixture and beat until thoroughly combined. Pat the dough into 2 squares, wrap in wax paper and refrigerate until firm, about 1½ hours.

5. On a well-floured surface, roll out each square to a 10½-by-6-inch rectangle, about ⅜ inch thick. Cut the dough in 1½-by-1¾-inch rectangles or in any similar-size shape you like. Transfer the cookies to the prepared baking sheets, spacing them about ½ inch apart. If desired, sprinkle the tops with the remaining 2 teaspoons sugar; then bake for 18 to 20 minutes, until golden at the edges.

6. Transfer the cookies to a rack to cool. *(The cookies can be stored for up to 1 week in an airtight container; their flavor improves with sitting.)*

—*Jerry Traunfled, The Herbfarm, Fall City, Washington*

• • •

DESSERTS

NUT-AND-BERRY BARK

Shiny red cranberries and brilliant green pistachio nuts are set off against a field of white chocolate. Wrap the bark in clear cellophane, gathered at the top with gold or silver ribbon for a stunning gift.

Makes 2 Pounds

1½ cups shelled raw, unsalted pistachios* (½ pound)
1½ cups dried cranberries* (6 ounces)
1¼ pounds white chocolate, finely chopped
****Available at specialty food stores***

1. Preheat the oven to 350°. Place the pistachios in a cake pan and bake for 10 minutes, stirring occasionally. Do not overcook, or the pistachios will lose their bright green color. Remove from the oven and set aside to cool.

2. Place a steamer basket in a medium saucepan filled with ½ inch of water; bring to a boil over moderately high heat. Place the cranberries in the basket, cover and steam until soft and moist, 3 to 4 minutes. Remove the basket and transfer the berries to a paper towel. Blot dry and let cool completely. Reduce the heat to moderately low to keep the water at a simmer.

3. Place about three-quarters of the white chocolate in a medium heatproof bowl set over the simmering water. Using a rubber spatula, stir the chocolate occasionally until it is about two-thirds melted, about 4 minutes. Remove the bowl from the water and add the remaining chocolate. Stir until the chocolate is completely melted and smooth. Insert a candy thermometer into the chocolate and set aside to cool to 83°, stirring occasionally.

4. Reserve 2 tablespoons each of the cranberries and the greenest pistachios. With a rubber spatula, stir the remaining nuts and berries into the chocolate. Scrape the mixture onto a large baking sheet lined with parchment paper or foil. Using a metal palette knife, spread it into a 10-by-14-inch rectangle about ⅜ inch thick. Scatter the reserved nuts and berries over the chocolate. Refrigerate until hardened, 20 to 30 minutes. Break the bark into large pieces. *(The bark can be stored in an airtight container for up to 1 week.)*

—*Peggy Cullen*

• • •

COCONUT "SUSHI"

These little confections look like the Japanese seaweed-wrapped rice rolls but taste like the coconut patties of Miami Beach, accented with candied ginger. Arrange the pieces in neat rows on a small rectangular tray or wooden board, just like a sushi chef, and garnish the tray with some candied ginger.

Makes 20 Pieces

½ cup heavy cream
¼ cup light corn syrup
⅔ cup sugar
1½ cups medium-shredded unsweetened coconut* (about 3½ ounces)
44 salted toasted almonds
3 pieces (¼ ounce) soft candied ginger, cut into fine strips
4 ounces semisweet chocolate, chopped
****Available at health food stores***

1. Lightly butter a medium bowl and set aside. In a small saucepan, combine the cream, corn syrup and sugar. Using a wet pastry brush, wash down the inside of the pan. Insert a candy thermometer. Bring the mixture to a boil over moderately high heat, occasionally washing down the inside of the pan with the pastry brush. Stir frequently to prevent scorching and boil until the mixture reaches 232°. Remove the pan from the heat, immediately stir in the coconut and pour into the buttered bowl. Cover with plastic wrap, prick a few holes in the top and set aside on a rack to cool completely.

2. Divide the cooled coconut mixture in two. On a work surface, roll one piece into a 10-inch log. Flatten slightly to form a 10-by-2½-inch rectangle. Arrange half the almonds, end to end and overlapping slightly, lengthwise down the center of the rectangle. Place half of the julienned ginger in a strip along one side of the almonds.

3. Slide a metal palette knife under the coconut rectangle to loosen. Bring together the long edges of the coconut rectangle up over the almonds and ginger to enclose and pinch the seams to seal. Roll the log back and forth to make it smooth and even, making sure that the length does not exceed 10 inches. Transfer the log to a baking sheet lined with parchment or wax paper and refrigerate. Repeat with the remaining coconut mixture, almonds and ginger. Transfer the second log to the baking sheet and refrigerate until firm.

4. Place three-fourths of the chocolate in a medium bowl. Set the bowl over a medium saucepan filled with ½ inch of simmering water and stir occasionally, until the chocolate is nearly melted. Remove the bowl from the heat and add the remaining chocolate; stir until the chocolate is melted and smooth. Scrape into a small bowl, insert a candy thermometer and let cool to 86°.

5. Using a dry pastry brush, brush the top and sides of the coconut logs with melted chocolate. Refrigerate for a few minutes until hardened. Turn the logs over and brush the bottoms with melted chocolate. Refrigerate until the coating is set and the centers are hardened, at least twenty minutes.

6. Place the logs on a work surface. Using a thin sharp knife and cutting straight down, trim the ends of the logs. Cut each log crosswise into ten 1-inch slices. Let the "sushi" come to room temperature before serving. *(The "sushi" can be stored in an airtight container for up to 1 week in a cool place or refrigerated.)*

—Peggy Cullen

• • •

PEANUT PENUCHE GOLD BARS

Penuche is technically a fudge made with brown sugar. In this variation, peanut butter penuche and mocha fudge are layered in a square pan, dusted with 22-karat gold powder and cut into little bricks.

Makes 40 Bars

PEANUT BUTTER PENUCHE:

1⅓ cups (packed) light brown sugar
2 teaspoons instant coffee granules
1 cup heavy cream
¼ cup light corn syrup
1 cup chunky peanut butter
1 teaspoon vanilla extract

MOCHA FUDGE:

¾ cup sugar
3 tablespoons unsweetened cocoa, preferably Dutch process
2 teaspoons instant coffee granules
Pinch of salt
½ cup heavy cream
3 tablespoons light corn syrup
2 tablespoons unsalted butter
22-karat gold dust, for decorating (see Note)

1. Line a 9-by-9-by-2-inch pan with a 12-by-16-inch sheet of foil, extending the foil over the edges. Lightly butter a medium bowl and set aside.

2. *Make the peanut butter penuche:* In a 2-quart saucepan, combine the brown sugar and instant coffee. Stir to break up any lumps. Stir in the cream and corn syrup. Using a wet pastry brush, wash down the inside of the pan. Bring the mixture to a boil over moderately high heat and insert a candy thermometer. Continue to boil, stirring occasionally and washing down the sides of the pan, until the temperature reaches 234°, about 10 minutes.

3. Without scraping the bottom of the pan, immediately pour the mixture into the buttered bowl. Place the peanut butter and vanilla on top, but do not stir them in. Place a candy thermometer in the bowl and set aside undisturbed on a cooling rack, until the temperature reaches 125°, about 25 minutes. Using a buttered wooden spoon or spatula, thoroughly stir in the peanut butter with a few quick strokes, just until the mixture thickens and lightens slightly in color, about 10 seconds.

4. Scrape the penuche into the prepared pan and press lightly with buttered palms to even it out. Bang the pan on the counter to release the air bubbles and place on a level surface to set.

5. *Make the mocha fudge:* Lightly butter a small bowl. In a small saucepan, whisk together the sugar, cocoa, coffee and salt. Stir in the cream and corn syrup; add the butter. Wash down the inside of the pan with a wet pastry brush. Bring the mixture to a boil over moderately high heat and insert a candy thermometer. Continue to boil the mixture, stirring occasionally and washing down the inside of the pan, until it reaches 234°, about 10 minutes.

6. Without scraping the bottom of the pan, immediately pour the fudge into the buttered bowl. Set the bowl on a rack to cool to 150°, 5 to 10 minutes. Using an electric mixer, beat the fudge on low speed until it thickens, loses its shine, lightens in color and becomes stringy, 6 to 8 minutes. Pour the fudge over the penuche layer and spread it with a buttered palette knife or fingers.

7. Dip a small paintbrush into the gold dust and tap it over the fudge to sprinkle. Set aside at room temperature for at least 4 hours or overnight. To serve, pull up the foil to lift out the fudge square and, using a sharp chef's knife, cut the fudge into quarters. Cut each quarter in half to make eight sections, then cut each section crosswise into 5 bars.

NOTE: *Nontoxic 22-karat gold dust can be found at art supply stores and stores that specialize in cake-decorating equipment.*

—Peggy Cullen

• • •

PINEAPPLE COLADA

4 Servings

1 medium pineapple
2 tablespoons fresh lime juice
2 tablespoons sugar
2 tablespoons shredded sweet coconut
2 tablespoons light or dark rum

1. Slice off the skin from the pineapple; using the tip of a vegetable peeler, remove the eyes. Quarter and core the pineapple. Slice each quarter crosswise ½ inch thick and cut each slice in bite-size wedges.

2. In a medium bowl, combine the pineapple and the remaining ingredients. Stir and let macerate at room temperature for 1 hour before serving.

—Stephanie Lyness

• • •

WINE-BAKED APPLES

8 Servings

¼ cup pine nuts (2 ounces)
8 medium Golden Delicious apples (about ½ pound each)
⅔ cup raisins
⅓ cup sugar
1½ cups dry white wine
4 whole cloves
1 cinnamon stick
Finely grated zest of ½ a lemon
2 tablespoons unsalted butter, melted

1. Preheat the oven to 375°. In a small skillet, toast the pine nuts over moderately low heat, shaking the pan often, until the nuts are fragrant and golden brown, about 6 minutes. Set aside to cool.

2. Butter a 9-by-13-inch glass or ceramic baking dish. Core the apples and peel them two-thirds of the way down. Arrange the apples in the prepared baking dish. In a small bowl, combine the raisins and pine nuts and stuff into the apple cavities. Sprinkle the sugar over the apples.

3. Pour the wine into the pan and scatter the cloves, cinnamon and lemon zest around the apples. Drizzle the melted butter over the apples. Bake for 45 to 55 minutes, basting occasionally, until the apples are tender when pierced with a knife. Let cool in their syrup to lukewarm before serving.

—Michele Scicolone

• • •

PEACHES IN PROSECCO

Prosecco is a dry sparkling wine from the Veneto region of Italy. It is the bubbly used to make a Bellini, the delicious white-peach cocktail.

6 Servings

6 medium peaches (about 2¼ pounds), peeled and thinly sliced
¼ cup sugar
¼ cup orange liqueur
1½ cups chilled Prosecco or other dry sparkling white wine

1. In a serving bowl, toss the peaches with the sugar and orange liqueur. Refrigerate for 1 hour.

2. Just before serving, spoon the peaches and their juice into individual bowls. Pour the Prosecco on top and serve immediately.

—Michele Scicolone

• • •

SLICED MANGOES WITH LIME AND GINGER

A ripe mango is one of the world's greatest delicacies. In equatorial regions, there are as many varieties of this "king of fruits" as there are apples in colder climates. Assemble this refreshing fruit salad just before serving.

4 Servings

2 large ripe mangoes, peeled and cut off the pit in ¼-inch slices
2 teaspoons minced fresh ginger
2 limes, halved
Fresh mint leaves, for garnish

Combine the mango slices and ginger and toss gently to mix. Squeeze the limes over the mangoes and garnish with mint leaves.

—Chris Schlesinger & John Willoughby

• • •

APRICOTS A LA MODE WITH CARAMEL PLUM SAUCE IN A GINGER BOWL

The ginger cookie "bowls" and the caramel-flavored plum sauce marry nicely with the fruity acidity of the lemon-poached apricots.

6 Servings

3 egg whites, at room temperature
1 cup sliced unblanched almonds (3½ ounces)
1 cup plus 2 tablespoons granulated sugar
4 tablespoons unsalted butter, softened
¼ cup (packed) dark brown sugar
2 tablespoons unsulphured molasses

½ vanilla bean, split lengthwise
1 tablespoon ground ginger
½ teaspoon cinnamon
½ cup all-purpose flour, sifted
6 fresh apricots
Juice of 1 lemon
2 pints vanilla ice cream, for serving
Caramel Plum Sauce (recipe follows)

1. Preheat the oven to 350°. In a small bowl, beat 1 of the egg whites with a fork until frothy. In another small bowl, moisten the almonds with about 1 teaspoon of the beaten white (discard any remainder). Sprinkle on 2 tablespoons of the granulated sugar and toss to combine. On a baking sheet lined with parchment paper, spread the almonds in an even layer. Toast the nuts for about 8 minutes, until just beginning to color. Remove from the oven and let cool, then break into small pieces. *(The almonds can be prepared up to 2 weeks ahead and stored in an airtight container.)*

2. In a medium bowl, using an electric mixer at moderate speed, cream the butter with the brown sugar until light and fluffy, about 2 minutes. Beat in the molasses and continue beating until blended.

3. In a small bowl, beat the remaining 2 egg whites with a fork until frothy; add them to the butter mixture in four batches, beating well after each addition. Scrape the seeds from the vanilla bean into the bowl. Add the ginger, cinnamon and flour and mix at low speed until blended.

4. Line a heavy baking sheet with parchment paper. Using a long narrow metal spatula, spread 2 heaping tablespoons of the ginger cookie batter in an even circle, about 6½ inches in diameter; be sure not to leave any bare spots. Sprinkle a ½-inch-wide ring of almonds around the edge of the circle, then sprinkle a 3-inch circle of almonds in the center. Bake for about 8 minutes, until the cookie begins to turn golden brown.

5. Remove from the oven and, working quickly, use a large metal spatula to peel the cookie off the parchment. Immediately place the cookie, almond side up, inside a 3-cup heatproof bowl. Press a small ramekin or custard cup into the center of the cookie for about 10 seconds to flatten the bottom. Let the cookie cool in the mold. Repeat with the remaining cookie batter and almonds, baking one cookie at a time. *(The cookies can be made up to 2 days ahead and stored in an airtight container at room temperature.)*

6. Quarter the apricots; discard the pits. In a medium nonreactive saucepan, combine the remaining 1 cup granulated sugar with the lemon juice and 3 cups of water. Bring to a boil over high heat and add the apricots. Remove from the heat and set aside until cooled completely. Drain the apricots and discard the liquid. *(The apricots can be prepared 1 day ahead and refrigerated, covered.)*

7. To serve, set the ginger cookie "bowls" on plates. Place a large scoop of ice cream in each bowl and spoon about 2 tablespoons of the Caramel Plum Sauce on top. Garnish with the apricots and serve immediately; pass the remaining sauce separately.

—Peggy Cullen

• • •

CARAMEL PLUM SAUCE

Makes 1⅓ Cups

¾ pound plums, quartered
½ vanilla bean, split
½ cup sugar
1 teaspoon almond liqueur (optional)

1. In a small nonreactive saucepan, combine the plums with ¼ cup of water and bring to a boil over high heat. Reduce the heat to moderate and cook until the plums are tender, about 10 minutes.

2. Transfer the plums and their liquid to a food processor and puree until smooth. Pass the sauce through a fine strainer into a medium bowl. Using a small sharp knife, scrape the seeds from the vanilla bean directly into the puree and stir to combine.

3. In a small heavy saucepan, combine the sugar with 2 tablespoons of water and cook over high heat without stirring until the sugar melts and just begins to turn golden, about 5 minutes. Remove from the heat, place the pan in the sink in case the caramel spatters and quickly stir in 2 more tablespoons of warm water. Return to the heat and stir to dissolve the caramel.

4. Stir the caramel into the plum puree. (If the puree is very sweet, you may not want to add all the caramel.) Add the almond liqueur. If the sauce is too thick to pour easily, thin it with a little water. *(The sauce can be refrigerated, covered, for up to 2 days. Bring to room temperature before serving.)*

—Peggy Cullen

• • •

FRESH BERRIES WITH RICOTTA CHEESE

4 Servings

1 pound fresh ricotta cheese
2 tablespoons finely grated orange zest (from 2 oranges)
2 tablespoons sugar
2 cups mixed berries, such as raspberries, blueberries, blackberries and strawberries
3 tablespoons fresh orange juice
Grated bittersweet chocolate (optional)

1. Press the ricotta cheese through a sieve set over a bowl. Stir in the orange zest and sugar.

2. Toss the berries with the orange juice and chocolate to taste.

3. Spoon the ricotta onto 4 dessert plates. Top with the berries.

—Stephanie Lyness

• • •

BANANA FRITTERS

4 Servings

Peanut oil, for frying
2 eggs, lightly beaten
½ cup cold milk
3 tablespoons light brown sugar
1 cup all-purpose flour
Pinch of baking powder
4 ripe bananas, sliced on the diagonal ¾ inch thick
2 tablespoons confectioners' sugar

1. In a deep medium skillet, heat 1 inch of oil over moderately high heat to 350°.

2. In a large bowl, mix the eggs, milk, brown sugar, flour and baking powder together until smooth.

3. Add the banana slices to the batter and stir gently to coat well. Spearing each slice with a fork, transfer half of the bananas to the hot oil and fry, turning once, until lightly browned on both sides, 2 to 3 minutes. Transfer the fritters to paper towels to drain. Repeat with the remaining banana slices.

4. Transfer the fritters to a warm platter and sift the confectioners' sugar over them. Serve at once.

—Jessica B. Harris

• • •

FRESH BERRIES WITH CHAMPAGNE ICE

Although seasonal berries need little to enhance their flavor, this Champagne ice, flavored with exotic-tasting rosewater, is a crowning complement. The ice can be made up to four days in advance.

8 Generous Servings

¾ cup sugar
1½ cups Champagne
2 teaspoons rosewater*
6 cups berries, such as blackberries, raspberries and sliced strawberries
****Available at specialty food stores and some Asian and Middle Eastern markets***

1. In a nonreactive saucepan, mix the sugar and 3 cups of water. Cook over moderate heat, stirring, until the sugar is dissolved, about 3 minutes. Remove from the heat and stir in the Champagne and rosewater. Pour into a 9-by-13-inch nonreactive dish, cover and freeze until firm, at least 4 hours.

2. Place the berries in 8 dessert bowls or goblets. Remove the Champagne ice from the freezer. Using a large spoon, scrape up about ½ cup of ice and spoon it over the berries in each dish. Serve at once.

—Janie Hibler

• • •

SWEET POLENTA CROSTINI WITH WINE-BAKED APPLES

Crisp, sugared slices of polenta are a pleasing contrast to the tender apples.

8 Servings

1¼ teaspoons salt
1 cup yellow cornmeal
3 tablespoons unsalted butter
1 tablespoon corn oil or other vegetable oil
2 tablespoons sugar
Wine-Baked Apples (p. 236)
Whipped cream, for serving

1. In a medium saucepan, bring 2 cups of water and the salt to a boil over moderately high heat. Place the cornmeal in a medium bowl and stir in 1½ cups of cold water. Gradually stir the cornmeal mixture into the boiling water. Cook over moderate heat, stirring frequently, until very thick, about 40 minutes. Scrape the polenta into an 8-by-4-inch loaf pan and smooth the top. Let cool slightly, then cover with plastic wrap, pressing it directly on the surface and refrigerate for at least 4 hours or up to 3 days.

2. Run a long, thin knife around the polenta and invert onto a cutting board. Cut the polenta crosswise into 16 slices. Arrange the slices on a wire rack and let dry out for 1 hour.

3. In a large nonstick skillet, melt 2 tablespoons of the butter in the oil over moderately high heat. Add half of the polenta slices and fry, turning once, until golden brown and crisp, 10 to 12 minutes. Transfer to a warm plate, sprinkle 1 tablespoon of the sugar on top and keep warm. Add the remaining 1 tablespoon butter to the skillet and repeat with the remaining polenta slices and sugar.

4. To serve, place 2 polenta crostini on each dessert plate. Top each serving with 1 warm Wine-Baked Apple. Drizzle any remaining wine syrup over the apples and garnish with a dollop of whipped cream.

—Michele Scicolone

• • •

STRAWBERRIES IN MARSALA WITH HONEYED MASCARPONE CREAM

Mascarpone, the extremely fresh cow's milk cheese from Italy, is blended here with whipped cream. You can use this creamy topping on other fruit desserts, tarts and cakes.

4 Servings

2 pints strawberries
¼ cup sweet Marsala
3 tablespoons sugar
¼ cup mascarpone cheese (2 ounces)
2 tablespoons honey
½ cup heavy cream, whipped

1. Set aside 4 perfect strawberries for garnish. Hull and slice the remaining berries. In a medium bowl, stir together the sliced strawberries, Marsala and sugar. Let macerate at room temperature for 30 minutes.

2. In a medium bowl, whisk the mascarpone and honey until smooth. Fold in the whipped cream.

3. Spoon the strawberries into 4 dessert bowls and top with a dollop of the mascarpone cream. Garnish with the reserved whole strawberries.

—Michele Scicolone

• • •

LEMON SORBET WITH RASPBERRIES AND CASSIS

4 Servings

½ pint raspberries
1½ teaspoons finely grated lemon zest
½ teaspoon sugar
⅓ cup crème de cassis (blackcurrant liqueur)
1 pint lemon sorbet

1. In a medium bowl, toss the raspberries with the lemon zest and sugar. Let sit for 5 minutes. Stir in the cassis and set aside for 10 minutes.

2. Scoop the sorbet into 4 dessert bowls. Spoon the raspberries and cassis on top and serve immediately.

—Susan Shapiro Jaslove

• • •

WARM CARAMELIZED PINEAPPLE WITH VANILLA ICE CREAM

8 Servings

1½ cups sugar
1 pineapple (about 3½ pounds)
4 tablespoons unsalted butter
1 tablespoon kirsch
Vanilla Ice Cream (p. 249)

1. In a heavy medium saucepan, cook the sugar over moderate heat, stirring, until it is a light gold color, about 15 minutes. Carefully stir in ¾ cup of water and cook, stirring, until the caramel is dissolved. You should have at least 1½ cups syrup (if not, add enough water to make up the difference). Set aside.

2. Trim off the top and bottom of the pineapple and slice off the skin. Using the tip of a vegetable peeler, remove the eyes. Quarter and core the pineapple. Cut each quarter crosswise in ½-inch-thick slices, then cut each slice into bite-size wedges. Reserve any pineapple juice.

3. Heat a large nonreactive skillet over moderately high heat. Add the butter and then the pineapple chunks and cook, stirring occasionally, until softened and browned, about 9 minutes. Add the reserved pineapple juice, caramel syrup and the kirsch and simmer until slightly thickened, about 3 minutes. Set aside until slightly cooled, about 5 minutes. Serve with the Vanilla Ice Cream.

—Lindsey Shere

• • •

WARM BERRIES WITH CINNAMON GELATO

Use whatever fresh berries are available, though a combination of tastes and textures is most interesting. The berry sauce is also delicious over good store-bought vanilla or fruit-flavored ice cream and frozen yogurt.

6 Servings

1 cup raspberries
1 cup blackberries
1 cup strawberries, hulled and halved or quartered if large
¼ cup sugar
Cinnamon Gelato (p. 249)

1. In a medium nonreactive saucepan, combine the berries, sugar and ¼ cup of water. Bring to a simmer over moderate heat. Cook, stirring occasionally, until the berries are soft and the liquid is slightly thickened, about 5 minutes. Let cool until just warm, about 20 minutes.

2. Ladle ½ cup of berries into each of 6 large goblets and top with a large scoop of the Cinnamon Gelato. Serve immediately.

—*Michele Scicolone*

• • •

MAINE WILD BLUEBERRY SLUMP

Slump, like cobbler, is a Down East term for various types of baked fruit desserts with some kind of batter topping. Maine wild blueberries are tiny and tangy-sweet with an intense flavor. Raspberries, blackberries and even pitted cherries could be substituted. Adjust the sugar according to the sweetness of the fruit.

6 Servings

4 cups Maine wild blueberries
1 cup sugar
1 cup all-purpose flour
1½ teaspoons baking powder
Pinch of salt
2 tablespoons unsalted butter
¾ cup milk
½ teaspoon vanilla extract
Vanilla ice cream, for serving

1. Preheat the oven to 375°. Generously butter a 7- to 8-cup baking dish. Gently toss the blueberries with ¾ cup of the sugar and turn into the prepared dish.

2. Using a fork, toss together the flour, baking powder, salt and the remaining ¼ cup sugar.

3. In a small saucepan, melt the butter in the milk over low heat. Add the warm milk and the vanilla to the dry ingredients and stir to blend. The batter will be thick.

4. Spread the batter evenly over the blueberries and bake for 45 minutes, or until the top is nicely browned. Let cool for 5 minutes, then spoon onto plates and serve with vanilla ice cream.

—*Nancy Harmon Jenkins*

• • •

NECTARINE NESTS

A serving of a nectarine half with lemon curd nestled in a round of crisp puff pastry is as satisfying as a hot fruit pie, especially when garnished with berries and served with ice cream. The difference is that this dessert takes only minutes to make.

6 Servings

2 eggs
2 egg yolks
Juice and grated zest of 2 lemons
1½ cups plus 1½ teaspoons sugar
1 tablespoon unsalted butter
¾ pound all-butter puff pastry, thawed if frozen
3 medium nectarines (about 6 ounces each), halved and pitted
¼ cup mixed blueberries and raspberries
1 pint vanilla ice cream, for serving

1. In a small nonreactive saucepan, whisk together the eggs, egg yolks, lemon juice and ½ cup of the sugar. Stir in the lemon zest. Cook over moderate heat, stirring constantly with a rubber spatula, until the curd thickens and just begins to bubble, about 4 minutes. Do not let it boil. Immediately remove the pan from the heat and strain the curd into a small bowl. Stir in the butter. Press a piece of plastic wrap directly on the surface of the curd. *(The lemon curd can be prepared up to 2 days ahead and kept, covered, in the refrigerator.)*

2. On a lightly floured work surface, roll out the puff pastry to an even ¼-inch thickness. Using a 4-inch round cookie cutter, stamp out 6 circles. Place a nectarine half, cut side down, on a work surface. Evenly drape a puff pastry circle over the nectarine. Holding the nectarine in the palm of your hand, cut side up, mold the dough around the nectarine, bringing a lip of dough around the cut edge; press lightly to adhere.

3. Place the nectarine nest, cut side down, on a heavy baking sheet lined with parchment paper. Repeat with the remaining nectarines and puff pastry circles. Arrange the nests at least 2 inches apart on the baking sheet. Refrigerate until chilled, at least 15 minutes or for up to 3 hours.

4. Preheat the oven to 425°. Pour the 1 cup sugar into a small bowl. Using a pastry brush, brush the rounded surface of the pastry lightly with water. Dip the nests, rounded side down, in the sugar and roll so that the sugar coats the surface of the puff pastry but not the fruit itself. Return to the baking sheet, cut side down. Repeat with the remaining nests. Reserve the sugar in the bowl.

5. Bake the nests for 15 to 20 minutes, turning the baking sheet once, until the puff pastry begins to brown. Reduce the oven temperature to 350° and remove the sheet from the oven. Working quickly, turn the nectarines cut sides up. Sprinkle each cavity with about ¼ teaspoon sugar and fill with about 1½ teaspoons of the chilled lemon curd and a few of the berries. Sprinkle

a little more sugar on top and bake for 10 to 15 minutes longer, until well browned. Remove from the oven and immediately transfer the nests to a cooling rack, cut sides up. Let cool slightly.

6. Set the nectarine nests, cut side up, on plates and serve warm with a scoop of ice cream on the side. Warm the remaining lemon curd briefly over low heat, stirring; place in a small bowl and pass separately.

—*Peggy Cullen*

• • •

GINGERED ICE CREAM WITH BERRIES

4 Servings

1 pint vanilla ice cream
Finely grated zest of 1 medium orange
1 tablespoon minced crystallized ginger
½ pint raspberries or other berries

1. Place the ice cream in the refrigerator until soft but not soupy, about 20 minutes.

2. Spoon the softened ice cream into a large bowl. Mix in the orange zest and crystallized ginger.

3. Scoop the ice cream into 4 glass bowls or goblets and sprinkle the berries on top. Serve at once.

—*Stephanie Lyness*

• • •

GINGERED BANANAS

4 Servings

4 firm-ripe bananas
2 tablespoons unsalted butter
2 tablespoons light brown sugar
1 tablespoon coarsely chopped fresh ginger
Vanilla ice cream, for serving

1. Halve the bananas lengthwise. Cut each piece in half crosswise. Set aside.

2. In a large heavy skillet, melt the butter over moderate heat. Add the brown sugar and stir to melt, about 15 seconds. Add the ginger and cook, stirring constantly, until the ginger releases its fragrance and begins to color, about 30 seconds.

3. Add the banana pieces and cook on one side until lightly browned, about 45 seconds. Flip over and brown the other side, another 45 seconds. Transfer the bananas to dessert plates, scraping up as much of the caramelized ginger as possible, and serve at once with ice cream.

—*Susan Shapiro Jaslove*

• • •

PRUNE CLAFOUTI

6 Servings

½ cup sugar
1½ cups pitted prunes (9 ounces)
3 eggs
1 tablespoon vanilla extract
¼ cup all-purpose flour
1 cup milk
1 cup heavy cream

1. Preheat the oven to 375°. Butter a 9-inch ceramic or glass pie or quiche pan. Sprinkle 2 tablespoons of the sugar inside the pan and tilt to coat. Scatter the prunes on top.

2. In a blender, combine the eggs, vanilla and the remaining 6 tablespoons sugar and blend until smooth. Add the flour and blend briefly. Add the milk and cream and blend until incorporated. Pour the mixture into the prepared pan and bake for about 45 minutes, until puffed and browned. Set aside to cool for 15 minutes before serving.

—*Stephanie Lyness*

• • •

FRESH PINEAPPLE FLAN

This wonderfully fresh-tasting, homey pineapple custard earns points on aroma alone. The French eat a great deal of fresh pineapple. It is in the market year-round, and it appears regularly as *ananas frais* on bistro menus throughout the country.

6 to 8 Servings

2 cups fresh pineapple chunks (1 inch)
2 cups milk
1 vanilla bean, split
3 whole eggs
3 egg yolks
⅔ cup sugar
2 tablespoons unbleached flour
2 tablespoons heavy cream

1. Preheat the oven to 400°. Butter a shallow, straight-sided 10½- or 11-inch round glass or ceramic baking dish. Scatter the pineapple chunks in the dish and bake for 20 minutes. Let cool slightly.

2. Meanwhile, pour the milk into a heavy saucepan. Scrape the seeds from the vanilla bean into the milk; add the bean. Bring just to a simmer over high heat. Remove from the heat, cover and let steep for 15 minutes. Remove the vanilla bean, rinse and save for another use.

3. Reduce the oven temperature to 350°. In a medium bowl, whisk together the whole eggs, egg yolks, sugar, flour and cream until thoroughly blended. Gradually whisk in the hot milk. Pour the custard over the pineapple and bake in the middle of the oven for about 30 minutes, or until just set. Serve the flan at room temperature, spooned directly from the baking dish.

—Patricia Wells

• • •

ALMOND CUSTARDS WITH DRIED FRUIT COMPOTE

You may use 12 ounces of any dried fruit for the compote.

8 Servings

COMPOTE:

¾ cup pitted prunes (5 ounces)
½ cup dried apricots (3 ounces)
¼ cup dried sour cherries or dried cranberries* (1 ounce)
¼ cup golden raisins (1 ounce)
¼ cup dark raisins (1 ounce)
¼ cup dried currants (1 ounce)
Boiling water

CUSTARDS:

1⅓ cups sugar
2 cups milk
½ cup heavy cream
1 teaspoon almond extract
3 whole eggs, at room temperature
3 egg yolks, at room temperature
****Available at specialty markets***

1. *Prepare the compote:* Put each of the dried fruits in a separate bowl and pour in enough boiling water to cover. Let soak overnight at room temperature.

2. *Make the custards:* In a small heavy saucepan, cook 1 cup of the sugar over moderate heat until it is a golden caramel color, shaking the pan occasionally when the sugar starts to melt and color, about 8 minutes. Stir in ½ cup of water, being careful to avoid the splatters, and simmer to dissolve the caramel. Remove from the heat and set aside to cool for 15 minutes. Spoon 1 tablespoon of the caramel into the bottom of each of eight ⅔-cup custard cups or ramekins and set aside.

3. Preheat the oven to 350°. In a medium saucepan, combine the milk, cream, almond extract and the remaining ⅓ cup sugar. Cook over moderate heat, stirring occasionally, until hot but not boiling, about 5 minutes. Remove from the heat.

4. In a medium bowl, whisk the whole eggs and egg yolks. Whisk in the hot milk mixture. Strain this custard into the caramel-lined custard cups set in a baking pan. Fill the pan with enough hot water to reach halfway up the sides of the cups. Cover loosely with aluminum foil.

5. Bake the custards for about 25 minutes, until set but still slightly wobbly in the center. Remove the custard cups from the pan and set aside to cool to room temperature; then cover and refrigerate overnight.

6. To serve, drain each of the fruits. Loosen the custards around the sides with a thin flexible knife and invert onto large plates; drizzle any caramel left in the custard cups over the tops of the custards. Scatter some of each of the fruits around the custards and serve.

—Lindsey Shere

• • •

BAKED QUINCES WITH CREMA CATALANA

Crema catalana, or "Catalan cream," is the Spanish cousin of crème brûlée—a rich, custardy affair with caramelized sugar on top. Some restaurants in Catalonia use the custard as a filling for baked apples, but quinces, also very popular there, offer a more dramatic contrast, with their fragrant, not overly sweet flesh.

6 Servings

3 large quinces (about ¾ pound each)—peeled, quartered lengthwise and cored
1 cup plus 2 tablespoons sugar
2 cinnamon sticks or a pinch of ground cinnamon
8 whole cloves
1 cup half-and-half or light cream
3 egg yolks
Sprigs of fresh mint, for garnish

1. Preheat the oven to 450°. Butter 6 shallow 5-inch-round porcelain quiche molds. Cut each quince quarter in 6 lengthwise slices. Arrange the quinces in the molds, fanning the slices. Place the molds on a heavy baking sheet and set aside.

2. In a small saucepan, combine 1 cup of water, ½ cup of the sugar, the cinnamon sticks and the cloves. Bring to a boil over moderately high heat and boil for 5 minutes. Reduce the heat to low and simmer until a light syrup forms, about 2 minutes. Strain the syrup over the quinces and bake for about 30 minutes, until the slices are tender. Set aside to cool for 15 minutes.

3. In a small saucepan, bring the half-and-half to a boil over moderate heat. Meanwhile, in a medium bowl, beat the egg yolks and ½ cup of the sugar with an electric mixer on high speed until thick, about 2 minutes. With the mixer running, add half of the hot half-and-half. Return the mixture to the saucepan with the remaining hot cream and cook, stirring constantly with a wooden spoon, until the custard reaches 170°, is slightly thickened and coats the back of the spoon, about 7 minutes. Strain the custard into a bowl and set aside.

4. Preheat the broiler. Spoon about 3 tablespoons of the custard over the quinces in each mold. Sprinkle each with 1 teaspoon of the remaining sugar. Broil until the top is caramelized, about 2 minutes. Serve warm, garnished with mint sprigs.

—*Colman Andrews*

• • •

CITRUS SPONGE PUDDING

This lemon-and-lime-flavored pudding separates into three distinct tiers as it bakes: a chewy meringue crust, a soft cakey center and a light creamy layer that acts as a sauce. It can be served warm or cold.

6 Servings

Juice and finely grated zest of 1 lemon
Juice and finely grated zest of 2 limes
2 tablespoons unsalted butter, at room temperature
¾ cup plus 5 tablespoons superfine sugar
4 eggs, separated, at room temperature
¼ cup all-purpose flour, sifted
1½ cups milk
Pinch of salt
Candied Citrus Peel, for garnish (p. 266)
Assorted berries, for garnish (optional)

1. Preheat the oven to 350°. Lightly butter six 1-cup ovenproof glass custard dishes and place them in a large roasting pan.

2. In a small bowl, combine the lemon juice, lime juice and the zests. Set aside. In a medium bowl, using an electric mixer at medium speed, cream the butter with ¾ cup of the sugar until blended, about 1 minute. Add the egg yolks, one at a time, beating well after each addition. Add the flour in two batches, alternating with the reserved citrus juices and the milk. Set aside.

3. In a medium bowl, using clean beaters, beat the egg whites at medium speed until foamy. Add the salt and continue beating until the whites hold soft peaks. Beat in the remaining 5 tablespoons sugar, 1 tablespoon at a time, until fully incorporated and the whites are stiff. Gently fold the whites into the citrus mixture until thoroughly incorporated. Transfer the mixture to the custard dishes in the roasting pan.

4. Pour 1 inch of warm water into the roasting pan. Transfer carefully to the oven and bake for about 35 minutes, until the custards puff up and brown and a small sharp knife inserted near the edge comes out clean. The puddings will crack and then sink when removed from the oven.

5. Immediately remove the dishes from the water bath and let cool on a rack for about 1 hour. Run the tip of a paring knife around the edge of each pudding to release it. Unmold the puddings onto serving plates and garnish with Candied Citrus Peel or berries. *(The puddings can also be made ahead and served chilled. Cover and refrigerate for several hours or overnight. Dip the bottom of each custard dish in warm water for several seconds to unmold.)*

—*Peggy Cullen*

• • •

GINGERSNAP HONEY CUSTARD

Make this dessert in plenty of time to let it chill properly. Generously dollop each serving of this silken custard with unsweetened whipped cream if desired.

6 Servings

¼ cup plus 2 tablespoons honey
12 gingersnaps (about 3 ounces)
4 eggs
¼ cup plus 2 tablespoons sugar
½ teaspoon salt
½ teaspoon vanilla extract
2½ cups milk

1. Preheat the oven to 350°. Generously butter six ½-cup custard cups. Spoon 1 tablespoon of the honey into the bottom of each cup. Break the gingersnaps into small pieces by hand or with a rolling pin and sprinkle the crumbs evenly on top of the honey. Place the cups in a baking pan and set aside.

2. In a bowl, whisk the eggs thoroughly. Whisk in the sugar, salt and vanilla. Stir in the milk until thoroughly blended and the sugar is mostly dissolved. Strain the mixture into the custard cups, filling them almost to the rims. The gingersnaps will rise to the surface. Pour enough hot water into the baking pan to reach halfway up the sides of the custard cups.

3. Bake the custards for about 30 minutes, or until a knife inserted in the center comes out clean. Let the custards cool in the water bath. Cover and refrigerate until chilled, about 4 hours.

4. To serve, run a knife around the edge of each custard and carefully invert onto individual plates, coating the custards with the liquid in the bottom of the cups.

—Lee Bailey

• • •

LOUISIANA BREAD PUDDING WITH PRALINE SAUCE

16 Servings

4 tablespoons unsalted butter, softened, plus 2 sticks (8 ounces), cut into small dice
1 loaf (1½ pounds) country-style Italian or French bread, thinly sliced and toasted
5 eggs
3 cups milk
1½ cups plus 3 tablespoons sugar
¼ teaspoon salt
3 tablespoons vanilla extract
1½ cups raisins
1 cup chopped pecans, lightly toasted
1 teaspoon cinnamon
½ teaspoon freshly grated nutmeg

PRALINE SAUCE:
2 sticks (8 ounces) unsalted butter
1 cup (packed) dark brown sugar
1 cup heavy cream

1. Preheat the oven to 350°. Butter a 9-by-13-inch glass baking dish with the softened butter. Set aside.

2. Tear the toast into bite-size pieces and place in a large bowl. In another bowl, whisk the eggs with the milk, 1½ cups of the sugar and the salt. Beat in the vanilla. Pour the mixture over the toast and set aside until it is completely absorbed.

3. Meanwhile, in a medium bowl, toss the raisins with the pecans. In a small bowl, mix the cinnamon, nutmeg and the remaining 3 tablespoons sugar.

4. Fold the raisins and pecans into the moistened bread and transfer to the prepared baking dish; pat down evenly. Sprinkle the spiced sugar and the diced butter over the bread pudding and cover with foil.

5. Set the baking dish in a larger pan of hot water and bake for 50 minutes to 1 hour, or until the pudding feels firm and a knife inserted in the center comes out clean. Remove the foil and let sit for 10 minutes.

6. *Meanwhile, make the praline sauce:* Combine all of the sauce ingredients in a saucepan and bring to a boil over high heat. Reduce the heat and simmer for 5 minutes.

7. Serve the pudding in squares, with the warm praline sauce spooned on top.

—Ferdinand Johnson, Chef Ferdinand's Restaurant, Harvey, Louisiana

• • •

TORRIJAS WITH ORANGE-FLAVORED SYRUP

Torrijas, a favorite Spanish home dessert, is reminiscent of *pain perdu*, or sweetened French toast.

6 Servings

1¼ cups fresh orange juice
1 tablespoon fresh lemon juice
⅓ cup plus 1 tablespoon Spanish brandy
⅓ cup plus 1 tablespoon orange liqueur
¼ cup plus 1 tablespoon port
Zest of ½ an orange, cut into fine julienne strips
⅓ cup plus 1 tablespoon sugar
4 cups milk
Zest of ½ a lemon
One 3½-inch cinnamon stick
Six ¾-inch slices of crusty Italian bread
¼ cup olive oil
3 eggs, well beaten

1. In a small nonreactive saucepan, combine the orange juice, lemon juice, brandy, orange liqueur, port, orange zest and sugar. Bring to a gentle boil over moderately low heat and simmer until the liquid has reduced to 1¼ cups, about 25 minutes. Set aside. *(The syrup can be made 1 day ahead and refrigerated. Reheat before serving.)*

2. In a medium saucepan, combine the milk with the lemon zest and cinnamon stick; bring to a simmer over low heat and let steep for 20 minutes.

3. Meanwhile, place 3 bread slices in a single layer in a baking dish. Pour half of the milk over the bread and let sit for a few minutes.

4. Heat a large heavy skillet over moderate heat until hot. Add 2 tablespoons of the olive oil. Carefully dip the soaked bread in the beaten eggs and turn to coat both sides, then place in the skillet. Cook, turning once, until nicely browned and firm, 3 to 4 minutes per side. Repeat with the remaining bread, milk, eggs and olive oil.

5. Arrange the *torrijas* on a platter and drizzle a little of the warm orange syrup on top. Pass the remaining syrup on the side.

—Ana Espinosa

• • •

Banana Fritters (p. 238).

Right, Strawberry and Passion Fruit Shortcake (p. 228).

Right, Gingersnap Honey Custard (p. 243). Far right, Apricots à la Mode with Caramel Plum Sauce in a Ginger Bowl (p. 236).

GINGER SOUFFLES WITH SPICED PECANS

6 Servings

¼ cup plus 2 tablespoons granulated sugar
1 tablespoon plus 2 teaspoons all-purpose flour
½ cup milk, at room temperature
1 egg yolk, at room temperature
1 tablespoon unsalted butter, at room temperature
1 teaspoon light rum
¼ teaspoon grated fresh ginger
5 egg whites, at room temperature
2 teaspoons minced crystallized ginger
Confectioners' sugar, for dusting
Spiced Pecans (p. 20)

1. Lightly butter the inside of six ⅔-cup ramekins (about 3¼ by 1¼ inches). Coat evenly with 1½ tablespoons of the sugar.

2. In a small nonreactive saucepan, toss the flour with 1½ tablespoons of the sugar. Stir in the milk and bring to a boil over moderate heat. Cook, stirring constantly, until very thick, about 2 minutes. Remove from the heat and quickly whisk in the egg yolk. Cook over moderate heat, stirring constantly, until very hot, about 1 minute.

3. Remove from the heat and stir in the butter, rum and fresh ginger. Transfer the mixture to a large bowl. Put a piece of plastic wrap directly on the surface and set aside to cool for 15 minutes. *(The soufflé base can be made to this point up to 2 days ahead; refrigerate. Bring to room temperature before proceeding.)*

4. Preheat the oven to 400°. In a medium bowl, beat the egg whites to soft peaks. Gradually beat in the remaining 3 tablespoons sugar until the whites hold soft peaks again.

5. Quickly and thoroughly fold about one-fourth of the whites and the crystallized ginger into the cooled soufflé base. Fold in the remaining whites until barely incorporated.

6. Gently scrape the mixture evenly into the prepared ramekins. *(The recipe can be made to this point up to 2 hours ahead; set the ramekins aside in a cool place.)* Bake in the upper part of the oven for about 10 minutes, until the soufflés are puffed, browned and barely set. Immediately set the soufflés on serving plates lined with doilies and dust the tops lightly with confectioners' sugar. Scatter the Spiced Pecans around the ramekins and serve at once.

—Lindsey Shere

• • •

VANILLA ICE CREAM

Makes 1 Quart

1 vanilla bean, split
2 cups heavy cream
1 cup half-and-half or light cream
⅔ cup sugar
6 egg yolks

1. Scrape the seeds from the vanilla bean into a medium nonreactive saucepan; add the bean. Stir in the heavy cream, half-and-half and sugar and cook over moderate heat, stirring occasionally, until the sugar is dissolved, about 5 minutes.

2. In a medium bowl, whisk the egg yolks to break them up. Gradually whisk in half of the hot cream, then pour the mixture into the remaining cream in the saucepan and cook over moderate heat, stirring constantly, until the custard coats a spoon and reaches 165° on a candy thermometer, about 6 minutes.

3. Strain the custard into a container and refrigerate until cold, about 2 hours. (Alternatively, chill the pan of custard in an ice water bath, stirring, for about 30 minutes.) Pour the custard into an ice cream maker and freeze according to the manufacturer's instructions.

—Lindsey Shere

• • •

CINNAMON GELATO

Makes 5 Cups

2 cups milk
1 cup heavy cream
2-by-¼-inch strip of lemon zest
½ teaspoon cinnamon
4 egg yolks
½ cup sugar

1. In a medium saucepan, combine the milk, cream, lemon zest and cinnamon. Warm over moderate heat until small bubbles form around the edge of the pan, about 5 minutes. Set aside to cool slightly.

2. In a large bowl, whisk the egg yolks and sugar until blended. Gradually whisk in the hot milk mixture.

3. Pour the mixture into the saucepan and cook over moderate heat, stirring constantly with a wooden spoon, until the custard thickens slightly and lightly coats the back of the spoon, about 5 minutes.

4. Strain the custard through a fine sieve into a large bowl. Let cool, then cover and refrigerate for at least 2 hours or overnight. (Alternatively, set the

Cherry-Frangipane Tart (p. 216).

bowl in a larger bowl of ice and chill, stirring, for 30 minutes.)

5. Transfer the custard to an ice cream maker and freeze according to the manufacturer's instructions. *(The gelato will keep for up to 2 days. Pack it into a container, cover and freeze; if the gelato becomes too firm, let it soften in the refrigerator for 30 minutes before serving.)*

—*Michele Scicolone*

• • •

VANILLA ICE CREAM WITH AMARETTO

4 Servings

1 pint vanilla ice cream
About 3 tablespoons amaretto liqueur
4 amaretti cookies, finely crumbled

Scoop the ice cream into 4 sundae dishes or glass bowls. Drizzle about 2 generous teaspoons of the amaretto over each serving and sprinkle the amaretti on top. Serve at once.

—*Susan Shapiro Jaslove*

• • •

LESS-CREAM, NO-EGG ICE CREAM OF THE PEACH VARIETY

Makes 1½ Quarts

1 pound ripe peaches, peeled and pitted
1½ cups sugar
1½ cups milk
1½ cups heavy cream
1 teaspoon vanilla extract

In a blender, puree the peaches until almost smooth. In a bowl, combine the sugar, milk and cream; stir until the sugar dissolves. Stir in the peaches and then the vanilla. Pour the mixture into an ice cream maker and freeze according to the manufacturer's instructions.

—*Mary Anne Dolan*

• • •

ONCE-A-YEAR CHEESECAKE ICE CREAM

Most of our family meals end sweetly but sensibly with fresh fruit, simple sorbets, frozen yogurt and a plate of cookies. But once a year we just have to have cheesecake ice cream, a fabulously rich dessert that's very easy to make and very hard to stop eating.

Makes 1 Quart

6 ounces cream cheese, preferably preservative-free, softened but still cool
¾ cup superfine sugar
1 cup cold sour cream
1 cup cold heavy cream
Pinch of coarse (kosher) salt
3 tablespoons fresh lemon juice
¼ teaspoon vanilla extract

1. Chill a medium mixing bowl and the beaters of an electric mixer. In the bowl, beat the cream cheese at medium speed until soft and smooth. Gradually add the sugar, ¼ cup at a time, beating well after each addition. Beat in the sour cream and then the heavy cream. Add the salt, lemon juice and vanilla and beat the mixture just until thick and smooth. Cover and refrigerate overnight, or until very cold. Wash and dry the mixer beaters and chill again.

2. Using the chilled beaters and gradually increasing the mixer speed from low to medium, beat the cold ice cream mixture until loose and creamy, about 3 minutes. Pour into an ice cream maker and freeze according to the manufacturer's instructions. Serve immediately, or pack the ice cream into a covered container and freeze for up to 24 hours. Allow the ice cream to soften in the refrigerator for 20 to 30 minutes before serving.

—*Leslie Newman*

• • •

ROASTED HAZELNUT ICE CREAM

What better way to make hazelnut ice cream than to begin with hazelnut butter, a deep-flavored cousin of peanut butter. You can make your own hazelnut butter or purchase it in health food stores. You'll need three-quarters of a cup for this recipe, plus two-thirds of a cup of chopped hazelnuts for texture.

Makes 1½ Quarts

4 cups milk
1¼ cups sugar
One 4-inch piece of vanilla bean, split
1½ tablespoons French- or Italian-roast coffee beans
5 egg yolks
⅔ cup heavy or whipping cream
2 cups hazelnuts (9 ounces)

1. In a heavy medium saucepan, heat the milk with the sugar, vanilla bean and coffee beans, stirring, until the mixture is hot and the sugar dissolves, 4 to 5 minutes.

2. In a medium bowl, lightly whisk the egg yolks. Whisk in 1 cup of the hot milk, then whisk the mixture back into the remaining milk in the saucepan. Cook over moderate heat, stirring occasionally, until the custard reaches 175°, thickens slightly and coats the back of a spoon, 8 to 10 minutes. (Do not boil or the custard will curdle.) Strain the custard through a fine sieve set over a medium bowl; discard the vanilla bean and the coffee beans. Stir in the cream and let cool to room temperature, then refrigerate until completely chilled.

3. Meanwhile, preheat the oven to 425°. Spread the hazelnuts on a baking sheet and toast in the middle of the oven until golden brown, about 8 minutes. Transfer the hot nuts to a kitchen towel and rub vigorously to remove the skins; let cool slightly. Set aside ⅔ cup of the toasted hazelnuts. Place the remaining hazelnuts in a food processor and process, scraping down the sides of the bowl once with a spatula, until a paste forms.

4. When the ice cream base is completely chilled, stir in the hazelnut butter until thoroughly incorporated. Coarsely chop the reserved hazelnuts and fold them into the ice cream base.

5. Pour the mixture into an ice cream maker and freeze according to the manufacturer's instructions. To store, transfer the ice cream to a clean, chilled container; cover tightly and freeze for up to 1 week.

—Carol Field

• • •

RICE PUDDING ICE CREAM

Italians actually make rice ice cream; it's a bit crunchy and as white as snow. However, this recipe is more a twist on the rice puddings of old. It's every bit as creamy and rich as they were, although no one ever soaked raisins in rum for those simple desserts.

Makes 2 Quarts

2 quarts milk
1½ cups sugar
½ teaspoon cinnamon
3 tablespoons long-grain white rice
½ cup raisins
5 tablespoons rum
One 4-inch piece of vanilla bean, split
1 cinnamon stick
5 egg yolks
⅔ cup heavy or whipping cream

1. Preheat the oven to 300°. In a buttered 2-quart baking dish or soufflé dish, combine 1 quart of milk, ¼ cup of the sugar, the ground cinnamon and the rice; mix thoroughly. Bake uncovered for about 2 hours, or until the pudding is creamy, the rice is very soft and the top is lightly browned. Set aside to cool to room temperature.

2. Meanwhile, in a small bowl, cover the raisins with the rum and let macerate until plump, at least 30 minutes.

3. In a heavy medium saucepan, combine the remaining 1 quart milk and 1¼ cups sugar with the vanilla bean and cinnamon stick. Cook over moderate heat, stirring, until the mixture is hot and the sugar dissolves, 4 to 5 minutes.

4. In a medium bowl, lightly whisk the egg yolks. Whisk about 1 cup of the hot milk into the yolks, then whisk the mixture back into the remaining milk in the saucepan. Cook over moderate heat, stirring constantly, until the custard reaches 175°, thickens slightly and coats the back of a spoon, 8 to 10 minutes. (Do not boil or the mixture will curdle.) Strain the custard through a fine sieve into a medium bowl. Stir in the cream and let cool to room temperature. Refrigerate until completely chilled, then stir in the rice pudding.

5. Freeze the mixture in two batches. Pour half of the mixture into an ice cream maker and freeze according to the manufacturer's instructions. To store, transfer the ice cream to a clean, chilled container; cover tightly and freeze for up to 1 week. Repeat with the remaining ice cream mixture.

—Carol Field

• • •

BALSAMICO ICE CREAM

On a sophisticated note, here is creamy vanilla ice cream flavored with a well-aged balsamic vinegar.

Makes 5 Cups

4 cups milk
1¼ cups sugar
One 4-inch piece of vanilla bean, split
5 egg yolks
⅔ cup heavy or whipping cream
1 to 1½ teaspoons balsamic vinegar

1. In a heavy medium saucepan, combine the milk with the sugar and vanilla bean and stir over moderate heat until the mixture is hot and the sugar dissolves, 4 to 5 minutes.

2. In a medium bowl, lightly whisk the egg yolks. Whisk 1 cup of the hot milk into the yolks; then whisk the mixture back into the remaining milk in the saucepan. Cook over moderate heat, stirring constantly with a wooden spoon, until the custard reaches 175°, is slightly thickened and coats the back of a spoon, 8 to 10 minutes. (Do not boil or the custard will curdle.) Strain the mixture into a medium bowl. Stir in the cream and let cool to room temperature. Refrigerate until completely chilled, then stir in the balsamic vinegar.

3. Pour the mixture into an ice cream maker and freeze according to the manufacturer's instructions. To store, transfer the ice cream to a clean, chilled container; cover tightly and freeze for up to 1 week.

—*Carol Field*

• • •

PANFORTE ICE CREAM

Siena is famous for its *panforte*, a dense Christmas fruitcake. *Panforte* is now available year-round in this country, providing an unending opportunity to put this ice cream on the table whenever you wish.

Makes 5½ Cups

4 cups milk
1¼ cups sugar
One 4-inch piece of vanilla bean, split
One ¾-inch cinnamon stick
⅛ teaspoon ground coriander
⅛ teaspoon ground cloves
⅛ teaspoon freshly grated nutmeg
5 egg yolks
⅔ cup heavy or whipping cream
¼ pound panforte,* cut into ⅓-inch dice
****Available at specialty shops and bakeries***

1. In a heavy medium saucepan, combine the milk, sugar, vanilla bean, cinnamon stick, ground coriander, cloves and nutmeg. Stir over moderate heat until the mixture is hot and the sugar is dissolved, about 5 minutes.

2. In a medium bowl, lightly whisk the egg yolks. Whisk 1 cup of the hot milk into the yolks, then whisk the mixture back into the remaining milk in the saucepan. Cook over moderate heat, stirring constantly with a wooden spoon, until the custard reaches 175°, thickens slightly and coats the back of the spoon, 8 to 10 minutes. (Do not boil or the custard will curdle.) Strain the custard through a fine sieve into a large bowl. Stir in the cream and set aside to cool to room temperature. Refrigerate until completely chilled, then stir in the *panforte* pieces.

3. Pour the mixture into an ice cream maker and freeze according to the manufacturer's instructions. To store, transfer the ice cream to a clean, chilled container; cover tightly and freeze for up to 1 week.

—*Carol Field*

• • •

PEAR SORBET

Any juicy, ripe pear—Anjou, Bartlett, Comice or Bosc—will lend itself to this elegant treatment.

Makes 1 Quart

3 pounds pears
1 lemon, cut into half
⅔ cup sugar

1. Peel, halve and core the pears, rubbing them with the cut side of a lemon half to prevent discoloration as you go. Cut the pears into 1-inch chunks and place in a medium nonreactive saucepan. Add ¾ cup water, cover and simmer over moderate heat until the pears are easily pierced with a knife, about 10 to 15 minutes.

2. Strain the pears through a coarse sieve set over a medium bowl. Stir the sugar into the hot cooking liquid until it dissolves completely; set aside.

3. In a food processor, puree the pears. Squeeze 1 tablespoon of juice from the remaining lemon half and add to the pears along with the pear liquid; process to combine. Scrape the puree back into the bowl and refrigerate until completely chilled.

4. Pour the mixture into an ice cream maker and freeze according to the manufacturer's instructions. To store, transfer the sorbet to a clean container, cover tightly and freeze for up to 3 days.

—*Carol Field*

• • •

PERSIMMON SORBET

Be sure to choose persimmons that are a deep orange and very soft.

Makes 1 Quart

3¼ pounds very soft, ripe persimmons (about 8)
⅔ to 1 cup sugar
2 teaspoons fresh lemon juice
4 teaspoons orange liqueur (optional)

1. Cut the persimmons in half lengthwise and scoop the flesh into a food processor; discard the skin and any seeds. Puree the pulp and transfer to a medium bowl. You should have 4 cups.

2. In a heavy, medium, nonreactive saucepan, combine 2 cups of the persimmon puree with ⅔ cup of the sugar. Cook over moderate heat, stirring, until the sugar dissolves and you can no longer feel any crystals between your fingers, about 3 minutes. Transfer to the bowl with the remaining persimmon puree. Stir in the lemon juice and liqueur; taste for sweetness, adding up to ⅓ cup more sugar. Refrigerate until completely chilled.

3. Pour the mixture into an ice cream maker and freeze according to the manufacturer's instructions. To store, transfer the sorbet to a clean container, cover tightly and freeze for up to 3 days.

—Carol Field

• • •

BLOOD ORANGE SORBET

Makes 1 Quart

4½ pounds blood oranges (about 16)
¾ cup sugar
⅛ teaspoon lemon juice

1. Lightly scrub the oranges in warm soapy water and rinse thoroughly. Dry well. Finely grate the colored zest of 4 of the oranges into a medium nonreactive saucepan. Be careful not to grate any of the bitter white pith. Set aside.

2. Squeeze all the oranges and strain the juice through a fine sieve into the saucepan with the zest. You should have about 3½ cups of juice.

3. Heat the juice and zest with the sugar over moderate heat, stirring, until all the sugar dissolves completely, about 2 minutes. Stir in the lemon juice. Refrigerate until completely chilled.

4. Pour the mixture into an ice cream maker and freeze according to the manufacturer's instructions. To store, transfer the sorbet to a clean container, cover tightly and freeze for up to 3 days.

—Carol Field

MEDLEY OF MELON SORBETS

A trio of fragrant melons—watermelon, honeydew and cantaloupe—are here transformed into sorbets and laced respectively with touches of Marsala, orange liqueur and dark rum.

6 Servings

Watermelon Sorbet (recipe follows)
Honeydew Sorbet (recipe follows)
Cantaloupe Sorbet (recipe follows)

Make each of the sorbets as directed in the recipes that follow. Then, 1 to 4 hours before serving, use a 4-ounce ice cream scoop to form nine to 10 balls of each sorbet. Place the balls on a large plate or tray and freeze until ready to serve. Present the balls of sorbet in a hollowed-out watermelon half or a large glass bowl.

—Peggy Cullen

• • •

WATERMELON SORBET

2 Servings

¼ of a large watermelon (about 2 pounds)
½ cup superfine sugar
1 tablespoon fresh lemon juice
1 tablespoon Marsala

1. Using a sharp knife, cut away the rind from the watermelon and discard. Cut the flesh into 2-inch chunks. You should have about 4 cups. In a food processor, puree the melon chunks with the seeds until liquefied. Strain the juice through a coarse sieve set over a medium bowl; discard the seeds.

2. In a small saucepan, combine the sugar with ½ cup of the strained watermelon juice. Dip a pastry brush in water and wash down the sides of the pan. Bring to a boil over moderately high heat, stirring occasionally; remove from the heat. Whisk this watermelon syrup into the remaining watermelon juice and stir in the lemon juice.

3. Pour the mixture into an ice cream maker and freeze according to the manufacturer's instructions. When the sorbet begins to set, after about 20 minutes, add the Marsala. When the sorbet is done, transfer to a tightly covered container and freeze overnight. *(The sorbet can be frozen for up to 1 week.)*

—Peggy Cullen

• • •

HONEYDEW SORBET

2 Servings

½ of a 4-pound honeydew melon
½ cup superfine sugar
1 tablespoon fresh lime juice
2 tablespoons orange-flavored liqueur

1. Scoop out and discard the seeds from the melon half. Using a large metal spoon, scoop out the flesh. You should have about 4 cups. In a food processor, puree the honeydew until liquefied. Strain the puree through a coarse sieve set over a medium bowl.

2. In a small nonreactive saucepan, combine the sugar with ½ cup of the strained puree. Dip a pastry brush in water and wash down the sides of the pan. Bring to a boil over moderately high heat, stirring frequently. Remove from the heat. Whisk this honeydew syrup into the remaining honeydew puree and add the lime juice.

3. Pour the mixture into an ice cream maker and freeze according to the manufacturer's instructions. When the sorbet begins to set, after about 20 minutes, add the liqueur. When the sorbet is done, transfer to a tightly covered container and freeze overnight. *(The sorbet can be frozen for up to 1 week.)*

—*Peggy Cullen*

• • •

CANTALOUPE SORBET

2 Servings

One 2-pound cantaloupe
½ cup superfine sugar
1 tablespoon fresh lemon juice
1 tablespoon dark rum

1. Cut the cantaloupe in half; scoop out and discard the seeds. Using a large metal spoon, scoop out the flesh. You should have 4 cups. In a food processor, puree the cantaloupe until liquefied. Strain the puree through a coarse sieve set over a medium bowl.

2. In a small saucepan, combine the sugar with ½ cup of the strained cantaloupe puree. Dip a pastry brush in water and wash down the sides of the pan. Bring to a boil over moderately high heat, stirring occasionally; remove from the heat. Whisk this cantaloupe syrup into the remaining cantaloupe puree and stir in the lemon juice.

3. Pour the mixture into an ice cream maker and freeze according to the manufacturer's instructions. When the sorbet begins to set, after about 20 minutes, add the rum. When the sorbet is done, transfer it to a tightly covered container and freeze overnight. *(The sorbet can be frozen for up to 1 week.)*

—*Peggy Cullen*

• • •

MELON SORBET WITH FRESH GINGER

Anyone who has ever visited Provence in the summertime remembers the little peppery, green-and-white striped Cavaillon melons that flood the markets at this time of year. In Provence, that's what I use for this sorbet, but any nice ripe cantaloupe, or muskmelon, makes a fine substitute.

4 Servings

4 cups cantaloupe cubes (1 large cantaloupe)
½ cup sugar
1 tablespoon plus 1 teaspoon fresh lemon juice
1½ teaspoons finely minced fresh ginger
Fresh mint leaves, for garnish

In a blender, puree the melon with the sugar just until smooth. Stir in the lemon juice and ginger. Transfer the mixture to an ice cream maker and freeze according to the manufacturer's instructions. Garnish the sorbet with mint leaves.

—*Ann Haskell*

• • •

GRAPEFRUIT-TEQUILA ICE

Texans are justifiably proud of their ruby grapefruit. Combined with tequila and lime, this dessert hints at a tall, refreshingly cold Margarita.

Makes 1 Quart

1¼ cups sugar
1 cup tequila
Juice of 4 large grapefruits (about 2½ cups)
Juice of 1 lemon

1. In a saucepan, combine the sugar with 1 cup water. Cook over high heat, stirring with a wooden spoon until the sugar dissolves. Bring to a full boil, remove the pan from the heat and let cool completely.

2. In a small saucepan, boil the tequila over high heat until it is reduced to ½ cup, 4 to 5 minutes. Set aside to cool completely.

3. Strain the grapefruit and lemon juices through a fine strainer set over a large bowl. Stir in the cooled sugar syrup and tequila. Freeze the mixture in an ice cream maker according to the manufacturer's instructions. Transfer the ice to a large bowl, cover and freeze for at least 1 hour or overnight. If frozen overnight, let the ice soften in the refrigerator for 30 minutes before serving.

—*Stephan Pyles*

• • •

SAUCES, CONDIMENTS & PRESERVES

PEANUT DIPPING SAUCE

Makes 1¼ Cups

2 teaspoons minced shallot
1 teaspoon vegetable oil
¼ cup plus 2 tablespoons creamy natural (unsalted) peanut butter
3 tablespoons unsweetened coconut milk*
2 tablespoons fresh lemon juice
2 tablespoons soy sauce
1 tablespoon (firmly packed) light brown sugar
½ to 1 teaspoon Asian chili paste*
2 tablespoons coarsely chopped fresh basil
****Available at Asian markets***

1. In a medium nonreactive skillet, cook the shallot in the oil over moderately low heat, stirring occasionally, until very soft, about 5 minutes. Whisk in the peanut butter, coconut milk, lemon juice and soy sauce until smooth. Stir in ¼ cup plus 2 tablespoons of water and cook, stirring often, for 5 minutes. Stir in the brown sugar and ½ teaspoon of the chili paste and cook for another 5 minutes.

2. Remove from the heat. Stir in the basil and another ½ teaspoon chili paste if desired. *(The recipe can be made up to 1 hour ahead; set aside at room temperature briefly.)* Serve warm.

—*Peter Merriman, Merriman's, Waimea, Hawaii*

• • •

RED CURRY SAUCE

This is also a good dipping sauce for raw vegetables.

Makes 1½ Cups

1 to 2 dried red chiles (árbol or cayenne)
1½ cups unsweetened coconut milk*
2 tablespoons palm sugar* or dark brown sugar
1 teaspoon tamarind pulp* soaked in 1 tablespoon warm water and strained, juice reserved
1 tablespoon fish sauce (nam pla)*
⅓ cup raw shelled and skinned peanuts, roasted (see Note) and coarsely chopped
****Available at Asian markets***

1. In a small skillet, toast the chiles over high heat until fragrant and blistered, about 30 seconds per side. Let cool, then finely chop with some of the seeds.

2. In a small saucepan, combine the chopped roasted chiles and coconut milk and bring to a boil over moderately high heat. Reduce the heat and add the sugar, stirring to dissolve completely. Stir in the tamarind juice and fish sauce and cook for 1 minute longer. Remove from the heat and stir in the peanuts. Pour into bowls and serve.

NOTE: *Freshly roasted peanuts have a wonderful flavor. Follow this method: In a small cast-iron skillet, roast the peanuts over moderately high heat, stirring constantly, until browned, about 5 minutes. Set aside to cool.*

—*Jeffrey Alford & Naomi Duguid*

• • •

TANGY LIME SAUCE

Makes ⅓ Cup

2 tablespoons fresh lime juice
1 tablespoon soy sauce
1 tablespoon fish sauce (nam pla)*
1 tablespoon palm sugar* or dark brown sugar
½ teaspoon cayenne pepper
2 tablespoons chopped fresh coriander (cilantro)
****Available at Asian markets***

In a small bowl, combine all the ingredients except the coriander leaves and mix well. Stir in the coriander and serve.

—*Jeffrey Alford & Naomi Duguid*

• • •

CILANTRO-SOY DRESSING

Makes ¾ Cup

3 tablespoons fresh lime juice
3 tablespoons soy sauce
1 tablespoon ginger juice (see Note)
1 tablespoon Oriental sesame oil
1 teaspoon minced garlic
Pinch of cayenne pepper
¼ cup corn or other vegetable oil
1 teaspoon minced fresh coriander (cilantro)

In a small nonreactive bowl, whisk together the lime juice, soy sauce, ginger juice, sesame oil, garlic and cayenne. Gradually whisk in the vegetable oil in a fine stream until blended. Stir in the coriander. *(The dressing can be made up to 3 hours ahead; cover and refrigerate.)*

NOTE: *To make ginger juice, grate fresh ginger on a small grater, then squeeze through a garlic press. Approximately 4 tablespoons grated fresh ginger yields 1 tablespoon juice.*

*—The Lodge at Koele,
Lanai City, Hawaii*

• • •

CHILE-LIME BASIL DRESSING

Makes 1 Cup

2/3 cup fresh lime juice
1/4 cup fish sauce (nam pla or nuoc mam)*
2 tablespoons sugar
1/8 teaspoon crushed, dried red Asian chile* or hot red pepper sauce
3 medium garlic cloves, coarsely chopped
2 to 3 small serrano chiles, coarsely chopped
1/3 cup (lightly packed) fresh basil leaves, preferably Asian*
****Available at Asian markets***

1. In a medium bowl, combine the lime juice, fish sauce, sugar and chile and stir to dissolve the sugar.

2. In a food processor, combine the garlic, serrano chiles and basil and pulse until minced. Add the lime juice mixture and process until blended, about 10 seconds.

—Linda Burum

• • •

FENNEL-MUSTARD DRESSING

Makes 1 1/2 Cups

2 teaspoons fennel seeds
1/2 cup Dijon mustard
2 teaspoons dry mustard
1/4 cup white wine vinegar
2 tablespoons sugar
2/3 cup extra-virgin olive oil

In a mortar or an electric grinder grind the fennel seeds to a powder. In a small bowl, combine the ground fennel, Dijon and dry mustards, vinegar and sugar. Slowly whisk in the oil until the dressing is creamy.

—Evan Kleiman

• • •

ROMESCO SAUCE

Dried ancho or pasilla chiles are most like the Spanish variety used in a *romesco* sauce. You can find them in the Mexican food section of supermarkets and at Hispanic groceries.

This sauce is wonderful served with Salt Cod Fritters (p. 27) or with steamed baby potatoes.

Makes 1 1/3 Cups

2 ancho or pasilla chiles
2 cups boiling water
About 1/2 cup extra-virgin olive oil
1 thick slice white peasant bread, crusts trimmed
20 whole blanched almonds
1/2 teaspoon salt
3 garlic cloves
1 medium tomato
1/8 teaspoon cayenne pepper
1 tablespoon red wine vinegar
Freshly ground black pepper

1. Break each chile into several pieces. Discard the stems and seeds. In a medium bowl, cover the chiles with the boiling water. Cover and set aside until soft, about 30 minutes. Drain and pat dry.

2. In a medium skillet, heat 1/4 cup of the oil over moderate heat until hot but not smoking, about 3 minutes. Add the bread and fry until golden, about 3 minutes on each side. Drain on a paper towel. Reduce the heat to moderately low, add the chiles to the skillet and cook for 2 minutes. Set the skillet aside.

3. In a food processor, mince the almonds with the salt and garlic, scraping the sides, about 1 minute. Break up the fried bread and add it, the chiles and their oil and process until a smooth puree forms.

4. Slice the tomato in half lengthwise. Squeeze out the juice and seeds and discard. Using the large holes of a metal grater, grate the flesh of 1 tomato half, leaving the skin intact in your hand; discard the skin. Repeat with the remaining tomato half.

5. Add the tomato and cayenne to the food processor. With the machine on, drizzle in as much of the remaining 1/4 cup oil as necessary to make a thick sauce. Stir in the vinegar and season with black pepper to taste. *(The sauce will keep for 5 days; cover and refrigerate.)*

—Sally Schneider

• • •

SORREL MAYONNAISE

Makes 1¼ Cups

1 cup mayonnaise
½ pound fresh sorrel, stems removed
2 tablespoons fresh dill
Salt and freshly ground pepper

In a food processor or a blender, puree the mayonnaise, sorrel and dill until the mixture is very finely speckled with green. Season with salt and pepper to taste. *(The recipe can be made up to 1 day ahead; cover and refrigerate.)* Serve at room temperature or chilled.

—Janie Hibler

• • •

WHITE BUTTER SAUCE

Makes 1½ Cups

¼ cup plus 2 tablespoons dry white wine
1 tablespoon distilled white vinegar
1 small shallot, minced
¼ cup plus 2 tablespoons heavy cream
3 sticks (12 ounces) unsalted butter, diced and chilled
½ teaspoon salt
¼ teaspoon ground white pepper

1. In a medium nonreactive saucepan, simmer the wine, vinegar and shallot over moderately low heat until the liquid is almost evaporated, about 5 minutes. Stir in the heavy cream, bring to a simmer and cook until reduced by one-third, about 5 minutes longer.

2. Whisk in the butter in 6 batches, adding each batch when the previous one is incorporated. Strain the sauce through a coarse sieve into a double boiler. Season with the salt and white pepper. *(The sauce will keep for up to 20 minutes over warm water.)*

—Roy Yamaguchi, Roy's, Honolulu, Hawaii

• • •

SUN-DRIED TOMATO BUTTER

Makes One 8-by-1-Inch Log

1 stick (4 ounces) unsalted butter, at room temperature
1 small garlic clove, minced
¼ teaspoon salt
1½ teaspoons fresh lemon juice
2 tablespoons finely chopped drained, oil-packed sun-dried tomatoes
¼ cup chopped fresh coriander (cilantro)
1 small tomato (about 3 ounces)—cored, seeded and finely chopped

In a small bowl, beat all the ingredients until well blended. Scrape the butter onto a sheet of wax paper and roll up into a 8-by-1-inch log. *(The butter can be made up to 3 days ahead and refrigerated. Let soften at room temperature before serving.)*

—Susan Costner

• • •

FRESH HERB BUTTER

Makes One 6-by-1-Inch Log

1 stick (4 ounces) unsalted butter, at room temperature
2 tablespoons finely chopped flat-leaf parsley
2 tablespoons finely chopped watercress leaves
1½ teaspoons minced fresh tarragon
1½ teaspoons minced fresh mint
1½ teaspoons anise-flavored liqueur, such as Pernod
1½ teaspoons freshly grated Parmesan cheese
½ teaspoon finely grated lemon zest
¼ teaspoon salt
¼ teaspoon hot pepper sauce
Pinch of freshly ground white pepper

In a small bowl, beat all the ingredients until well blended. Scrape the butter onto a sheet of wax paper and roll up into a 6-by-1-inch log. *(The butter can be made up to 3 days ahead and refrigerated. Let soften at room temperature before serving.)*

—Susan Costner

• • •

HAZELNUT-HONEY BUTTER

Makes 1 Cup

1 cup hazelnuts
1 stick (4 ounces) unsalted butter, softened
¼ cup honey

1. Preheat the oven to 350°. Spread the hazelnuts on a small baking sheet with sides and roast for 10 minutes, or until golden brown and fragrant. Transfer the hot nuts to a kitchen towel, wrap them up in the towel and set aside to steam for 10 minutes. When the nuts have cooled, rub them together vigorously in the towel to remove the skins.

2. In a food processor, process the hazelnuts until finely ground. Add the butter and honey and process briefly to blend. Scrape the butter into a ramekin. *(The honey butter can be made 1 day ahead; cover and refrigerate. Let soften to room temperature before serving.)*

—Lee Bailey

• • •

BERTUCCI'S TOMATO SAUCE

Long cooking allows this sauce's flavors to blend properly.

Makes 4 Quarts

½ cup olive oil
3 garlic cloves, halved
3 medium onions, chopped
4 large scallions, chopped
2 cans (6 ounces each) tomato paste
½ cup chopped parsley
1 tablespoon plus 1 teaspoon salt
1 teaspoon freshly ground black pepper
½ teaspoon crushed red pepper
2 cans (35 ounces each) crushed tomatoes
3 tablespoons sugar
About 8 cups boiling water

1. In a large nonreactive casserole, heat the olive oil over low heat. Add the garlic and cook until browned lightly, about 3 minutes. Add the onions and scallions and cook, stirring, until thoroughly wilted and browned, about 20 minutes.

2. Stir in the tomato paste, parsley, 1 teaspoon of the salt, ½ teaspoon of the black pepper and the crushed red pepper. Cook over low heat for 20 minutes, stirring frequently to prevent sticking.

3. Stir in the crushed tomatoes. Add 2 tomato cans' worth (8¾ cups) of water and bring to a boil over high heat. Reduce the heat to moderate and stir in the sugar and the remaining 1 tablespoon salt and ½ teaspoon black pepper. Simmer uncovered for 1 hour, scraping the casserole frequently.

4. Stir in 2 cups of boiling water. Cook, stirring, for a total of 4 hours, adding 1 cup of boiling water about every 45 minutes, or as the sauce thickens. The sauce can cook for another hour if desired; add more water, if necessary, to maintain a good consistency. *(The sauce can be frozen for up to 1 month.)*

—Diane Darrow & Tom Maresca

• • •

PINEAPPLE SALSA

Makes 3 Cups

½ of a medium pineapple—peeled, cored and cut into ¼-inch dice (about 2 cups)
½ of a large sweet onion, such as Maui, cut into ¼-inch dice
2 medium tomatoes, seeded and cut into ¼-inch dice
1 jalapeño pepper, seeded and minced
¼ cup chopped fresh coriander (cilantro)
1 teaspoon coriander seeds, crushed
¾ teaspoon cumin
½ teaspoon minced garlic
½ teaspoon salt

In a medium nonreactive bowl, stir together all the ingredients. Cover and refrigerate for at least 30 minutes and up to 2 hours.

—Peter Merriman, Merriman's, Waimea, Hawaii

• • •

SALSA VERDE CRUDA

This refreshing uncooked green sauce goes well with almost all Mexican dishes, especially those made with cheese and tortillas.

Makes 1½ Cups

½ pound fresh tomatillos—husked, rinsed and quartered
2 garlic cloves, coarsely chopped
½ cup fresh coriander (cilantro) leaves
3 to 4 serrano chiles, seeded and coarsely chopped
1 teaspoon salt
¼ teaspoon sugar

Combine all of the ingredients in a food processor and puree until almost smooth. If the salsa is very thick, add a few teaspoons of water to thin it out. Serve immediately or cover and refrigerate for up to 4 days.

—Chata DuBose

• • •

SALSA RANCHERA

Unlike many other salsas, this one calls for roasting the tomatoes and chiles before combining them with the other ingredients.

Makes 2 Cups

2 large tomatoes (1½ pounds)
3 serrano chiles, stemmed
½ of a small onion
1 garlic clove
Salt

1. Heat a griddle or cast-iron skillet over moderate heat. Add the tomatoes and chiles and roast, turning frequently, until blistered and slightly charred. Peel off and discard as much of the tomato and chile skins as possible.

2. In a food processor, puree the tomatoes, chiles, onion and garlic. Transfer the salsa to a bowl and season with salt to taste.

—*Chata DuBose*

• • •

RED TOMATO SALSA

Red tomato salsa is a staple in southwestern cooking; with the addition of cilantro, it is known as *pico de gallo*, a popular, all-purpose salsa.

Makes 2 Cups

2 garlic cloves, unpeeled
1 pound small, ripe red tomatoes, seeded and cut into ¼-inch dice
3 tablespoons finely diced red onion
2 tablespoons finely diced red bell pepper
1 teaspoon fresh lime juice
1 fresh red jalapeño pepper, seeded and finely diced
½ teaspoon salt

1. Preheat the oven to 400°. Loosely wrap the garlic cloves in foil and roast until very soft, about 25 minutes. Squeeze the garlic pulp from the skins into a small bowl and mash to a paste.

2. In a medium bowl, combine all of the remaining ingredients. Add the garlic pulp and stir to blend.

—*Stephan Pyles*

• • •

GARDEN SALAD SALSA

This salsa is based on a recipe from my friend Danny Matthews. If you like a more fiery salsa, use a medium-size jalapeño pepper.

Makes 3½ Cups

1 small jalapeño pepper, including seeds, coarsely chopped
2 medium garlic cloves, halved
¼ cup (packed) fresh coriander (cilantro) leaves
4 large plum tomatoes (about 1 pound)—cored, seeded and quartered
1 medium carrot, cut into chunks
1 medium red bell pepper, cut into large chunks
½ cup fresh, thawed frozen or canned (rinsed) corn kernels
4 scallions, thinly sliced
2 tablespoons white wine vinegar
1 tablespoon fresh lime juice
1 tablespoon olive oil
Salt

1. In a food processor, process the jalapeño, garlic and fresh coriander until finely chopped. Add the tomatoes, carrot and bell pepper and pulse about 15 times, scraping down once, until the vegetables are coarsely chopped. Transfer the mixture to a large bowl.

2. Stir in the corn, scallions, vinegar, lime juice and oil until combined. Season with salt to taste.

—*Susan Shapiro Jaslove*

• • •

TOMATILLO SALSA

Makes 2 Cups

4 large garlic cloves, unpeeled
4 scallions, finely chopped
1 pound fresh tomatillos—husked, rinsed, cored and cut into ¼-inch dice
2 tablespoons chopped fresh coriander (cilantro)
3 to 4 serrano chiles, seeded and finely diced
2 teaspoons fresh lime juice
½ teaspoon salt

1. Preheat the oven to 400°. Loosely wrap the garlic cloves in foil and roast for about 25 minutes, until very soft. Squeeze the garlic pulp from the skins into a small bowl and mash to a paste.

2. In a medium bowl, combine all of the remaining ingredients. Add the garlic pulp and stir to blend.

—*Stephan Pyles*

• • •

YELLOW TOMATO SALSA

Yellow tomatoes are softer and sweeter than red tomatoes, and this salsa makes a wonderful accompaniment to grilled fish.

Makes 2 Cups

1 pound yellow tomatoes or 1 pint yellow plum tomatoes, seeded and diced
2 serrano chiles, seeded and finely diced
2 tablespoons finely diced yellow bell pepper

3 tablespoons finely diced mango
2 teaspoons fresh orange juice
½ teaspoon salt

Combine all of the ingredients in a medium bowl.

—*Stephan Pyles*

• • •

JICAMA-MELON RELISH

Makes 1½ Cups

1 small mango, peeled and flesh cut from seed
1 serrano chile—seeded, deribbed and minced
2½ tablespoons fresh lime juice
2 tablespoons finely diced red bell pepper
½ cup finely diced cantaloupe
½ cup finely diced honeydew
2 tablespoons finely diced, peeled and seeded cucumber
½ cup finely diced jicama
2 teaspoons chopped fresh coriander (cilantro)
¼ teaspoon salt
¼ teaspoon freshly ground black pepper

In food processor or blender, puree the mango with the serrano chile and lime juice. In a bowl, combine all the remaining ingredients and add the puree. Cover and refrigerate for up to 4 hours.

—*Stephan Pyles*

• • •

FRESH MINT CHUTNEY

Makes ⅔ Cup

2 cups (packed) fresh mint leaves, rinsed and dried thoroughly
¼ cup fresh lime juice
2 tablespoons fresh coriander (cilantro) leaves
3 small shallots, coarsely chopped
1 medium jalapeño pepper, finely chopped
1 teaspoon sugar
½ teaspoon salt

Combine all the ingredients in a food processor. Process until almost pureed, about 20 seconds. Serve immediately, or cover and refrigerate until ready to use.

—*Jeffrey Alford & Naomi Duguid*

• • •

PAPAYA-TOMATILLO CHUTNEY

Chutneys and salsas are used extensively in southwestern cuisine and are common accompaniments to grilled meats and fish.

Makes 5 Cups

¾ pound tomatillos—husked, rinsed, cored and quartered
1 large papaya, peeled and cut into ½-inch dice
2 small red bell peppers, cut into ½-inch dice
1 small green bell pepper, cut into ½-inch dice
8 scallion whites, thinly sliced
2 small jalapeño peppers, seeded and minced
¾ cup red wine vinegar
½ cup diced fresh pineapple
½ cup (packed) light brown sugar
1 tablespoon chopped fresh coriander
1 teaspoon salt
1 garlic clove, minced
¼ teaspoon cumin

In a large, heavy, nonreactive saucepan, combine all of the ingredients. Bring to a boil over high heat, stirring frequently. Reduce the heat to moderately low and boil gently, stirring occasionally, until thick, 30 to 35 minutes. Transfer to a bowl and let cool completely. Cover and refrigerate for up to 5 days.

—*Stephan Pyles*

• • •

RED BANANA-CURRY KETCHUP

The sweetness of this tropical ketchup provides a nice contrast to the heat of spicy-hot food. If red bananas are not available, use yellow bananas instead.

Makes 2 Cups

2 tablespoons vegetable oil
1 medium onion, coarsely chopped
3 ripe red bananas (about 1 pound), sliced ½ inch thick
1 can (6 ounces) guava nectar
¼ cup fresh orange juice
1 tablespoon dark brown sugar
1½ teaspoons curry powder
1 tablespoon white vinegar
2 tablespoons fresh lime juice
Salt and freshly ground pepper

1. In a medium nonreactive saucepan, heat the oil over moderate heat. Add the onion and cook until softened, 5 to 7 minutes. Add the bananas and cook, stirring frequently, for about 5 minutes. Add the guava nectar, orange juice, brown sugar, curry powder and ½ tablespoon of the vinegar. Bring to a boil over high heat. Reduce the heat and simmer gently until the ketchup thickens to the consistency of applesauce, about 10 minutes.

2. Remove from the heat and stir in the remaining ½ tablespoon vinegar and the lime juice. Season with salt and pepper to taste. Serve hot or at room temperature. *(The ketchup can be refrigerated, covered, for up to 6 weeks.)*

—Chris Schlesinger & John Willoughby

• • •

CRANBERRY-MAUI ONION COMPOTE

Serve this accompaniment warm with roast pork or game birds.

Makes 3 Cups

½ cup dry white wine
½ cup sugar
¼ cup rice vinegar
1 cinnamon stick
One 2-inch strip of lemon zest
2 whole cloves
¼ teaspoon salt
Pinch of thyme
3 Maui onions or other large sweet onions, quartered lengthwise and thinly sliced crosswise (5½ cups)
1 medium garlic clove
2 cups cranberries, picked through

1. In a medium nonreactive saucepan, stir together the wine, sugar, vinegar, cinnamon stick, lemon zest, cloves, salt and thyme. Bring to a simmer over moderately high heat and cook until slightly syrupy, about 5 minutes.

2. Stir in the onions and garlic and reduce the heat to moderately low. Cover and cook until the onions are crisp-tender, about 12 minutes. Stir in the cranberries and cook, uncovered, until they burst, about 6 minutes. *(The compote can be made up to 2 days ahead; cover and refrigerate. Reheat gently over low heat before serving.)* Discard the garlic and cloves. Serve warm.

—Werner Boettner, The Dining Room, Hotel Hana-Maui, Maui, Hawaii

• • •

WINTER FRUIT COMPOTE WITH MUSTARD SYRUP

Makes 3 Cups

2 pounds firm pears—peeled, cored and cut into ⅓-inch dice
⅓ cup sugar
1 tablespoon finely grated lemon zest
1 cup fresh or frozen (not thawed) cranberries
1 teaspoon minced candied ginger
1 tablespoon dry mustard

1. In a medium nonreactive saucepan, combine the pears, sugar, lemon zest and ¼ cup of water. Stir with a wooden spoon to mix well and bring to a boil over moderate heat, then cook until the pears are just tender, about 8 minutes. Stir in the cranberries and candied ginger and cook until the cranberries pop, about 4 minutes longer.

2. Using a slotted spoon, transfer the fruits to a medium bowl. Boil the liquid in the saucepan over high heat until syrupy, about 2 minutes. Stir the syrup into the fruit. Set aside to cool for 15 minutes, then stir in the mustard until thoroughly combined. Serve at room temperature. *(The compote can be made up to 2 days ahead; cover and refrigerate.)*

—Lee Bailey

• • •

APRICOT-FIG BLATJANG

Blatjang is a spicy, vinegary condiment based on the chutneys that were brought to southern Africa by Malaysian slaves. Dried apricots and raisins are typically used. We have added figs, which figure prominently in several northern African cuisines, but you can substitute any other dried fruit.

Makes 1½ Cups

2 tablespoons blanched almonds
5 ounces dried apricots, cut into ½-inch dice (about ¾ cup)
1½ ounces dried figs, cut into ½-inch dice (about ¼ cup)
¼ cup golden raisins (2 ounces)
½ of a small onion, finely diced
About ¼ cup red wine vinegar
1½ teaspoons minced garlic
¼ teaspoon cayenne pepper
Salt

1. Preheat the oven to 350°. Spread the almonds on a baking sheet and bake until toasted, about 10 minutes. Let cool.

2. In a medium nonreactive saucepan, combine the apricots, figs, raisins, onion and ¼ cup vinegar. Add enough water to just cover the fruit and bring to a boil. Reduce the heat to moderate and simmer, stirring frequently, until the mixture is the thickness of honey, about 15 minutes. (Do not overcook; the mixture will thicken as it cools.) Remove from the heat.

3. In a mortar, pound the garlic, cayenne and toasted almonds until a coarse puree forms. Stir the puree into the apricot mixture. Season with salt and additional vinegar to taste.

—Chris Schlesinger & John Willoughby

• • •

HARISSA

In this Tunisian-inspired version of *harissa*, caraway seeds provide a subtle flavor. Choose your chiles based on your heat tolerance.

Makes ½ Cup

¼ cup coarsely chopped fresh red or green chiles
2 tablespoons chopped fresh coriander (cilantro)
2 tablespoons distilled white vinegar
1 tablespoon caraway seeds
1 tablespoon cumin
1 teaspoon minced garlic
½ teaspoon salt
¼ teaspoon freshly ground pepper

In a food processor or blender, combine all the ingredients and puree. *(This condiment can be refrigerated, covered, for about 1 month.)*

—Chris Schlesinger & John Willoughby

• • •

CHILE PASTE

Makes ¼ Cup

4 small Thai, or bird, chiles, finely chopped
2 garlic cloves, finely chopped
1 tablespoon fresh lime or lemon juice
Salt

In a mortar, pound the chiles and garlic, adding the lime juice to make a paste. Add salt to taste. Serve in one or more small condiment dishes.

—Jeffrey Alford & Naomi Duguid

• • •

PARSLEY PESTO

Makes ½ Cup

1½ cups coarsely chopped flat-leaf parsley
1 large garlic clove, coarsely chopped
3 tablespoons freshly grated Parmesan or Asiago cheese
1 tablespoon red wine vinegar
¼ cup olive oil
Salt and freshly ground pepper

In a food processor or blender, combine the parsley, garlic, cheese and vinegar and puree just until combined. Scrape down the sides and, with the machine on, add the oil in a slow steady stream and process until emulsified. Season with salt and pepper to taste.

—John Ash & Sid Goldstein

• • •

CHILI-LEMON OIL

This spicy lemon oil is great for basting fish and poultry.

Makes 2 Cups

1½ cups corn or peanut oil
2 tablespoons Japanese sesame oil*
⅓ cup thinly sliced scallions
2 plump stalks of fresh lemon grass,* pounded with a meat mallet and cut crosswise into finger lengths
¼ cup dried red chili flakes*
2 tablespoons slivered fresh ginger
1 tablespoon Szechuan peppercorns*
1 large garlic clove, lightly smashed and peeled
Finely minced zest of 3 to 4 lemons*
****Available at Asian markets***

1. Combine all the ingredients except the lemon zest in a heavy nonreactive 2-quart saucepan. Heat to 225° over moderately low heat, about 15 minutes. Let the oil bubble for 10 minutes. Remove the pan from the heat and let stand for 5 minutes, then stir in the lemon zest. Set aside until cool.

2. Discard the lemon grass. Scrape the oil and seasonings into an impeccably clean glass jar and store at room temperature.

—Barbara Tropp

• • •

CHILI-ORANGE OIL

This flavorful oil is wonderful in cold dishes, marinades and sauces. The cooked seasonings in the oil can be used to accent cold noodle dishes, meat loaves and dumplings.

Makes 2½ Cups

2 cups corn or peanut oil
¼ cup Japanese sesame oil*
½ cup dried red chili flakes*
3 tablespoons Chinese fermented black beans* (do not rinse them), coarsely chopped
1 to 2 large garlic cloves, peeled and lightly smashed
Finely minced zest of 3 large navel oranges
****Available at Asian markets***

1. In a heavy nonreactive 2-quart saucepan, combine all of the ingredients and heat to 225° over moderately low heat, about 20 minutes. Remove from the heat and set aside until cool.

2. Scrape the oil and seasonings into an impeccably clean glass jar and store at room temperature.

—Barbara Tropp

• • •

MARINATED FRESH GINGER

Makes ¼ Cup

One 2-inch piece of fresh ginger, peeled
⅓ cup rice vinegar
1 tablespoon sugar
1 teaspoon soy sauce

Thinly slice the ginger on the diagonal into long ovals. Cut the slices into very thin strips. In a small bowl, combine the vinegar, sugar and soy sauce, stirring until the sugar is dissolved. Add the ginger and marinate for several hours or overnight.

—Linda Burum

• • •

HOMEMADE PICKLED GINGER

Use the juice from this easy-to-make condiment in dressings and sauces. The ginger and juice can be refrigerated indefinitely, although the juice may turn cloudy.

Makes ½ Pound

10 ounces fresh ginger, peeled
Boiling water
1⅓ cups unseasoned Japanese rice vinegar
3 tablespoons cider vinegar
2 tablespoons distilled white vinegar
½ cup plus 1 tablespoon sugar
1 tablespoon plus 1 teaspoon coarse (kosher) salt

1. Slice the ginger crosswise against the grain into paper-thin coins. Place in a heatproof bowl, cover with boiling water and let stand for 2 minutes. Drain.

2. In a medium nonreactive saucepan, combine all the remaining ingredients. Stir over moderate heat until the sugar and salt dissolve and the liquid is near steaming.

3. Put the ginger in an impeccably clean glass jar and pour in the hot liquid. Let stand until cool, then cover and refrigerate.

—Barbara Tropp

• • •

PRESERVED LEMONS

Preserved lemons can be used in many recipes. Try them in a black bean salad or a warm lentil and sausage salad. They are also wonderful in a lamb stew or when added to the pan juices of a roast leg of lamb. Finely diced, they add zest to many soups, especially tomato or leek and potato.

Makes 1 Quart

4 large lemons (about ¾ pound)
⅔ cup coarse (kosher) salt
⅓ cup sugar
3 large shallots, minced
3 tablespoons minced garlic
Olive oil

1. Bring a medium saucepan of water to a boil over high heat. Add the lemons and boil for 5 minutes. Drain and set aside until cool enough to handle.

2. Trim the ends off the lemons and, using a very sharp thin knife, slice the lemons crosswise ⅛ inch thick. Discard the seeds as you slice.

3. In a small bowl, combine the salt, sugar, shallots and garlic. Layer the lemon slices in a wide-mouth quart-size glass or porcelain jar, sprinkling each layer lightly with some of the salt mixture. Press down lightly on the lemon slices and pour enough olive oil over them to cover by 1½ inches. Cover securely and refrigerate at least overnight and up to 1 month.

—Perla Meyers

• • •

PICKLED JALAPENOS

Serve this incendiary delight with scrambled eggs, hamburgers and fajitas. These pickles are more flavorful and firmer than any you can find in a jar.

Makes 2 Pints

1½ cups cider vinegar
2 tablespoons honey
1 tablespoon pickling spice*
1 teaspoon salt
4 garlic cloves
1 pound green jalapeño peppers, stemmed and sliced ⅛ inch thick
****Available at most supermarkets***

1. Sterilize two 1-pint preserving jars and their lids.

2. In a nonreactive saucepan, combine the vinegar, honey, pickling spice, salt, garlic and ¾ cup of water. Bring to a boil over high heat, then set aside to steep for 10 minutes.

3. Pack the jalapeños to within 1 inch of the rim of the hot jars.

4. Return the brine to a boil. Pour the hot brine over the peppers to within ½ inch of the rim of the jars, dividing the spices and garlic cloves evenly between the jars. Run a small knife or spatula around the inside of the jars to release trapped air bubbles. Wipe the rims clean and seal with the lids. Let cool slightly, then refrigerate.

—Jonathan Locke & Sally Gutiérrez

• • •

OLIVE OIL PICKLED BEANS

The olive oil in this brine congeals once the beans are refrigerated. Allow a little time before serving for the oil to soften. These pickles are delicious, brine and all, in marinated salads or as a sandwich garnish.

Makes 2 Pints

1½ cups white wine vinegar
¼ cup olive oil
¼ cup brown sugar
1 teaspoon celery seeds
1 teaspoon mustard seeds
⅛ teaspoon crushed red pepper
¾ pound unblemished green beans
1 small yellow onion, sliced lengthwise

1. Sterilize two 1-pint preserving jars and their lids.

2. In a medium nonreactive saucepan, combine the vinegar, olive oil, brown sugar, celery seeds, mustard seeds, red pepper and 1 cup of water. Bring to a boil over high heat, then cover and set aside to steep for at least 10 minutes.

3. Trim the stems off the beans and cut any long beans to stand within ¾ inch of the rim of the preserving jars. Stand the beans upright in the hot jars and pack in the onion.

4. Return the brine to a boil. Pour the hot brine over the beans and onions to within ½ inch of the jar rim. Run a small knife or spatula around the inside of the jars to release trapped air bubbles. Wipe the rims clean and seal with the lids. Let cool slightly, then refrigerate.

—Jonathan Locke & Sally Gutiérrez

• • •

DILLED CARROT STICKS

Try these pickles in place of dilled cucumber pickles. Serve as an hors d'oeuvre or alongside burgers and other grilled meats.

Makes 2 Pints

1½ cups cider vinegar
6 garlic cloves
3 tablespoons dill seeds, lightly crushed
2 tablespoons honey
1 teaspoon salt
1 pound medium carrots, cut into 4-by-⅜-inch sticks

1. Sterilize two 1-pint preserving jars and their lids.

2. In a small nonreactive saucepan, combine the vinegar, garlic, dill seeds, honey, salt and ¾ cup of water. Bring to a boil over moderate heat, then set aside to steep for at least 10 minutes.

3. Meanwhile, pack the carrot sticks upright in the hot jars.

4. Return the brine to a boil. Pour the hot brine over the carrots to within ½ inch of the rim of the jars, dividing the dill seeds and garlic evenly between the jars. Run a small knife or spatula around the inside of the jars to release trapped air bubbles. Add more brine if necessary to top off the jars. Wipe the rims clean and seal with the lids. Let cool slightly, then refrigerate.

—Jonathan Locke & Sally Gutiérrez

• • •

PICKLED BEETS

This Scandinavian-inspired recipe pairs well with pâté and a variety of meat sandwiches.

Makes 2 Pints

1⅓ pounds beets
1⅓ cups apple cider vinegar
1⅓ cups honey
¾ teaspoon whole cloves
1 cinnamon stick, broken in half

1. In a large pot, cover the beets with water and bring to a boil over high heat. Reduce the heat to moderately low and simmer until tender, about 45 minutes.

2. Meanwhile, sterilize two 1-pint preserving jars and their lids.

3. In a small nonreactive saucepan, combine the vinegar, honey, cloves and cinnamon. Bring to a boil over moderately high heat, then set aside to steep.

4. Drain the beets, rinse under cold water and slip off the skins. Halve any large beets, then slice the beets ¼ inch thick and pack them in the hot jars.

5. Return the brine to a boil. Pour the hot brine over the beets to within ½ inch of the rim of the jars, dividing the cloves and cinnamon stick evenly between the jars. Run a small knife or spatula around the inside of the jars to release trapped air bubbles. Wipe the rims clean and seal with the lids. Let cool slightly, then refrigerate.

—Jonathan Locke & Sally Gutiérrez

• • •

OLD-TIMEY CORN RELISH

If you do not have a proper canning kettle with a rack, you can use any large stockpot and a round cake rack. Use tongs to handle the hot jars. Down South, this vinegary corn relish is served with baked ham, roast pork, turkey and chicken. This recipe can be doubled.

Makes 3 Pints

8 large ears of fresh corn
2 cups cider vinegar
8 medium celery ribs, finely diced
1 large green bell pepper, finely diced
1 large red bell pepper, finely diced
1 large yellow onion, finely diced
½ cup sugar
1 tablespoon salt
1 teaspoon celery seeds
2 tablespoons all-purpose flour
1 tablespoon dry mustard
½ teaspoon turmeric

1. Bring a stockpot of water to a boil. Drop in the corn, cover and boil for 10 minutes. Drain well, then cool in a large pot of ice water; drain thoroughly. Stand an ear of corn in a large shallow bowl, holding it by the pointed end. Using a small sharp knife, cut straight down the rows of kernels, slicing off about 3 rows at a time. Do not scrape the cobs (the pulp will cloud the relish). Set aside 4 cups of corn kernels and save the remainder for another use.

2. In a 4-gallon canning kettle (or stockpot fitted with a rack) of boiling water, immerse three 1-pint preserving jars and their lids; cover and boil for 5 minutes. Reduce the heat to low and keep at a simmer until ready to use.

3. In a large nonreactive saucepan, combine the vinegar, celery, green and red bell peppers, onion, sugar, salt and celery seeds. Bring to a boil over moderate heat and boil gently for 5 minutes.

4. In a small bowl, combine the flour, mustard and turmeric. Using a fork, stir in 3 tablespoons of cold water to form a paste. Whisk about 1 cup of the hot pickling liquid into the flour paste until smooth, then mix the paste into the vegetables and boil, stirring, until slightly thickened, 2 to 3 minutes. Stir in the corn kernels, cover and boil for 5 minutes, stirring once or twice.

5. Remove 1 hot jar from the kettle and using a wide-mouth canning funnel or a ladle, fill the jar with enough hot relish to reach ¼ inch from the top. Run a small spatula around the inside of the jar to release air bubbles, wipe the jar rim, then seal the jar with the lid. Repeat with the remaining jars.

6. In the canning kettle, immerse the jars in enough boiling water to cover by at least 1 inch and boil for 15 minutes (make sure that the jars do not touch one another or the sides of the kettle).

7. Transfer the jars to a work surface covered with a kitchen towel and let cool to room temperature. Check the seal on each jar (see Note), then label and date the jars and store in a cool, dark spot for at least 3 weeks and up to 1 year.

NOTE: *The lids of properly sealed jars will be concave and will make a "ping" sound when tapped with your fingers. Any jars that have not sealed can be emptied, the jars sterilized again in boiling water, then refilled, resealed and processed as before.*

—Jean Anderson

• • •

OVEN-DRIED CHERRY TOMATOES

Much like sun-drying, oven-drying preserves tomatoes while intensifying their acidity and flavor.

Makes 2 Cups

8 pints red and/or yellow cherry tomatoes (5½ pounds), stemmed and halved lengthwise
Salt

Preheat the oven to 200°. Lightly sprinkle the tomatoes with salt and place, cut side up, on 2 large nonreactive baking sheets. Bake the tomatoes for about 7 hours, until they are free of juice when squeezed. Check them every 45 minutes or so, turning the pans so that the heat is evenly distributed. Remove from the oven and let cool. *(The tomatoes can be stored in a glass jar, covered with vegetable or olive oil, in the refrigerator for several months.)*

—Stephan Pyles

• • •

CANDIED CITRUS PEEL

Makes 1 Cup

1 lemon
1 lime
1 navel orange
⅓ cup sugar

1. Using a sharp paring knife, trim off the ends of the lemon, lime and orange. Make 4 vertical cuts in the skins, cutting through to the fruit. Peel off the skin in 4 sections with the white pith attached. Cut the skins lengthwise into ⅛-inch strips.

2. In a small saucepan, cover the citrus strips with cold water and bring to a boil over high heat. Reduce the heat to moderate and simmer for 5 minutes. Drain and return the citrus strips to the pan. Cover with cold water and repeat the blanching process 4 more times.

3. In the saucepan, sprinkle the drained softened peel with the sugar and 3 tablespoons of water. Bring to a boil over high heat, reduce the heat to moderately high and boil, stirring occasionally, until the peels are glazed and translucent and the liquid has been absorbed, about 8 minutes. Do not let the sugar caramelize. Strain through a coarse sieve, separate the zests with a fork and place on a rack to dry. For a frosted look, roll the cooled dried peel in granulated sugar. If the candied peel is to be used immediately, it can still be slightly moist. Alternatively, dry it thoroughly on the rack for at least 6 hours or overnight, and store for up to 6 months in an airtight container.

—*Peggy Cullen*

• • •

CANDIED APPLE SLICES

Makes 5 Cups

5¾ cups sugar
1 tablespoon corn syrup
6 medium Granny Smith or other tart green apples

1. Set 2 large cooling racks over baking sheets and set aside. In a 6-quart nonreactive saucepan or stockpot, combine 2½ cups water with 5 cups of the sugar and the corn syrup. Wash down the inside of the pan with a wet pastry brush and bring to a boil over moderately high heat. Insert a candy thermometer and boil, occasionally washing down the inside of the pan, until the syrup reaches 250°.

2. Meanwhile, peel, core and quarter 2 of the apples. Cut each quarter lengthwise into four slices. When the syrup has reached 250°, stir in the apples with a wooden spoon, separating the slices. Boil without stirring, occasionally prodding the apples gently to keep them submerged. When the slices are white, puffy and have transparent streaks throughout, after 6 to 7 minutes, remove the pan from the heat. Using a skimmer or slotted spoon, transfer a few apple slices at a time to the cooling rack, separating them with a fork or a table knife; be careful not to pierce the apples.

3. Bring the syrup back to 250°. Core, peel and slice 2 more of the apples and repeat the poaching process. (The apples will cook more quickly this time, in about 5 minutes.) Transfer the slices to the cooling rack, arranging them without touching. Finally, repeat the process with the remaining 2 apples, which will cook in 3 to 4 minutes.

4. Set the apples aside on a clean, dry rack in a warm, dry place until the exteriors are dry, about 12 hours. Turn the apples once after 6 hours. (As the apples cool they will turn pale green and look jelly-like and translucent.)

5. Place the remaining ¾ cup sugar in a small bowl and toss the apples in the sugar to coat each slice. Transfer the slices to a clean dry rack until completely dry, about 24 hours longer. *(The candied apples can be stored for up to 2 weeks in an airtight container in a cool place.)*

—*Peggy Cullen*

• • •

CANDIED CRANBERRIES

Makes 3 Cups

1 package cranberries (12 ounces)
3¼ cups sugar

1. Place the cranberries in a medium heatproof bowl and set aside. (If using frozen berries, do not thaw.) In a medium nonreactive saucepan, combine 2½ cups of the sugar with 1¼ cups water. Wash down the inside of the pan with a wet pastry brush and bring to a boil over moderately high heat. Remove from the heat and then pour the syrup over the cranberries.

2. Place a small, flat-bottomed heatproof bowl upside down in a large saucepan and set the bowl with the berries on top. Pour 1 inch of water into the saucepan and cover the pan with a tight-fitting lid. Bring the water to a boil over moderately high heat. Reduce the heat to moderately low and steam the cranberries in the syrup for 40 minutes. Transfer the bowl of cranberries to a cooling rack and let cool undisturbed.

3. Set the cooled cranberries aside in a warm, dry room. Stir occasionally for 2 to 3 days until the syrup thickens and is somewhat jelled. Drain the berries in a colander. Spread them out on a cooling rack or on trays lined with parchment paper and let air dry for 2 to 3 days.

4. Place the remaining ¾ cup sugar in a medium bowl. Toss the cranberries in the sugar, a few at a time, to coat completely. *(The cranberries can be stored on a tray for up to 1 week in a dry place.)*

—*Peggy Cullen*

• • •

CANDIED ORANGE PEEL

Makes 4 Cups

6 large navel oranges
4 cups sugar
3 tablespoons light corn syrup

1. Using a small paring knife, score the oranges lengthwise into quarters. Peel off the skin and slice each quarter lengthwise into ¾-inch-wide strips.

2. In a medium saucepan, cover the orange peel with water and bring to a boil over moderately high heat. Boil the peel for 6 minutes, then drain in a colander. Repeat this blanching and draining process two more times to tenderize the peel and to remove bitterness.

3. Place 1 cup of sugar on each of 2 heavy baking sheets. In the saucepan, combine the remaining 2 cups sugar with the corn syrup and 1 cup water. Bring to a boil over moderately high heat, occasionally washing down the inside of the pan with a pastry brush. Add the orange peel and cook, stirring occasionally, until the peel is somewhat transparent and most of the syrup has been absorbed, 40 to 50 minutes. During the last 10 minutes, stir frequently and watch carefully to make sure that the peel doesn't burn.

4. Drain in a colander and, using a fork or tongs, transfer one at a time onto the sugared baking sheets. As they begin to cool, after about 15 minutes, roll the peel in the sugar to coat completely. Let cool thoroughly in the sugar, then transfer the peel to a cooling rack to dry overnight. *(The candied orange peel can be stored in an airtight container for up to 1 week in a dry place.)*

—*Peggy Cullen*

• • •

LAVENDER SYRUP

The syrup is a gorgeous purplish pink color with an intense lavender aroma and a delicate floral flavor. For a simple, elegant dessert, drizzle it sparingly over slices of honeydew melon, and garnish the plate with fresh mint leaves. Any impeccably fresh fruit will pair beautifully with the syrup.

Makes 1 Cup

½ cup sugar
¼ cup sweet dessert wine, such as Riesling or Sauternes
2 tablespoons fresh orange juice
2 tablespoons dried lavender

1. In a medium nonreactive saucepan, bring the sugar, wine, orange juice and ½ cup of water to a boil over moderately high heat. Reduce the heat to moderately low and simmer, stirring occasionally, until the sugar has dissolved, about 5 minutes; do not let the liquid reduce. Remove the syrup from the heat and stir in the lavender. Cover and set aside to infuse for at least 2 hours.

2. Strain the syrup through a sieve into a small bowl or jar, pressing on the lavender to extract all the liquid. Set aside to cool to room temperature, then cover tightly and refrigerate for at least 1 hour or up to 2 weeks. Serve the syrup slightly chilled.

—*Renée Shepherd, Shepherd's Garden Seeds, Felton, California*

• • •

INDEX

C

D-E

F

G-H

I-J

K-L

M

N-O

P

Q-R

S

T

U-V

W-Y

CONTRIBUTORS

Jeffrey Alford and **Naomi Duguid** are cookbook authors, food writers, photographers and the authors of *Tastes of Travel 1992* (Dharma Enterprises) and an upcoming book tentatively titled *Basic Kneads: A Book of Flatbreads* (Morrow).
Jean Anderson is a food/travel writer and the author of numerous cookbooks. She is currently working on *German Cooking Today* for HarperCollins.
Colman Andrews is a critic and the author of *Everything on the Table: Plain Talk About Food and Wine* (Bantam), *Catalan Cuisine* (Atheneum) and an upcoming book from Bantam on contemporary Spanish food and wine.
John Ash and **Sid Goldstein** are co-authors of *American Game Cooking* (Aris).
Lee Bailey is a designer and the author of nine cookbooks, including the recent *Cooking for Friends* (Clarkson Potter). He is currently working on four more books (all for Clarkson Potter), including *Lee Bailey's New Orleans* and *Lee Bailey's Corn*.
Lidia Bastianich is chef/owner of Felidia in New York City.
Rick Bayless is the chef/owner of Frontera Grill (Chicago) and the author of *Authentic Mexican* (Morrow).
Werner Boettner is executive chef at Hotel Hana-Maui on Maui in Hawaii.
Jennifer Brennan is the author of numerous cookbooks, including *The Original Thai Cookbook* (Perigee), *One-Dish Asian Meals* (HarperCollins) and an upcoming book from HarperCollins called *Tradewinds and Coconuts: The Foods, Cultures and Customs of the Pacific and Oceania*.
Linda Burum is a cooking teacher, food journalist and the author of a number of cookbooks, including *Brownies* (Scribners), *Asian Pasta* (Aris), *Frozen Delights* (Scribners) and *The Guide to Ethnic Food in Los Angeles* (HarperCollins).
Hugh Carpenter is a cooking teacher, food writer and the co-author of *Chopstix: Quick Cooking with Pacific Flavors* (Stewart, Tabori & Chang).
John Phillip Carroll is the author of *California the Beautiful Cookbook* (HarperCollins) and a number of books in the Williams-Sonoma Kitchen Library Series (Time-Life), including *Grilling* and the upcoming *Muffins & Quick Breads*.
Bob Chambers is a New York-based chef and food stylist.
Susan Costner is the editor of *Tables* magazine (for Beringer Vineyards) and the author of *Great Sandwiches* and *Good Friends, Great Dinners* (both from Crown).
Peggy Cullen is a baker, candy maker and food writer.
Diane Darrow is a food writer and co-author (with Tom Maresca) of *La Tavola Italiana* (Morrow) and the upcoming *The Seasons of the Italian Kitchen* (Grove Press).
Tony DiLembo is a Los Angeles-based baker and restaurateur. He is also the author of *California Bistro* (Contemporary Books).
Mary Anne Dolan is a writer, syndicated newspaper columnist and television commentator currently working on a book about the role of food rituals in family life.
Chata DuBose is a Houston-based cooking teacher.
Billy and Tracy Fava are the owners of Mayers Famous Plate Lunches and Mayers Catering, both in Lafayette, Louisiana.
Dean Fearing is chef of The Mansion on Turtle Creek in Dallas.
Carol Field is a food writer and the author of *The Italian Baker* (HarperCollins), *Celebrating Italy* (Morrow) and the forthcoming *Merenda: Italy in Small Bites* (Morrow).
Michael Flynn is executive chef at Sonoma Mission Inn and Spa in Sonoma, California. He is also the author of *Spa Food* (Clarkson Potter).
Susanna Foo is chef/owner of Susanna Foo in Philadelphia.
Susan R. Friedland is a senior editor at HarperCollins Publishers and is the author of *Ribs* (Harmony) and *Caviar* (Scribners).
Teresa Gannon is pastry chef at Haliimaile General Store on Maui in Hawaii.
George Germon and **Johanne Killeen** are chefs and co-owners of Al Forno (Providence, Rhode Island) and the co-authors of *Cucina Simpatica* (HarperCollins). They are currently working on a second book.
Camille Glenn is a cooking teacher and the author of several cookbooks, including *The Heritage of Southern Cooking* (Workman).
Marcy Goldman is a food writer, pastry chef and cooking teacher (Cuisine d'Or Specialty Bakery, Montreal).
Sally Gutiérrez is a Minneapolis-based food writer.
Barbara Lee Hanson is a food writer and the editor of a newsletter called *Eating New York*. She is working on a book called *MicroQuick* to be published in 1993 by Wellspring Press.
Jessica B. Harris is a food writer, culinary historian and the author of *Tasting Brazil* (Macmillan), *Sky Juice and Flying Fish* (Fireside), *Iron Pots and Wooden Spoon* (Atheneum) and a forthcoming book on the heritage of African-American cooking from Simon and Schuster.
Ann Haskell is a teacher of medieval gastronomy (State University of New York at Buffalo) and the author of two books of Provençal cooking, as yet unpublished.
Janie Hibler is a cooking teacher, food writer and the author of *Dungeness Crabs and Blackberry Cobblers* (Knopf).
Susan Shapiro Jaslove is a food writer and recipe developer.
Nancy Harmon Jenkins is a food writer and culinary historian. She is currently working on a book on American ethnic groups and their foods, to be published in late 1993 by Bantam.
Ferdinand Johnson is the chef/owner of Chef Ferdinand's Restaurant in Harvey, Louisiana. He is currently working on a cookbook called *Chef Ferdinand's Blend*.
Baba S. Khalsa is the author of *Great Vegetables from Great Chefs* (Chronicle).
Evan Kleiman is executive chef and owner of the Angeli restaurants in Los Angeles.
Leslie Land is a gardening and food writer and the author of, most recently, *Modern Country Cook*.
Jonathan Locke is a food writer, cooking teacher and chef of August Moon (Golden Valley, Minnesota).
Susan Herrmann Loomis is a food writer and the author of *Farmhouse Cookbook, The Great American Seafood Cookbook* and the forthcoming *The Clambake Book* (all from Workman).
Sheila Lukins is food editor of *Parade Magazine*, the co-author of

The New Basics Cookbook, The Silver Palate Cookbook and *The Silver Palate Good Times Cookbook* (all from Workman).
Stephanie Lyness is a food writer and cooking teacher.
Nick Malgieri is a pastry chef, cooking teacher and the author of *Great Italian Desserts* (Little, Brown) and *Nick Malgieri's Perfect Pastry* (Macmillan).
Tom Maresca is the author of *The Right Wine* (Grove Weidenfeld), *Mastering Wine* (Bantam) and co-author (with Diana Darrow) of *La Tavola Italiana* (Morrow) and the upcoming *The Seasons of the Italian Kitchen* (Grove Press).
Elin McCoy and **John Frederick Walker** are contributing wines and spirits editors for *Food & Wine* and the authors of *Thinking About Wine* (Simon and Schuster).
Rose Marie Nichols McGee is president of Nicholas Garden Nursery in Albany, Oregon.
Perla Meyers is a food writer, cooking teacher (The Seasonal Kitchen, Washington, Connecticut), consultant and the author of numerous cookbooks, including most recently *The Art of Seasonal Cooking* (Simon and Schuster).
Leslie Newman is a novelist, screenwriter, food writer and the author of a cookbook called *Feasts* (HarperCollins). She is currently working on a second cookbook called *The Family Table*.
Adam Odegard is the executive chef at Peninsula Spa in the Peninsula Hotel in New York City.
Tim Patton is chef/owner of Patton's Caterers in Chalmette, Louisiana.
Jacques Pépin is a cooking teacher, newspaper columnist and the author of numerous cookbooks, the most recent of which are *Cuisine Economique* (Morrow) and two volumes of *Today's Gourmet* (KQED, Inc.), the companion books to his PBS series of the same name.
Stephan Pyles is a chef/restaurateur, cooking teacher and the author of the forthcoming *The New Texas Cuisine* (Doubleday).
Tracy Pikhart Ritter is a consulting chef to spas and the fitness industry and is the chef/owner of Stamina Cuisine in San Diego.
David Rosengarten is a cooking teacher, food writer, wine columnist and the author of *Food & Wine*'s "Food & Drink" column, *Red Wine with Fish* (Simon and Schuster) and the forthcoming *Crashing the Borders* (Crown Harmony).
Amy Scherber is the owner of Amy's Bread in New York City.
Chris Schlesinger and **John Willoughby** are co-authors of *The Thrill of the Grill* (Morrow) and two forthcoming books, both from William Morrow: *Salsas, Sambals, Blatjangs and Chow-Chows* and *Born Under a Hot Sun*.
Sally Schneider is a food writer, consultant, food stylist and the author of *The Art of Low Calorie Cooking* (Stewart, Tabori & Chang) and the forthcoming *A New Way to Cook* (Morrow).
Michele Scicolone is a food and travel writer and the author of *The Antipasto Table* and the forthcoming *La Dolce Vita* (both from Morrow).
Renée Shepherd is president of Shepherd's Garden Seeds (Felton, California) and is the co-author of *Recipes From a Kitchen Garden: Volumes I, II and III* (Shepherd's Garden Publishing).
Lindsey Shere is a pastry chef, the co-owner of Downtown Bakery & Creamery (Healdsburg, California) and Chez Panisse (Berkeley, California), and the author of *Chez Panisse Desserts* (Random House).
Martha Rose Shulman is a food writer and the author of numerous cookbooks, including *Martha Rose Shulman's Feasts & Fêtes* (Chapters Publishers), *Entertaining Light* and *Mediterranean Light* (both from Bantam) and an upcoming book, *The Bread Book*.
Nancy Silverton is pastry chef and co-owner of Campanile in Los Angeles.
Barbara Tropp is chef/owner of China Moon Cafe in San Francisco and the author of *The Modern Art of Chinese Cooking* (Morrow) and *The China Moon Cookbook* (Workman). She is currently working on a book titled *The China Diet*.
Patricia Wells is a Paris-based food journalist and the author of *Simply French* (Morrow), and *Bistro Cooking, The Food Lover's Guide to Paris* and *The Food Lover's Guide to France* (all from Workman). She is currently working on a book titled *Trattoria Cooking* for Morrow.
Alan Wong is chef at CanoeHouse in the Mauna Lani Bay Hotel (Kohala Coast, Hawaii).
Roy Yamaguchi is a Hawaii-based chef/restaurateur.
Eileen Yin-Fei Lo is a cooking teacher (China Institute in America, New York City), food writer and the author of *Eileen Yin-Fei Lo's New Cantonese Cooking* (Viking), *The Dim Sum Book* (Crown) and *The Chinese Banquet Cookbook* (Crown).
Andrew Ziobro is a New York-based chef and food writer.

We would also like to thank the test kitchen (Diana Sturgis, director; Marcia Kiesel, associate director; Tracey Seaman, recipe tester-developer) and the following restaurants and individuals for their contributions to *Food & Wine* and to this cookbook: **Terrance Brennan**, Prix Fixe, New York City; **Tom Colicchio**, Mondrian, New York City; **Rose Daley; Roberto Donna; Ana Espinosa; Araceli Filguiera; Graham Griswold; Ramon Flores Guerrero; Hay Day,** Westport, Connecticut; **Greg Higgins; Ron Hook; MaryLee Johnson; Jean-Marie Josselin; John Ed Laborde; The Lodge at Koele,** Lanai, Hawaii; **Pepe Marin; Patricia Martell; Kazuto Matsusaka; Peter Merriman; Bradley Ogden**, The Lark Creek Inn, Larkspur, California; **Georges Paineau**, Bretagne, Brittany, France; **Maria del Carmen Pérez; Pilar Plana; Michael Romano**, Union Square Cafe, New York City; **Jimmy Schmidt**, The Rattlesnake Club, Detroit; **Bernd Schmitt; The Sign of the Dove,** New York City; **Jerry Traunfeld; Vilai Yenbamroong.**

PHOTO CREDITS

Cover: Jerry Simpson. **Page 33:** Mark Thomas. **Page 34:** Maria Robledo. **Page 35:** Mark Thomas. **Page 36:** Cynthia Brown. **Pages 53-55:** David Bishop. **Page 56:** Jerry Simpson. **Page 73:** Jerry Simpson. **Page 74:** Mark Thomas. **Page 75:** Dennis Galante. **Page 76:** Jerry Simpson. **Page 93:** Mark Thomas. **Pages 94-95:** Maria Robledo. **Page 95:** William Abranowicz. **Page 96:** Mark Thomas. **Page 113:** Dennis Galante. **Pages 114-115:** Lisa Charles Watson. **Page 115:** Jerry Simpson. **Page 116:** Dennis Galante. **Page 149:** Mark Thomas. **Pages 150-151:** Robert Jacobs. **Page 151:** Dennis Galante. **Page 152:** Jerry Simpson. **Page 169:** David Bishop. **Pages 170-172:** Jerry Simpson. **Page 189:** David Bishop. **Pages 190-192:** Maria Robledo. **Page 209:** Jerry Simpson. **Pages 210-211:** Susan Goldman. **Page 211:** David Bishop. **Page 212:** Jerry Simpson. **Page 245:** Jerry Simpson. **Page 246 bottom:** David Bishop. **Page 246 top:** Robert Jacobs. **Page 247:** Deborah Denker. **Page 248:** Robert Jacobs.